# Methods and Nations

*Cultural Governance and the
Indigenous Subject*

# Methods and Nations
## Cultural Governance and the Indigenous Subject

Michael J. Shapiro

ROUTLEDGE
NEW YORK AND LONDON

A volume in the *Global Horizons* series, edited by Richard Falk, Lester Ruiz, and R.B.J. Walker.

Published in 2004 by
Routledge
29 West 35th Street
New York, NY 10001
www.routledge-ny.com

Published in Great Britain by
Routledge
11 New Fetter Lane
London EC4P 4EE
www.routledge.co.uk

Library of Congress Cataloging-in-Publication Data

Shapiro, Michael J.
   Methods and nations : cultural governance and the indigenous subject / Michael J. Shapiro.
       p.   cm.—(Global horizons)
Includes bibliographical references and index.
   ISBN 0-415-94531-3 (alk. paper)—ISBN 0-415-94532-1 (pbk. : alk. paper)
   1. Postcolonialism and the arts.   I. Title.   II. Series.
   NX180.P67S48   2003
   700′.1′03—dc21
                                                          2003013950

To the memory of Harry J. Friedman
mentor, friend, and colleague

# Contents

# Preface
## Politics, Methods, and Loci of Enunciation

When I began my research and teaching career at the University of Hawai'i in the mid-1960s, I was confident that my social science education and research orientation were universally relevant; I was there to assert my newly minted, social science self, a product of the knowledge culture into which I had been initiated. As the years passed, and I became less enthralled by the epistemological premises of an explanatory social science, and increasingly influenced by post-Kantian practices of critique, I became attentive to my complicated loci of enunciation—the historically and territorially complex spaces that articulate the political relevance of my work. The contingencies associated with my location had begun to assert themselves. As a result, I find it necessary to begin by situating my arguments in the conceptual and territorial spaces that provide the context for the analyses that follow.

Conceptually, critical perspectives challenging traditional approaches in the social sciences in general and political studies in particular are primarily a legacy of the trajectory of German philosophical thinking in the eighteenth and nineteenth centuries. Kant's insights into the aporias of knowledge and Hegel's Kant-inspired rendering of the dilemma of epistemology (in brief, that any criterion of knowledge must be predicated on a claim to knowledge that must itself be proven) introduced uncertainties into knowledge enterprises that social science practitioners have been reluctant to acknowledge. Once the Kantian revolution was elaborated and its implications extended by twentieth-century philosophers, especially Martin Heidegger, the epistemological conceits informing "method" in the human sciences were confronted with their ontological predicates: the web of practices or involvements (linguistic and otherwise) mediating the ways in which objects become available to knowing subjects.

In the later decades of the twentieth century, a critical philosophical tradition, practiced most notably by French post-phenomenologists and poststructuralists, reflected on the role of historically situated genres and discourses.[1] Their philosophical, historical, and sociopolitical analyses presume that concepts are historically and politically predicated, that loci and modes of enunciation are inextricable mediations that render knowledge claims historically and spatially contingent. Consequently, left without foundational guarantees for certifying the known, philosophically informed inquiry has been coerced into continuous self-reflection, and the cast of negotiators dealing with the value and implications of knowledge claims (knowledge for what, for whom, and how?) has been broadened. The diminution of the certitudes of epistemology has weighed as heavily on ethical inquiry as it has on social and political inquiry. The suspicion that the world does not tell us how we should act has accompanied the loss of faith in a search for worldly signs that tell us what we should know. Ultimately, instead of a search for warrants, ethico-political inquiry requires a recognition of radical contingency and the need for new ways to negotiate the implications of theory.

More recently, Third World scholars have issued an additional challenge to the mainstream epistemological practices of the Anglo-American social sciences (which I address in chapter 1). Noting that "Epistemology is not ahistorical" and that it is also "geographical in its historicity," Walter Mignolo refers to the epistemological divide between the former colonial powers and their former colonized peoples. He notes that the "densities of the colonial experience" have given risen to "emerging epistemologies." As a result, he argues, Frantz Fanon's writings constitute an epistemological revolution that is equivalent to the impact of Kant's. Moreover, they reflect a historicity that Kant's formalisms lack. Although Kant's introduction of temporality as immanent in a productive version of human apprehension was part of the radicalizing effect of his critique of empiricist epistemology, time for Kant is a formal aspect of consciousness. In contrast, Fanon's texts inaugurate a time consciousness whose radicalizing effect is realized in the differences of the "being and time"of the colonizer and that of the colonized and formerly colonized.[2]

Apart from my resistance to a pre-Kantian/pre-Fanon social science, my ethical, political, and conceptual concerns are deployed on a complicated conjunction between methods and nations within two historical registers. The first and main concern, treated in chapter 1, involves the coincidence of two developments: the emergence of contemporary, scientifically oriented social science in the twentieth century and one of the primary deployments of its methods: an explanatory comparative politics whose major focus has been on "nation building" in the "Third World." Within the second register, treated in subsequent chapters, my focus is on the methods (or "policy" in a broad sense) of states, or at least of those groups placed to determine the direction of state policy. Especially since the nineteenth century, state representatives have been active in various modes of cultural governance, seeking to complement coercive monopolies with diverse modes of cultural containment.

Nestor Garcia Canclini's treatment of some of the mechanisms of cultural containment, in a discussion of the way elites control the production and reception of visual culture in Latin America, provides an apt illustration of cultural governance. Latin American elites, he states, "spiritualize cultural production under the guise of artistic 'creation'"...imposing a "division between arts and crafts"; they "freeze the circulation of symbolic goods in collections, concentrating them in museums, palaces, and other exclusive centers"; and they "propose as the only legitimate form of consumption of these goods the also spiritualized, hieratic method of reception that consists in contemplating them."[3] To illuminate this second register, from which Garcia Canclini offers one example in a diverse history of methods that the governing arms of states have employed to become "nation-states," my major focus in chapters 2–6 is on state-sponsored and encouraged developments of the artistic forms through which they have sought to create the unitary and coherent national cultures that are implied in the nation-state conjunction.

At the same time, because this is a work of critique (a practice explicated in chapter 1), much of my attention is on artistic productions that operate outside of state cultural governance, articulate alternative modes of attachment, and contest forms of state-sponsored and -encouraged symbolic production aimed at forging homogenous national cultures. The oppositional modes of artistic production on which I focus constitute instances of what Gilles Deleuze calls "counterinformation," because, as he suggests, "information [is] the controlled system of order-words that are used in a given society."[4] Accordingly, to propagate information uncritically is to reaffirm the dominant order within which the information is intelligible. No one has said it more succinctly than Fanon, as he points to the paradoxical competence with which colonized peoples participate within the system of intelligibility that subordinates them: "to speak means to be in a position to use a certain syntax, to grasp the morphology of this or that language, but it means above all to assume a culture, to support the weight of a civilization."[5]

Similarly, within the first register, my main effort is to expose and counter the results of what can best be termed the "cognitive imperialism" of a state-centric social science, which has been involved in attempting to universalize and render self-evident its practices of space and intelligibility. In enacting a critique of the history of modern social science, I seek to bring to recognition forms of political expression—alternative modes of intelligibility for things, people(s) and spaces—that have existed on the margins of the nationhood practices of states and the complicit nation-building and nation-sustaining conceits of social science. In making legible parts of the world that have been overcoded by dominant discursive modes for framing "the political," I am not merely attempting to redeem a neglected supplement of political relationships in order to render a more extensive and whole political world. Rather, as I note in my treatment of critical translation in chapter 1, critique is aimed at resisting closure, at challenging the assumption that there is a political vocabulary which, once achieved, can be adequate to a common political experience. Contrary to the conceits of those who see their task in terms of achieving a discursive universality, political division cannot be reduced to idiomatic disparity.

In addition to addressing the silences imposed by those who seek to achieve a historically unsituated, universal political discourse, I am concerned in chapter 1 with a specific mode of political expression; I offer a critique of the traditional liberal political discourse within which the consequences of state formation for indigenous peoples are not discernible. This aspect of my focus articulates a complex conceptual and locational interconnection, which I address in this preface.

**The Location**

My historical/territorial predicates are implicated in my conceptual ones. I am situated in Hawaii, an archipelago in the mid-Pacific, which provides me with an ambiguous locus of enunciation. Although, temporally, I write in what Walter Benjamin has called "now time," I am also located in the geopolitical, cultural, and economic history of migration and encounter through which the human population of the islands was assembled and shaped. Until recently, the most prominent public articulations of politics in Hawai'i reflected the traditional political imaginaries that had been deposited by Euro Americans in what was to become the fiftieth U.S. state. The long history in which Pacific peoples, especially those who greeted the settler populations in Hawaii, were constructed within perspectives other than their own is too extensive to summarize. Suffice it to say that Native Hawaiians were largely regarded as ineligible to articulate their mode of governance, their land use practices, and their ways of valuing things and persons, within the emerging political and moral economies that took shape throughout the nineteenth and twentieth centuries. The substantial Asian in-migration fared differently. They integrated themselves more successfully, ideationally, economically, and politically, into a Euro American modernity, after beginning as low-end labor, initially on plantations and subsequently in hotels. In general, the perspectives and interests given weight in the historical rendering of Hawai'i's disjunctive entry into a capitalist modernity have been those of the people who emigrated from the writing cultures of established nation-states.

At present, however, Pacific cultures in general and Hawai'i in particular are experiencing a newly politicized climate. An increasingly unruly Pacific is hearing voices that challenge the Euro American codes through which Pacific imaginaries—the meanings of land, of bodies, and of politically relevant cultural authority—have been understood. In the early 1990s, for example, Epeli Hau'ofa came to Hawai'i from Fiji, and, in a series of speeches on the "Big Island" (Hawai'i), contested "the idea that the countries of Polynesia and Micronesia are too small, too poor, and too isolated to develop a meaningful degree of autonomy." Going back to the "myths, legends, and oral traditions and cosmologies of the peoples of Oceania," Hau'ofa discovered a world conceived of as quite large compared with those of nation-states. It is a world "comprised not only of land surfaces, but the surrounding ocean as far as they could traverse and exploit its underworld with its fire-controlling and earth-shaking denizens, and the heavens above with their hierarchies of powerful gods and named stars and constellations that people could count on to guide their ways across the seas."[6] In short, Hau'ofa discovered a vast world. His discovery poses a challenge to the Euro American perspective in which the Pacific contains "islands in a far sea." Instead, he asserts, the Pacific is a very large "sea of islands," a turn of phrase that overturns the view that has "confined ocean people to tiny spaces."

In a another ocean venue, Antonio Benetez-Rojo also supplies a critical intervention into traditional territorial imaginaries. Calling attention to the distinctiveness of the Caribbean, he states that "[t]he culture of archipelagos is not terrestrial;" rather, "it is fluvial and marine . . . a culture of bearings, not of routes; of approximations, not of exactitudes;" it is a culture in which "the world of straight lines and angles . . . does not dominate; here rules the fluid world."[7] As a result, he suggests, one can think of the Antilles as a "meta-archipelago." Its disruptive character is constituted by the way in which it serves as "an island bridge, connecting . . . North to South America." Like Hawai'i's situation *vis á vis* Asia and North America, the Antilles is a "discontinuous conjunction of . . . empty spaces, unstrung voices, ligaments, sutures, voyages of signification," a place that "has the virtue of having neither a boundary nor a center."[8]

While the implication of Hau'ofa's challenge is that the space from which I write can be seen differently from its traditional relegation to a small, politically insignificant domain, the implication of Benetez-Rojo's is that to write from the mid-Pacific is to write from a spatially disruptive imaginary, one that reinflects the epistemic significance of enunciations and challenges the codes within which the cultural/political habitus of pre-settler Hawaii was devalued within the discourses that shaped the dominant intellectual strategies of my original discipline, a state-centric, social science-oriented political science.

In order to set a context for my departure from the dominant conceits of that discipline, I return to the initial deployment of political science in Hawai'i in chapter 1, in which I use the contemporary, politically contentious situation in Hawaii as a context for elaborating a critique of both the social sciences and the neoliberal approach to political equality which, together, disqualify the claims of Hawaiian political movements and thereby support the extension of the two-century history of the colonization of Hawai'i. Subsequent chapters deal with the cultural governance theme, beginning with a general treatment of the genre-nation states relationship, with special emphasis on the novel and the theater, proceeding to other artistic genres—music, landscape painting and photography, and film— and ending with the way the genre nation-state relationship pertains to contemporary issues in states' global management of violence in the post cold war, post-9/11, securitized world.

## A Few Words about Method

Having evoked the concept of method to apply to the way states seek to govern the cultural coherence of their citizen-inhabitants, it is appropriate in these introductory remarks to address myself to *my* "method." Such a disclosure is especially necessary because I inaugurate my investigation in chapter 1 with a critique of the purported objectivity of a social science that, in the twentieth century, distinguished itself by its departure from superstition, ideology, and arbitrarily selected empirical indicators—by, in short, the objectivity of its methods. It was a social science designed to provide an unbiased approach to reality and therefore an unambiguous frame within which "the real" could be communicated. What I want to note is that a rejection of a referential model of the real does not constitute a rejection of realism. Throughout my analyses, my approach to the real presumes a semiological rather than a referential real.

The most significant implication for "comparative politics" that I derive from a semiotic approach to the real is a displacement of what Walter Mignolo has referred to as the "monologic and universal subject of knowledge"[9]—which has been presumed during the period of European colonization and has been reenacted in modern social science discourses— by a focus on semiotic interactions. To treat "semiotic interactions" is to be concerned with encounters between peoples who use different modes of meaning production and different approaches to what is involved in events of understanding.[10] For example, when Third World intellectuals have approached historical encounters of alternative systems of meaning production, those with a politicized perspective have noted that alternative narratives of the emergence of modernity are involved. For example, speaking of the politics of writing history, Dipesh Chakrabarty asserts that it requires a "political-ethical task" effected by "attending to the fractures of the semiotic field called 'history' so that what is unrepresented is at least allowed to make visible the laws and limits of system of representation."[11]

What is a "semiotic field," and how does it differ from a field of communication? While those who treat language as communication focus on the relationship between statements and their referents, a semiological approach treats intelligibility on the basis of the interrelationships within a system of signs rather than in terms of the word-object relationship and, in addition, regards meaning systems as productive rather than merely referential. For purposes of illustration, I introduce here the approach of Georges Didi-Huberman to Dutch landscape painting (which I treat more elaborately in chapter 1). Didi-Huberman shows how the meaning of particular signs, for example streaks of white paint in Pieter Brueghel's painting *Landscape with the Fall of Icarus*, are discernible, although unstably so, when each sign is seen in the context of its relationship with other material signifiers within the painting. It would seem obvious to those who are familiar with the mythical account of Icarus's fall that each feather in a series of them, which seem to be following more slowly, Icarus's descent, supplies "an iconographic attribute necessary to the representing of the mythological scene." But, as Didi-Huberman's cogent reading indicates, the painting does not achieve its signifying ability through mere representational depiction because "the materiality of the paint . . . the details we have called 'feathers' have no determining feature which might 'separate' them completely from the foam the falling body produces in the sea."[12] We are prone to seeing the streaks as feathers, not because we are familiar with the mythological story and because each mark is a discrete representation of some-thing, but because of relationships among the signifiers in the painting—"because, the same mark is repeated in a constellation of marks, and sets itself off against a background other than the sea," for example, a "mark individualiz[ing] itself in front of a boat."[13]

Ultimately, read from a semiological point of view, the painting's pictorial signifiers cannot be treated as discrete representations. Their indeterminacy, as bits of materiality, places the burden of meaning on the interrelationships among the signs. Significantly, the painting does not simply represent; it displays a process of meaning production. It shows the activity of its making. Similarly, reading history as what Chakrabarty calls "a semiotic field" should turn our attention to the conditions under which historical accounts are produced. Rather than seeing historical discourse as a set of statement about events, each kind of historical discourse should be treated as a historical event of event-making, as the scripting of statements that reflect an exercise of control. The discursive contribution to event-making is not politically innocent. As Michel Foucault has shown, the historical productions of discourses of knowledge are power-invested enactments. They produce new discursive objects and new and privileged locations from which speakers can make intelligible and legitimate utterances.[14]

Signifying practices do not simply disseminate information, as neo-Enlightenment theorists presume; they contain, as Foucault has put it, "coercive power;" they impose an order with respect to who can perform speech acts with significant collective consequences. In short, a critical view of discourse requires a shift from discourse as a mode of communication about things to one that raises the questions of "power and eventualization"[15]—that treats the ways in which a particular account points to a process of imposing an order of meaning at the expense of other possible orders. The most relevant consequence of this perspective is that, to appreciate how the signifying practices contained in alternative historical narratives yield insights into the politics of knowledge, attention must be on the interests that a discourse, historical or otherwise, serves. One of Foucault's remarks (in one of his earlier works) on the value of statements locates the issue effectively:

> To analyze a discursive formation . . . is to weigh the 'value' of statements. A value that is not defined by their truth [here he contests empiricism], that is not gauged by the presence of a secret content [and here he contests traditional hermeneutics]; but which characterizes their place, their capacity for circulation and exchange.

A statement is therefore to be understood, Foucault adds, as "an asset." To interrogate statements in this way is to pose "the question of power," for a statement is "an asset that is, by nature, the object of a struggle, a political struggle."[16]

How can one move from such a general characterization of the politics of discourse to a focus on the redistribution of political assets? The study that follows is addressed to this question but, to provide a brief preview, I call attention to an analytically disenabling perspective on the world's spaces to which Akhil Gupta and James Ferguson have addressed themselves. They note that:

> Representations of space in the social sciences are remarkably dependent on images of break, rupture, and disjunction. The distinctiveness of societies, nations, and cultures is predicated on a seemingly unproblematic division of space, on the fact that they occupy 'naturally' discontinuous spaces.[17]

Within such a spatial commitment, which is delivered within the traditional discourses of comparative politics and international studies, the process by which societies form modes of economy and governance are attributed to their collective national character. As a result, the more centrifugal aspects of difference contained within state societies (different peoples whose histories and modes of attachment are not contained within the dominant divisions of geopolitical space) become invisible. By contrast, in this investigation I treat governance not as the management of a people who belong by dint of character or other distinguishing attributes within a discrete territory, but rather as a historical process in which boundaries are imposed, and peoples are accorded varying degrees of cultural coherence and political eligibility—not on the basis of natural divisions, but as a result of the exercise of power. This alternative perspective makes possible a critical approach to governance, an approach I inaugurate in chapter 1, which is introduced with a gloss on the legitimating discourses attending the Euro American dispossession of the Hawaiian nation.

# Acknowledgments

I owe the title of this study to my former colleague Rudolph Rummel, who was responsible for instituting a course entitled "Methods and Nations" in the University of Hawai'i's graduate catalogue. A few years ago, as I prepared to teach a graduate seminar, the design for which helped me to formulate the investigations in this book, I used Professor Rummel's course title. At the time, I thought the fit might be awkward, but at least it would allow me to avoid the cumbersome bureaucratic process (involving feisty faculty committees and surveilling deans) of having a new course added to the graduate curriculum. Rummel's purpose in instituting the course was primarily to teach multidimensional scaling techniques, with nations and what he calls their "attributes" and "behaviors" as his units of analysis, an approach to method quite different from my own.

However, the more I labored under the title I had appropriated, the more I liked its fit. "Method," in my approach to comparing nations, turns out to have a productively double resonance. It refers to both *my* focus on critical translation (explicated in the critique of twentieth century social science in chapter 1) and to the methods that developed during periods of "nation-building," as states mobilized diverse modes of cultural governance to invent culturally coherent nations (the primary "empirical" focus of subsequent chapters).

Other debts are owed to colleagues and students, who in some cases solicited prototypes of some of the chapters and in others read and reacted to parts or the whole of this book or to oral presentations, based on the ideas in the book. I am grateful to John Agnew, Jane Bennett, Bill Callahan, David Campbell, Bill Chaloupka, Bill Connolly, Mick Dillon, Tom Dumm, Jenny Edkins, Jorge Fernandez, Jon Goldberg-Hiller, Manfred Henningsen, Sankaran Krishna, Walter Mignolo, Neal Milner, Konrad Ng, Thad Oliver, Paul Patton, Noenoe Silva, Nevzat Soguk, Manfred Steger, Hannah Tavares, Rob Walker, and Geoff Whitehall. And, finally, I want to thank the Routledge staff, particularly Angela Chnapko and Donna Capato for a smooth and efficient production process.

CHAPTER **1**

# Social Science, "Comparative Politics," and Inequality

## Introduction: Biopolitical Conceits and the Colonization of Hawaii

*Colonial thugs with their bible and drugs—snitches, dopers, religious interlop-ers. The mission to seize secure ka aina pa'a i ka [the land and thus the nation] native pure . . .*

*Skippy Ioane*

As the contemporary music of Native Hawaiian activist Skippy Ioane sug-gests, colonialism in Hawai'i is, for some, a live issue. But its recognition remains fugitive for many because colonialism is not easily accessible within the dominant neoliberal discourse on the rights and privileges of individ-uals. The initial colonizing of Hawai'i was a "century-long project driven first by merchants and missionaries, then by the demands of whale fishery, and ultimately and most powerfully by the expansion of capitalist agricul-ture in the plantation production of sugar."[1] Among the most significant consequences for the native population was the displacement of Hawaiian commoners from the lands held on the basis of ancient grants bestowed by Hawaiian chiefs. Along with the spiritual and material consequences at-tached to the land grab was an altered context for the connections between culture and political economy. The colonial encounter favored interpreta-tions of sexual, working, and citizen bodies that comported with an imposed, capitalist economic hierarchy, blessed by a supportive, expansion-oriented religious organization.

1

Although there is a growing body of work on the implications of the Euro American colonizing of Hawai'i, especially from the points of view of culture and economy, the primary focus here is on the role of the nascent discipline of political science, whose initial deployment in Hawaii provided an ideational legitimation for the displacement of the Hawaiian political order and one of whose major products (along with the other social sciences) in Hawai'i and elsewhere, has been the warranting of forms of political and cultural domination under the guise of objective analysis.

In order specifically to contest the historical role political science has played in Hawaii and generally to provide a narrative of the parallels between social science and political domination, I begin with a critique of a (highly schematic) trajectory of discourses on political inquiry, nation building and equality/inequality, throughout the twentieth century, to which the primary contributions have been from American social science. I then work toward an ethico-political sensibility, presenting an approach to inequality that challenges the predicates of state-centric discourses on rights and equality before the law and end by making a case for critical translation as a method to displace an empiricist comparative political analysis. The historical section is instrumental to the sections on equality and translation, because my critique of a historical trajectory of social science discourse is focused especially on the traditional practice of a "comparative politics" within which the inequalities visited on nations without states are legitimated. As a disciplinary focus, comparative politics was invented by those who, regarding themselves as prophets, approached the problem of difference in a way well summarized by Caribbean writer Edward Glissant: "'I can acknowledge your difference and continue to think it is harmful to you. I can think that my strength lies in the Voyage (I am making History) and that your difference is motionless and silent.'"[2]

Glissant's words capture particularly well the perspective of one of the founders of modern comparative politics, Daniel Lerner, whose mid twentieth-century writings receive extended treatment later in this chapter. Here, the Hawai'i portion of the narrative continues with an examination of an earlier version of political science, which made its debut on the Hawaiian scene in an exchange of letters between Sanford Dole and John W. Burgess, near the end of the nineteenth century. Dole, the head of the provisional government of Hawaii and leader of the coup that overthrew the Hawaiian monarchy, wrote to ask Burgess, dean of the political science faculty at Columbia University (and a widely acknowledged founder of American political science), about the form Hawai'i's new government should take, if he and his cronies were to dominate the new political order. Although Dole's letter was somewhat elliptical, couched as it was in the rhetoric of good government, Burgess got the gist of the inquiry. After reviewing the information Dole conveyed about the Hawaiian ethnoscape, he wrote: "I understand your problem to be the construction of a constitution which will place the government in the hands of the Teutons [read whites], and preserve it there, at least for the present." Being wholly sympathetic to Dole's et al. problem—he was of the view that "the Teuton really dominates the world by his superior political genius"[3]—Burgess responded with suggestions about how to impose voting qualifications and governance structures that would politically disqualify a substantial portion of Hawaii's non-white population ("Teutons" numbered only 4,533 out of a total population of 89,990, of which 40,622 were Hawaiians and part Hawaiians).[4]

Burgess's responses partake of the same rhetorical dissimulation as Dole's queries. His partisan racial and ethnic tropes are presented in the discourse of good governance, which foregrounds such crotchets as the virtues of a "strong presidency." And, as was the case throughout Burgess's intellectual and pedagogical career, part of his rationale for preserving structures of white dominance was what he regarded as the unquestionable value of stability, which he believed was to be achieved by the consolidation of the European state form of political organization. According to Burgess, "the national state is... the most modern and the most complete solution of the whole problem of political organization which the world has yet produced." Coupled with his practical and metaphysical commitment to state-controlled nation building, was Burgess's biopolitical agenda. Appended to his remark about the state as "the most complete solution... to political order" is the phrase, "and the fact that it is a creation of Teutonic political genius stamps the Teutonic nations as the political nations *par excellence*." This biopolitical observation carries with it a legitimating corollary; Burgess was of the opinion that the historical warranting of the Teuton's "political genius"... "authorizes them... to assume the leadership in the establishment and administration of states."[5]

Biopolitical conceits as well as notions about governmental forms were thus integral aspects of political science's contribution to the colonization of Hawai'i. Now that Hawaiians are involved in movements aimed at decolonizing their ancestral lands (in the case of the more radical movements) or recovering "ceded lands" (in the case of less radical ones),[6] another version of biopolitics is being articulated to discredit their claims. More than a century after the Dole-Burgess exchange, and after the subsequent political suppression and economic degradation experienced by the Hawaiian people, who first lost their government and then lost their lands to the depredations of a coalition of economic predators and politically collusive white American leaders, another Burgess, H. William, a lawyer involved in suits that oppose any form of Native Hawaiian legal entitlement, participated in a much less congenial conversation. In an exchange with Haunani-Kay Trask, a Hawaiian academic and activist committed to the restoration of Hawaiian sovereignty, Burgess argued against a bill before the American Congress

(S.B. 2889 and H.R. 4904) that would lend federal recognition and a measure of self-governance to Native Hawaiians. Invoking the Fourteenth Amendment, Burgess asserts that the bill would allow the federal government to violate the Equal Protection Clause by funding "racially defined 'Native Hawaiians."[7] He added that it would create a "new tribe out of thin air."[8]

Significantly, Trask's remarks are dominated by historical rather than legal tropes. And, when she does refers to law, it is to international rather than U.S. law. Instead of invoking the U.S. Constitution, she refers to a "continuing assault on Native Hawaiian entitlements and institutions," which began with the missionary descendants (those involved in the overthrow of the Hawaiian monarchy), and to the violence associated with the founding of the U.S. as a "white country."[9] Crucially, instead of referring to Hawaiians as a "race," she identifies them as a nation, whose nationhood was stolen.[10] This discursive gesture reorients the spatial predicates of the issue. For Trask, a critique of U.S.-Hawaiian relationships is a critique of U.S. foreign policy. Because there has been no space for such gestures within the post-John Burgess period in which American social and political science has been institutionalized, it's necessary to return to that period, which witnessed the emergence of American social science, in order to open a discursive space within which to treat more elaborately the implications of the Burgess-Trask encounter for thinking about territorial control, bodies, and inequality.

## The Development of American Social and Political Science

John Burgess's focus on political genius was short-lived within the discipline of political science. Public policy making, understood as a problem of rational political planning and management, displaced Burgess ethno-political conceits. Among those shaping this phase of the discipline in the early decades of the twentieth century was Burgess's student, Charles Merriam, who had entered Colombia University in 1896 and was subsequently to carry on the legacy of Burgess's shift from a juristic to a social science-oriented understanding of governance. During the period of his tutelage of the young Merriam, Burgess's orientation toward political science had changed: "Despite his conservatism (a Hegelian-inspired metaphysics grafted onto the historical method), Burgess began to shift from a juristic formal political science to one that envisioned a synthesis of the social sciences."[11]

Merriam, an urban reformer, the first political scientist at the University of Chicago, a leader of the American Political Science Association, and a founder of the Social Science Research Council, was also a planner in President Franklin Roosevelt's administration. In the last role, he helped create "a historically distinct form of national planning to fit the American setting," seen as a rapid movement toward an urban-industrial complex in need of a new form of (guided) liberalism. As a historian of the Roosevelt years puts it, "Merriam, an advocate of professional expertise in the making of public policy, sought to reformulate the American liberal tradition by professionalizing social science, using research in public-policy making."[12]

Merriam's approach to method is described in his "Progress Report of the Committee on Political Research," in a 1923 issue of the *American Political Science Review*. Arguing that social science research has no partisan agenda, he suggests that it be evaluated on the basis of its "utility in the development of the more accurate study of social phenomena."[13] Among the subdisciplines Merriam singles out for their policy-relevant objectivity is political psychology, which, he notes, "has become an increasingly significant field for the student of government."[14] Without going into elaborate historical detail, it should be recalled that it was an American social psychology that modernization theorists often employed to discredit indigenous political initiatives in the decolonizing movements of the "Third World" and to counter the influence of communist and socialist movements. Social psychology, as Ellen Herman has pointed out, was a cold war weapon represented as objective science. For example, Leonard Doob, an exemplary cold war psychologist, one who "held tightly to the vision of an objective and nonjudgmental behavioral science" ascribed Third World impoverishment to the psychological deficits that abound in 'uncivilized' societies. He, like many of the "development theorists," saw receptivity to revolutionary Marxist or socialist movements as an indication of rigid and dogmatic thinking.[15]

While Merriam's primary concern was the American polity, the role of political science's outward gaze during the cold war period is manifested in the dominant methods-oriented thinkers in the subdiscipline of comparative politics. Again, the Social Science Research Council is a major venue for political science's role in legitimating power structures. As Timothy Mitchell observes, in the 1940s and 1950s, "[p]olitical science had to expand its boundaries to match the growth of postwar U.S. power, whose ambitions it would serve."[16] By 1955 the comparative politics committee of the SSRC, chaired by Gabriel Almond, sought to go beyond mere institutional analysis because "the basic problems of civic loyalty and political cohesion lie in large part outside of the formal government framework." In a "memo," written by Almond and his colleagues, Taylor Cole and Roy Macridis, they state (while claiming to champion "objective method"):

> This memo arises from more urgent practical considerations. The survival of parliamentary and democratic institutions on the European continent is by no means to be taken for granted. The political communities of the major Western European countries—France, German, and Italy—are fragmented into exclusive ideological movements. Large bodies of opinion appear to be alienated from the West, politically apathetic, or actively recruited to communism.[17]

The writers go on to speak of the inability of a "legal-historical-philosophical approach to discover how serious these cleavages and alienations are."[18] Although the very idea of the "West" as a separate geographical area and as a separate thought-world is conceptually flawed, for want of a familiar and intelligible alternative, I too resort to it as a geographical/conceptual marker to identify European and American locations and perspectives throughout this investigation. Among other disciplines, a highly institutionalized "area studies" within the academy has made "the West" an almost irresistible discursive gesture.

Like the subdiscipline of comparative politics, the impetus to knowledge production in area studies, which also developed during the cold war and articulated the idioms of political science with those of other social science disciplines, partook of an undisguised, geopolitical partisanship. For example, an analysis of key area studies methods texts reveals that "just as the humanities were meant to cultivate a self that was authorized to transmit the legacy of the past, area studies would develop a body of elite scholars capable of producing knowledge about other nations to the benefit of our nation."[19] Moreover, there was an identity angst animating the look outward, for as Vincente Rafael notes, "most area studies programs in the United States were conceived at a moment in American history when liberal ambitions for enforcing a global peace necessary for capitalist expansion coincided with liberal anxieties over desegregation, spurred by the successes of the civil rights movement."[20]

There is a variety of ways to situate and render political the loci of enunciation that have governed political knowledge in the social sciences. A sensitivity to movements that have historically resisted state consolidation (what Almond et al called "cohesion") reveals how "knowing the world and producing knowledge" requires "the interplay of continually shifting positions and perspectives"[21] Insofar as a narrow range of perspectives has dominated, it has been largely a function of "the geohistorical locations of the social sciences" in which there have been, for the most part, five countries and four languages that have "saturate[d] academic production."[22] A small set of "textual national legacies,"[23] has produced a state- and Euro-centric political discourse. Pierre Bourdieu has pithily summarized one of the consequences: "if the state is so difficult to think, it is because we are the state's thinkers, and because the state is in the head of the thinkers."[24]

## The New Deal and the Emergence of Social Science

To elaborate on the implications of Bourdieu's remark, it is necessary to specify some of the ways that the modern state—often misleadingly rendered as a "nation-state"—is in the "head of thinkers." In the social sciences in general, and especially in a national sovereignty-enthralled comparative politics and international studies, the state dominates conceptions of political space. To the extent that one adheres to a simplistic narrative of nation building, in which states are seen as the consummation of more or less consensual political developments, the space of the state is rendered politically incontestable. However, as one counter narrative would have it, the state has, in numerous cases, been a "nation killer" rather than a "nation builder."[25] While "traditional empires were generally tolerant of, or at least indifferent to, ethnic, linguistic, or even religious diversity,"[26] and therefore contained a plurality of cultures and even nations, the violent process of state consolidation was in part driven by legitimation-oriented projects. The intent was to create states that contain unitary and coherent national cultures. Neglecting the institutionalized violence exposed in the counter-narratives pointing to the violence of state consolidation, much of American social and political science has been "professional" in the sense that what has been professed is a trained inattention to the historical meta-politics of their political imaginaries.

To engage the implications of the unproblematic reproduction of state space in professional political science, I begin with a consideration of what political scientists regard as "domestic politics" and examine and contest the partisanship of the "objective" and "disinterested" American social science, to which Charles Merriam, as both a social scientist and New Deal policy maker, was committed. While the New Deal is often thought of as a historic victory for the forces of democratic equality, there are some consequences of New Deal agriculture policy that are underappreciated in the mainstream historical and political studies that perpetuate the egalitarian narrative. As Clyde Woods has shown, agricultural policies developed under the New Deal were instrumental to the destruction of African American agricultural livelihoods, particularly in the area of the Mississippi delta. They provided inducements for white southern planters to demote their workers to the status of casual laborers, employed only seasonally. "Eventually millions [of African Americans] drifted out of the South all together, probably the largest government-impelled population movement in all our history."[27] The diminution of their agricultural livelihoods, along with other, more violent white practices that made the South increasingly inhospitable to African Americans, led to the diaspora northward.

The impact of the New Deal on the well being of southern African Americans is Woods's specific political concern in his analysis of the arrested development in the Mississippi delta. His epistemological contribution stems from his juxtaposition between "plantation bloc explanation" and "blues epistemology." According to Woods, the plantation has persisted not only as a "monopoly over agricultural manufacturing, banking, land, and water," but also as a "world view."[28] From the point of view of the plantation bloc, for example, the federal policies, which influenced agricultural developments in the Mississippi delta region, enabled a capitalist enterprise with a "natural" organization structure: "the planter as the heroic master of a natural ethnic, class, gender, and environmental hierarchy." By contrast, for the "blues bloc," the plantation system is a system of exploitation and repression. Practicing the blues as not simply an aesthetic but also as an ontology and way of knowing, African American communities in the rural south (and in a state of diaspora throughout the post-slavery period) turned to blues epistemology to provide a "constant reestablishment of collective sensibility in the face of constant attacks by the plantation bloc and its allies" and to reaffirm "the historic commitment to social and personal investigation, description, and criticism present in the blues."[29]

The African American blues involvement is therefore an articulation of knowledge with a "structure of feeling"; it enacts a lived experience that resists the explanatory monopoly of the plantation bloc's absorption of southern agriculture into a narrative of economic development, in which diasporic black bodies have no political standing. While within the locus of enunciation of white planters, agriculture is a set of issues related to national "economic policy," the issues are different from the perspective of displaced African American farmers. For them, as Woods puts it, "these issues meant the difference between leaving and staying."[30] Woods's political act, articulated through the invention of a new epistemological concept, consists in denaturalizing a dominant system of explanation: "The planter's mythical ethno-regional system of explanation."[31]

Woods's analysis also bears significantly on the political role of American social science. He points out that while the blues developed "as a theory of African American aesthetics" in literature and the arts—for example, Richard Wright's treatment of "the blues as social criticism"—"the social sciences remained unscathed."[32] Taking up this challenge, he proceeds with a scathing critique of the collusive role of American social science with "the planters' mythical ethno-regional system of explanation."[33] Allowing the "plantation"as a system of explanation to migrate into a general frame of public policy discourse, Woods discovers its social science epistemological fellow-travelers in a history of research running from the mid nineteenth century (e.g., George Fitzhugh's *Sociology of the South or the Future of Free Society*) through the twentieth century, for example "modernization theory," which supported the "false belief that industrial growth would eliminate racial inequality."[34]

Woods's treatment of the complicity of the social sciences in the modern history of white domination goes well beyond indictment. Parallel to his discussion of the ideational supports of the plantation bloc (writ large) is his treatment of the redemptive quality of "the blues tradition of social explanation."[35] And importantly, for purposes of my concern with the politics of inequality (taken up later in this chapter), Woods's study stands as an instance of this tradition. His *Development Arrested* is an enactment of a politically inspired mode of "subjectification;"[36] it articulates and includes voices that have been outside the dominant order, enacting an intervention that brings into political discourse the concerns of those who, in Jacques Ranciere's terms, have "made themselves of some account" by "placing in common a wrong,"[37] and in Woods's terms, have been "seen as a threat to the legitimacy of the plantation bloc."[38]

I treat some of the implications of the African American blues aesthetic in chapter 3. Here, I consider another register of the development of modern social science, its outward-looking gaze, as it was articulated in the modernization theory that Woods indicts and, more generally, in a comparative politics focused on the problem of nation building. For this purpose, an inspection of some of the influential writings of the earlier-mentioned Daniel Lerner serves to strike comparative politics at its exemplary center. Lerner famously elaborated the main doctrines through which an explanatory social science was to dominate the discipline of political science (formerly a more descriptive discipline involved in mapping the structural elements of modern governments) from the mid twentieth-century onward. He also helped, with his study of nation building in the Middle East, to inaugurate a comparative politics concerned with nation building within the postwar, three-world global imaginary. For Lerner, as for Merriam before him, the New Deal was an unmitigated blessing, establishing a nonpartisan social-science-governance relationship. "The New Deal," he asserted, "codified a relationship between social research and social policy which had developed through preceding decades under the regime of both major parties."[39] Lerner situated his research endeavors within the domain of official foreign policy as well. He regarded his government's technical assistance program—"aid from richer to poorer countries"—as a significant policy aspect of the "political development" concept that was at the center of his understanding of global geopolitics.[40]

Apart from the uncritically accepted models of space and time upon which Lerner's discourse on political development is based, is a failure to acknowledge what a subsequent generation of "dependency" theorists was to point out: the complex interactions that constitute being a richer versus a poorer country. Without summarizing all the important work on global political economy, it should be noted, at a minimum, that instead of looking for economic success within particular state infrastructures, one needs to treat poverty as a relationship. Given the ways in which global capital has been controlled, some nations are poor *because* some are rich. In contrast with Lerner et al's emphasis on motivational and communicational resources, the way a country's economic fortunes evolve cannot be attributed only to local sources. Without treating the historical shifts through which powerful nations degrade labor abroad, a brief look at the consequences of contemporary indebtedness should suffice to challenge the psychological conceits of the modernization theorists. As "new interstate collaboration, multililateral networks, and global capitalism have tied the world tighter," and the economically powerful states in "the north [have] increasingly pressured the south to open its economies to foreign corporations," a main consequence has been the production of a "hyper-indebtedness" that paralyzes the economies of "poorer" countries in ways that no amount of enterprising motivation can overcome.[41]

## Epistemic Commitments: A Critique of Pre-Kantian Realism

Although Lerner's epistemological, historical, and political commitments, in both his substantive and methodological writings, may now seem passé, given subsequent decades of critical work on global political economy, they nevertheless provide exemplary insight into the social science-policy nexus that shaped much of American political science. As Herbert Schiller notes:

> Lerner was among the first to grasp and articulate the geopolitical strategy of securing the excolonial world for Western-structured 'development'... he helped found the new field of development communication that incorporated this strategy into its underlying assumptions and practices.[42]

In addition, much of Lerner's focus was on the tension between Islam and modernity, which has emerged in the twenty-first century as a primary issue in the worlds of official policy making, academia, and popular culture. And, apropos of the focus here on the politics of social science knowledge, although one might hope that Lerner's pre-Kantian reliance on the self-evidence of observation has been superceded in political studies, it remains the dominant epistemological model for social scientists. After Lerner and his generation's elaboration of a scientifically oriented comparative politics, lodged within a development narrative, the comparative data archive-driven method dominated until late in the twentieth century, when a "crisis of developmentalism" became also "a crisis of the comparative method."[43] Although a "critical globalism"[44] has largely supplanted the mid twentieth-century developmentalist, modernization theory among comparativists, many—even those who shift the locus of enunciation to Third World voices—continue to focus on a map of national cultures, neglecting the centrifugal attachments within states, which speak to the absence of the level of collective coherence that the conjunction "nation-state" implies. And even though the cold war context within which Lerner's major writing was undertaken is no longer a significant policy frame (despite remaining for some a residual geopolitical imaginary), the more general state-oriented, geophilosophy guiding Lerner's efforts persists in the ways in which social scientists and policy makers make their worlds.

The two narratives, which more or less exhaust Lerner's corpus, remain central to mainstream American political science. The first is a celebration of the "new" social science, which is distinguished by its displacement of dubious modes of speculation with an epistemological commitment to systematic observation: "Social science is a genuinely new way of looking at the world—replacing the successive methods of magic, religion, philosophy by the method of observation."[45] The second is what he refers to as the setting for the new social science, "the drama of modernization," the process through which, in his view, static and inert societies are being mobilized to join a capitalist modernity, based on an articulation of an industrializing economy and a modernizing-accepting psychology that is growing within the social order. As the title of his major work, *The Passing of Traditional Society,* implies, history is on the side of a modernity defined by the "Western" highly industrialized countries.

Doubtless, Lerner's "drama" narrative seemed incontestable to him because of his epistemological story, the triumph of an exemplary empiricism, with its commitment to an unsituated scientific mode of observation. Philosophically, an effective challenge to the empiricist faith in observation has been developed by those thinkers who have effected a "dislocation between seeing and saying," showing, with historical treatments of changes in knowledge problematics, that "the problem of knowledge (or rather 'knowledges')" cannot be effectively approached by treating language as representational, "by invoking a correspondence or conformity of terms."[46] Although the philosophical critique of representation has yet to have a significant impact on the social sciences, its implications are well elaborated by theorists of visual culture. In particular, there are significant challenges to correspondence notions of realism in the critical perspectives evinced by art historians, for example, in Georges Didi-Huberman's analysis of Jan Vermeer's painting *View of Delft* (1658) (treated briefly in the preface), and Michael Fried's of Thomas Eakins's painting *The Gross Clinic* (1876)—a medical scene with doctors operating and medical students observing—both of which are exemplary.

Didi-Huberman begins his analysis by contesting the representational approach of another art historian, Svetlana Alpers, who, in her discussion of Vermeer's *View of Delft,* is at pains to show the representational verisimilitude between the painting and the town itself, presuming, as Didi-Huberman puts it, that the painting is faithful depiction:

> As if the visible world were a surface . . . as if paint had nondensity. As if a flow of pigment had the legitimacy of a topological projection: such is the hidden ideal underlying the notion of technical skill, which requires that the hand itself be turned into a 'Faithful eye'; that is to say an organ independent of a human subject.[47]

In contrast with Alpers's descriptive approach to Vermeer's painting— her capitulation to the "primacy of the referent"[48]—Didi-Huberman calls attention to an enigmatic patch of yellow on the canvas. Looking for clues within the painting instead of examining (as did Alpers) the topographical features of the city of Delft, Didi-Huberman notes that seemingly accidental patches of color in Vermeer have the effect of unsettling a mimetic approach to the objects in the painting, of making those objects unstable. Vermeer's color patches are "intense representational voids" that call attention to "painting in action."[49] Didi-Huberman's search for what he calls "semiotically unstable elements" is, effectively, a search for "*the symptom of painting within the picture.*"[50] He shows how painting, like writing, is a productive, meaning-generating vocation rather than an activity governed by its referents.

Fried's treatment of Eakins's painterly practice provides a similar critique of a representational model of realism. He shows that "crucial aspects" of the painting's "significance . . . can be brought out only by bracketing its supposed dependence upon the scene it claims to represent and by comparing it instead with a considerable number of works in Eakins's oeuvre . . . "[51] Two details in Eakins's canvas, which are crucial to Fried's critique of a representational realism, accord well with the insights in Didi-Huberman's analysis of Vermeer's *View of Delft*. First, instead of connecting the painting's configuration with the actual medical event that is its subject, Fried points to patches of color that occur not only in *The Gross Clinic*, but also in other Eakins paintings: "Coloristically," he notes, "the works in question are dark, with black or brown shadows enveloping much of the image. . . . punctuated by patches of white as well as by areas of bright warm red that are surely meant to mediate between dark and light but often seem almost to leap out of the painting." Fried infers from the color treatment that Eakins's paintings are "frankly painterly," that they belong to "a tradition that goes back at least to Caravaggio and Courbet."[52] Second, Fried calls attention to Eakins's appearance within the painting, noting that beyond the mere fact that Eakins represents himself in the painting is the issue of *how* he represent himself. Given Eakins's long-standing preoccupation with the coordination of hand and eye (owed to his early education), his placement in the scene, sitting in a wholly detached manner with pen and writing tablet, thematizes the scene as a whole within the painterly problematic of the co-ordination of hand and eye, instead of, for example, seeking a faithfulness of representation.

The most relevant implication of Didi-Huberman's and Fried's critiques of realist painting as mere depiction is their substitution of the paint-ing as a presentational act for painting as representational. In this sense, they are post-Kantians inasmuch as Kant, with his notions of *Ercheinung* (a bringing into appearance) and *Darstellung* (making present) establishes the primacy of presentation over representation. Accepting this model of meaning-production, Didi-Huberman and Fried recognize that phenom-ena do not make an unaided appearance. Because their focus is on the action of presentation, they are able to treat Vermeer's and Eakins's painting prac-tices instead of blaming Delft and medical practices respectively for the ways they appear in the paintings.

However, the displacement of simplistic, observational, or referential models of reality, effected by art historians, needs a critical supplement, which emerges from the analysis of the cinematic object. In particular, Gilles Deleuze's gloss on Italian neorealism provides a different view of semiotic realism, based on the cinema's use of moving images. Recognizing that with Italian neorealist cinema, the process of meaning making shifts from its dependence on the movement of characters involved in a dramatic narra-tive, within a stable interpretive frame, to a destabilized set of time images, constructed with "irrational cuts and incommensurable relations between images," Deleuze resists the totalizing frame within which semiotic image analyses tend to work.[53] Without treating the intricacies of his elaborate no-tion of cinema's time image, suffice it to say, for purposes of a discrediting of referential realism, Deleuze's analysis of time images shows the ways in which the technologies that are the vehicles for imaginaries (models of the world) create their objects, in contrast with the assumption of traditional realism, which "presupposes the independence of its objects."[54]

Moreover, and most significantly, Deleuze's emphasis on the time image, which is owed in large measure to Henri Bergson's philosophy, explicates the ways in which modern film—in contrast with its earlier construction through movement images—shows the past within the present. The concept of the "temporalization of the image,"[55] central to Deleuze's critical philos-ophy of film, can be used to undermine essentialized notions of, among other things, the bodies deployed in a nation-state model of geopolitical space. For example, if we consider the history of encounter, which contin-ues to haunt the present, we can see in much of the world's ethnoscape a dynamic of "creolization," a historical process of "the construction of cul-ture out of fragmented, violent, and disjunct pasts," rather than seeing a static national culture or set of racial and ethnic maps superimposed on state-administrated territories.[56]

The examples from art historical and cinematic critique have significant critical implications for Lerner's faith in the gift that social science bestows on rational public policy—"candid and comprehensive observation."[57] At a minimum, they encourage us to inquire into the observational practices he deploys and the spatiotemporal commitments those practices presume rather than holding the world responsible for his conclusions about it. What are those conclusions, and what observational predicates animate them? Spatially, Lerner practiced the three-world model (the "West" as the first world, the Soviet bloc as the second, and the former colonies as the third) that dominated the postwar geopolitical imaginary shared by policy makers and those academics who articulated the dominant policy discourses. Certainly the three-world model does not strike the eye. Rather, it emerged as a global cartographic practice within the social science discourses of the 1950s and '60s, especially within modernization theory. The political investments that such a division of the globe reflected for American social scientists are unmistakable. The three-world model was animated by the "presumed imperial ambitions of the Soviet Union" and "the prospect of decolonization and the transfer of responsibility for much of the former British Empire to the United States."[58]

The three-world spatial model is intimately connected with a temporal one, reflected, in Lerner's case, with his "drama of modernization" narrative, his world divided into those countries that have successfully entered modernity and those that must overcome an antimodernizing mentality in order to participate in the ineluctable future of a modern urban and industrial oriented nationhood. More specifically, seeing Middle Eastern populations as "the inert peoples of the underdeveloped world,"[59] Lerner sought to distinguish those with progressive as opposed to "traditional" attitudes in order to find vestiges of a character that would lead to the kind of mobilization necessary for an entry into an economic and political modernity for which Islam had failed to provide. And, holding to a linear narrative of political development, he expressed confidence that Islamic, clerically oriented polities, which have failed to provide plausible models of political modernity, had no future; the "infusion of a rationalist and positivist spirit," is a force against which "Islam is absolutely defenseless," Lerner insisted.[60]

### Alternative Political Narratives

Certainly, one can easily use hindsight to impeach Lerner's intrepid forecast. But his narrative commitments, the way he constructs historicity rather than his specific model of futurity, are more to the point. Although Lerner addresses himself to an array of Middle Eastern polities—Turkey, Lebanon, Egypt, Syria, and Iran—his approach to Turkey, the site where his research had the most ethnographic and historical depth, provides the best example of his theoretical/ideational commitments. As has been the case with many "Western" intellectuals, the Ottoman Empire is the great "Other" to contrast with the emergence of the modern nation-state. For Lerner, who prized the communication structures necessary to accelerate social mobility, the Ottoman Empire, his version of Turkey's antimodern past, represents a tradition of communicative stasis; it was, he stated, "not merely a variety of illiterate populations but an *anti*-literate elite," which controlled communication through oral dissemination as a means of social control.[61]

Lerner's gloss on the Ottoman Empire (for which he supplies scant evidence) can be effectively challenged by even a cursory treatment of its cultural policies. For example, for those who prize the freedom of expression that they think is an exemplary condition in modern democratic states, Ottoman Turkey provides a counterintuitive historical example. Before Kemal Ataturk's revolution, which displaced the Ottoman Empire with a European style secular state, Ottoman Turkey reflected an extraordinary cultural heterogeneity:

> From the beginning the Ottoman state was a heterology. . . . From all over the Islamic world it attracted adventurers interested in the profits of legitimate warfare against the Christian west . . . [it contained a] hodgepodge of languages, religions, ethnicities, cultures that seem to typify the late Middle Ages, and as it forced its way into the power vacuum left by the decline of the Byzantine Empire, it inscribed its originary heterogeneity on the fundamental structure of the state.[62]

Moreover, and in contrast with Lerner's presumption, "the Ottomans most often permitted a high degree of self-control to local groupings and tended to avoid enforcing homogeneity (except occasionally in questions of the practice of Islam among Muslims)."[63] The centripetal forms of expression within Ottoman Turkey were often expressed in poetic traditions. In contrast with the identity policing in the contemporary Kemalist state, which manifests an exemplary intolerance of cultural diversity, the Ottoman Empire supported an "astounding complexity of identity—multi-cultural, multi-confessional, multi-lingual." For example, reflecting the identity tolerance of the Ottoman period, a genre known as *divan* poetry expressed an exemplary alienation from any single identity space. Focusing on mobile characters such as vagabonds and exiles, it celebrated ambiguity and resisted efforts to encode bodies within any stable semiotic order imposed by a central authority.[64]

In contemporary Turkey, which is rife with the communication structures that Lerner attributes to a developed modernity, cultural governance weighs heavily on most artistic productions. To cite one instance: Yessim Ustaoglu's contemporary film (discussed in chapter 5), which treats the plight of Turkey's politically and culturally suppressed Kurdish minority, has been kept out of Turkish theaters by a regime that wants films to express the nation's founding ideals.[65] And more recently, a "pro-Islamic politician" had his political activities restricted by the highest Turkish court because of an earlier conviction "for threatening the secular government by reciting a poem deemed seditious."[66] At a minimum, Lerner's linear historical narrative, in which the Ottoman imperial system reflects an authoritarian past whose vestigial modes of informational hegemony retard Turkey's entrance into modernity, is both conceptually and historically obtuse.

As has been the case in many historical venues, a tradition-modernity tension was manifested *within* Ottoman Turkey. Rather than steadfastly resisting modernization, the Ottoman court sought to both welcome and control new technologies. For example, contrary to Lerner's unsupported claim that "the Ottoman Imperium" was "an *anti*-literate elite" that controlled communication by suppression writing in order to use oral dissemination as a means of social control is the record of Ottoman publishing.[67] Recognizing that "printing demanded a substantial ethical and cultural change within the Islamic culture of knowledge," the Ottomans nevertheless permitted its rapid development.[68] Certainly there were controls. In 1727, Sultan Ahmad III prohibited the printing of texts that dealt with the Koran.[69] But by the early nineteenth century, even the Koran could be discussed in print, and by 1848, a wide variety of texts, totaling 514 and covering diverse topics in science, literature, and language, among others, were printed and marketed.[70]

While the production and dissemination of print media under the Ottomans definitively impeaches Lerner's claim about the communicational hegemony practiced by the Ottoman elite, the print revolution in the Ottoman Empire provides a more thoroughgoing challenge to Lerner's meta-history, his tradition-modernity duality, in which, over time, the latter displaces the former. When faced with the social implications of printing, the Ottomans sought not simply to preserve tradition. Rather, regarding printing as part of "the new," they vigorously debated its implications, allowing it to pervade the social order. Manifesting an emphasis on logic and rhetoric, "the production of printed books [became] a part of the existing social system without destroying its foundations."[71]

In effect, the print revolution in the Ottoman Empire raises the question of "tradition" and contrary to simplistic models that ascribe the concept to an outmoded past, reveals the ways in which what constitutes tradition is an ever-changing process of negotiation. Why relegate tradition to an outmoded past? In a remark that effectively captures much of the impetus of Lerner's project, Reinhart Schulze notes that the use of "tradition" as a simple designation of the past is:

> the means by which the subject liberates himself from history . . . [it] allows him to believe that he is part of modernity, of a modern history and culture which have nothing in common with former periods and states.[72]

Having challenged Lerner's locus of enunciation (which he claims that his "observational viewpoint implies no ethnocentrism"[73])—his status as one who occupies a more or less completed modernity as he views a social order struggling to leave a traditional past—what are alternatives? A far different political understanding of "modernity" emerges when one heeds the writings of intellectuals from a "world" that Lerner and his social science colleagues merely anthropologized. According to Lerner and his generation of development theorists, Western social science produces effective knowledge, while the "Third World" generates modernity-resistant cultures. Focusing on the psychological requisites a person needs to participate in the mobility that is congenial to modern capitalist modes of production and exchange, Lerner saw no need to inquire into alternative historical narratives that might challenge his linear story of the "drama of modernization." However, the Third World produces not only cultures [to be anthropologized] but also anthropologists, ethnohistorians, and other scholars active in a wide variety of intellectual disciplines.[74] A brief look at their writings reveals a pluralistic world containing disjunctive temporalities, or perhaps better put, alternative modes of worlding. For example, in contrast with what he calls "imperial history writing" Indian historian Dipesh Chakrabarty, who worlds from the point of view of a "subaltern 'real' labor that capital subsumes and overcodes, but which it cannot quite contain," constructs history as a set of conflicting and colliding temporalities that reflect "heterogenous social worlds" that cannot be subsumed within a unilinear historical drama.[75]

Mexican anthropologist Garcia Canclini makes a similar case for the Latin American experience. Resisting a linear historical account of modernity applied to that continent, he shows that "Latin America [is] a complex articulation of traditions and modernities (diverse and unequal), a heterogeneous continent consisting of countries in each of which coexists multiple logics of development."[76] Like Chakrabarty, Garcia Canclini refers to a 'hybrid history," an "intersection of different historical temporalities." To heed such a model of history is to invalidate the perspectives within which the former colonies constitute a "belated modernity," and that accordingly lump together such countries as "India, Columbia, and Turkey."[77]

Making the same case about the African experience, African postcolonial theorist Achille Mbembe provides a view of African societies that emerges when, instead of relying on the Western "literature of political science and development economics," one takes into account "*time as lived*" and heeds "the criteria that African agents accept as *reasons for acting.*" Contrary to the view from the West, which ascribes African practices to "the blind force of custom," as though African societies have been inert and lacking in historical depth, Mbembe reveals a complex temporality governing the immense changes in African social, political, and economic orders. Providing a strenuous critique of "theories of evolutionism and ideologies of development and modernization," he shows how African social orders are rooted in a multiplicity of times, trajectories, and rationalities that, although particular and sometimes local, cannot be conceptualized outside a world that is, so to speak, globalized."[78] Instead of the concept of hybridity, Mbembe refers to a "*time of entanglement.*" He notes that every age "is in reality a combination of several temporalities,"[79] and shows, more specifically (and in a way commensurate with Gilles Deleuze's insights into time images), how African modernity, which articulates a complex mix of dynamics, occasioned by interactions between local and global forces, cannot be subsumed into a linear narrative.[80] There is no "distinctive historicity,'" he insists, that is not "embedded in times and rhythms heavily conditioned by European domination."[81]

In addition to demonstrating that the Western social science narratives of modernity, which purport to articulate a universal locus of enunciation, are rather best understood as local idioms, Mbembe exposes the Western models of personhood that have structured the social science gaze. In noting that the dominant Western perspective on Africa assumes that Western societies have freely reasoning "individuals," while African societies have merely "entities, captives of magical signs," he evokes a concept that is the crux of the Euro American states' (and Western political thought's) inability to come to terms with issues of inequality.[82] That individual, as the dominant narrative would have it, is one who:

> has gradually freed her/himself from the sway of traditions and attained an autonomous capacity to conceive, in the here and now, the definition of norms and their free formulation by individual, rational wills.[83]

Mbembe's observation about the West's autonomous individual, which has been part of the discourses used historically to disqualify African societies from the respect accorded to "Western" ones, provides the hinge for the analysis here. That model of the "individual," which Mbembe invokes to provide a critique of the Western gaze on sub-Sahara Africa, also serves to dehistoricize and delegitimate inequalities *within* Western societies.

Mbembe's critique can be turned inward and connected with the treatment of indigenous peoples with which this chapter began. To make the connection, it is necessary to treat the modern state not simply on the basis of its sovereign or external exclusions but also as a set of homogenizing practices *within*—as an active producer of biopolitical distinctions. With respect to the biopolitical enactments associated with nation building, the nineteenth-century American scene provides an exemplary case.

### Critique: Law Making and Law Preserving Violence

During the period of European colonization of the North American continent, "the constructed category 'Indian' occupied the space of the quintessentially 'foreign.'"[84] Subsequently, however, political forces, driven by predatory economic interests among others, domesticated the Native American population. And the discipline of anthropology (as well as those of other social sciences) was conceptually complicit in the adjustment. By the nineteenth century, "the European concept of a 'polity,' organized by a sovereign, territorial state was juxtaposed to the Indian's lack of territorial organization, which, in turn, made Indians, in the words of Chief Justice John Marshall in 1831, into a 'domestically dependent nation.' as opposed to a foreign state."[85]

The continuing domestication (and thus political disqualification) of Native American nations has involved an inter-articulation of juridical and social science modes of knowing. This epistemic collusion was rendered unambiguously evident when, in 1976, a group representing a branch of the original Pequot nation, the Mashpee Wampanog Tribal Council, filed suit in federal court for possession of 16,000 acres of "land constituting three-quarters of Mashpee, 'Cape Cod's Indian Town."[86] During the trial, social scientists and historians testified for both the plaintiffs (the Mashpee) and the defense (the officials of the town). The defense, advised by political scientists and historians, made reference to research into "the 'complete' documented record of Mashpee history" while the plaintiffs placed more reliance on the oral testimony of living Mashpee Indians and on anthropological accounts of Native American life in Mashpee and other comparable cultures.[87] As has been the case with other Native American nations, Mashpee identity has involved a process of partial assimilation and partial boundary maintenance.

The Mashpee counter-narrative to the one told by political scientists and historians, who found no evidence of a continuous Mashpee political organization, was that historically, the Mashpee maintained their integrity but did not choose isolation. They had a dilemma from the point of view of those imposing a cultural essentialism: "caught between a local past and a global future; they either hold onto their separateness or enter the modern world.."[88] However, the Mashpee's did not practice an "either/or." As the trial showed, they were "people who were sometimes separate and 'Indian' sometimes."[89]

Ultimately, the court's unwillingness to acknowledge Mashpee political integrity constitutes an exemplary case of what Walter Benjamin calls "law-preserving violence," which, along with "lawmaking violence," according to Benjamin, constitutes the only forms of "violence as means" that sustain the validity of the law.[90] Apart from the particular light that his approach to the violence of the law sheds on the Mashpee case, Benjamin's insight provides a conceptual vehicle to oppose the historical role of social science in normalizing state space and imposing a benign version of the process of state-nation building that provides the current context for the conceptual disqualification of indigenous claims. In contrast with the approach to such political entities as states by an empiricist social science committed to "theory building," Benjamin opted for "critique," which requires a historico-philosophical consciousness:

> The critique of violence is the philosophy of its history—the 'philosophy' of this history, because only the idea of its development makes possible a critical, discriminating, and decisive approach to its temporal data.[91]

A primary aspect of Benjamin's approach to "critique"—"from the Greek *krinein* (to cut, rift, separate, discriminate, but also to decide)"[92]—for social science knowledge is captured in Foucault's remark that "knowledge is not made for understanding; it is made for cutting,"[93] and by Derrida, who applies the implications to the problem of justice: "Justice as law is never exercised without a decision that *cuts*, that divides."[94] The other important implication, which derives from Benjamin's evocation of historical consciousness, allows us to situate critically the Trask-Burgess conversation on Hawaiian sovereignty with which this chapter began. In effect, Benjamin's argument about the historical consciousness necessary for critique vindicates Trask's emphasis on historical rather than rights-oriented tropes.

Trask resists the application of a juridically-oriented treatment of Hawaiian entitlements, which raises the specter of "racial preferences," because she is aware of the "founding violence of the law," which has historically imposed "a language on national or ethnic minorities. . . ."[95] To put Trask's critique of the "racial preference" discourse in a historical context, one needs a politically informed grasp of the historical emergence of the "racial state."[96] Within the contemporary discourse of public policy, there exists the issue of "managing racial diversity." Within such a dehistoricized perspective, the evocation of the issue can be regarded as an antiracist initiative. However, within a historical perspective one can see the existence of diverse "racial" minorities within the state as something that the state created. Moreover, as Paul Gilroy has noted, anthropological and geographical disciplines, since Kant's writing on "national character," were involved in inter-articulating "character" with national-racial boundaries.[97] To recover the production of such a thought model is to recognize "the co-articulation of race and the modern state.;"[98] it is to recognize that, as Anthony Marx puts it, "selective exclusion was not tangential to nation-state building, as liberals argue, but was instead central to how social order was maintained."[99]

To now seek a model of justice and fairness that does not discriminate on racial grounds is therefore to beg a prior political issue—the deployment of privilege that resulted when various peoples or nations were racialized, as states sought to impose unitary cultural nations. On the one hand, there is a politics associated with opposing unfair racial preferences, a politics that responds to the "exclusion" to which Marx refers. But, on the other hand, there is a historically informed politics associated with the biopolitical predicates of nation building and a recognition of the grievances of those whose racialization has amounted to political disenfranchisement.

Paradoxically, in the case of Hawaii, the imposition of a racial model at the level of public policy was aimed in part at providing Hawaiians with entitlements. In 1920, for the first time, Hawaiianness was defined by "blood quantum" in an act establishing the Hawaiian Homes Commission to provide housing benefits, initially to "full-blood" Hawaiians, and eventually to those with one-half Hawaiian blood.[100] Ignoring Hawaiian forms of identification and "Hawaiian sovereign claims to land," both of which are based on a genealogical rather than a blood quantum model of Hawaianness, the act "constructed Hawaiians as a racialized beneficiary class."[101] In addition to its local and primary economic effect—imposing a model of Hawaiianness that ultimately privileged "white property interests"[102]—the blood quantum criterion for racializing indigenous peoples is part of history of the obliteration of rival nations throughout the Euro American nation-building process. In the case of Native Americans, for example, a blood quantum model of racial construction was part of strategy to make Native American nations effectively disappear. Legislative and judicial acts, based on this model, were the primary policy instruments that dispossessed Native Americans from their lands by seeking to dissolve their historico-cultural continuity.[103]

The expectation behind racialization was similar in Hawai'i. "Hawaiians were positioned much like American Indians, as native and inevitably disappearing."[104] Once claims based on Hawaiian models of a genealogical connections (a performatively-oriented approach to kinship relations and, by implication, to ancestral lands) were dismissed, Hawaiians, except for that diminishing group with at least a 50 percent "blood quantum," could be constructed as merely individual citizens. Within this status, which effectively effaces the political integrity of Hawaiian nationhood, Hawaiian land claims would be construed, as H. William Burgess does, as demands for racial preferences, as an affront to the juridical principle in which everyone is equal before the law. A historically produced inequality is thereby displaced by a formal, ahistorical approach to political equality, a "formal equality" which, in David Theo Goldberg's terms, serves "to veil substantive inequality' and thereby to "legitimate it."[105] To challenge the legitimating and depoliticizing effect of the neoliberal, formal, and juridically-oriented approach to equality, I stage an encounter between Ronald Dworkin's thorough and intricate elaboration of that approach—an assiduously developed political arithmetic, which incorporates the West's invented model of the person, the autonomous, ahistorical "individual"—and Jacques Ranciere's radical rejection of such ahistorical, arithmetic solutions in his treatment of "disagreement."

### Dworkin versus Ranciere

Appropriately entitled *Sovereign Virtue,* Dworkin's investigation reaffirms the conventional "jurisdictions": the legal/spatial boundaries of the state and the privileged political discourses that the boundaries entail. His geophilosophy has, at its center, what he calls "the prosperous democracies," which, he states, "seem to be able to provide a decent minimal life for everyone."[106] As is the case with the geophilosophy on which empiricist comparative politics has been traditionally predicated, Dworkin fails to discern the unprosperous worlds sequestered within the "prosperous ones"—for example, an unregistered alien labor force living a "Third World" existence within the First World and a surviving "Fourth World" of First World Nations that have been transformed into domestic burdens. Ignoring those who do not seem to share, even minimally, in the prosperity of "the prosperous democracies" (one can add here the partially employed, the unemployed, those out in the streets, the thousands without medical benefits), Dworkin seems also unaware that "prosperity" is a relationship; among other things, capital flows, which are largely provoked by the prosperous democracies, affect those outside as well, as capital rearranges identity spaces, opportunity for kinds of work, and land use patterns all over the globe.

Dworkin's anaemic model of global political economy, his limited imagination of the forces affecting the lives of the unprosperous, is doubtless connected with his anaemic version of political life in general. Biopolitically, life for Dworkin features an "ethical individual"[107] who deserves to be accorded equal opportunity, if not an equal measure of success or pleasure. Where is Dworkin's "life" deployed? His political lives are constituted as a group of autonomous individuals, enclosed within the boundaries of static territories. By contrast, when sovereignty is seen as a dynamic process, "life" becomes unstuck; it is subject to the vicissitudes of sovereignty-related enactments (an issue to which I turn in chapter 6). Dworkin's adherence to a static geophilosophy, a world of state-enclosed citizen lives, is an affirmation of a static and uncontested territoriality within which the virtue of fairness is to be deployed. If instead one recognizes sovereignty as episodic, as moments of violent enforcement or legal affirmation and counter-sovereign episodes of resistance, political life becomes an unstable set of events. However, before treating the eventualities of politics, which are accessible within the frame of Ranciere's notion that "the political" is a rare enactment, Dworkin's geophilosophy of equality requires further critical attention.

Dworkin's insensitivity to sovereignty as the enactment of power (power is evacuated in his notion that sovereignty is simply the space for administering justice and fairness) is also evident in his treatment of the linguistic register. Failing to heed what Foucault has called "the coercive structure of the signifier,"[108] Dworkin reduces political equality to the opportunity that individuals have to express their political preferences. His failure to recognize the power of discourse is evident in his articulation of the seemingly unproblematic premise that "people have . . . political preferences."[109] Dworkin's grammar here is analytically disenabling. It is more politically perspicuous to say that political preferences have people. By privileging subjective agency as his primary model of political enactment, Dworkin bars access to the entrenched models of political intelligibility available to subjects. He recycles the traditional liberal democratic model of politics that only warrants those distributions of preference related to the policy issues that achieve public articulation—for example, preferences about limiting or extending welfare entitlements.

Unless an unusual political movement takes place to change the discursive terrain within the "prosperous nations" control meanings, political participation remains circumscribed within the dominant language of politics, which constitutes what a "preference" can be and determines which subjects' noises constitute politically relevant expression. If instead of regarding a preference as an emanation from an individual consciousness, one sees it as an expression whose political legitimacy is warranted by the authoritativeness of a discursive terrain, the discourse-power relationship, which is inaccessible within Dworkin's frame, becomes manifest. Preferences have people because the conditions of possibility for being a politically relevant subject exist within the authoritative language of public policy.

Ultimately, Dworkin offers a sophisticated and elaborate treatment of a wide variety of conditions impinging on the traditional dimensions of equality—equality of resources, of outcomes, of access, of psychological enablements, and of talents—assessing each in relation to the established ideals of a democratic liberalism that homogenizes citizen subjects. Aside from the limitations that his commitment to a state-oriented territoriality impose, Dworkin's reliance on an arithmetic version of equality, within which disparities among citizen bodies are effaced, constitutes his most egregious failure to countenance a political margin existing outside a statist policy monopoly.

Dworkin's resort is to the model of the "auction" to treat the equality of resources[110] and to the model of the insurance actuarial to analyze the issue of whether an equality of opportunity for weathering a catastrophe reigns: "[I]f everyone had an equal risk of suffering some catastrophe that would leave him or her handicapped, and everyone knew what the odds were and had ample opportunity to insure—then handicaps would pose no special problem for equality of resources."[111] Here Dworkin supplies a political arithmetic that effaces the history of violence. Effectively, he obscures the institutionalized catastrophe visited on those wronged during what social science has euphemistically constructed as the period of "nation building" and affects their subsequent supply of economic and social capital (a voiced perspective that would be heeded by authorities) to insure themselves, even when they know the "odds."

To consider the relationship of the history of wrong to the problem of inequality, while at the same time exploring an alternative to an arithmetic imaginary of the political, it is appropriate to contrast Jacques Ranciere's radical egalitarianism, which is elaborated within a model of the political-as-episodic. For Ranciere, "politics exists when the natural order of domination is interrupted by the institution of a part of those who have no part,"[112] and "political activity is whatever shifts a body from the place assigned to it or changes a place's destination."[113] Contesting liberal democratic approaches to a universality applied to political communities such as "the reign of law" or "the process of governing," Ranciere sees the only universal in politics as equality.[114] And he rejects the traditional meta-politics within which "man and citizen are the same liberal individual enjoying the universal values of human rights embodied in the constitutions of our democracies."[115] Recognizing the history of wrong involved in the founding violence of the law (e.g., constitution making) and in the preservation of the law, a form of policing or "policy" that functions within a traditional meta politics, Ranciere evokes the distinction between "a logic of subjectification and a logic of identification."[116]

The logic of identification is the typical political arithmetic within which everyone is a subject before the law or has a political preference to be counted along with the others. In contrast to "the arithmetic of shopkeepers and barterers" (or insurance companies, as in Dworkin's model), Ranciere speaks of "a magnitude that escapes ordinary measurement," a "paradoxical magnitude" that escapes a logic that equates "the equality of anyone at all with anyone else."[117] The logic of subjectification derives from a pluralism of disparity. Resisting metaphysical foundations, Ranciere sees the social order as sheer contingency. There are no political parties with an existence prior to "the declaration of a wrong." Thus, to take one of Ranciere's examples: "Before the wrong that its name exposes, the proletariat has no existence as a real part of society."[118] Similarly (to treat my primary case) the political articulations of Hawaiian sovereignty activists are instances of subjectification. Their evocation of the history of a wrong constitutes them as political subjects. They become "indigenous subjects" when they contest their existence within a state political organization. Prior to the coup, in which a planter-led militia overthrew the Hawaiian monarchy in the late nineteenth century, Hawai'i's had international recognition as a nation-state.

To return again to the Trask-Burgess encounter and locate it in the context of Ranciere's approach to inequality, we can regard it as an encounter between "police logic and political logic." The policies, referenced by Burgess, within which Hawaiians have no separate standing, are part of a historical trajectory of "policy," an institutionalized wrong within which Hawaiians, as political subjects, have no part. Whereas the historical reference to the stealing of nationhood by Trask enacts a disruption of policy and evokes "democracy," understood not as a system of equal opportunity of access by anyone in relation to anyone else as governed by the law's founding or preserving violence, but as a moment in which a part that has had no part asserts itself. Ranciere summarizes this model of democracy:

> Democracy is not a regime or a social way of life. It is the institution of politics itself. The system of forms of subjectification through which any order of distribution of bodies into functions corresponding to their 'nature' and places corresponding to their functions is undermined, thrown back on its contingency.[119]

Ranciere's "subjectification" is therefore the opposite of subjection. It exists only in those instances when different worlds collide, not when already recognized subject positions are involved in a power struggle. By subjectification, Ranciere means not the imposition of already recognized social identities but the introduction of new voices that are at once expressive and disruptive. Subjectification involves articulations from a part that has not been a recognized part of public deliberation.

In accord with my treatment of the historical role of social science, Ranciere points out that social science has historically assisted a "modern parapolitics," an effacement of the contingencies of political encounter in favor of "the problematization of origins of power and the terms in which it is framed—the social contract, alienation, and sovereignty.."[120] Social science takes as its starting point an "individuality," where entitlement is simply "the *entitlement* of anyone at all to question the state or to serve as proof of its fidelity to its own principle."[121] In contrast, politics, in Ranciere's sense, escapes the compass of social and political science's concern with policy. "The political" makes an appearance through a "polemicization,"[122] an action in which a part that has had no part makes itself manifest. The political is therefore not a set of structures or a continuing process accessible to an application of disinterested knowledge to the arithmetic distribution of identical bodies, or to the reality expressed in the discourses of individuals and modes of governance. Ranciere's challenge to conventional modes of political calculation, and his evocation of disparity have radical implications for comparative method. Rather than seeking a universal political language within which political systems and processes can be arrayed, what his methodology implied is a way to treat historical encounters between disparate modes of making meaning. If Ranciere's insights about disparity are to be heeded, rather than imposing a single meaning frame on disparate episodes, in order to standardize communication at various levels of political inquiry (in order, for example, to manage "aggregate data"), one must turn to the problem of translation.

## Conclusion: Critical Translation versus the Convergence of Meaning

The dominant perspective in the social sciences in general and political science in particular remains disinterested, utilitarian, and geophilosophical in a statist sense. Charles Merriam's commitment to "utility in the development of the more accurate study of social phenomena." and a misleading narrative of "nation building" continue to hold sway. To the extent that the social sciences see the world as a relatively quiescent array of territories, which somehow achieved "integration,"[123] and whose primary mode of difference consists in idiomatic disparity, better "communication" becomes the issue for those who seek to make "policy" more "efficient." This depoliticizing rhetoric has been the constitutive agenda of an international group of scholars participating in COCTA, the Committee on Conceptual and Terminological Analysis, a research group in the International Political Science Association. As one recent version would have it, "Global issues confronting the world as the 20th Century ends can be understood when scholars working in all the social science disciplines, and in all countries of the world, learn how to communicate clearly and efficiently with each other and to focus on politics that require cross-disciplinary interactions."[124]

There is a radically different way of characterizing the discourse issue. It is suggested in a remark by Judith Butler, which is predicated on the recognition of a world-wide struggle to resist the entrenched vestiges of colonialism. Instead of communication, Butler evokes the process of translation:

> The task of the postcolonial translator . . . is precisely to bring into relief the non-convergence of discourses so that one might know through the very ruptures of narrativity the founding violences of the episteme."[125]

What is the consequence of such a bringing into relief of nonconvergence? The traditional, empiricist assumption animating the drive of the political science terminology project is that the researcher is situated in a coherent and unitary culture that requires untainted information to assist a governmentally-oriented mode of "policy formation." Within such a locus of enunciation, the trope of communication is the logical resort. But if language is regarded not as simply a tool for communication but as a dynamic, growing phenomenon that is continually altered by encounters between different articulations of alternative life worlds, and interlingual encounters can be exploited to learn about incoherences, translation, seen as a component of a politics of interpretation, offers itself as a mode of critical self-reflection. At a minimum, an emphasis on translation contrasts markedly with the closural emphasis of empiricists who seek commensurability of concepts across cultures and politics. James Clifford's reflections on his use of concepts achieves the appropriate level of epistemic caution:

> Comparative concepts—translation terms—are approximations, privileging certain 'originals' and made for specific audiences. Thus the broad meanings that enable projects such as mine [rethinking spatiality as itinerary—an immanent temporalization of a specific set of spatial relations] necessarily fail as a consequence of whatever range they achieve. This mix of success and failure is a common predicament for those attempting to think globally—globally enough—without aspiring to overview and the final word.[126]

And Walter Benjamin goes further in his reflections on translation between different languages. Rendering the translator as vulnerable as well as humble, he asserts that the translator should be "powerfully affected by the foreign tongue," and should "expand and deepen [her or his] language by means of the foreign language."[127] It is not wholly clear what Benjamin means by an expanded and deepened language, but, at a minimum, his approach to translation implies that the translator operates precisely the opposite way from those involved in fixing definitions in order to facilitate comparative analysis in empirically oriented disciplines.

From a methodological point of view, the implication of Benjamin's approach is that translation should "dislocate . . . definitions rather than establishing them"[128] and, perhaps most tellingly, the process itself should call into question the presumed stability, the self-assured sense of coherence and intelligibility, that one ascribes to one's own frame of meaning. In short, the implication to be derived from the phenomenological view of translation that Benjamin articulates is that what is to be achieved by linguistic self-reflection is an appreciation of aspects of ambiguity, incoherence, and otherness within the practices of intelligibility we call language and within the institutional loci that give language its points of departure. To translate, in Benjamin's sense, is to engage in a politics of interpretation by challenging the authority of privileged loci of enunciation.[129] This sense of translation does not, therefore, derive from the project of simply improving communication across languages. Rather, it seeks to politicize the question of meaning, to enact the same consequence that derives from critical interpretation in general: treating the issue of meaning as a political intervention, which requires, in some cases, "the political rewriting of the text and its destination."[130]

To appreciate what is meant by translation-as-political intervention, we can first consider an instance of translation-as-critique in which the Hebrew Bible's standard political significance is challenged. In a thoroughgoing intervention into that venerable compilation, literary scholar Harold Bloom and translator David Rosenberg have dramatically reordered the text's voices.[131] Arguing that the text ultimately given to modernity has been fashioned to accommodate the imperatives of a priestly authority, they extract a different author with their translation. They name that author J, and identify her as a woman whom they surmise to have been a member of King Solomon's court. J emerges in their translation as an ironist rather than a mere chronicler. Among other things, she produces a wholly different, more capricious Yahweh.

The challenge of the Bloom/Rosenberg translation, which (to some) provides a heretical affirmation of the Hebrew Bible as a multiauthored text containing Gnostic perspectives, which are disjunctive with the normative Judaism made familiar by Judeo-Christian theologians, goes beyond a confrontation with religious piety. In effect, they engage in an act of subjectification that reorders the gender contribution to centuries of the culturally and politically significant interpretive practices that have lent almost exclusive authority to men. The Bloom/Rosenberg resurrection of a gendered otherness within a history of spiritual authority provides a model for encounter across spatial as well as temporal boundaries.

National languages, which have largely displaced spiritual discourses and the authorities they warrant, can also be subjected to a politics of translation. "How should we move away from the 'natural' connections between structures of knowledge and national-imperial languages," asks Walter Mignolo.[132] Not by seeking communicative convergence, by standardizing meanings in order to improve the interpretive climate for social science practitioners to pursue the familiar and authoritative policy problematics. By staging crossings of what Mignolo calls "the epistemological divide,"[133] one affirms the ambiguities and lack of closure that must persist "at the intersection of two or more languages"[134] and thereby resists the "cognitive imperialism" practiced by social science empiricists, operating within the dominant languages and viewing the world from their privileged loci of enunciation. From the point of view of a politics concerned with broadening the sphere of subjectification, of creating spaces for silenced voices, a critical approach to translation must displace a "comparative politics" driven by a fantasy of delocalized or universally valid conceptual mastery.

Some of the relevant implications emerge in a commentary by Andrea Opitz, whose task it was to translate a Native American novel, James Welch's *Fools Crow,* into German. Finding no ready-to-hand German equivalents for Welch's use of language, especially the descriptive qualities of his naming, Opitz discovered that no word-for-word approach would suffice. She discovered that "*[F]ools Crow* does not simply offer an alternative vision but an alternative space in which the reader dwells."[135] Seeking to come to terms with the novel's "foreignness," even though it is written in English (her primary language), Optiz discovered the articulation of a precolonial world within a colonized one:

> In the novel, culture is imagined from inside. . . . The points of reference exist mainly in the Blackfeet universe. The Blackfeet in this novel are not seen or portrayed with a colonial mind-set, as neither the noble nor the displaced silent minority. They inhabit their world with a confidence, relying on themselves rather than whites for their sense of self, of belonging.[136]

Accepting her alienation from the world created in *Fools Crow,* Opitz tried, in her translation, to capture the ways in which the novel's "language speaks directly from the land Welch's ancestors inhabited and exemplifies the relation between the Blackfeet and the world around them."[137] Transcending "existing territorial boundaries," the novel imagines a 'Native textuality' that reclaims the land and its lost culture within it."[138] As a result, like the Bloom/Rosenberg translation, the novel enacts a subjectivization; it evinces voices from and maps of the spaces of an "other" America. To restore that otherness, Welch's novel creates a different temporality, "a world, and experience, that is altogether 'other,' disconnected from the contemporary world."[139]

There are similar effects with different temporal strategies. While Welch's novel challenges a state's conceptual/territorial dominance by evoking a precolonial past, some writers who write from a resistant locus of enunciation within a dominant language, produce that challenge from alternative temporal points of view. For example, in her *Free Enterprise,* Jamaican novelist Michelle Cliff's narrator reflects on the historical role of each language's participation in the imperial domination of her homeland. "English," she says, "was the tongue of commerce. . . . Spanish was the language of categories" (by which she means the creation of a biopolitical matrix of economically and politically ineligible, miscegenated blood types), and Latin was the language of Christian spiritual hegemony. "Against these tongues," she adds "African of every stripe collided."[140]

In contrast, some plurilingual colonial subjects write from the point of view of an imagined, postcolonial future.[141] Exemplary in this respect is the Algerian feminist novelist Assia Djebar, who, like Welch and Cliff, writes in a way that *highlight[s] the epistemic violence of colonialism.*"[142] Seeking to invent a postcolonial, feminist Algeria, Djebar "Arabizes" her written French to supply voices to those who have not been part of the "Algeria" historically constructed by France. Writing a "multilingual French," Djebar, as she summarizes it, employs "French for secret missives; Arabic for our stifled aspirations towards God; Lyico-Berber which takes us back to the most ancient of our mother idols. The Fourth language, for all females, young or old, cloistered or half-emancipated, remains that of the body."[143]

Djebar's writing explores the political implications of critical interpretation within a translation idiom. Her texts are a vehicles for articulating the "political context and power relations with which language acquisition takes place" for the "plurilingual subjects" who have absorbed their different languages in a colonial context.[144] Djebar is an acculturated North African who resists "the assimilationist role assigned to the North African elite by French colonizers."[145] Although she continued to write in French after her 1962, postindependence return to Algeria, her prose stages encounters between alternative constructions of Algeria not only by occasionally arabizing French but also, more elaborately, by creating a text that "moves between the written French . . . of the colonizers, the oral 'Arabized' French of the Algerian women [for example, the main subjects in her *Fantasia*], the cries of love of the *fantasia* (cavalcade) of the Algerian tribes."[146]

If, after Benjamin's provocative treatment of the "task of the translator," one focuses on the historical background of a text's performativity rather than thinking of translation as merely a communicational or representational problem, Djebar's French must be regarded as untranslatable in the commonly understood sense.[147] To bring the text into a context that seeks the commensurability of the words in different languages (the way data archives of those investigating "comparative politics" have worked) is to conjure away the deeply historicized life worlds that "Third World" subjects have experienced. Djebar's writing, like that of many "colonial subjects" seeks to perform a reinflection of the language of the colonizer, or, in the words of Caribbean writer Maryse Conde'—reflecting on her Creolization of European languages—to subject language "to a certain violence," to make it "strange, so that it becomes the writer's own singular language...."[148]

At a minimum, the political significance articulated in the writing of formerly colonized subjects lies in their challenge to the fantasy that the modern state contains a unitary and coherent national culture of communication, forged by a single system of meaning. A focus on the issue of translation, from a critical interpretive perspective reveals not only "the irremediable distance between language and the world of reference" but also that there are voices that will remain silenced by projects that seek a universal, conceptual mastery of political experience within the fantasy that all significant political expressions are contained within unitary national cultures. In chapter 2, I continue my approaches to critical interpretation and translation with a focus on diverse genres—especially novels and plays—that are part of the methods shaping the dominant imaginaries of nation-states. I also treat the methods of those who supply counter-memories to contest those instances of a state's cultural production that are designed to show that the state contains an unproblematic and completed nation culture.[149]

CHAPTER **2**

# Nation-States
## *Drama and Narration*

### A Peruvian Prelude

> Behind patriotism and nationalism there always burns the malignant fiction of
> collectivist identity, that ontological barbed wire which attempts to congregate
> "Peruvians," "Spaniards," "French," "Chinese," et cetera, in inescapable and un-
> mistakable fraternity. You and I know that these categories are simply abject
> lies that throw a mantle of oblivion over countless diversities and incompatibil-
> ities. . . ."
>
> Mario Vargas Llosa[1]

These lines, by a Peruvian writer and former presidential candidate (and
former radical turned counterrevolutionary) reflect more than a desire to
demythologize patriotism. The eloquent and hyperbolic statement, in a
novel focused primarily on familial love triangles, conveys an appreciation
of the work of fiction, which is integral to the contemporary nation-state's
maintenance of its existence. The style of Vargas Llosa's novel, "a rich confusion of art and fact, fiction, and reality,"[2] mimics the contemporary state's
performance of nationhood, which also bundles "art and fact, fiction and
reality," in a variety of genres of expression, not as in Vargas Llosa's novel,
to disclose the ways in which fantasy mediates erotic encounters, but to perpetuate itself as the container of a coherent and cohesive national culture.[3]
Yet, as Vargas Llosa clearly appreciates, the tasks, though disparate in their
aims, produce similar, hybrid modes of expression.

   Although I have begun this treatment of the nation-state with a literary
voice, situated within the global literary culture in general and the Peruvian

politico-intellectual culture in particular, there is a multitude of *locations* (loci of enunciation) from which diverse kinds of voices emerge and bear on the status of nation-states. There is also a variety of texts in diverse *genres* (modes of enunciation) that articulate the issues surrounding the status of nation-states. In this chapter I invoke a variety of loci and modes of enunciation for two reasons, one theoretical and the other historical. Theoretically, multiple positions are required because of the essential contestability of the meaning and status of the nation-state. Historically, the political, geographic, and economic prerogatives of the contemporary nation-state have been increasingly contested. In response, states have been required, now more than ever, to perform their identities, to maintain their ontological as well as their practical statuses as "nation-states." Although state control over the meaning of spaces and bodies is increasingly challenged by globalizing forces, "the concept-metaphor 'nation-state,'" as Gayatri Spivak puts it, continues to manifest a "ferocious re-coding power."[4]

While the initial aggregations forming the dominant model for subsequent states—the European state system established by the Treaty of Westphalia in 1648—involved military and fiscal initiatives, coercive and economic aspects of control have been supplemented by a progressively intense cultural governance, a management of the dispositions and meanings of citizen bodies, aimed at making territorial and national/cultural boundaries coextensive. State cultural governance has been aided and abetted by academic discourses on state sovereignty, which reify sovereignty, turning it into a unproblematic expression of modern politics. This has the effect that Michael Hardt and Antonio Negri address; it "weed[s] out every residue of social antagonism." Therefore, they note:

> The nation is kind of an ideological shortcut that attempts to free the concept of sovereignty and modernity from the antagonism and crisis that define them. National sovereignty suspends the conflictual origins of modernity . . . and it closes the alternative paths within modernity that had refused to concede their powers to state authority.[5]

This chapter addresses two concerns. At a simple level, the aim is to bypass that "ideological shortcut" and illustrate the contentious process accompanying the emergence and persistence of nation-states. At another, more elaborate and specific level, and in keeping with Vargas Llosa's critically disrupting mixed metaphor, the aim is to cut the "ontological barbed wire" surrounding the metaphysical nation-state in order to disclose the *methods,* a dense set of interpretive and material practices, through which the (misleading) nation segment of the hyphenated term, nation-state, achieves its standing. At the same time, those methods are contested with a treatment of the methods through which the nation-state's metaphysical standing is challenged. "Nations"—at least those that are arguably contained within states—should be regarded as dynamic and contentious domains of practice, not as autonomous entities to be treated as objects of analysis, as they are within the empiricist, "comparing nations" perspective that dominated political studies throughout the twentieth century.[6] At a symbolic level, they are imaginaries (abstract domains of collective coherence and attachment), which persist through a complex set of institutionalized practices.[7]

However, to simply refer to the nation as an imaginary is insufficient for supplying a critical perspective on nation-states. Adding a historical perspective on the media through which the imaginary is created and sustained, which will occupy much of this chapter, moves in the direction of a historically and politically informed purchase on the contemporary nation-state. The "ontological barbed wire" to which Vargas Llosa refers has been installed by the largely symbolic, self-inscribing practices through which modern states claim nationhood. But the historical emergence of a nationalizing "statecraft," a term for a complicated territory- and people-managing mode of governmental practice, must be understood in the context of the variety of specific material as well as symbolic conditions shaping the contemporary political entities recognized (in varying degrees) as nation-states.

The historical trajectory and social dispersion of the practices supporting state claims to containing coherent national communities, which is elaborated in a comparative frame in this chapter, is focused rather than comprehensive. Accordingly, in order to supply a sufficient context for Vargas Llosa's skepticism, I turn first to the functioning of statecraft during its most crucial nation-building stage in his homeland, Peru. As a polity that emerged from colonial rule, the boundaries of the Peruvian state resulted initially from Spanish imperialism, then from contests among Creole functionaries to manage a fairly amorphous territory, and then from conflicts between Peru and other states. Forging a *nation*-state, however, has been more complicated. It cannot be claimed that the Peruvian case is exemplary because there are different strategies that states have employed in their attempts at becoming nation-states. Nevertheless, Peru's nationalizing process warrants scrutiny because conceptualizations (as opposed to generalizations) are best developed in the context of specific historical episodes.

In the Peruvian case, the state's governing elite began its nationalizing initiatives in the face of a set of regional power configurations that were a legacy of the colonial period. Peru's relatively late independence (1824) came about as the result of a bourgeois revolution that displaced the pre-capitalist, colonial-imposed oligarchy (of planters, mine owners, and wool merchants).[8] Inasmuch as virtually all interdependencies—material, social, political, and religious—functioned within regions, the process of nationalizing the Peruvian population necessitated a wresting of control from various regional elites. To express it in terms of geographical dynamics, the state sought effectively to reterriorialize attachments and structures of exchange through the "annihilation of regional space by state power."[9]

There have been significant aspects of political economy impelling that geographical dynamic. In the nineteenth century, the Peruvian state had maintained its bureaucratic and fiscal controls through a set of clientele relationships. The ruling elites were required to manage such state administrative functions as revenue collection and peacekeeping in exchange for being allowed to control their regional affairs. At the end of the century, however, "the massive expansion of North Atlantic capital into Peru ... initiated a process of social transformation and national consolidation that brought to an end the fragmented conditions that had dominated the 19th century."[10] The subsequent process of centralization, in which the state expanded fiscal, bureaucratic and cultural controls, involved a complex set of shifting alliances among different classes and different locales. In the center, the Lima ruling class has controlled credit and commercial structures, and in the periphery, different regions, villages, and groupings have had a history of unstable partisanship with respect to local interdependencies and varying degrees of cooperation and resistance with respect to state centralization.[11]

While the historical process of centralization in Peru, as in other cases, speaks to the emergence of the modern fiscal-military state (a more or less continually contested "emergence" in Peru's case, for as late as the 1990s the state military fought a Maoist insurgency, instituted a period of terror against suspected collaborators, and wiped out much of the black economy, based on coca production), the story of the coherence of the nation segment of the Peruvian nation-state is case-specific and has been historically unstable. The process of integrating the diverse population of Creoles, "Indians," and *Mestizos* into a coherent citizen body has been contested at both elite and mass levels at every stage. At the elite level, the Creole nation-building strategy has been inconsistent. State-oriented intellectual discourses constructed the problem of indigenous citizenship (*indigenismo*) in very different ways, during the mid-1940s and early 1970s periods, as the state attempted to achieve nationhood through "revolutionary social and educational reforms."[12]

In the1940s, a conception of a dual citizen body was perpetuated: "The Ministry of Education ... implemented an educational policy infused with a purist, anti-*Mestizo* ideology that sought to forge a State out of two physically and culturally separate nations."[13] Twenty plus years later, however, the biopolitical dimension of the state's nation-building initiative (the state's warranting of politically eligible identities)[14] was radically reversed. Whereas before, educational policy attempted to reinstall a "pure" Indianness as a separate cultural existence within the state, under the revolutionary regime of Juan Velasco Alvarado, "Indian" was abolished as an official term and replaced with the term peasant (*compesino*). Although this displacement was effected primarily through the national educational curriculum, it was also implemented through a variety of other genres with which states have historically scripted the characteristics of their nationhood, for example, national *fêtes*. In Peru, June 24, which had previously been "the day of the Indian," was now to be "The day of the peasant."[15]

This seemingly trivial politics of representation points to an important contingency afflicting attempts to impose essences on the identities that states have historically produced to invent national bodies. It is such episodes of identity instability that the expose the arbitrariness of attempts to provide foundational anchors to contentious interpretive practices. For example, in a fictional commentary on the new attachments developing during the disintegration of the Austro-Hungarian Empire, writer Joseph Roth provides a telling reflection on the arbitrariness of attempts to lend historical weight to a newly emerging Czech national identity. He introduces a character, Heinrich P. a decommissioned officer and occasional writer, existing at the moment when a newly formed Czech nation falls out of the old Austro-Hungarian Empire, a time when many who spoke Czech only as a second language were now making it their first. Heinrich, a man of "shallow affect," drifting around the periphery of events, writes a personal "account of his experiences in a local paper" and exaggerates "the enthusiasm and confusion" he has observed surrounding the revolution. His reference to "people reeling and intoxicated" catches the eye of officials in the new Czech government, who attempt (unsuccessfully, for he flees to Switzerland) to recruit him as a writer to help script a popular and widespread emotional depth "for the new so-called autonomous Czech people."[16]

Roth's ironic scripting of the events surrounding state formation in middle Europe is one among many cases of opposition to a state's scripting of cultural nationhood. In the case of the Peruvian state's attempts at lending a foundational spatiotemporality to its nationhood since independence, such opposition has been pervasive. Spatially, the state's dominant geographic imaginary, the imposition of a coincidence between state and nation, has been countered by the "cartographic practices of indigenous groups," who privilege local rather than national "geographies of identity."[17] And temporally, the "Creole nationalist 'discursive frameworks' of the liberal republican state," which have lent the Peruvian state a macro-level, "republican history," have been opposed by an alternative "history of indigenous rights and property," which can be discovered when one descends "from elite texts" (for example, the successive drafts of the Peruvian Constitution beginning in 1822) to a genre that mixes elite and vernacular idioms: "the petty archives of local courts and notaries where peasant voices were registered."[18]

In short, the existence of a distinctive postcolonial Peruvian nationhood has been contested and negotiated in a clash between alternative writing performances (or modes of enunciation), and between alternative loci of enunciation, those issuing from either official/national or local space. Official republicanism, defined in legal texts ranging from the founding constitution to a historical archive of tax codes, has been opposed by an indigenous version of "Indian republicanism" (*indios republicanos*),[19] which, though invented in part by a state taxing authority, took on local meanings, registered within local ledgers. Despite historical attempts by Creole nationalists to negate "the historical agency of republican Indians" (for example, constructing them as "pre-political beings"[20] during the early twentieth-century *indigenismo* educational initiative already noted), the local ledgers of the nineteenth-century nation-building period stand as a challenge to "the teleological historicity of Creole nation-building."[21]

The unstable nation-building dynamic evident in the case of postcolonial Peru, where "political keywords like *republic* and *nacion* resisted univocal definition,"[22] reflects a situation of incomplete national integration, which the ever skeptical Vargas Llosa has attributed to his subcontinent as a whole: "We in Latin America do not yet constitute real nations . . . our countries are in a deep sense more a fiction than a reality."[23] But while Vargas Llosa departs from traditional Creole nationalists, his self-ascribed realism, with which he claims innocence of ideological taint, masks a neoliberal ideological agenda that articulates itself in (among other places) his fantasy that Peru and other Latin American states "can *choose* to be prosperous" by entering the global economy as open competitors.[24]

Although in his novels Vargas Llosa resists and even impugns such simplistic ideological cant, his autobiographical reflections on the political conditions in Peru are insensitive to both the inequalities imposed within a global political economy and the continuing Creole oppression of the Indian population. As one critic puts it, "Vargas Llosa the realist story-teller eludes Vargas Llosa the counter-revolutionary ideologue."[25] For example, although he was an early admirer of the novels of José Maria Arguedas, whose writing has articulated the situation of Indian immiseration in Peru, Vargas Llosa went out of his way to discredit Arguedas's literary mapping of Peru's racial-spatial order:

> Neither Indian nor White, neither indigenist nor hispanic, the Peru which is emerging to last is still a mystery of which we can only say for certain but with absolute certainty, that it will have nothing to do with the images used by José Maria Arguedas in his works to describe it—to fabulate it.[26]

In opposition to Vargas Llosa's claim, I turn here to some aspects of Arguedas's Peru, which, like the earlier mentioned "local ledgers," also contests "the teleological historicity of Creole nation-building." His "images," which Vargas Llosa disparages, are based on a rapport with the Indians of Peru that is outside the experiences of most Creole Peruvians, Vargas Llosa included. Arguedas explains that he acquired this rapport because he was "the handiwork" of his stepmother, who consigned him to a living space with her indigenous servants in the kitchen of her hacienda, where he slept in a "wooden trough . . . of the kind used to knead bred." But Arguedas's young life spent in "Indian country" (which in Peru exists primarily in "the highlands," but also in the kitchens of haciendas), turned out to be both emotionally and linguistically enriching. The Indians, especially the women, gave him "tenderness and limitless love . . . the love they feel for each other and also for nature, the highlands, rivers, and birds."[27] And, he learned the Indian language, *Quechua,* which influenced his use of Spanish by providing much of the syntax as well as the imagery in his novels.

Arguedas's novels disclose a Peru that fails to achieve recognition within the perspectives of the dominant Creole governmentality. He wrote to "transmit to the reader of Spanish not only compassion for the oppressed, but a sense that the latter also had a perception, a world view of their own, in which people, mountains, animals, the rain, truth, all had dimensions of their own, powerful, revealing, and utterly unlike Iberian ones."[28] As John Murra explains:

> [Arguedas] took the very turns of phrase for which Andean speakers of Spanish are mocked, and used them in his fiction, so that their outlandishness, their 'incorrectness,' conveys to the middle-class reader of Spanish that he is missing another cultural context.[29]

Cleaving to the "the ethical as well as the grammatical requirements of Andean speech," Arguedas summons an alternative worldview unfamiliar to the Creole Peruvian.[30] A brief illustration from his novel *Deep River* conveys the significance of his hybrid Spanish-*Qechuan* textualization. When a landscape is described, Arguedas, following the practices of the highland Indians, views it from the perspective of the birds who inhabit it in varying ways, depending on their preferences:

> The *Tuyas* prefer tall trees; the goldfinches sleep or rest in the yellow bushes; the *Chihuaco* sings in the dark-leaved trees such as the alder, the eucalyptus, or the *lambras;* it doesn't go to the weeping willows. The doves seek out the old, hollowed-out walls . . .[31]

The novel's challenge to Creole dominance works thematically as well as formally; following the travels of the novel's main character, Ernesto, who, like the young Arguedas, is "a child tortured by a double origin, a child with roots in two hostile worlds,"[32] it has Ernesto confront the spaces of Peruvian injustice. The novel therefore not only challenges, with its very form, the dominant Creole way of making the world intelligible, but also displays a great divide that impeaches any attempt to treat Peru as a completed cultural nation.

### Achieving an Appropriate Grammar: Nationhood as State Practice

The case of Peru points to the pervasive incompleteness of state nationalizing initiatives, an incompleteness that has challenged the traditional grammar of questions posed about nation-states. In recognition of the limitations of traditional queries, Walker Connor has changed the nation-state question from "what is a nation?" to "when is a nation?," because, as he puts it, "it is problematic whether nationhood has even yet been achieved."[33] Connor's alteration of the question of nationhood provides a threshold for a critical analysis of nation-states. His displacement of the "is" with a temporal trajectory challenges the ontological status of nations by shifting attention from the ideal of the nation to the historical vagaries of nation building. But while historicizing rather than reifying is an important step in resisting ideological complicity with "the state effect" (the representational practices through which nation-states appear as an autonomous, self-contained agents, separate from the activities that constitute them),[34] the "when" question is an analytic dead end unless coupled with an emphasis on an inquiry-empowering "how" question. "We should not," in the words of Rogers Brubaker, "ask 'what is a nation' but rather: how is nationhood as a political and cultural form institutionalized within and among states?"[35]

Once attention is historically oriented and focused on the "how" question, it becomes possible to generate conceptions with which to elaborate state nation building as practice. A preface to the conceptual task is supplied in Ana Maria Alonso's reflections on the "politics of space and time" involved in the nationalizing aspects of state formation. Referring to "the cultural inscription of the idea of the state," she notes that it "has in part been secured through the spatialization of time."[36] Alonso's use of the writing metaphor provides a effective frame for treating state practices. At a concrete historical level, it accords with Benedict Anderson's insights into the role of print technology and its various genres of expression—especially novels and newspapers—in the creating and consolidating of national consciousness.[37] At a conceptual level, it articulates well with Gilles Deleuze and Felix Guattari's way of construing the state as a scripting machine that "overcodes"[38] alternative ways of encoding bodies and territories. Manifesting a "dread" of uncoded flows,[39] states have historically constituted themselves through the production of increasingly dense systems of inscription, not only for creating and policing boundaries but also for coding the movement of bodies. Effectively, nationalizing states translate biological bodies into social bodies.[40] The Deleuzian state is therefore a machine of capture.[41] In Alonso's terms, it spatializes time; it turns an dynamic of self-production into a reified, unproblematic existence. To capture its "people," whose coherence is based on a narrative of its historical assemblage, the state must also capture time; it must monopolize the temporal trajectory through which its existence is made natural and coherent.[42] To denaturalize that coherence and pursue the capture metaphor that Deleuze and Guattari employ, one must turn to perspectives of those whose relationships and movements are constrained by the state's methods of capture. Consequently, in the following section, I relate the story of "the assassin," Demetrios Tsafendas, and others who have been victimized by the physical and symbolic capture mechanisms of states.

## A Fatal Unease

"The migrant is an uncertain and incomplete man.
He lives in an inveterate state of unease."[43]

In a stunning literary performance, Henk van Woerden reconstructs the fatal encounter between two immigrants. A "half-Greek," Demitrios Tsafendas, who was born to a Greek father and an African mother in Lourenco Marques (now Maputo), the capital of Portuguese East Africa, killed Henrik Verwoerd, the "half-Dutch" prime minister of South Africa and architect of Apartheid, who was born in Amsterdam. As Tsafendas, employed as courier in the Cape Town parliament building, approached Verwoerd on September 6, 1966, observers assumed he was delivering a message. Instead, he mortally wounded Verwoerd with four thrusts of a long knife. Tsafendas struck at the man whom he saw as the cause of his nearly life-long malaise. He saw himself as a victim of the Verwoerd-initiated racial separation decrees. But the killing of Verwoerd had no immediate effect on racial division. The Apartheid policy remained in place as Verwoerd was succeeded by the Nationalist Party's minister of justice, Balthazar Vorster, while the official biography of Tsafendas (the spin the event was given in the South African press) consigned his act to the irrationality of a madman. Transferred from the place of his original confinement on Robben Island to Pretoria Central Prison, Tsafendas was "placed in a cell next to death row and forgotten."[44]

As a thirteen-year-old, Henk van Woerden had experienced the disruption of Verwoerd's implementation of "racial" separation directly. A South African white and, like Verwoerd, "a half-baked Hollander" (who had emigrated with his family at age nine to South Africa), he lived in "the racially mixed" suburb of Cape Town when, in the early 1960s, his Cape Coloured neighbors disappeared. Ultimately, three to four million South Africans were "chased out of their cities." And for many like van Woerden, the separation was inexplicable:

> The differences between the 'poor white' Afrikaners and the Coloureds, especially, were not all that easy to make out, on either side of the colour line. Both groups spoke the same language and felt the same longing for a recognition of the wrongs done to them in the past.[45]

As van Woerden's experience attests, contrary to the conceits of Verwoerd's Nationalist Party, many of the "Whites" and "Coloureds" (to use the local idiom) shared a "structure of feeling;" what was "actively lived and felt," did not conform to the ideological underpinning of the Apartheid policy.[46] What was officially articulated was disjunctive with "discordant elements in exemplary personal experience."[47] And, for van Woerden, the discord only deepened. He returned to Europe shortly after the assassination but remained unable to quench a "great thirst," a "nostalgia for the future ... left behind."[48] By writing a Tsafendas biography, van Woerden implies that he is restoring a level of political consequence that impersonal accounts of South Africa's Apartheid years have left out, "visceral forms of human connectedness."[49] The viscera in question belong primarily to Tsafendas, for shortly after the account begins, van Woerden abandons a first-person grammar as he is displaced in the experiential narrative by Tsafendas.

The politics of writing in van Woerden's biography of Demitrios Tsafendas constitutes a epistemic shift from that of a state-oriented public policy perspective. Rather than rendering South Africa's Apartheid policy within a discourse dominated by a state system mode of explanation (in which geopolitical and geo-strategic conceptions dominate), van Woerden focuses on the consequences of the policy for an exemplary body. His story foregrounds the ways in which the (varying) national and racial identities lent to Tsafendas, at different times and in different places, affect his ability to dwell, to move, to work, and to form attachments. Leaving aside for the moment Apartheid's system of racial exclusion, the story of Tsafendas peregrinations reveals a world of state boundaries, a normative grid that retards movement, particularly for one with an ambiguous national lineage. On the geopolitical map, South Africa, Greece, Portugal, Egypt, Turkey, Germany, the U.S., and Canada are nation-states. For Tsafendas, who resided briefly in each, they were complex zones of exclusion—at times allowing brief periods of entry and residence (as a youngster in Alexandria, a schoolboy in the Union of South Africa and an adult in many of the world's coastal cities), at times rejecting him, and at times holding onto to him. The details of

Tsafendas's continually arrested and enforced movements, throughout four continents, map a world of geopolitical constraints. One exemplary episode stands out:

After spending a month under arrest in Oporto Portugal (because his refugee passport revealed episodes of deportation from the U.S.), "his putative Portuguese citizenship was investigated and confirmed from Lourenco Marques."[50] He then sought to return to Africa. After getting no response from his family, then living in Pretoria, he took a ship to Lourenco Marques, but was denied entry after a series of negotiations with the consular office. Relating this part of the story, van Woerden writes, in one of the most poignant and telling moments in the narrative: "Not long after this episode the authorities returned him to Lisbon. He was trapped like an eel in a basket, it seemed he would never escape."[51] Tsafendas did escape from the "basket." Eluding the confinements of state boundaries and their citizen codes, he eventually made his way back to Africa and even into South Africa, a state from which he had been permanently banned (from 1951 onward), thanks to the negligence of an agent in the Lourenco Marques consulate, who failed to find his name on the "stop list."[52]

As I have noted, nation-states are more than merely juridical entities in the process of constituting and administering citizen bodies; they are also "biopolitical" actors.[53] Included and excluded bodies are tracked and segregated not only through the use of a legal paper trail but also with a genealogical one. In Tsafendas's case, he entered a state within which the normative grid was extraordinarily dense, surveillant, and discriminatory. As van Woerden notes:

> The South Africa that Demitrios was entering was in most respects the same country as the one he had left two decades before—only worse. The Afrikaner Nationalist Party, under Verwoerd, was still in the saddle and ruling as relentlessly as ever. Segregation was enforced even more strictly than before: laws against mixed marriages and sexual acts between different races were in effect, as were draconian pass laws ('movement control' was their stated aim).[54]

Involved with a "Coloured woman" and declaring his dedication to a future in which "complete mingling of the races would finally take place in Africa,"[55] Tsafendas applied to the Population Registration Office to be reclassified as "Coloured." and, ultimately, planned the assassination of the architect of South Africa's racial separation. Ironically, because his request rang warning bells within the interior ministry (where it was discovered that he was on the banned list), an order to deport him was executed. The day Tsafendas killed Verwoerd, the letter informing him that he was to be deported was sitting in an official's "out-tray."[56]

## Other Racial-Spatial Orders

Although the killing of Verwoerd serves as a denouement to van Woerden's story, the bulk of the narrative addresses itself, through its biographical focus, to the question of how nationality and race are lived, which constitutes an alternative way of looking at the relationship between "race" and nationhood. In contrast, the dominant discourse on partition in the political science literature is state-centric. Like the basket in which Demitrios Tsafendas was, in van Woerden's terms, "caught like an eel," political science discourses, particularly the subfield specializations of comparative politics and international relations, assist in the historical process by which the state captures bodies, not only through its policing mechanisms but also through the ways in which it dominates codes, the way it "overcodes" alternative ways of encoding bodies and territories.[57]

At different times, state coding has had different kinds of emphasis. For example, as James Scott points out, "[t]he nineteenth-century Prussian state was very much interested in the ages and sexes of immigrants and emigrants but not in their religions or races; what mattered to the state was keeping track of possible draft dodgers and maintaining a supply of men of military age."[58] Effectively, nationalizing states translate biological bodies into social bodies in ways that reflect the particular state project at the time.[59] Inasmuch as the state is, like van Woerden's eel basket, a machine of capture, in the twentieth century, the machine has been increasingly employed to produce the myth that the state contains a unitary ethno-national culture.[60]

The state-as-machine of capture was strikingly in evidence during one episode in another partitioned global venue, the normative and geopolitical separations involved in the long-running Israeli-Palestinian conflict. In 1992, 415 Palestinian men were expelled from Israel as "security risks." Sent across the northern border into the "security zone" in southern Lebanon and prevented from further entry into Lebanon, they were effectively desubjectivized mobile bodies, trapped in a narrow, liminal zone between states.[61] Treating the men's liminality in discourse as well as in space, Samira Kawash points out that in their abjected condition, they were perceptible but not representable.[62] They were moving bodies that could not be located as citizen subjects within the discourses of states. Their expulsion, and thus their "desubjectification," placed them symbolically as well as spatially in a "no-man's land;" "forced into motion," they ceased to occupy an identity space. They could not *be* within the familiar political discourse applied to a world of governmental states.[63]

To the extent that one perceives or recognizes such abjected bodies, which "expose[s] a fizzure in the totalizing edifice of state and subject,"[64] one has access to what is unthought within geopolitical discourses. Serving as a relay for the mode of capture experienced by the Palestinian men, the geopolitical approach to partition in the academy sees it "like a state." This was nowhere more apparent than in the way many in the field of international studies rendered structure of antagonism in the recent Bosnian war. As David Campbell points out, "conventional renderings of the Bosnian war . . . inject ontological presumptions (about ethnicity, nationalism, identity, violence, etc.) into their claims of actuality without disclosing their complicity in the representational process."[65] Among other things, the characterization of the Bosnian war as a "civil war," based on ancient ethnic hatreds by many in the media and academia constituted a redeployment of the dominant modern state project. And in so doing, these state-form representations had the effect of making much of Bosnia "invisible."[66]

Geopolitically, then, partition is simply "policy," what one international studies analyst calls, "a common political practice."[67] Treating the motivations leading to partition, he speaks, within the language of the nationalizing state project (of developing a unitary national culture that is coextensive with state boundaries) of a desire for "self-determination."[68] Yet almost invariably the selves that nationalists seek to separate are ambiguously mixed rather than ethnically pure selves. The drive to partition and abjection constitutes a denial of a history of intermingling and acculturation. The voices of those who have been forcibly separated tell a different story than the tales emerging from the geopolitical conceits of the state-form and its collusive cultural agents—for example, one who states, baldly, that India "had the most successful ethnic partition" (because it allowed the British to leave and because the resulting conflict "was contained").[69]

The voices of displaced people, who are no longer able to enjoy the intimacies of former attachments sing a different tune rather than amplifying "the noise of the state."[70] Those who convey these voices seek to overcome the silence to which they have been consigned by state-form explanations. For example, seeing the partition of India as "one of the great human convulsions of history,"[71] Urvashi Butalia takes us to the other side of the silence by extracting stories from many who experienced the convulsion:

> The suffering and grief of Partition are not memorialized at the border, nor publicly, anywhere else in India, Pakistan, and Bangladesh. A million may have died but have no monuments. Stories are all that people have, stories that rarely breach the frontiers of family and religious community: people talking to their own blood.[72]

For those who redeploy the state form, whether peace advocates or security-minded conflict managers, the consequences of partition are a matter of either politically contested or uncontested borders in the sovereign units that remain. Thus, for example, Robert Schaeffer describes what is left, after the century's experience of "severed states" as "thirty-seven successor states,"[73] while for those like Urvashi Butalia's family, whose life worlds have been divided, what is left is a condition of broken attachments. The same experience of broken attachments is evident in the Bosnian case, which, when seen from the perspective of the abjected bodies, challenges the policy grammars of nation-states.

One such challenge is articulated by the Bosnian poet, Semezdin Mehmedinovic, who became an exile after the wars in the former Yugoslavia swept into Sarejevo:

> *I saw things no one wanted to see*
> *From the day I was born to my*
>   *Judgment day*
> *When I'm to get a reward or pay my dues*
> *And no matter what it takes*
> *I'll keep my Bosnian blues.*[74]

Ironically, as Robert Hayden has noted, "the wars in the former Yugoslavia since 1991 have taken place almost entirely within regions that were among the most 'mixed'—those in which the various nations of Yugoslavia were most intermingled."[75] As a result, the "violence of ethnic cleansing," at a conceptual level, "may be seen as deriving from the clash of a prescriptive model (culture-as-ideology) with what exists on the ground (culture-as-lived), but is not in accordance with the prescription."[76] In short, the violent attempts to create homogeneous national cultures that are coextensive with state boundaries required an unmixing to satisfy ideological requirements belied by lived experience.

In keeping with Hayden's observation, Radovan Karadzic, the leader of the Bosnian Serbs and "the most vocal champion of absolute separation along 'cultural borderlines,'" comes from an extraordinarily mixed heritage. When Mehmedinovic checked the Sarajevo phone directory under the surname Karadzic, of the twenty-two entries he found, there were ten Muslims, nine Serbs and one Croat. "On the basis of such a Bosnia ethnic inventory," he concludes, "any racist idea—of necessity—becomes grotesque."[77] Mehmedinovic has traced the lived experience of the various migrations imposed by the violent, pseudo-ethnic divisions resulting from the Bosnian war. Although many simply left the country, many others migrated within Bosnia: "People leave one part of town for another, seeking cover in 'less threatened areas,' in quieter neighborhoods."[78]

As a writer, Mehmedinovic is sensitive to the disjuncture between the ideology of cultural separation animating the war and what, in Hayden's terms, has existed "on the ground." The national literature, he points out, cannot be divided along ethnic lines:

> In the case of Bosnia, you simply could not say that the literature written in Sarajevo or Bosnia-Herzegovina was Bosnian or Croatian or Serbian. But this is precisely what has happened as a result of the war, that on the borders of culture all kinds of divisions and separations have been made. When you force these kinds of sharp divisions—in this case within the same language—the results are bloody. The best of what I see here demonstrates a model that can only benefit all cultures.[79]

And other genres speak to the same cultural sharing as literature. A convergence of cultural tastes in the decades of the '70s and '80s provides further evidence against Karadzic's injunction about the impossibility of a multicultural state: "The late 1970s and 1980s saw a great interest in comic book art, rock music, and film, that's what me and my generation educated ourselves on . . . there was intense communication between like-minded people because we were essentially brought up with similar aesthetic interests."[80]

While presenting his observations of the effects of pseudo-ethnic separation on the social order, Mehmedinovic mounts a challenge through a change in the locus of enunciation. He shifts the focus from the level of national politics to the consequences of geo-strategic action for families. He notes, for example, "[t]his morning, I compared my palm with my son's palm: the lines embedded in our skin are of the same depth. In terms of suffering, my son and I are twins."[81] In shifting the focus, Mehmedinovic achieves an effective politics of interpretation, or, more specifically, what Mieke Bal, in her feminist reading of the Book of Judges, calls a "counterco-herence." In contrast with a nationalist reading of Judges, which emphasizes the conquest of territory, Bal shifts the spatial emphasis to "the houses to be conquered," the places where, among other things, "daughters . . . meet their undoing,"[82] places, moreover, where, more generally, "the interaction between the political and the domestic is located."[83] This countercoherence theorized by Bal describes well the significance of much of Mehmedinovic's treatment of "Sarajevo blues" and exemplifies the primary politics of partition emerging from Urvashi Butalia's interviews with women, whose bodies were among the primary casualties in India's post-partition violence—in numerous episodes of abduction, rape, and murder—but whose voices have not hitherto carried from households to public arenas. Contrasting women's narratives with "official discourses of history,"[84] Butalia demonstrates not only how a different politics of partition becomes available when one crosses over to "the other side of silence," but also the more general political understanding one can achieve with a contrast between official historical accounts and "women's time."[85]

There are states whose "partition" exists within the state and is wholly normative and experiential rather than juridical. In the case of the post-slavery U.S., for example, within the official story—told from the point of view of antidiscrimination legislation, court decisions, and executive orders—the historical narrative is one of the overcoming of racial division. However, from the point of view of a set of individual experiences, which have been chronicled in a series of investigations reported in the *New York Times,* racial division remains a dominant feature of American life.[86] For example, when two friends from Cuba, Achmed Valdes, a white Cuban and Joel Ruiz, a black Cuban, emigrated to the U.S., they discovered that it was virtually impossible to maintain what had been a close and intimate friendship because of the ways in which white and black America constitute separate life worlds. Ruiz

> discovered a world that neither American television nor Communist propaganda had prepared him for. Dogs did not growl at him and police officers did not hose him, But he felt the stares of security guards when he entered a store in a white neighborhood and the subtle recoiling of white women when he walked by.[87]

Similarly, Valdes experienced the black sections of Miami as intimidating and inhospitable. As a result, "his contacts with African Americans are limited to chance encounters at work, his relationships with blacks to those he knows from Cuba."[88] Although unlike the South Africa of Verwoerd's South Africa, the U.S. (no longer) has no antimiscegenation laws and other official racial separation injunctions, many U.S. venues are effectively in a state of practiced and thus experienced Apartheid. At a minimum, such separations impugn the dominant temporality of the modern state, its narrative of evolving cultural cohesion.

## From Spatiality to Temporality

Pursuing the temporal aspect of state nation building, we can note that state attempts to control temporality have produced not only the familiar "invention of tradition" that Hobsbawm has analyzed in his historical treatment of nationalism,[89] but also attempts to control interpretations of the future. States have put considerable energy into managing anticipation as well as historical memory. For example, as Reinhart Koselleck has pointed out, European states, after the establishment of the Westphalian system in the seventeenth century, instituted controls over astrological readings. They sought to maintain their people's focus on national rather than apocalyptic futures.[90]

By heeding the temporality associated with nation building, we can therefore discern a disjuncture between the state and nation portion of the hyphenated nation-state. The spatial discourse which identifies the state system is uneasily articulated with a temporal one. The state, in its contemporary realization, is understood as a territorial entity, even though it has a history of emergence, having gradually or rapidly, as the case may be, expanded its political, legal, and administrative control by monopolizing violence and incorporating—by statute, by force, and/or by other means—various sub-units into a legal and administrative entity with definitive boundaries. The primary understanding of the modern "nation" segment of the hyphenated term is that a nation embodies a coherent culture, united on the basis of shared descent or, at least, incorporating a "people" with a historically stable coherence.

Inasmuch as few if any states contain coherent historically stable communities of shared descent, the symbolic maintenance of the nation-state requires a contentious management of historical narratives as well as territorial space. Effectively, state aspirations to nation-state existence are realized in various modalities of collective autobiography. The nation-state is scripted—in official documents, histories, and journalistic commentaries, among other texts—in ways that impose coherence on what is instead a series of fragmentary and arbitrary conditions of historical assemblage. At the same time, other modalities of writing—e.g., journals, diaries, novels and counter-historical narratives—challenge the state's coherence-producing writing performances.

To resist the metaphysical hypostatization of the nation-state and, at the same time, to appreciate the dynamic of scripting and counter-scripting, as the state has attempted to achieve nation-state coherence and has faced challenges to its self-production, we must again look at concrete historical instances. And, as was noted in the treatments of the Peruvian case, where state constitutions and tax codes have met a challenge at the level of the local ledger, and where the Creole version of Peruvian becoming is contested by an indigenous locus of enunciation, we must pay attention to the diverse writing genres within which the ongoing contest over the nation-state political form has been conducted. The significance of writing, as both a technology for the production of national consolidation and as a potentially subversive form, became apparent to the nationalizing state quite early in the European nation-building process. For example, in England, in the early sixteenth century, the state sought to repress oppositional cultures by extending "the scope of treason . . . to encompass treason by word as well as overt deed," in addition to making other "sustained attempts . . . to suppress oppositional writing."[91]

## Scripts and Counter-Scripts: State Initiatives and Oppositional Forms

The contemporary nation-state's departure from the premodern state consisted in both its establishment of clearly marked borders rather than ambiguous frontiers and its development as a political form that became increasingly associated with territorial rather than dynastic markers.[92] By the Renaissance, for example, the geopolitics scripted by European cartographers began to reflect a diminution of the significance of emperors and monarchs. In the case of Britain, the spaces on official maps, which had previously been assigned to "insignia of royal power," decreased as the maps increasingly emphasized the markers of land configuration and the boundaries of national territory.[93] By the seventeenth century, the succession of images on maps reflected a historical sequence "from universal Christendom, to dynastic state, to land centered nation."[94]

French national territory was also inscribed cartographically, but key episodes in the genealogy of French cartography reflect a significant difference in the mode of French nation building, which stemmed from a revolutionary change in the class basis of national legitimation. Rather than a shift from monarchical inscription to a land-based territory, the key changes in French cartographic practices were aimed at displacing the spaces of aristocratic privilege with a uniform space in keeping with a republican ideal: "the uniform application of law and administration."[95] Accordingly, the new national cartographic surveys repressed regional differences in order to depersonalize the former hierarchically-oriented social order.[96] In effect, the "redrawing of France's administrative boundaries in the late 18th century was a moral act inspired by and symbolizing the highest political ideals;" it reflected a state in the process of producing a modern politico-moral territoriality, one in which the "subordination of the bourgeoisie to the nobility and church" would be overturned.[97]

Mapmaking has been only one of the early genres of state nation building. In subsequent periods, as I have noted, the state's cultural governance has been a major aspect of its modern form of management and legitimation. In Europe, the cultural production aspect of its nation-building practices intensified in the nineteenth century when, as Ernest Gellner points out, states found it necessary to produce homogeneous national cultures, not only to legitimate and celebrate their "essential" national characteristics but also to mobilize their population for work and military service. In the case of an industrializing Europe, the state's scripting was often aided and abetted by the development of national arts programs—for example, national theater initiatives in both England and France.

But in both states, "theatrical nationhood" (national theater developments beginning in the mid-nineteenth century) was contested. The inauguration of national theaters took place amid a struggle "between advocates of a centralized national theater that might reconcile the nation from above and rival, perhaps antagonistic, 'popular' cultures on the social and geographic periphery which resisted this reconciliation under duress."[98]

Both movements drew their legitimation from the developing ideology of nineteenth-century nationalism, the idea that the state contains a coherent nation, a "people" that provides the basis of its authority. But, as Loren Kruger has pointed out, "notions of the 'people' offer no stable ground or ruling principle on which to erect the nation or the nation's theater, but rather a battleground of intersecting *fields* on which the legitimacy of national popular representation is publicly contested."[99]

In the French case, the legitimations associated with the struggle over the national theater reflects the same impetus that is evident in the post-revolutionary cartographic genre. Advocates of a national theater saw it the way they saw the *fêtes publiques,* as a way to "invite the people into the nation,"[100] In the English case, the National Theater initiative was not republican in spirit. Rather, the theater was designed to hail an exemplary and "qualified" class of landed aristocrats rather than to shape a popular constituency.[101] Eventually, however, the theater's "patrician hegemony" was to be challenged from "class and colonial margins."[102] To situate that challenge, I turn to the latter and treat a recent rehearsal of that challenge in a contemporary Irish play, Brian Friel's *Translations* (1980). The play speaks to the significance of drama in the development of English nationhood and is an exemplar of the way Irish literatures and dramas have mounted critiques of England's imperialist nation-building project.

To situate Friel's play both conceptually and historically, one must appreciate the role of disparaged others in the construction of national imaginaries in general and, more specifically, the place that Ireland has held within self-representations that have informed English nationhood. As Michael Neill notes in his analysis of the place of Ireland in Shakespeare's historical plays, Ireland played a crucial role in the English nationhood project. England's control over Ireland was:

> a prerequisite for the idea of an English national body politic in principle separable from the body of the monarch—the idea of the nation, that is, as a 'commonwealth' with an essential and permanent existence distinct from the king's estate and determined by something other than the dynastic accidents that fixed the boundaries of the feudal kingdoms . . .[103]

At the same time, however, Irishness served as the negative other to Englishness:

> It was the Irish 'wilderness' that bounded the English garden, Irish 'barbarity' that defined English civility, Irish papistry and 'superstition' that warranted English religion; it was Irish 'lawlessness' that demonstrated the superiority of English law and Irish 'wandering' that defined the settled and centered nature of English society.[104]

Although England needed Ireland as part of its self-constitution, it needed at the same time to maintain a distance if it was to nurture a national imaginary based on the differences constituting its national character. Hence, reflecting England's anxiety about resisting pollution from its Celtic fringe, Shakespeare's *Richard II* has "barbarous speakers of foreign tongues, unreliable Welsh and treacherous Irish, who do not properly belong to the English nation," playing peripheral roles in the play.[105] Indeed, central to the nationhood impetus in early modern English drama is a linguistic romanticism. It is manifested in *Richard II* when Mowbray's imminent banishment from England is most keenly felt as an alienation from his home language. He is to suffer "an enforced geographical translation" from, as he puts it, "The language I have learnt these forty years.. . ."[106] And because much of English national attachment was realized as an attachment to a language, an anxiety about the encroachment of foreign tongues was manifested. By the early seventeenth century, there were significant expressions of anxiety about "[t]he influx of thousands of new words from Latin, Greek, French, Spanish, and Italian."[107] One of the more vociferous and politically charged reactions imagines an ungoverned circulation of non-English words: "foreign signifiers floating 'without a Parliament, without any consent or allowance, establish[ing] themselves as Free-denizens on our language.'"[108]

The historical trajectory of England's linguistically oriented nationhood provides the context for Brian Friel's critical intervention into the language-nationhood nexus in his *Translations*. However, the play must be understood not only in the context of England's language hegemony but also in the context of a shift from the Irish nationalism of the postindependence period to a contentious "culturalist paradigm" within which the "language question" in Ireland has been negotiated within the civic sphere.[109] Accordingly, the play's emphasis on language draws its political force from a focus on Irish resistance to English language imperialism. It opens with a "glimpse of a linguistic Eden, an Irish-speaking Ireland," And in a scene focused on a language lesson, there is a parody of English "as foolish gibberish."[110] Emphasizing Ireland's distance from English literary culture, for example, one character reacts to an Englishman's mention of Wordsworth by remarking: "Wordsworth? . . . No I'm afraid we're not familiar with your literature, Lieutenant. We feel closer to the warm Mediterranean. We tend to overlook your island."[111] And when an English character expresses his sense of being an outsider in Ireland, his interlocutor challenges commitments to a language-nationhood relationship by emphasizing the historical contingency of linguistic codes: "I understand your sense of exclusion, of being cut off from life here; and I remember that words are signals, counters. They are not immortal. And it can happen—to use an image you'll understand—it can happen that a civilization can be imprisoned in a linguistic contour which no longer matches the landscape of . . . fact."[112]

Friel's dramatic challenge is therefore not only to England's sense of civilizational superiority and English linguistic imperialism but also to *any* romanticization of a language-nationhood connection. Rather than seeking to trump Englishness with an Irishness based on an injunction to return to Gaelic, "the play," as Josephine Lee rightly puts it, "is full of moments which destabilize meanings and authority of words . . . [forcing the audience] to be self-conscious about language."[113] Because the issue of translation consumes the play's narrative and engages the audience through the repeated ambiguities arising in the dialogues, Friel's *Translations* achieves a Brechtian, critical effect. Instead of opting for one versus another language culture as a foundation for nationhood, it disables the audience's ability to connect words and meanings, encouraging a critical reflection on language.[114]

In other nation-state contexts, Brechtian, critically-oriented drama goes well beyond a disruption of the methods, linguistic and otherwise, through which states construct national cultures. In the Columbian case, for example, the avowedly Brechtian playwright, Enrique Buenaventura, has aimed his dramas at disrupting the racial, class, and gender orders constituting male Creole dominance over the Columbian national imaginary. Foregrounding "the concepts of 'tradition,' 'history,' and race, class, and gender 'difference' which sustain the power elite," Buenaventura's plays, for example, his *Los Papeles del Infierno,* which addresses a contemporary period of Colombian violence, puts the audience in the position of the historian.[115] The many brief vignettes in *Papeles* present documents designed to provoke interpretive reactions in the audience, which must impugn official Columbian history.

While there are numerous other national venues within which theatrical nationhood has been an arena of confrontation between state nationalizing initiatives and critical, deconstructive reactions, particularly in postcolonial contexts, I turn here to the "American" case because U.S. domestic colonial history provides a critical comparison with the English/Irish example. In the U.S., the most familiar national theater initiative is associated with the cultural governance policies enacted as part of Franklin D. Roosevelt's New Deal. Unlike the English case, in the U.S. there was no "a hegemonic elite culture"[116] capable of controlling the federal theater initiative, which was inaugurated in the 1930s. As a result, although the Roosevelt administration sought to create a theater that would shape "a national audience out of local and regional audiences,"[117] it lacked a "monopoly on legitimacy."[118] Instead, the theater was shaped in a climate of compromise between political forces contesting inequities and those seeking to contain radical political initiatives.

However, a focus on the theater's role in the nationalization of American culture in the twentieth century finesses political issues associated with the Euro American assault on indigenous nations. While Ireland was a significant (and disparaged) other in the case of early modern English drama's role in nation building, in the U.S. case, the nationhood project's construction of otherness was more complicated. On the one hand, there is the legacy of conquest. The destruction of the first nations and the seizure of their lands obstructs, or at least compromises, the democratic revolution and cultural expansion narratives through which American nationhood is valorized as pervasive and exceptional.

In the key nineteenth-century nation building period, "Americans," as Susan Scheckel notes, "attempted—in popular fiction, legal argumentation, and official Indian policy—to come to terms with the restless ghosts of the national past, the legacy and history of conquest and revolution that threatened the moral foundations of nationhood."[119] At the same time, Indians were accorded a privileged place in some versions of the national narrative. If, as some would have it, America is to be "nature's nation"—an identity willingly taken on by white colonialists wanting to distinguish themselves from their British connection (in contrast with the Irish, who have had to struggle to shed the mantel of naturalness that England bequeathed with its civilizational model)—the Native American's presumed attunement to the natural world provided an exemplary symbolic resource. Accordingly, "[m]any literary nationalists in the early nineteenth century suggested that the history and myths of American Indians could provide the new nation with a sense of 'primitive origins.'"[120]

However, although the Indian-as-symbolic-narrative resource served to help free America from its reliance on English patrimony, English inheritance could not be wholly rejected because it served to buttress Euro American claims to Indian lands. As a result, artistic productions complemented legal and governmental discourses in the nineteenth century as they addressed the complex location of Euro America, within disjunctive narratives *vis á vis* England and Native America. For example, James Fenimore Cooper's novels—especially *The Pioneers*—seek to contain the contradictions in America's Indian policy by establishing interrelationships between English and Native American heritages. In addition, various dramatic versions of the Pocahontas-John Smith story do the same, while elaborating the feminine side of Native America as a mode of Indianness that extends a hospitality denied by the masculine, warrior mode.[121] Arguably, no class of dramas has addressed itself to the Indian difference and the troubling position of Native America in Euro American nation-building narratives more consistently that various versions of the Pocahontas story. Here, I want to contrast one nineteenth-century version that legitimated Euro American expansion, and a contemporary one that provides a parodic critique of Euro America's historical use of the Pocahontas myth.

Pocahontas, the "singular most popular subject of Indian dramas during the nineteenth century," was inaugurated on the American stage with James N. Barker's *The Indian Princess; or, La Belle Sauvage: An Operatic Melodrama in Three Acts*.[122] As is the case in Cooper's novels, the play situates itself in the midst of America's two modes of otherness, England and Native America. The play's version of Captain John Smith articulates a new national order that is "distinctly American," and which "[l]eav[es} behind the 'shrill war-cry' of New World natives and the vices of 'old licentious Europe.'"[123] As for the "Indian Princess," her role here, as in other nineteenth-century Pocahontas dramas, is to seal the connection between nationhood and a romantic domesticity. Pocahontas's amorous connection with white America enacts the feminine side of Native America's hospitality and thereby contributes to a domestication of a former "wilderness," to which Indian men will not accede. The twentieth-century version of the story (for example the 1998 Disney feature film), which was already well articulated in the nineteenth century, has perpetuated a "mythohistory . . . comfortable and comforting to the dominant group, white Euro-Americans."[124] In contrast with the comforting story of Pochahontas's heartfelt hospitality toward a future whitening of the American continent, the evidence, while equivocal, favors another interpretation. As Daniel Richter puts it:

> [I]t seems plausible that, far from being a youthful rebel who defied her father's will to join the English invaders, Pochahontas was a dutiful child who fulfilled a very traditional function in Native politics and diplomacy. Her role . . . defined [Captain John Smith] as her adoptive parent, and this established kinship relations between him and her biological father and, presumably, her mother's clan as well.[125]

In addition, the legitimating effects of white America's versions of the Smith-Pocahontas story have not gone unchallenged in the theatrical genre. Reacting to white America's historical use of the Pocahontas myth, Native American actress-playwright Monique Mojica produced a dramatic version of Pocahontas entitled *Pocahontas and the Blue Spots*.[126] While the play effects a recovery of aspects of Native American history left out of Euro American versions—one character is "a modern Native woman on a journey to recover the history of her grandmothers as a tool towards her own healing" (14)— it's primary mode is parody. Written for two women playing multiple roles, the characters include: "Princess Buttered-on-Both-Sides," who is "One of the many faces of the trickster, Coyote. She is a contestant in the Miss North American Indian Beauty Pageant and she is stuck in the talent segment." And a "Storybook Pocahontas". . . . "The Little Indian Princess from the picture books, friend of the settlers, in love with the Captain." She "comes complete with her savage-Indian-Chief father."

The vehicles of the play, thirteen transformations, one for each moon in the lunar year, provide a narrative sequence that moves from scenes in which Pocahontas characters enact the roles that Euro America scripted for them to scenes in which they take control over their identities. Thus for example, in transformation 5, the "Storybook Pocahontas" is in love with the Captain. She coos, "He's so brave his eyes are so blue, his hair is so blond and I like the way he walks." And she does some swooning. In transformation 10, which takes place in a contemporary setting, America's exemplar remains white. The Pocahontas version named Princess Buttered-On-Both-Sides says "I wanna be the girls next door. . . . I wanna have lots and lots of blonde hair. I wanna be—Doris Day, Farah Fawcett, Daryl Hannah. . . ." But by transformation 13, the border theorist and critic of Euro America's racist exclusions, Gloria Anzaldua, appears, and two contemporary women react: contemporary [Native America] woman #1 says "This ain't no stoic look, this is my face" after having said "What I want is the freedom to carve and chisel my own face. . . ." And contemporary [Native American] woman # 2 sings (in untranslated Spanish) "Una nacion no sera conquista . . . hasta que los corazones de sus mujeres caigan a la tierra [A nation will not be conquered until the hearts of its women have fallen]."[127]

## From Dramatic Performance to Spatial Practice: The Novel and the Nation-State

There is a significant homology between theatrical dramas and the nation-shaping methods of the state. Inasmuch as coherent nationhood requires that the state engage in a continuing performance, that it stage nationhood, the state's performance is the larger drama within which artistic dramas are performed and upon which they are often led to reflect. When they do, and when they're politically engaged, the theater sometimes supports and sometimes contests the state's performances of nationhood. In the case of the novel, a different mode of the nation-state's construction of its status is enacted, it's spatiotemporality. And as in the case of national theater initiatives, the contention between state nationalizing and modes of resistance are in evidence. Here, I treat briefly the role of the novel in a variety of national venues, beginning with an emphasis on novelistic space and with the case of the United Kingdom in the nineteenth century.

With respect to the relationship between the novel and the nation-state, the novel's "literary geography," the ways in which it encodes territory, is, as Franco Moretti investigation has shown, one of its most significant attributes. In his treatment of the British case, Moretti focuses on the nineteenth-century novel and begins with some observations on the remarkable exclusions in the novelistic geography of Jane Austen's plots. Her Britain has no Ireland, Scotland, or Wales, and her England is missing its industrial North. The sentimental novel, the genre to which Austen's works belong, is focused on social rather than national issues. As a result, the "small homogeneous England of Austen's novels"[128] represents a marriage market for the families, ranging from local gentry to national elite, living in England's most well-to-do and populated area. Given Austen's "ideology of space," there is little concern with British nation building as whole, much less with Britain's management of its colonial possessions. When the men in an Austen novel travel abroad, the writer's purpose is not to map global space or to elucidate the political economy of colonialism but either to remove the character from the plot or to allow the character to acquire wealth. And wealth in Austen's plots have nothing to do with economic imperialism and everything to do with funding a character in order to enable him to participate effectively in the social relations of his class.

In contrast with the geography of the sentimental novel, which is concerned primarily with social rather than nation-state space, are nineteenth-century historical novels, for example, Sir Walter Scott's, which offer "a veritable phenomenology of the border."[129] Scott's novels evoke a complex bordered world at a time in which the nation-state system is being reconfigured, as some borders are hardened and others contested. His novelistic geography treats most of Britain and is concerned with the delineation of its internal, anthropological boundaries. Moreover, the historical novels of Scott and other nineteenth-century writers do not simply tell static stories of borders; their plots are associated with a nation building, geographic dynamic, a process of erasure of borders "and of the incorporation of the internal periphery into the larger unit of the state;"[130] they reflect and reinforce the geopolitical preoccupations of the nineteenth-century nation-state. The historical novel therefore exceeds Jane Austen's "middle sized-world."[131] It articulates a highly politicized geography in comparison with the depoliticized, social geography of the sentimental novel, and the enlarged space it references enunciates the political consolidation of the state system.

The nineteenth-century English historical novel, exemplified by those of Sir Walter Scott, therefore aided and abetted two major dimensions of the British nation-building project. In their general preoccupation with boundaries, Scott's novels mapped state territorial space, and with their erasure of internal anthropological divisions, they complied with the state's domestic biopolitical project, its attempt to fashion a homogenous national culture.[132] However, Scott's literary geography was not uncontested both within Britain's Celtic fringe and in her colonies. Pointing toward an alternative, "bardic nationalism," which was developed in a nativist, antiquarian literature, Kate Trumpener describes the nature of the literary opposition in nineteenth-century romantic novels to Scott's implied narrative of a progressive British cultural nationhood. The antiquarian revival in the works of such writers as James Macpherson, Sydney Owenson, John Galt, and Charles Maturin valorized disparate folk communities. Their novels were aimed at preserving the separate cultural spaces that Scott's novels sought to consolidate within a unified British national culture.[133]

Yet despite significant opposition by writers in Britain's colonies (as well as within the British Isles), Scott's novelistic approach to national history—his placement of fictional characters in actual historical situations—has been appropriated to other nation-building contexts in former colonial states. For example, in twentieth-century Spanish America, the project of consolidating unitary "American" national cultures "propelled the formation of national literatures and histories . . . seeking to display each country's uniqueness,"[134] and many Spanish American authors saw Scott's historical novels as a model. However, as Nina Gerassi-Navarro points out, "unlike England or France, where the distant past had the ability to awaken a consonant patriotic fervor [as Scott's Waverley novels did in the English case], the colonial past in Spanish America was a much more controversial period." As a result, in her reading of twentieth-century pirate novels "as metaphors for the process of nation building in Spanish America,"[135] Gerassi-Navarro found a nationalist ideology evinced not as a play of identity/difference within the state but as an ambiguous play of association and disassociation between local and European cultural attachments.

Inasmuch as "Spanish American republics were seen as being contingent on existing European models," the novels tended to articulate the problem of the political and cultural gap between the former colonial powers and the new Spanish American states.[136] Characteristically, twentieth-century pirate novels used history not to find national origins but to define their national orders *vis á vis* "other identities."[137] Nevertheless, in Spanish America as well as in many other newer states, which have extracted themselves from colonial rule, literary culture in general and the novel in particular, which during the emergence of Third World states "quickly predominated as a privileged narrative form," became a site of resistance after having been initially a form that supported the colonizing process.[138] Arguedas's earlier-noted *Deep Rivers* is an example in the Latin American context.

In the case of Middle Eastern states the "master narrative of imperialism" has been challenged by writers whose novels violate the narrative containments that had formerly served as agencies of colonialism—for example, the novels of Palestinian writer Ghassan Kafani.[139] Moreover, in contrast with those Middle Eastern novelists who write realist fiction within a stable geopolitical locus—for example, the novels of the Egyptian, Naguib

Mahfouz—Lebanese and Palestinian novelists, who experience a sense of territorial instability, articulate their precarious geopolitical status with a tendency toward "parody and exaggeration," as they reflect on the violence attending the clash of Arab and Israeli national projects.[140] For example, in Lebanese novelist Elias Khoury's *Little Mountain,* the reliance on liberating Arab armies is parodied. After a tank breaks down, two characters become distracted by a concern with aesthetics (which displaces ethnic difference onto color coding):

> I want a tank made of all colors. Do you know colors, says the young African boy. I don't know them. I don't know what colors mean. Everything is colored as it can be. And Talal wants a colored tank.[141]

There are also exemplary instances of novelistic opposition to nation-building projects in African states. Effectively, as Rhonda Cobham summarizes it, "the transformation of the anti-imperialist struggle in Africa into a nationalist movement exacerbated a crisis of individual and collective identity that is staged in the African novel."[142] The novels of Nahruddin Farah are exemplary in this respect, for they have provided a counter-script to that developed during Somalia's most intense nation-building period under General Siyad Barre in the postindependence period (1969–1991). Faced with a population of people with a disjunctive set of attachments—a social order composed of lineage clans and subclans, different classes with, among others, a huge noble-commoner divide, as well as a north-south divide as a colonial legacy—Barre employed educative as well as coercive strategies. While mounting a military irredentist campaign to recapture the Ogaden territory under Ethiopian rule, he also mounted a literacy campaign, seeking to displace tribal attachments with national ones by, among other things, having everyone learn to read and write [an adopted] Somali language, Amharic.[143]

In his novels, especially *Sweet and Sour Milk* and *Maps,* Farah contests the imposition of a uniform cultural space in Barre's nationalizing project. In *Maps,* for example, the main character, Askar, is the posthumous offspring of two patriotic martyrs with Somali nationalist attachments. At the same time, however, he is intimately connected with a foster mother and uncle whose backgrounds do not fit the new Somali national profile in terms of heritage or language.[144] And most significantly there is a disjuncture between the novel's structures of intimacy and the new imposed cultural/political map. For example, speaking to his surrogate mother, Misra, Askar notes that on the one hand, he has intense bodily dependence on her, but at the same time there are "the maps which give me the distance between you and me" and that as a result "we are a million minutes apart, your 'anatomy' and mine."[145] And, in turn, Misra refers to the divisive forces of the nationalizing campaign, telling Askar "when you do well, the credit is not mine but your people's that is your [Somali] nation whose identity I do not share."[146]

Ultimately, the interacting characters in Farah's *Maps* reflect the instabilities of the identities of the people contained within the nationalizing state. Through the characters' queries about their attachments and interrelationships and their confusions about shifting designations of place, Farah challenges the presumption of a coherent Somali nation and resists complicity with the project of imposing an unambiguous nation-state frame on a complex African intercultural order, whose spatial predicates are disjunctive with statist geopolitics. For example, Askar's Uncle Hilaal sees a map in Askar's room in which the word Ogaden has been erased and replaced by the term "Western Somalia."[147] However, in addition to the critical spatial reconfiguration that Farah's novels enact, much of the critique they supply to Barre's version of the Somalian national imaginary focuses on biopolitical issues, especially the significance of raced and gendered bodies. Picking up on this dimension, I turn to the novel's role in the biopolitics of nation building, which of necessity evokes the tensions between national and novelistic modes of temporality as well as space.

### The Nation-State and Its Others: Biopolitical Enterprises

In a telling response to Jurgen Habermas's recent gloss on the "European Nation-State,"[148] Timothy Mitchell points out that contrary to Habermas's implication, imperialism, rather than being incidental to state nationalisms, was the context shaping them.[149] As my analysis thus far has implied, this is also true of a major dimension of imperialism's legacy, racism. Rather than merely a policy problem for the nation-state (as implied in much of official and academic policy writing),[150] racism has been a fundamental shaping force, although in different ways in different state nation-building venues. In Ecuador, for example, the institutionalized "ideology of national identity results in a racial map of national territory: urban centers . . . are associated with modernity, while rural areas are viewed as places of racial inferiority, violence, backwardness, savagery, and cultural deprivation."[151]

The Ecuadorian "racial/spatial order," which is reflected in a regional cultural genre, a beauty contest that is significantly racially coded, contrasts with the way the U.S. racial/spatial order is often addressed—through erasure—as in the mid-twentieth-century production of *Oklahoma!* But as the Ecuadorian beauty contest example suggests, there remains an additional shaping context to be addressed in this analysis of the state's nationalizing project, its management of the meaning and role of women, particularly with respect to the relationship between "nationalism and sexualities."[152] For example, treating nations as "elaborate social *practices* enacted through time," and expressed in diverse media and print genres, Anne McClintock, in her analysis of the case of South Africa, points out the ways in which women have been confined within the state's national story to the role of "biological producers of National groups . . . transmitters and producers of cultural narratives, . . . and reproducers of the boundaries of the nation by accepting or refusing sexual intercourse or marriage with prescribed groups of men."[153]

In general, state nationalizing initiatives have manifested a striking gender-oriented biopolitics. They have often constructed good versus bad women on the basis of their relationship to a racial, ethnic, or class-legitimated familial sexuality. The nation-building impetus of this construction was evident in the Broadway musical, *Oklahoma!* (treated at length in chapter 3) at the point where a choreographed dance routine has "bad women" (prostitutes and dancehall girls in skimpy outfits and mesh stockings), being displaced by farmers' wives in long calico dresses. It is a construction also evident in the case of Argentina, where the state's nationalizing discourse was shaped by locating women's appropriate versus inappropriate sexuality: "The issue of 'bad women' triggered the discourse on female nationality" at a historically crucial moment in Argentina's nation-building process, a time in the nineteenth century when "thousands of women left their European homelands . . . in search of a better life in the Americas." Argentina's imagined community therefore owed much of its contour to the regulation of women's sexual identities: "the Honor of the nation" required a particular practice of sexual virtue.[154]

Because the kinds of regulation of women in state nation building and maintenance varies considerably, I want to conclude by contrasting two disparate cases, India and the U.S., beginning with India, which, during its industrializing period, has had no state-sponsored "welfare system." As a result, the situation for many women has been one of an exploitable dependency that is far more pervasive, uninhibited, and violent than in countries with elaborate systems of financial aid. The exploitation is especially severe in the case of "tribal" women who, as writer and tribal activist Mahashweta Devi points out, have not been a part of "the decolonization of India."[155] Many tribal women end up as prostitutes in "the bonded labor system," handed over by their families to pay off a debt that can never be fully paid because the accounts carry compounded interest.[156] While Indian nation building is valorized in official texts as a case of successful development, Mahasweta has described her counter-hegemonic task as, among other things, resistance to "development" because of the state's complicity in the devastating effects of the capitalist market on tribal women and children.[157]

In addition to her strenuous political organizing among "tribals," Mahashweta's writing constitutes an exemplary counter-script to that of the nationalizing state, which has exploited indigenous bodies, while, at the same time, engaging in a biopolitical, nationalizing discourse that erases their presence. In her story *Douloti the Bountiful,* Mahashweta displaces the state's national cartography with "the socially invested cartography of bonded labor,"[158] and she challenges the state's biopolitical discourse by showing how women's bodies are casualties of "national industrial, and transnational global capital."[159] Her Douloti, the daughter of a tribal bonded worker, is sold into prostitution. She dies on a journey homeward, after having given up on being taken in by a hospital to be treated for venereal disease.

Ultimately, therefore, to describe nationhood as the mere aggregation of diverse groups, or to use such cleansing language as "the forging of a national culture," is to launder some of nation building's catastrophic effects. Mahashweta supplies a powerful recognition of the violence of a nationalizing state. Her Douloti, exploited and ravaged by illness, lies down to die on a large map of India that a teacher, Mohan, has inscribed for his students in a clay courtyard to celebrate Independence Day. As Mahashweta puts it (in the last lines of the story):

> Today on the fifteenth of *August,* Douloti has left no room at all in the India of people like Mohan for planting the standard of the Independence flag. What will Mohan do now? Douloti is all over India.[160]

Gayatri Spivak's characterization of Douloti's final gesture eloquently captures this chapter's theme: the contentious cartographic and biopolitical scripting involved in the struggle between nation-states and those who resist them. Douloti, Spivak writes, "reinscribes this official map of the nation by the zoograph of the unaccommodated female body restored to the economy of nature."[161]

## Nationhood as an Ambiguous Achievement: Toni Morrison's *Paradise*

The case of Douloti provides an effective threshold for treating one of the most politically perspicuous American novels of the twentieth century, Toni Morrison's *Paradise,* another treatment that summons the abjected female. I end this chapter with a treatment of *Paradise,* not only because it provides a significant challenge to one of America's foundational legitimating narratives but also because it is an example of an approach to critical interpretation and translation that this investigation as a whole endorses and articulates. Moreover, the lived experiences of the characters in the novel, are examples, like that in the earlier treatment of Demetrios Tsafendas, of bodies whose trajectories of movement have been enforced by structures of exclusion. Through its characters' experiences, framed within a politics of interpretation and translation, Toni Morrison's *Paradise* constitutes a challenge to foundational national imaginaries in general. And with its contorted and elliptical narrative of intersecting lives, it supplies a counter-narrative to a specific foundational American story, "American exceptionalism," the ideological assumption that the national culture is a consequence of a unique mission that must be continually sacrilized by a romanticization of the past.

To situate the challenge of Morrison's novel to the ideology and story of American exceptionalism, one has to appreciate not only its origins but also its persistence. Initially, the religious, patriarchal leaders of the early New England settlers strove to inculcate the presumption that American was to be a new Jerusalem, "a site specifically favored by God—perhaps the very place that he had chosen to initiate the millennial Kingdom of Christ."[162] Subsequently, from the early nineteenth century on, a secularized version of American exceptionalism has held sway among many American historians who have been vehicles of "the assumption that the United States, unlike European nations, has a covenant that makes Americans a chosen people who have escaped from the terror of historical change to live in timeless harmony with nature."[163]

In addition much of the writing in the Euro American segment of the American literary tradition has reinforced the national eschatology that was designed and elaborated by the early New England settlers. Nathaniel Hawthorne's departure from the historico-literary consensus is therefore striking. His fiction offers, in Lauren Berlant's terms, "a counter-National Symbolic." He "opens up other political vistas," and a "politics . . . that might or might not refer to or reauthorize the national horizon."[164] Hawthorne's counter-nationalism is conveyed, as Sacvan Bercovitch has famously noted, through his sense of irony. Moreover, as Bercovitch puts it, "[Hawthorne] was too good a historian wholly to espouse the American teleology, too concerned with personal relations to entertain the claims of the American self;" indeed "[h]is lifelong struggle with the typology of mission is a measure both of his own integrity and the power of the myth."[165]

Hawthorne's ironic detachment from the covenant philosophy of the Puritans and his recognition of the violence that must attend the worship of pure origins, especially as it reached its inevitable realization in the oppression of Hester Prynne in *The Scarlet Letter,* are reenacted and reinflected in Morrison's *Paradise.*[166] The idea of the covenant and the imperatives that flow from it—the need to resist change and the need to maintain the purity of the lineage that is charged with the special mission—produce the woeful consequences described at the beginning and end of Morrison's novel. The novel suggests that at best the exceptionalist narrative stifles politics and at worst it leads to violence. In addition to the closure of the political, the other consequence provides the chilling opening to the novel, whose first line is, "[t]hey kill the white girl first." Thereafter, an understanding of this opening event requires that the reader follow a complex and shifting narrative that eventually explains a deadly attack by a group of men from a covenanted, all-black community in Oklahoma on the women in a nearby convent that has served as a women's shelter.

The attackers are from Ruby, a small western all-black community in which the older members situate themselves in a self-described historical narrative that celebrates the perseverance of their ancestors in the face of rejection and their subsequent redemption through adherence to the codes of a special mission. Descended from former slaves, the town's ancestors left post-Reconstruction discrimination in the late nineteenth-century American South only to be denied entry into both white and black communities in Oklahoma, which, as Morrison had learned, had twenty-six all-black towns at the turn of the twentieth century.[167] The Rubyites special mission, a black version of American exceptionalism, is engendered by their rejections, to which they refer as the "disallowing." Having walked from Mississippi to Oklahoma, attracted by an advertisement about an all-black town, they discovered that their blackness was a threat to the lighter-skinned "Negroes" who shunned them: "The sign of racial purity they had taken for granted had become a stain."[168]

Coping with the shock of a rejection (which they had expected only from whites), they founded their own all-black community of Haven in Oklahoma and subsequently moved even farther into western Oklahoma to found Ruby, which they regarded as the fulfilment of their ancestors' intention to construct an Eden, a paradise on earth run by a group of racially pure blacks. The town chronicler, Patricia, summarizes the "8-rock's" (descendants from the original founders) model for maintaining purity: "Unadulterated and unadulteried 8-rock blood held its magic as long as it resided in Ruby. That was their recipe. That was their deal for immortality."[169] But while "Ruby" ("Who can find a virtuous woman? for her price is far above rubies." Proverbs 31: 10) contains paradisaical signs (for example, the soil seems almost miraculously fertile, so that while Haven had only barren muddy ground, Ruby has flourishing gardens). It also turns out to be a stiflingly conservative, patriarchal, and even misogynist community. Rather than turning inward to confront divisive issues, when the younger Ruby generation departs from the original covenant with a different interpretation of its imperative, the patriarchs of Ruby displace their problems on a nearby community functioning with a different covenant. The assault with which the novel begins is on a shelter for women whose inhabitants have had intimate connections with some of the town's men. The shelter is in a former convent (in a mansion that had once served as a "cathouse") outside the town.

Most of the novel's chapters are named for women whose experiences of abuse are narrated as they seek shelter in the convent. In contrast with Ruby—rendered by Morrison as one kind of "convent," a place where an adultery-avoiding (and denying) community will never again be brought to their knees[170]—is a convent in which no kind of adulterated past can render the members unwelcome. But although some of the men of Ruby are charmed by the differences in the convent's women, they ultimately replay the typical articulation between gender dominance and national narratives; they construct them as "bad women" whose existence undermines Ruby's covenanted community. As Patricia, Ruby's chronicler notes, "everything that worries them must come from women."[171]

As this second convent is filled with these "worrying women," who become victims because their experiences are disjunctive with the codes of Ruby, whose men cannot tolerate facing their own contradictions and disjunctures, the novel's narrative structure manifests a homologous disjunctiveness; it is filled with centrifugal, fragmenting voices in an overall, nonlinear narrative that continually inhibits the reader's attempts at assembling a coherently and simply themed story. The novel therefore manifests the Bakhtinian insight that a novel's many contending voices (it's "heteroglossia") pulls away from a community's verbal/ideological center.[172] The clash of perspectives it articulates constitutes a critique of the Rubyite's drive to stifle conflicting interpretations of its mission.

The other formal aspect of the novel, its disjunctive narrative structure, contributes to the delegitimating of Ruby's commitment to racial purity. Inasmuch as novels (at least the most familiar, realist type) tend to operate within a "genealogical imperative" by placing their acts and images in "a dynastic line that unites the diverse generations of the genealogical family,"[173] the disruptions in the family stories in the narrative structure of *Paradise* constitutes a challenge both to the purity conceits of the Rubyites and to the traditional way that novels have reinforced ethno-national imaginaries. And to reinforce her narrative challenge to Ruby's purity commitment, Morrison has Patricia, the community's keeper of the family genealogies, burn her genealogical records, as she heaps scorn on the community's attempts to maintain pure bloodlines:

> Did they really think they could keep this up? The numbers, the bloodlines, the who fucks who? All those generations of 8-rocks kept going, just to end up narrow as bale wire.[174]

Patricia's burning of the records accords with the politics of interpretation in *Paradise*, which, along with its critique of exceptionalist nation- or community-building narratives, be they black or white, constitutes the novel's most significant attack on foundational narratives. The foundation constructed by Ruby's founding families bears a similarity to that of the ancient Israelites. The Rubyites too have an "ark of the covenant," which in their case is a communal oven, which they had made originally in Haven and had then moved to Ruby. It was a "flawlessly designed oven that both nourished them and monumentalized what they had done."[175] To hold their past as a fixed monument, they took it apart brick by brick as they left Haven and reassembled it in Ruby. The oven/ark's original text, inscribed on the oven's iron plate read, "Beware the furrow of His brow." But as succeeding generations began to contest the covenant and to see their relationship with their past and with white America differently, the conflict plays itself out in the civic sphere (the space of the communal oven), articulated as a textual battle, a contest over how to translate foundational commitments. A younger generation paints a black power symbol, a black clenched fist, on the oven and wants to revise the text to read, "Be the furrow of His brow."

Morrison's treatment of the text of Ruby's covenant is remarkably similar to a radical strain within the Talmudic tradition. In particular, Patricia's burning of the Rubyite's genealogical record accords with the Talmudic scholar, Marc-Alain Ouaknin's evocation of a "burnt book" to help narrate an approach to Talmudic interpretation that resists "the various measures [of conservative scholars] aimed at petrifying Jewish tradition."[176] Affirming that aspect of Talmudic interpretation that celebrates change, Ouaknin's exemplar, a burnt book, has a historical referent. The eighteenth-century scholar, Rabbi Nahman of Bratislav, burned one of his books as a gesture of moving beyond fixed interpretive tradition. Accordingly, the Talmudic text, for those who follow Nahman's lead, is treated not as an original and sacrosanct monument but as a changing script, which departs from its origin as it experiences ongoing interpretations. Rather than a fixed object, then, the "book" should attract active contention. In Nahman's view, "the Book has/is a 'mouth';" it can serve as "the course of the opening of a mouth, if it creates, generates speech."[177]

Precisely in accord with this spirit of textual practice, the younger generation of Rubyites want to treat the oven/ark of the covenant as a place for negotiating meanings, while most of their elders seek to stifle any talk aimed at critical interpretation rather than reverence for the original founding acts and injunctions. Thus, at one point, when the younger members are contesting their elder's version of the past, while congregated at the site of the oven, they are told that there is only one way for things to mean. Their talk is described as simply "backtalk." After admonishing a youth with the remark, "what is talk if its not back," one of the elders asserts, "[n]obody, I mean nobody, is going to change the Oven or call it something strange."[178] However, one of the elders contests this position and affirms the value of continuing interpretive change (thereby representing both the more radical

Talmudic tradition and Morrison's critique of foundational exceptionalism): "Seems to me . . . they are respecting it. It's because they do know the Oven's value that they want to give it new life."[179]

Ultimately, like the interpretive practice of radical Talmudic scholars, who want words to live, who regard "divine speech" as "plural speech,"[180] Morrison's novel affirms a critical hermeneutics. She contests, at once, the Puritan reading of American exceptionalism and the African American attempt to simulate that exceptionalism and to treat it as a dogma by attempting to preserve or freeze the meanings generated in founding acts. The covenant for Morrison is an injunction to continual self-inspection and change rather than stasis. She recognizes that the covenants of nationhood are ambiguous achievements. To the extent that they abject those—for example, the women in the other convent—whose lives fail to conform to the founding injunctions, covenants foster antipolitics and violence. Morrison's other convent serves effectively as what Michel Foucault has called a "heterotopia," a place of otherness from which one can gain an appreciation of the normalizing practices of the dominant, institutionalized, covenanted spaces.[181] In addition to requiring a stance outside its imposed dogmas, community, or nationhood, as Morrison's last unnamed and redemptive section of the novel implies, requires "endless work,"[182] a process of negotiation and contestation rather than mythologizing. Morrison's fictional intervention is opposed to "the malignant fiction of collectivist identity" to which Vargas Llosa refers in the fragment from his novel with which this chapter begins. In chapter 3, I turn to musical nationhood, another genre within which the fiction of collectivist identity is produced and contested. Accordingly, I summon both musical forms that have served as agents of national consolidation and those that disclose the ambiguities in those processes and/or reveal alternative loci of attachment.

# CHAPTER 3

# The "Musico-Literary" Aesthetics of Attachment and Resistance[1]

## Introduction: World Music and (Post) National Attachments

Developing its central themes from the lives of those associated with "world music," a "universal pop aesthetic"[2] influenced by the globalization of Western musical idioms, Salman Rushdie's novel *The Ground Beneath Her Feet* begins with the death of a world renowned rock singer, Vina Apsara, who is swallowed up in a Mexican earthquake. Although much of the novel is centered around a love story involving Vina and the composer, Ormus Cama, a relationship modeled in part on the Orpheus myth, it also contains a more decentered story, which is articulated through the narration of Vina's occasional lover, the photographer Rai (undoubtedly named after a famous Indian photographer, Raghu Rai).[3] Rai, who decides, he says, to "end my connection with a country, my country of origin as we say now, my home country," finds that his move is enabling for his photographic practice. Only those, he insists, who step out of the frame have access to "the whole picture."[4]

Disparaging Hindu nationalism in particular and national attachments in general, Rai and other significant characters in Rushdie's novel value "multiplicity." That multiplicity, Rai informs the reader, is realized musically, especially in the "earthquake songs" of Ormus Cama, which "are about the collapse of all walls, boundaries, restraints."[5] Rai serves as Rushdie's alter ego. His post-national perspective, like Rushdie's, is forged in the cosmopolitan city of Bombay, where through the viewing of foreign films, among other things, he develops the global imaginary that energizes his photographic practice. His photography, like Ormus Cama's music, deploys creative acts of imagination aimed at provoking a reception that will counter dangerous, exclusionary (especially nationalistic) myths. Similarly, Rushdie, also a permanent exile from his home country, attributes his creativity as a writer to his resistance to the "reason" of any particular nation-state. *His* critical posture also stems from his existence "outside of the frame," which allows him to resist the tendency of the state, which, he says, "takes reality into its own hands, and sets about distorting it."[6] In imagery that provides the governing trope of his novel, Rushdie, speaking of cosmopolitan exilic writers, states:

> We are now partly of the West. Our identity is at once plural and partial. Sometimes we feel that we straddle two cultures; at other times, that we fall between two stools. But however ambiguous and shifting this ground may be, it is not an infertile territory for a writer to occupy.[7]

In *The Ground Beneath Her Feet*, Rushdie intensifies the imagery of a shifting ground. The earthquake with which the novel opens migrates conceptually into a mode of global, or in the contemporary idiom, "world music," which, because of its "hybridization," the mixing of diverse musical genres within the arena of a musical utterance, shakes up networks of national attachment and encourages (for some) the development of a supra-national sense of affiliation.[8] Implicitly juxtaposing cracks and fissures, which result from arbitrary episodes of encounter among diverse forces and idioms, with national boundaries, Cama's "quake songs," Rai informs us, show us a different world from that confined within state. It is a world with a different ethical and emotional valence, one both "worthy of our yearning" and productive of selves "worthy of the world."[9]

Rushdie's novel enacts the very multiplicity to which it refers. His commitment to a transnational world is articulated through his writing style as well as in the utterances of his alter ego, Rai. Expressing the hybridity he prizes, Rushdie's sentences contain American and British idioms, and Bombay argot, as well as various other idioms from diverse language formations. *This* Rushdie is stylistically homologous with the music of his Ormus Cama, who admits at one point that his lyrics, "cockeyed words" and "vowel sounds," are simultaneously his and someone else's.[10] Like Rushdie's prose, the world's musical hybridity is always already present in the premusical sounds of many national patrimonies. As the narration notes, Ormus's incorporation of so-called "Western sounds" in his music is not a betrayal of a preexisting purity:

> The music he had in his head during the unsinging childhood years, was not of the West except in the sense that the West was from the beginning, impure old Bombay where West, East, North, and South had always been scrambled, like codes, like eggs.[11]

Rushdie's novelistic invocation of world music is not an idiosyncratic fantasy. "World music" emerged in the late 1980s, primarily as a marketing expression to refer to popular music produced by other than Anglo-American sources, for example, "Rai music" from Algeria (perhaps an additional encouragement for the name of Rushdie's character).[12] And certainly the Algerian Berber singer, Djur Djura, provides an apt model for Rushdie's Vina Apsara. Having grown up in France, Djura's bicultural identity has given rise to a version of world music that combines genres while at the same time aspiring to a universality of appeal. From Djura's perspective, her music partakes of a "universal language of emotions."[13] This notion is not unlike that applied to the music of Rushdie's fictional global pop bands, a few of which "reach the rhythm center of the soul."[14]

Despite current tendencies to treat world music as a new genre, analyses of the compositions have shown that it preexisted its expression. Various past episodes of globalization have created the influences that have made many existing musical forms hybrid. Acknowledging this historical trajectory of globalizing influences, Rushdie's novel registers contemporary globalization's impact on musical idiom by posing some of the same questions about national identities and attachments that have been raised in contemporary, expressly political discourses. For example, suspecting that contemporary globalization poses new challenges to a hospitable international civic order and, like Rushdie, opposed to ethno-nationalism, Jurgen Habermas has attempted to theorize a post–nationalistic version of state sovereignty. Arguing that political subjects ("citizens") receive a "double coding," Habermas goes on to suggest that the state portion of the nation-state term provides a territorial identity while the nation portion implies a shared cultural community with a historical trajectory. Like Rushdie, however, Habermas is wary of a politics of identity based on shared cultural characteristics. In search of a frame for communal attachment that is not the organic one in which collective solidarity is predicated on the myth of a "prepolitical fact of a quasi-natural people,"[15] he advocates a civic as opposed to an ethno-oriented mode of national attachment. Rushdie, who is similarly suspicious of the myths of an ethnic coherence model of nationhood, expresses his wariness of national mythologies with a gloss on the critical reader who manifests a "willing, disbelieving . . . in the well told tale."[16]

However, the world music that Rushdie uses as a metaphor for cosmopolitanism has a different significance when articulated through struggles of indigenous peoples rather than through contentions between nationalists and cosmopolitans. When linked to indigenous political initiatives, "world music" constitutes a counterforce to contemporary *neo*-imperialism rather than serving as an ecumenical, border-effacing aesthetic. Indigenous nations are engaged in a different musical appropriation from the cosmopolitan, supra-nationalistic one that motivates Rushdie's narrative. As one analyst has put it, "popular forms of music have become an effective site of enunciation and people involved in indigenous struggles have mixed traditional elements of music with rock to reach a mass audience through the circulation of world music."[17] And as George Lipsitz has pointed out, although popular music has been appropriated in different ways in "different national circumstances" for nation-state building, it has also been used by indigenous people to reassert their presence. They have produced "distinctly different kinds of political music" because of their "very different relationships to narratives of national identity."[18]

The absorption of dominant commercial musical genres into indigenous movements is not, then, simply an extension of the existing structure of global hegemony. The staging of such music, which effectively fuses local and global concerns within different cultures and moments of reception, changes its significance, as in the case of indigenous Australian [Aboriginal] musicians, whose music articulates their "participat[ion] in inter-ethnic ecological and anti-racist coalitions."[19] Among others, the Aboriginal rap performers, Blackjustis, have incorporated some of the musical style of the African American rap group, Public Enemy (who performed in their urban Sydney ghetto), and have given it a content that speaks to a history of the Euro Australian appropriation of Aboriginal lands.[20]

The indigenous music-nationhood connection and, more specifically, the appropriation of musical genres throughout the history of the Hawaiian nation's resistance to Western colonization, is the ultimate part of my analysis in this chapter. However, to provide a conceptual and historical context and to pursue the central concern in this chapter—the music nationhood connection—I turn first to the use of musical genres in the production of national allegiance in Europe in the nineteenth century. Thereafter, I consider two forms of musical production in twentieth-century America, the national allegiance-inspiring ethnic songs and theater music, produced primarily by assimilationist Jewish Americans, most notably Irving Berlin, and the trajectory of centrifugal forms of African American music from blues through jazz to hip-hop.[21] As was the case with my treatment of the Rushdie-world music connection, for each phase of the analysis I turn to exemplary forms of writing that parallel the musical genres: those Jewish American novels that are homologous with the allegiance-seeking of many Jewish American musical forms, those African American novels that enact a blues and/or jazz aesthetic, and finally, in the last phase of the analysis, contemporary Hawaiian poetry, which is lyrically homologous with some of the contemporary Hawaiian musical sounds of resistance.

## Music and Nationhood: The Production of Allegiance

At the beginning of his influential *Noise: The Political Economy of Music,* Jacques Attali asserts that "all music, any organization of sounds is . . . a tool for the creation and consolidation of a community."[22] Attali may be correct when he notes that Bach and Mozart's music "reflect the bourgeoisie's dream of harmony better than and prior to the whole of nineteenth-century political theory," but his emphasis on the implication of music in the production of consensuality—his suggestion that "the entire history of tonal music" involves "an attempt to make people believe in a consensual representation of the world"—is belied both by the development in musical (and accompanying literary) forms in the nineteenth century and by the controversies and adjustments in even those forms of music dominated by state institutions. Rather than always regarding "national music as the homogenising imposition of a nation-building elite," it is more sensible, as Peter Wade puts it, to attain an "appreciation of the diversity contained *within* the nationalist music or discourse about music."[23]

Certainly there are diverse venues which provide historical validation for Attali's position. Grieg's music served Norwegian nationalism, Sibelius's was instrumental in the production of a Finnish national identity, a diverse group of Slavic and Hungarian composers created music that aided and abetted national attachments in middle European states, and in Columbia in the nineteenth century, *bambuco,* a culturally hybrid, melodic music, that "counts all Columbians among its authors," was "integrated into the discourses about national identity."[24] And the promotion of a homogeneous musical culture in England was very much a part of the agenda of some nineteenth- and early twentieth-century composers. For example, according to the English composer (and activist in the cause of English musical nationalism), Ralph Vaughan Williams, music ought to aim its idioms in the direction of creating a "homogeneous community." Arguing against those who promoted a cosmopolitan view of music, Vaughan Williams saw a nationally framed and biologically-culturally encouraged commonality, particularly in the compositions of German and English composers, based on the tendencies of the composer's music to evoke "the sympathy of others . . . who by race, tradition, and cultural experience are nearest to him."[25]

However, it is doubtless the French case that most profoundly influences Attali's perspective. After the French Revolution, he points out, there were vigorous attempts by the state to "nationalize" music and musicians in order both to insulate musical production from solely commercial forces and to promote the statist ideology of a centralized, unitary national culture.[26] Although Attali comments on the subversive as well as the allegiance-inspiring aspects of music,[27] his analysis is highly abstract, and his brief sketch of the genealogy of musical space fails to register the specific historical instances of musical resistance to French national consolidation. The history of French national opera provides an antidote for Attali's totalizing gloss and, at the same time, speaks to the music-nationhood relationship he seeks to illuminate. In nineteenth-century Europe, generally, musical productions often treated the theme of finding the people's authentic voice. As a result, a politicized national musical idiom developed, and, in particular, operatic narratives were enlisted to help articulate national identity.[28]

This insight is applied in Jane Fulcher's comprehensive historical treatment of nineteenth-century musical theater in Paris. She indicates how French grand opera "was a subtly used tool of state."[29] Much of Fulcher's treatment plays into Attali's hands inasmuch as a changing structure of legitimation, attending the shift from a monarchical to a republican form of governance, was implicated in the contestations that developed over operatic libretti. During the new republican era, pressures were mounted to make the opera complicit with an emphasis on a new locus of sovereignty, "the voice of the 'people.'"[30] Yet it was also the case that, functioning at the intersection between political and aesthetic impulses, French opera manifested an ongoing struggle in the first half of the nineteenth century between the demand that it assimilate a commitment to a national political culture and that it register protests against such a commitment.[31] Continual contention over the proprieties of the way libretti treated French prerevolutionary history, especially the roles of the monarchy and the church, and struggles over opera's role in assimilating a proletarian constituency into the audience of national arts, shaped the alternatively legitimating and subversive nature of French musical theater.

In addition to an almost continuous governmental intervention into the shaping of French opera, journalists were major players in the struggle. In the 1840s, when the new *Opera National* was created, with the aim of integrating French workers into forms of cultural attendance that would produce a national culture by helping to evince passions associated with collective goals, journals enlisted themselves in the project. They urged workers to take advantage of the cultural forms and their readers to support the new opera, noting, for example, "the theater's function of linking the real nation with the French state by revealing the glorious facts of our history."[32] Ultimately however, despite the high level of contention associated with the development of nineteenth-century musical theater in France, the bulk of nationally produced operas, framed and reinforced by literary forms, especially journalism, served national legitimation rather than subversion.

In the nineteenth-century European nation-building context, control over operatic performances articulate with the relationship between a governmentality that reflected a concern with then details of the national population and the attempt to build a national culture. However, the migration of operatic performances into postcolonial states involves a somewhat different nation-building problematic. For example, the staging of Italian opera in nineteenth-century Mexico, "a calculated plan on the part of the regime at the moment," was part of the government's "civilizing mission" and its decolonizing agenda. The governing elite wanted to create a Euro-oriented national culture in a pluricultural context and, at the same time, to import a cultural idiom that would allow the new state to assert its difference from Spanish culture.[33]

In general, it has been historically rare for opera to mount a challenge to state nation building, but there is one notable example in Canada in the twentieth century. Representing a "fractious history of linguistic, regional, ethnic and political difference" in its plot, a Canadian composer's opera, *Louis Riel* "enacts the nation's diversity" both thematically and linguistically. Portraying the story of the first nation (Cree) rebel, Louis Riel, the opera is written in English, French, and Cree. Its linguistic and musical cacophonies destabilize the Euro-oriented consensual national narrative.[34]

Although nineteenth-century operatic productions tended to lend themselves to nation-building initiatives—differently in different national venues—when one looks at other nineteenth-century musical and literary developments, the picture becomes less clear. In particular, I want to call attention to the co-emergence of symbolist poetry and music in France during the latter half of the nineteenth century. David Michael Hertz has pointed convincingly to a parallel between Mallarme's poetry, in which he obfuscates the "syntactic hierarchy of a poetic line"[35] (in contrast with Baudelaire for whom the "period," the same quadratic form, which organizes orthodox music, structures his poetry), and the "fracturing of the musical period in Wagner,"[36] which was influential in the subsequent departures from orthodoxy of the musical compositions of French symbolists such as Debussy.[37] Referring to Roland Barthes's argument about the origin and positioning of modern writing such as Mallarme's—that it lies "in the cracks between the orderly progression of the classical text, in the exploitation of ambiguity in the act of signification"[38]—Hertz provides the same imagery for convention-breaking meaning systems as Rushdie.

The crack or fissure, which is characteristic of the boundary breaking, world music of Rushdie's fictional Ormus Cama, is also a figure for the convention breaking of the symbolist movement in nineteenth-century French poetry and music. However, in the case of Rushdie's supra-national cosmopolitanism, the innovative novelistic and musical texts are almost literally deterritorializing; Rushdie's writing and Ormus Cama's music are signifying assaults on state borders. Nineteenth-century French musical developments function *within* a state, challenging the rhythms and tonalities that support ethno-nationalism and the dominant French territorial imaginary.

Much of the innovative challenges to musical intelligibility in nineteenth-century France is attributable to the French reception of Wagnerian music. For example, influenced by the Wagnerian disruption of the musical period, Debussy's music (like Mallarmé's poetry) disrupts familiar meaning conventions. Specifically, Mallarmé's poetry disrupts syntactic expectations—for example, substituting a chain of nouns in places where the reader expects adjectives,[39] or inserting "the silence of the 'blank space' " instead of producing an elaborate symbolism.[40] In effect, Mallarmé's aesthetic ambiguities, which violate poetical conventions, also disrupt the orders of meaning. By creating disjunctures between the "flow of semantic movement" and "the standard code of cultural references,"[41] he negates the allegiance-affirming aspects of language.

Debussy's music has a similar negating effect. Just as "Mallarmé's imagery is not contingent upon a rigid narrative structure . . . Debussy's melodic ideas are not contingent upon a rigid tonal scheme."[42] In ignoring the norms of musical periodicity, Debussy's music resists expectations of closure. Rejecting the authority of conventional tonality, his scales have no conventional points of beginning and ending; for example, they often have whole-note intervals, a practice that violates the tonality conventions through which musical spacing and narrative had been commonly understood.[43] In addition, Debussy uses a "reiterative phraseology" with "oscillating chords" which constitute "a mode of musical continuity that is diametrically opposed to the goal-directed syntactical harmony of traditional tonal music."[44] Instead of developing themes, Debussy creates musical fragments, a multiplicity, a nonlinear set of musical associations that resist instead of moving toward a stable narrative or a stable set of references. Like Mallarmé's poetry, Debussy's music continually blocks rather than fulfills expectations.[45] The result is a disruption of conventional musical intelligibility and, by implication, the production of a system of counter-intelligibility to those musical genres to which Attali refers when he attributes to them an encouragement of collective allegiance.

Debussy's challenges to conventional musical intelligibility was not ignored by the official protectors of French nationhood. Critics complained about his music's "indecisive tonality and formal disorder."[46] And Alfred Bruneau, the Inspecteur General des Beaux-Arts and a spokesperson for a republican musical aesthetic, was distressed that one of France's most talented composers was producing a music that could not be unambiguously appropriated to an espousal of genuinely French republican traits. Because "he could construe Debussy's innovations only within the narrow framework of his own aesthetic-political discourse," he, like other spokespersons for the republic, was upset by the resistance of the compositions to an nationalist cultural politics.[47]

The lyricism of ambiguity and resistance to closure contained in the musical and poetic texts of the nineteenth-century French symbolists provide a conceptual frame for considering the resistance to American national allegiance in African American music. For example, one can observe a parallel between the symbol-resistant blank spaces in Mallarme's poetry and the pauses in Thelonious Monk's jazz compositions and between Debussy's disruptions of tonality and production of fragments with different musical associations and John Coltrane's jazz compositions, which similarly develop fragments of musical association, for example, his multiple riffs on "My Favorite Things" (discussed later in this chapter). Edified by the musical disruptions to intelligibility and, by implication, to territorial and national/collective allegiance, I turn to a contrast between the stable referentiality of the music of Irving Berlin and other artists associated with Broadway musical theater, and the intelligibility-shattering of the signifying play in much of the tradition of African American music, from blues, through jazz, to hip-hop. Jumping from the musical developments and national appropriations of France in the nineteenth century to competing musical genres in the U.S. in the twentieth century, my concern is also with diverse literary and musical personae who have been implicated in both assimilative and disruptive moments in American collective nationhood: assimilative Jewish Americans, assimilation-denied Afro-Americans, and, ultimately, colonization-resistant Native Hawaiians.

## Becoming American: Irving Berlin's Music and the Jewish American Novel

By the mid twentieth century, American Jews—at least those who were third generation Americans—had, for the most part adopted the mainstream American national identity. There is perhaps no better expression of the assimilationist sentiment than that of Nathan Zuckerman, the author's alter ego in Philip Roth's novelistic treatment of the red scare years of the early 1950s:

> I was a Jewish child, no two ways about it, but I didn't care to partake of the Jewish character. I didn't even know clearly what it was. I didn't want to. I wanted to partake of the national character.[48]

Nathan Zukerman's assimilationist sentiment is much more exacerbated among the first and second generation Jewish characters in Jewish American fiction. For these characters, "America" was a reprieve from a history of discrimination in Europe. It was a place of freedom or emancipation as compared, for example, with czarist Russia. For diasporic Jews in the late nineteenth and early twentieth centuries (in contrast with the more contemporary diasporic Third World intellectuals such as Rushdie), there was a strong impulse to become an unambiguously national citizen, to form a bond with the new host country. This impulse to what Sam Girgus has called a "new covenant," articulated itself in both the novels and the musical compositions of many Jewish Americans.[49]

The drive to assimilation shaping the American Jewish novel has resulted in a particular, ethnic version of what M.M. Bakhtin has identified as the *bildungsroman*, whose "organizing force" as a genre, according to Bakhtin, is "held by the future," a historical future in which "the very foundations of the world are changing, and man must change along with them."[50] Wanting to be an integral part of a new American political culture, many Jewish novelists and composers sought, Gurgus argues, to "recreate American themes and values in the form of a new language that is now part of American consciousness and culture."[51] In the case of the novel, early twentieth-century Jewish writers such as Abraham Cahan and Henry Roth constructed young Jewish characters who were in the process of escaping the still alien environment of their families to become converts to American culture.[52] These novelists were not simply treating "America" as a context for the dramas of their characters; they were helping to invent a version of America as a myth and idea, as a historically unique venue and a model for the politics of the future.[53]

Irving Berlin's music was also involved in inventing this kind of America. He said, in 1915, that he was "writing American music,"[54] and like many of the Jewish novelists, his early ethnic songs contained a pedagogy about becoming American; they often contained a narrative in which a young ethnic is being absorbed into American culture. Berlin, as Christian Appy notes, "was a gifted assimilator of a variety of musical traditions and an equally eager champion of dominant American institutions and values [for example, his well known] "White Christmas" is a supreme example of Berlin's attraction to a vision of America devoid of all evidence of fundamental difference and conflict."[55] However, I want to call attention to one of Berlin's lesser known early songs, "Jake! Jake! The Yiddisher Ball-Player,"[56] because it articulates with an exemplary American Jewish novel that treats the same theme in the same time period.

Participating in or becoming a fan of baseball, the quintessential "American pastime," constitutes an exemplary gesture for assimilating into American culture. Accordingly, in his contemporary novel, *The Celebrant*,[57] Eric Greenberg reproduces the early twentieth-century Jewish version of the *bildungsroman* in a novel about a Jewish baseball fan. The story line features the New York Giant's Christy Mathewson, who, at the turn of the century, was one of baseball's premier pitchers, and Jackie Kapp, an immigrant Jew who, having failed to realize his dream of becoming a major league pitcher, becomes instead one of Mathewson's devoted fans. Having joined his family's jewelry business, he uses his design skills to fashion and present to the great pitcher commemorative rings to celebrate each of his no-hit games.

Like the characters in the early Jewish American novels, Jackie Kapp is in the process of extracting himself from the values and cultural attachments of his "Old World" parents. When he tells them he wants to play professional baseball, they respond that "we had not crossed the ocean to find disgraceful employment,"[58] And, although he is at times rebuffed and reminded of his marginal status as he tries to establish his bond with America through his devotion to Mathewson and his pitching prowess—"Listen Jew . . . stay away from Matty," he is told by team agents—he uses his attachment to the American pastime to effect his transition from immigrant Jew to mainstream American. The transition is symbolized at one point when he and his brother, attending a ball game, sing "take me out to the ball game," in both English and German, the language of their European patrimony: "For it's ein! zwei! Drie strikes unt raus At the old ball game."[59]

Irving Berlin's ethnic baseball song about "Jake, the Yiddisher ball-player" effects a similar mixing; in this case it's American vernacular idiom and Jewish/Yiddish syntax:

> Go on and give it a smack, crack! That's a l-la-paloos-a!
> Run, you son of a gun, Run,—you son of a gun,
> What's that I hear the people shout?
> You're out! Jake, I lose my half a dollar,
> Poi-son you should swal-low; Jake, Jake,
> You're a reg-u-lar fake . . .

However, by 1914, Berlin had ceased writing ethnic novelty songs. His movement through musical styles was not unlike the movement of the characters in the Jewish American *bildungsroman,* which, in its early version inaugurated by such writers as Abraham Cahan, is organized around a story of the vertical movement of young Jews up the status hierarchy.[60] While his earlier ethnic novelty songs were performed in vaudevillian theaters, thereafter Berlin moved into mainstream American music, and his music was performed in respectable musical theater venues such as Broadway. And at this point, having left his ethnic preoccupation behind, he began to develop a distinctive American voice. While some more critically oriented theater productions "were experimenting with flashbacks, broken time lines and the projection of a character's interiority on stage, all devices which manipulated the artificiality of the theater in order to express the contingent quality of all we think we 'know'," mainstream Broadway musical theater worked with simple, linear narratives and uncomplex musical voices.[61]

Of course, Berlin constructs a hybrid musical voice. Like others who wrote for the musical theater (for example, Jerome Kern and George Gershwin), he incorporated African American musical styles in his songs. Nevertheless, Berlin saw himself as one constructing a unitary national voice. Once he ceased writing his ethnic novelty songs, he forged ahead with the intention of creating nothing less than a musically inspired American public culture, a "culture" that was one among many subcultures in an increasingly urban-dominated nation. Berlin's intention was largely realized. While, as Mark Steyn notes, Habsburg Austria expressed itself as a nation in the nineteenth century in operatic and waltz time, the United States in the twentieth expressed its national coherence—at least for much of white America—with the music of Irving Berlin.[62]

In contrast with the French symbolists' disruption of collective structures of intelligibility, and in keeping with Attali's argument about the allegiance-producing effects of music-as-the-the-organization-of-sound, Berlin's music is territorializing; it is complicit with the official mythology of the state as a container of a unitary national culture because it is musically simple; it is designed so that anyone, anywhere in the country, can sing or hum it; it is structured to incorporate rather than disrupt familiar musical styles. Moreover, it is thematically as well as musically territorializing in two important senses. First, its literary geography is national in scope. Berlin's patriotic songs: "God Bless America," "The Freedom Train," and "Song of Freedom," among others, map an ideationally undifferentiated national space.[63] Second, its personae are protagonists rather than antagonists. In accord with the ideological frame of the Jewish American *bildungsroman,* Berlin's early songs were usually written as the expression of a single protagonist "whose identity," as Charles Hamm puts it, "was encoded into the text and music, then projected, clarified, or even changed in the act of performance."[64]

Of course, among the Jewish American contributions to musical theater are those productions, particularly during the period of the labor movements of the 1930s, that have a radical, allegiance-disturbing impetus. Exemplary in this respect is Marc Blitzstein's *The Cradle Will Rock,* which, like other examples of Popular Front music, "borrowed the forms of Tin Pan Alley and turned them inside out."[65] A "proletarian opera," whose theme deals with union organizing in "Steeltown USA," its disruptive effects on an American national consensuality are owed in part to its Brechtian influences. While capturing vernacular speech styles, it locates them in a series of disjunctive encounters among representatives of different classes, who speak in different idioms, and all are articulated within a narrative that resists reconciliation.[66] The circumstances of the initial performances of the play are as politically significant as its theme. Originally supported by the Federal Theater Project (part of the New Deal WPA initiative), it was canceled, doubtless because of its radical political import. Thanks to the perseverance of director Orson Welles, it had its opening in a vacant theater nearby, without scenery and props. Although the play manifested the social realism favored by those running the Federal Theater Project, the conflictual relationships it portrayed between labor and capitalist enterprise violated the national consensus orientation to which the FTP was dedicated.[67]

However, despite such exceptional, highly politicized examples, which proliferated in the 1930s, by the 1940s, the bulk of Broadway productions exemplified the musical theater's construction of a unitary American identity. As the cold war developed in the mid-1940s, plays with radical themes were discouraged, for they were deemed unpatriotic. The nation-building sentiments in the Broadway musicals in this period are articulated primarily through narratives in which diverse types become exemplary Americans. Yet, at the same time that they were inventing particular versions of Americanness, the writers of the musicals imagined themselves as contributors to a unitary and ethnically blind national culture.[68] The Rodgers and Hammerstein musical *Oklahoma!* is an exemplar of the unreflective nation-building Broadway musical of the 1940s. In its approach to American nationhood, the expansion of Euro America is foregrounded, and the complex and mixed ethnoscape of the former "Indian Territory" is erased. I turn here to a reading of *Oklahoma!* not only because of the exemplary way that it constructs American nationhood but also because of the absences it reflects.

### Rodgers and Hammerstein's *Oklahoma!*

Opening in New York in 1943, *Oklahoma!* portrayed the Euro American fantasy of an attunement between domestic and national life. Although focused on the Oklahoma Territory just before statehood in the early part of the century, its geographic imaginary is the "American" nation-state as a whole:

> The apparently modest and homely social world that *Oklahoma!* dramatically produces and enacts has a more fundamental, symbolic reality as the realisation of the American dream. The domestic world of *Oklahoma!* is also the hoped and promised 'land of the free' which is to be wrought in the USA by civilising nature. This is to be accomplished democratically by the individual and collective labour of its inhabitants, and will make the USA the earthly Garden of Eden that is both 'God's own Country' and the world's first, modern nation-state.[69]

From its opening, lyrical ode to daily life with "Oh What a Beautiful Morning" to its closing celebration of conjugal fulfillment with a communal dance routine, *Oklahoma!* suppresses a history of usurpation, displacement, and violence. What was to become "Oklahoma" in the early twentieth century was peopled largely by western and displaced eastern Native American nations by the mid nineteenth century (and was in fact officially designated as "the Indian Territories"). The wholly white Oklahoma depicted in the Broadway musical (and subsequent film version) reflects a sudden white population surge—the 1889 "land rush" provoked when President Benjamin Harrison "announced [in violation of the treaties with the displaced eastern nations] that the 'Unassigned Lands' would be opened for public homesteading at noon on April 22."[70]

Ignoring this violent historical process and the still-mixed ethnoscape—of eastern nations, western nations, a large number of all-black communities, and a considerable population of "Negro cowboys"[71]—the drama of *Oklahoma!* unfolds as a containment of threats to a unified and integrated white national culture. The dangers to an accord between person and nation include a rapidly developing modernity (in such places as the "up-ter date" Kansas City, which must be carefully and slowly integrated with the simple pastoral life on the plains), the intrusions of urban and foreign seducers of gullible women (*viz* the crafty Ali Hakim), other outsiders (e.g., Jud Frye, who is neither a cowboy nor a farmer, and whose "primordial instinctuality"[72] is a threat to a communal libidinal order), and, more generally, any representative of extra-familial sexuality (e.g., the temptations of prostitutes and dancehall women, shown in a choreographed dance).

The songs and dance routines in *Oklahoma!* are addressed to a crucial stage in Euro American nation building, the period when Oklahoma experienced a rapid white in-migration and was about to change from territory to state. In addition to celebrating a peaceful accord between cowmen and farmers, the music and choreography are aimed at integrating potentially centrifugal elements of the social order, at maintaining coherent community in the face of change. The choral song style celebrates the transition from territory to state (in "Many a New Day . . ."), and as people arrive by train from such places as Kansas City, the dance routines present, side-by-side, alternative dance idioms that then become integrated routines. In each staging of music and dance, the implicit narrative is a movement from separate idiom to integrated genre, a movement toward an organic whole, representing "the prevailing ideological commitment in the USA to an integration of its constituent states into a unified society, able to both acknowledge and reconcile its differences."[73]

Of course, the emerging, Euro-dominant West of the turn of the twentieth century, which *Oklahoma!* reflects, had already been invented in literature. The basic tenor of Theodore Roosevelt's epic *The Winning of the West*, which simultaneously celebrates Euro American cultural and territorial expansion and evacuates the Native American presence, is reproduced in the popular fiction of Owen Wister, who, like his friend Roosevelt, chronicled the coming of the heroic, self-sufficient Anglo male. Wister's vision of the West parallels that of *Oklahoma!*; it is a "wide, wild farm and ranch community, spotted with remote towns and veined with infrequent railroads."[74] Although Wister includes a Native American presence, the Indians serve the same function in Wister's fiction that they do in Roosevelt's epic; they are props against whom the cowboy's heroism can be realized.

However, the West of Wister and Roosevelt (treated more extensively in chapter 6), as well as of Oklahoma, has been glossed from alternative loci of enunciation. In particular, Wister's revealing essay, "The Evolution of the Cow-Puncher,"[75] which like his stories and novels invents the heroic, adventurous Anglo Saxon male, can be juxtaposed with the figure of the Anglo cowboy offered by the Creek poet journalist Alex Posey. Posey, whose satiric writing was aimed at asserting the Indian presence in Oklahoma and, at the same time, chastising white America for its appropriation of the lands of the tribal nations, reacted this way to the cowboy's incursion into Oklahoma:

> Whoop a time er two fer me!
>   Turn me loose an' let me be!
> I'm Wildcat Bill
>   From Grizzle Hill,
> A border ranger; never down'd;
>   A western hero all around;
> A gam'ler, scalper; born a scout;
>   A tough; the man ye read about . . .
>   Afeard o' nothin; hard to beat;
> Kin die with boots upon my feet—
>   An' like a man![76]

Posey's literary path was a journey between two worlds. He adopted some of the conventions of Euro American literary traditions, especially the poetry of Walt Whitman, Emily Dickinson, and Robert Burns, while also transforming the trickster styles of Creek orality and incorporated them in his writing.[77] Africa American musical styles often effect a similar bicultural encounter. For example, such an encounter is realized in jazz musician Sonny Rollins's rendering of songs from Rodgers and Hammersteins' *Oklahoma!* While "The Surrey with the Fringe on Top," serves in the Rodgers and Hammerstein musical as a romantic ballad to express a desire for a communal witnessing of an inchoate marriage bond, Rollins's version of the song is a parody of a singularly white narrative of the settling of the West. His riff on "The Surrey with the Fringe on Top" articulates well with the visual and musical intent of his *Way Out West* album, which contains "aberrant readings of 'I'm an Old Cowhand' and 'Wagon Wheels'" and features him on the cover—a "Negro cowboy" enacting an "appropriation of the iconography of the American West."[78]

Rollins's western musical gestures exemplify the manner in which African American jazz musicians have resignified the music of Tin Pan Alley. They reflect not only an alternative musical idiom but also a different political sensibility. In the case of Rollins's "Western music," the political agenda is a critique of *Oklahoma!*'s evacuation of the dark bodies from the ethnoscape of the "Indian territory," which, as a result of the white land grab, was incorporated into a Euro American-dominated USA. But Rollins's musical critique is a very small part of an African American musical politics. Recognition of an "America" that emerges when the jazz tradition is in focus requires attention to a domestic diaspora, a movement of African Americans from the South and Southwest to northern and Midwestern cities. This movement tells a different story than the integrative nation-building story that supplies *Oklahoma!*'s implicit narrative.

My scene therefore shifts from Oklahoma to Kansas City, Missouri, which is treated in Robert Altman's feature film, *Kansas City*. As Altman's filmic narration makes evident, it was a city that was in the 1930s a crossroad of diasporic African American musicians as well as of diverse Euro Americans involved in national election politics. Ironically, many of the black musicians in Altman's story hail from the very Oklahoma that the Rodgers and Hammerstein musical treated as an overwhelmingly white ethnoscape. Although rarely seen in this light, the state of Oklahoma contributed significantly to diverse aspects of American popular culture, including singing cowboys, folksingers, country and western vocalists and, most significantly jazz musicians, many of whom had thrived in a "biracial" musical setting in Oklahoma and subsequently migrated to Kansas City to help create the "Kansas City style" of jazz. For example, Benny Moten's famous Kansas City jazz band, which is the historical basis for the group in the black Hey Hey Club in Altman's film, was comprised largely of musicians that Moten acquired when he raided the Oklahoma "Blue Devils," which operated from Oklahoma City. Moreover, Moten's band pioneered the musical battle of bands and musicians that came to be identified as a typical Kansas City musical phenomenon (featured in the film).[79]

## Another Racial/Spatial "America"

The Kansas City scene constructed in Robert Altman's feature film constitutes a political challenge to *Oklahoma!* Through both its treatment of spatial history and its presentation of alternative domains of intelligibility, the film offers a different America from *Oklahoma!*, or more generally an alternative to the dominant American national narrative.[80] In contrast with *Oklahoma!*'s story of Euro American nation building, for example, *Kansas City* provides a key moment in the story of African American musical development, which is intimately connected with a history of black cultural (as opposed to territorial) nationalism. Although the filmic story has only a two-day duration, situated during the 1934 presidential campaign, the black nightclub and music scene it features reflects a significant period in the earlier noted movement of the African American population from the South and Southwest to the major urban areas of the north and Midwest. And in the particular case of Kansas City, it shows the result of an in-migration of scores of talented black musicians who shaped the Kansas City version of jazz.

While most of the major U.S. American cities were still reeling from the Great Depression, Kansas City was relatively prosperous, due in large to the political influence of the boss of the local Democratic machine, Thomas J. Pendergast, whose delivery of Missouri votes in national elections was redeemed in the form of federal money for local projects. Pendergast created an economic oasis in Kansas City by attracting New Deal labor-intensive public works programs. As a result of the Pendergast-sponsored availability of jobs, Kansas City became "a Mecca" for black jazz musicians, among whom were Benny Moten, Count Basie, Lester Young, Eddie Durham, Jesse Stone, Walter Page, Oran "Hotlips" Page, Mary Lou Williams, Eddie Barfield, Henry "Buster" Smith, Ed Lewis, and Charlie Parker.[81]

However, the influx of African Americans—musicians among others—to Kansas City and other urban centers was the result of a push as well as a pull. Interestingly, in different, indirect ways, President Franklin D. Roosevelt's administration played a role in the developments of both *Oklahoma!* and Kansas City jazz. In the case of the former, Roosevelt's New Deal policy included a "Federal Arts Project" (1935–1943), "which encouraged a form of democratic realism in art as a means of rhetoricising the economic and social transformations needed to relocate capitalism as a morally defensible economic system for a democratic society."[82] It created an accepting climate for the production of *Oklahoma!*. Like the other funded projects, aimed at developing a "vernacular tradition of representation" in response to "the perceived dominance of European art forms,"[83] *Oklahoma!* exemplifies this version of an American vernacular and represents the power of an American communality of values to retard threats to the new order. In the case of the latter, the agricultural policies developed under the New Deal (as was noted in chapter 1) provided inducements for white southern planters to demote their workers to the status of casual laborers, employed only seasonally. "Eventually millions [of African Americans] drifted out of the South altogether, probably the largest government-impelled population movement in all our history," according to historian Donald Grubbs.[84] The degradation of African agricultural work, the restrictions and exclusions imposed by the Jim Crow laws, and other, more violent white practices that made the South increasingly inhospitable to African Americans, led to the large-scale movement northward.

The African American movement to northern and Midwestern urban centers is intimately connected with Afro-American musical developments. Instead of a state-oriented, nation-building geographical dynamic, African American music articulates a musical geography that reflects the black diaspora (a diaspora that contrasts with the musical geography mapped by Salman Rushdie, a Third World migrant intellectual with an anti-nationalist, cosmopolitan agenda). Moreover, African American music is associated not only with a domestic U.S. diaspora, but also with a geographically extensive movement of black bodies (and consequently musical idioms) through the Atlantic region. Despite the diaspora, however, there remains a coherent supranational dispersion of "structures of feeling," constituting what Paul Gilroy calls a "black Atlantic" with cultural forms that are "stereophonic, bilingual," and "bifocal."[85]

The music in Altman's *Kansas City* therefore speaks to developments well outside the particular vignettes in the film's story line. While virtually all the action within the camera's frame takes place in Kansas City, the film makes extensive use of the two dimensions of cinematic space famously elaborated by Noel Burch, "that included within the frame and that outside the frame."[86] What is taking place in Kansas City in 1934, is, among other things, the preparation for a presidential election. The city's main train station appears in several scenes as white power brokers and shipped-in voters connected with national politics enter the film's frame as they head into the city, while, at the same time, black clients, musicians, and refugees also enter the film's frame as they arrive in Kansas City. As was the case in the film version of *Oklahoma!*, the railroad tracks represent links between what is inside and what is outside of the frame, serving simultaneously as vehicles for the movement of key characters (the in-migration of people with domesticity-destabilizing, modern values in the case of *Oklahoma!*), and as a symbolic linkage between the local and national forces shaping the lives in the filmic narratives. In the case of *Oklahoma!*, the consummated marriage bond reflects a triumph of domesticity and homogenous communal values over outside, disruptive forces, while in the case of *Kansas City,* the marriage partners—whose relationship ends in their deaths rather than an anticipation of the marital bliss toward which *Oklahoma!* gestures—serve as vehicles to highlight the immense gulf between the white and black commercial and political cultures of Kansas City and, by implication, America as a whole.

The domestic pairings in *Oklahoma!* and *Kansas City* therefore constitute a contrast between two very different American stories. Briefly, the action in *Kansas City* is generated by an episode taking place during two days of the 1934 presidential primary. The husband, Johnny, robs a black tourist/gambler headed for Seldom Seen's black Hey Hey Club, while wearing blackface to make it appear to be a black-on-black crime. After he is found out and apprehended by Seen's henchmen, Johnny's scrappy and resourceful wife, Blondie, kidnaps Carolyn, the wife of Henry Stilton, an influential politician who has connections with boss Pendergast, the governor, and the local Italian crime syndicate, and is headed to Washington, D.C., to confer with President Roosevelt. Blondie's plan is to coerce Stilton to use his connections to rescue Johnny. Stilton is telegraphed at an intermediate station and tries to meet Blondie's demand. But the "rescue" ultimately fails; Johnny comes home mortally wounded and Carolyn ends up shooting Blondie to death as she lies prostrate over her dying husband. Moreover, the kidnaping drama is less significant than the way Johnny and Blondie's story illuminates the disjunctures between white and black Kansas City.

The film narrative provides a mapping of white election politics as it traces the influence peddling and corruption that attends the contests for national, state and local offices. The Pendergast machine is shown in operation, employing political and criminal connections and violence to steal the forthcoming election. But, at the same time, the film depicts the black music scene enacted within Seldom Seen's Hey Hey Club. Through the cuts and juxtapositions, Altman's film speaks of the separations and encounters that constitute the exemplary racial/spatial order of Kansas City in the 1930s: on the one hand, a white society caught up in an election contest and, on the other, what LeRoi Jones/Amiri Baraka has called the black "meta-society" articulating its within-group solidarity and its highly coded relationship with white society through its music.[87]

As the film narrative develops, the pervasive historical doubleness that Kansas City represents is shown to persist. Missouri contained both sides of the slavery conflict in the nineteenth century, and in the twentieth, its most vibrant city contained a juxtaposition of two exemplary racial orders. It is important to note, however, that the form of *Kansas City*'s film narrative is the primary way in which the film speaks of a politically divided American nation. This is the second dimension of Altman's implicit challenge to the musical *Oklahoma!* The film version of *Oklahoma!* makes use of master shots. The viewer is situated panoptically, in front of an unfolding panorama of an increasingly homogeneous social order as it overcomes threats to an attunement between domestic and national life. *Kansas City,* by contrast, tells a double story cutting back and forth between Johnny's and

Blondie's participation in the events; it tells, in the words of one critic: "two meandering, sometimes violent stories that finally come together near the end of the picture."[88] And, in further contrast with the filming of *Oklahoma!*, Altman employs multiple camera positions. As was the case in his filming of *Nashville*, which also explores a racial/spatial order in an American city, Altman resists what his *Nashville* editor, Sid Levin, calls "the classic style . . . the conventional use of master, medium and close-up shots." Rather, there are "three or four different master angles of the same sequence, each with a slight variation in camera angle."[89]

Altman's approach to sound and meaning produces a multiplicity that is of a piece with his approach to the pluralistic situating of angles of vision. In a seemingly trivial yet exemplary moment of filmic and aural montage in *Nashville*, for example, the scene cuts from a hospital, where a husband weeps over the news that his wife has just died to a festive gathering in which someone is laughing in precisely the same rhythm. In *Kansas City*, Altman produces a similar double resonance. In a scene in which Seldom Seen's henchmen are knifing to death the cab driver (who had conspired in the robbery of Seen's black gambling customer) in an alley, the film narrative cuts to the Hey Hey Club, where "at the same time the two saxophonists try to outdo each other with a rapid exchange of short phrases. [Coleman] Hawkins and [Lester] Young engage in a cutting contest of their own,"[90] and their intensity produces the same rhythm as the killing.

As was the case in his *Nashville*, Altman's focus in *Kansas City* is on encounters between two systems of meaning-making, two domains of discourse, economy and music, which distinguish the white and black ethnoscapes of an American city. In *Nashville*, Altman achieved an improvisatory climate for his filmic narrative by letting his actors function without a fixed script and by complimenting the multidimensional ethnoscape he achieved in the visual register with a plurality of camera angles with the use of many microphones placed to pick up peripheral conversations (a technique used in *McCabe and Mrs. Miller* to convey the complex cacophony of voices structuring the turn-of-the-century West).[91] But Altman's approach to the complexity of voices is deeper in *Kansas City* than it is in *Nashville*. The film as a whole is structured like jazz. While the surface plot maps the Kansas City-Washington connection and provides insight into the white election politics of the corrupt, Pendergast-run Democratic machine, the aural rhythms of the film provide a glimpse of another America with a politics coded in sound. Simply put, the voices of *Kansas City*'s characters double the voices of the performing jazz musicians.

The "story" in the film as a whole, as Altman puts it (in response to complaints that the plot of *Kansas City* is thin): "is just a little song, and it's the way it's played that's important."[92] More elaborately, Altman's approach was to make the movie itself into a kind of freewheeling jazz improvisation."[93] Altman again:

> A song is usually about three minutes long . . . but when jazz guys work on it, the song takes 17 minutes. I decided to make a song out of the story of the two women. As it developed, the whole movie is jazz. Harry Belafonte [who plays Seldom Seen] is like a brass instrument—when it's his turn to solo, he does long monologues like riffs—and the discussions of the two women are like reed instruments, maybe saxophones, having duets.[94]

Aware of both the history of jazz and of its central role in the highly coded (musical) languages with which much of African American political culture expresses itself, Altman creates an effective inter-articulation between African American spatial history (the historical emergence of the Kansas City style of jazz as black musicians migrated into the city) and a distinctively African American approach to musical intelligibility: elements of blues, emanating primarily from the Mississippi Delta but also from the distinctiveness of the southwestern bands that had remained true to the old blues tradition,[95] ragtime developed in the Midwest, and New Orleans jazz are fused in the Kansas City style of jazz. However, in addition to its complex spatial history, the music reflects a history of what Ben Sidran calls "black talk"[96] a form of counter-intelligibility (or what George Lipsitz calls a "strategic anti-essentialism")[97] on the American scene, which is owed in part to its African discursive heritage and in part to the necessarily coded form of discourse that developed among people who have not, in varying degrees and at different historical moments, been free to express themselves directly and, as a result, have been often excluded from participation in mainstream forms of Euro American civic expression.

A treatment of the history of jazz is beyond the scope of this chapter. What I want to note at a minimum is that the music derives from a complex set of forces imposed from the outside on African American music and from within, as musicians created a synthesis between black vernacular modes of expression and the European musics that were also a part of the America's musical heritage. Among the synthesizers of the articulation of black orality (in its musical mode) and European based musical forms was Louis Armstrong, who "combined the oral approach to rhythm and vocalization with an intuitive grasp of Western harmonic structure, creating a new synthesis acceptable to both blacks and whites."[98] But the synthesizing did not simply aid and abet the music-nationhood relationship to which white composers had contributed. While granting that "[a] nation's emergence is always predicated on the construction of a field of meaningful sounds," Houston A. Baker, Jr., points out that the black musical contribution creates a disjuncture. He notes that the "*national* enterprise of black artists and spokes persons, since the beginning of the century, have been involved in "a mode of *sounding* reality," that resists the Euro American state's desire for a unitary nationalizing enterprise.[99]

The Broadway musical form, of which *Oklahoma!* is an exemplar, was of course not wholly outside the influence of the African American musical development. For example, Gershwin's *Porgy and Bess* is also a synthesizing artistic production. It represents Gershwin's attempt to "forge an American musical language," to achieve an artistic unity out of a diversity. Gershwin wanted an articulation of black and white music to represent what he called the "the rhythms of these interfusing peoples . . . clashing and blending."[100] But apart from whatever degree of musical fusion Gershwin achieved, the racist stereotypes in his "folk opera" drew substantial and warranted criticism from the black newspaper community.[101] And Duke Ellington staged his own musical, *Jump for Joy*, because he wanted, in his words, "to take Uncle Tom out of the Theater."[102]

Ellington was also critical of attempts at white-black musical fusion. As he surmised, and as the musical developments of the jazz age have shown, American musical nationhood resists an easy synthesis. Jazz development represents a different set of voices and a different mode of articulation than what can be apprehended in the consensus-building chorus-oriented mode of Tin Pan Alley music. And its trajectory has consisted of a resistance to a uniform national musical language. According to John Gennari, its hallmark has been "its role as a progenitor of new forms, and inventor of new languages, a creator of new ways to express meaning. The blue notes, microtones, polyrhythms, and the extended harmonies of jazz constitute a musical vocabulary and grammar that cannot be accurately represented by the standard notational systems of Western music."[103]

In addition, therefore, to the spatial history that provides much of the context of African American music in general and jazz in particular, locating the significance of jazz requires attention to its improvisatory approach to musical intelligibility. While the Broadway musicals of the Tin Pan Alley composers work from a precomposed score that is subsequently enacted after numerous rehearsals, jazz performances ambiguate the boundary between composition and performance. It is because of his appreciation of this aspect of the music, that Altman insisted on using only live footage of the jazz performances in his *Kansas City*. Nevertheless, the swing era, Kansas City style of jazz, which contained some moments of clashing, improvisatory musical voices, functioned primarily as an entertainment and dance-facilitating club genre. As a result, in the film, the music's role alternates between background mood and foreground statement. It is the subsequent "hard bop" and "free jazz" developments in the 1960s, associated to a degree with some Kansas City musicians (for example, Ornette Coleman), but more thoroughly present in the composition/performances of Miles Davis and John Coltrane, that exemplify a distinct counter-intelligibility to the national consensuality-inspiring style of other musical genres.

To treat this genre of musical expression and its political implications, I turn to the jazz improvisations of John Coltrane, who dedicated himself to incessant movement beyond what had already been musically said. To witness a Coltrane performance—on the tenor, alto, or soprano saxophone—is to watch and hear someone attempting to make an instrument speak in a way it has never spoken before and (often) to hear someone intensely involved in changing a "piece of music" into a questioning of its boundaries and coherence. By the time he played the lead in his own quartet (with McCoy Tyner on piano, Elvin Jones on drums, and Jimmy Garrison on base), Coltrane's "musicking"[104] constituted the kind of performance that contrasts dramatically with the traditional European-inspired approach to music: the "piece" that is performed as a fixed accomplishment.[105] As his drummer, Elvin Jones, has noted, Coltrane would typically begin playing and expect the rest of his ensemble to enter the process without a map of where they were going or how long the journey would be. On one occasion, the group was commissioned to perform several songs for a three-hour television program but never got off the first one. Coltrane just kept working on it.[106] In contrast with the Euro American tradition, in which composition is an autonomous activity, Coltrane's jazz performances are enactments of composition. They reflect what Christopher Small calls a "struggle between freedom and order" in that the playing of jazz involves a movement back and forth between the spaces of black vernacular orality and the values and assumptions of the white social order.[107] Rather than a musical fusion, Coltrane's playing was a musical semiosis, an encounter staged between a system of meaning characteristic of African American culture and the institutionalized referentiality of the dominant white culture.[108]

But to appreciate the formal particulars and political implications of Coltrane's semiotic encounters with the white social order, it is necessary to treat the details of a particular composition. For this purpose, Coltrane's extended repetitions of the song, "My Favorite Things" from the Rodgers and Hammerstein musical, *The Sound of Music,* serves well. It is in such seemingly nonpolitical musical compositions that one can appreciate the political impetus of Coltrane's jazz. Certainly there are more explicit political referents in his repertoire. Although he was vague about his political ideas, in one instance he addressed a song to violence against African Americans in Alabama after the Klansman, "dynamite Bob" (and at least two others) blew up a black church, killing four young girls on September 15, 1963. The dirge-like mood in Coltrane's "Alabama" exemplifies the somatic resonances of jazz. His composition, he said, was an attempt to capture both his own emotional reactions to the event and the rhythms of Martin Luther King's eulogy at the children's funeral.[109]

Nevertheless, the political significance of what appears to be a simple parody of the socially trivial theme of the song, "My Favorite Things," constitutes a more thoroughgoing statement of jazz politics. To elaborate this claim, it is useful to return to Jacques Attali's analysis of the political economy of Western music, specifically where he deals with the relationship between "value" and "things:"

> The entrance of music into exchange implicitly presupposes the existence of an intrinsic value in things, external and prior to their exchange. For representation to have a meaning, then, what is represented must be experienced as having an exchangeable and autonomous value, external to the representation and intrinsic to the work.[110]

Were Coltrane's approach to the "things" to which the song refers merely representational, he would simply play the song as originally composed as an affirmation of the value attributed to the "things." What Coltrane does instead is to repeat rather than represent. To the original tune, he adds seven bars in E minor and twenty-three in E major, repeating the melody within different chordal harmonies. Moreover, there is a hint of a different musical geography framing his renditions for, as one commentator notes, he makes it "sound more like an Indian raga than a Rodgers and Hammerstein waltz."[111]

There is a variety of conceptual frames one could evince to treat Coltrane's radical approach to musical intelligibility. First, his resistance to representation evokes Attali's point about the relationship between representation and harmonious consensuality. "Representation," asserts Attali, "doubly implies harmony . . . it enacts a compromise and an order society desires to believe in, and to make people believe in."[112] Desiring to keep the issue of belief and the authority of dominant structures of (musical) intelligibility open, Coltrane evinced a nonclosural musical grammar. As he put it, he wanted to "learn how to start in the middle of a sentence and move in both directions at the same time."[113] That commitment, along with his repetitions and recontextualizations constituted a challenge to extant structures of meaning and the things to which allegiances are attached. Accordingly, his "My Favorite Things" belongs to what Gilles Deleuze calls the theater of repetition instead of the theater of representation within which allegiances are deepened.

> The theater of repetition is opposed to the theater of representation . . . in the theater of repetition we experience pure forces, dynamic lines in space which act without intermediary upon the spirit, and link it directly with nature and history, with a language which speaks before words, with gestures which develop before organised bodies, with masks before faces, with specters and phantoms before characters—the whole apparatus of repetition as a 'terrible power.'[114]

Valuing the act of saying over the already said, the habit-resistant "singularity of repetition"[115] over representation, and dedicated to enacting the contingency of the musical statement, Coltrane's constant exploration of the boundaries of musical meaning seemed aimed at resisting the authority of the social reality recycled in representational compositions. He would begin within a musical reference but then say it differently in a cyclical moving away (a saying) and then coming back to the original melody. Coltrane's resistance to merely repeating the already said opens up another line of critique, which is reflected in Michel Foucault's treatment of the writing of Raymond Roussel. Much like Coltrane, Roussel did not want, as Foucault puts it, "to duplicate the reality of another world, but, in the spontaneous duality of language, he wants to *discover* an unexpected space and to *cover* it with things never said before."[116] Roussel's writing, like Coltrane's music, has a reference in the already said but it engages in incessant repetitions that alter the said's significance and context before recovering it. As Foucault puts it:

> In certain of Roussel's works, nothing is given at the beginning except the possibility of encountering the "already said" and with this "found language" to construct, according to his rules, a certain number of things, but on the condition that they always refer back to the "already said."[117]

If we heed Roussel's remarks on his method, the homology between his writing and Coltrane's music becomes strikingly evident. Roussel refers to his use of "metagrams" (words that are altered by changing one letter) so that, for example, billiard (as in a game) becomes pillard (plunderer).[118] And in his more complex substitutions, phrases are involved, as Roussel, who was originally trained as a musician,[119] improvises with what he calls "phonic combinations."[120] For example, in *Impressions de Afrique,* the expression, "*Ma chandelle est*" (my candle is), becomes "*Marchand zelee*" (zealous merchant),[121] and the story moves on with an incorporation of such a character as Roussel follows the trajectories of the alternative meanings that are phonically implicated. In this respect, the flow of Roussel's narratives also bear comparison with Debussy's musical scores. "[E]mancipat[ing] pitch and rhythm as well as harmonies from relationships defined by tradition and rules," Debussy's "sequence of sounds is suggested by their gradual unfolding, one from the next, permitting new and unexpected sounds and colors to emerge from the actual (if not natural) and non-artificial character of sound."[122]

As is the case with Debussy's musical scores, both Roussel's and Coltrane's explorations in sound and meaning have a clear structural effect. Their departures can be understood in the context of the "patterning and functioning of language"[123] explicated by Roman Jakobson and Morris Halle in their analysis of types of aphasia. Jakobson and Halle's approach articulates particularly well with the earlier noted struggle between order and freedom that the hard bop/free jazz movement exemplifies. The capacity to speak intelligibly, they point out, operates on an "ascending scale of freedom."[124] While the freedom with respect of available phonemes is "zero," the "freedom to combine phonemes into words is [merely] circumscribed . . . limited to the marginal situation of word coinage," and, finally, "in the combination of sentences into utterances, the action of compulsory syntactical rules ceases, and the freedom of any individual speaker increases substantially."[125]

Most significantly, for a treatment of the license taken by Roussel with language and Coltrane with music, Jakobson and Halle distinguish two axes of linguistic selection; the first is the vertical axis in which selection involves the substitution of one meaning for another with roughly the same sound, and the second is the horizontal axis on which temporal sequencing or concatenation is effected. When these axes are distinguished, it becomes evident that Roussel's improvisations take off from his explorations along the vertical axis. He exacts his degrees of freedom and thereby his creativity from ritualized and expected meanings from the vertical or "concurrence" dimension of intelligibility. This is also the case for Coltrane, much of whose musical creativity derives from a vertical rather than horizontal series of improvisations.

At the risk of oversimplifying, we can distinguish Thelonious Monk's and John Coltrane's improvisational strategies as horizontal and vertical, respectively. Monk's reinterpretations of standard tunes usually involve changes in the temporality of their phrasing. In the words of one critic, Monk "makes hesitation eloquent."[126] For Monk, "space and its intrusion meant more than just the handling of chords."[127] In contrast, Coltrane's improvisations are primarily vertical; they emphasize "aggregations" and the articulation of chords with selective pitches or differing accents. Although, like other jazz performers, Coltrane also effects changes in rhythmical movement along the melodic line, his is better known for the verticality of his improvisations.[128]

Like other musicians playing free jazz, Coltrane's music is influenced by the call and response, statement/counter-statement styles of black orality. His music therefore articulates with a tradition that values the "rhizomatic structure" that Slavoj Zizek has ascribed to Schuman's romanticism, a music with intertwining sections with multiple repetitions and contrasts.[129] But Coltrane's version of repetition has special debts to an African American practice of playing with intelligibility, a process of "signfyin'," a doubleness involving "assertions and counter-assertions" with strong resonances in what Henry Louis Gates, Jr., calls "The African American discursive forest."[130] There is, in short, a strong relationship between jazz performance and "the play of black language games,"[131] a "telling misuse inflicted on English, an abuse which brings the referent more explicitly to light."[132]

However, Coltrane's musical explorations exceed this signifying style. Just as he changed instruments—moving, for example, to a soprano saxophone in "My Favorite Things"—in search of freedom from modes of sound-making, he attacked basic musical structures, seeking, for example, to "demolish the chord barrier"[133] and show how, by varying chord combinations, meanings can be multiplied within the vertical dimension of musical signification. This vertical play, involving a strenuous substitutions of chords and "harmonic extensions upon a harmonic structure,"[134] relocated the "things" in "My Favorite Things," which in the original song were frozen into a simple melodic narrative that had "little chordal motion,"[135] into a complex set of repetitions, giving them a multiplicity of meanings. Jazz artist Miles Davis, in whose ensemble Coltrane played before assembling his own quartet, aptly describes Coltrane's innovations:

> What he does, for example, is to play five notes of a chord and then keep changing it around, trying to see how many different ways it can sound. It's like explaining something five different ways.[136]

## From Semiosis to Politics

I referred to Coltrane's riffs on familiar songs as a "semiosis," a semiotic event/encounter. Rather than merely fusing different musical styles or genres, Coltrane's repetitive work on the simple show-tune melody of "My Favorite Things" is a clash between a musical realization of "black talk" and the presumptively universalized, referentiality of Euro American music. In such encounters, a dual confrontation takes place, one between alternative spatial histories and one between alternative practices of intelligibility. As a result, a challenge is mounted to the fantasy structure of a unitary American nationhood. The political challenge to the dominant narrative of American nation building provided by such encounters between alternative meaning worlds becomes especially evident when we consider the parallel between the degrees of semantic freedom exacted in Coltrane's jazz improvisations and Altman's filmmaking.

Jakobson and Halle make the case that their treatment of linguistic degrees of freedom is as relevant to film making as it is to jazz improvisation. They note that the "art of cinema," can function primarily vertically—with its capacity for "changing the angle, perspective, and focus of 'shots,'" with, among other things, a set of substitutions along a vertical axis—with "metaphoric 'montage'" and "lap dissolves" that provide "filmic similes."[137] If we heed this dimension of filmic improvisation and compare the film version of *Oklahoma!* with Altman's *Kansas City*, we observe an *Oklahoma!* that consists primarily of close-up, framing shots. With the exception of a few long views of the vast plains, the viewer's perspective is claustrophobically locked into a romantic narrative in which the familial bond that eventuates is an allegory for a national cohesion. Insofar as the collection of scenes are composed with cuts from one to another, the narrative remains continuous and thematic. The cuts serve simply to fill in the cultural unity-valorizing, narrative sequence.

In contrast, in *Kansas City* (as noted earlier), the viewer is offered alternative perspectives from varying cameras angles, and the montage, which is realized as a set of metaphoric substitutions, serves to question any story of the emergence of a unitary political culture. Altman's *Kansas City* is therefore structurally homologous with Coltrane's jazz improvisations. And it has the same political impetus; it accords with the oppositionality of much of African American music, which must be understood in terms of its challenge to the historical trajectory of American nation building and the contemporary illusion of a unitary territorial citizen attachment. At a minimum, a treatment of the political significance of Coltrane's musical explorations requires an analysis of a distinctive relationship between African American music and nationhood.

Approaching the issue of this distinctiveness, while articulating the relationship between hip-hop and African American nationhood, Touré suggests that *this* nation is constituted as a series of musical events rather than in terms of territorial extension:

> I live in a country no map maker will ever respect. A place with its own language, culture and history. It is as much a nation as Italy or Zambia, a place my countrymen call the Hip-Hop Nation ... We are a nation with no precise date of origin, no physical land, no single chief ... The Hip-Hop Nation is a place as real as America on a pre-Columbus atlas.... The Nation exists in any place where hip-hop music is being played or hip-hop attitude is being exuded.[138]

Similar insights can be derived from a trajectory of African American musical genres that runs from the blues through jazz and bebop to hip-hop. To appreciate the political predicates of the black national separateness articulated by Touré, one needs a view of "the political" that contrasts with the simplistic homogenizing gloss on the American polity that animated the musico-literary aesthetics of the Jewish American novelists and composers I have treated.

The primary difference between the politics of the Jewish American and African American musico-aesthetics I have analyzed thus far relates to a difference in the locus of wrongs the two groups have experienced. The vertical movement of the Jewish American, which is part of the thematic of the exemplary Jewish American novel, and is intrinsic to Irving Berlin's construction of musical America, has been largely realized despite significant levels of discrimination. At a minimum, the American scene has been relatively liberating for this group compared with the European scene they left behind. Spatially as well as in terms of outcome, the African American case is quite different. Most of the wrong that focuses their politics has been experienced on the American scene.

Turning again to Jacques Ranciere's radically egalitarian approach to "the political" (elaborated in chapter 1), we can construe politics as not mere "policy" or the enactment of the principles of democratic norms: "Politics is not the enactment of the principle, the law, or the self of a community," he argues; it is something instituted by those who heretofore have had "no right to be counted as speaking beings" and have, accordingly, made themselves "of some account" by "placing in common a wrong."[139] This account of politics resonates well with the African American experience. The trajectory of African American music in this century has not articulated a felicitous view of American nationhood. As Amiri Baraka (aka LeRoi Jones) has argued, the structure and thematics of blues, for example, reflect the historical pressures on African Americans and the structure of their adaptations.[140] As a result, the political predicates of African American musical forms are perhaps best captured in Ranciere's summary of the form that politics takes when it is applied to its irreducible problematic, that of "equality." Politics is deployed, he asserts, on the "processing of a wrong."[141]

Certainly many white Americans have also been excluded from the America that Irving Berlin tunefully invented. White composer/performers from Woody Guthrie to Bruce Springsteen have constructed counter-Berlin tunes ("This Land is Your Land" and "Born in the USA," respectively), which speak to the parts of the nation that have not enjoyed Irving Berlin's "freedom train" ("where the en-gen-eer is Un-cle Sam").[142] Guthrie and Springsteen, like African American blues composers, "use geographic makers"[143] to identify spaces where people are left out of the "American dream." But while the focus of Guthrie and Springsteen has been on working people, the blues genre has derived its forms as well as its objects of attention as a result of racism. The African American experience, from slavery onward, which has been wholly incommensurate with that of other Americans, has given rise to distinctive literary and musical genres. Although, as Touré suggests, African American nationhood is often realized in moments rather than in an institutionalized territorial extension, there are distinctive spatial predicates of black politico-musical forms. As is the case with Rushdie's attachment to world music, the African American relationship to blues (and subsequent blues-inflected musics) arises from their dual diasporic experience—from Africa to the American South and, subsequently for many, to northern U.S. cities. The blues speaks, as LeRoi Jones puts it, to African peoplehood; "the history of the music, he argues, "is the history of the people . . . the Afro-American people as text, as tale, as story, as exposition, or narrative, or what have you." It is "the score, the actually expressed creative orchestration, reflection of Afro-American life, our words, the libretto, to those actual lived lives."[144]

The spatial contrast between the way African American blues developed and the music of Irving Berlin is telling. While Berlin's music spoke to the vertical movement of immigrant protagonists, precisely at the time of Berlin's ethnic novelty songs, African American movement was horizontal, from a marginalized status in the South to a similar one in the North. By 1914, Jones/Baraka points out, "masses of Negroes began to move to the Northern industrial centers such as Chicago, Detroit, New York,"[145] and what was vertical was not their movement but the city, whose "verticality" divided the blues into different types[146]—the older, more expressive and vocal forms and the newer, highly instrumentalized, jazz-oriented kind that incorporated aspects of white music. However, despite the increasing hybridity of African American blues and bluesy jazz, as it departed from its predominantly African-inspired vocal and rhythmic forms, it remained a resistant, highly coded mode of signifying musical expression of the African American "meta-society."[147] It reflected the situation of a people whose music enacted their sense of difference and their struggle for solidarity.

The signifyin' style of African American musical forms, in blues through hip-hop—a quintessentially African-inspired mode of expression[148]—contrasts markedly with the representational and narrative orientations of many white musical forms. As the music of the "other" on the American scene, African American music manifests a fugitivity. Rather than seeking, like the protagonists in Berlin's music, to mature into a fundamentally American mode of intelligibility, the music seeks to evade the normal structures of meaning. Like the linguistic play of blacks during the slavery period, when spoken and musical forms contained a "willful abuse,"[149] designed to construct the referents of the language within a different meaning context. The subsequent blues through jazz compositions and performances contain multiple riffs on the same themes and contradictory clashes of musical voice designed to reflect the resistant singularity of an African America way of being. It can be construed as a form of nationhood within a nation that achieves its coherence through a struggle against imposed interpretations of African American identity and against the white, commercial appropriation of the musical expressions of their peoplehood.

Accompanying the urbanization of blues and jazz, evident in the musical styles ultimately elaborated by Miles Davis, John Coltrane, and Thelonious Monk, among others, was an African American literary outpouring, especially by writers associated with what came to be known as the Harlem

Renaissance of the 1920s. A blues aesthetic is manifest in the novels and poetry of Langston Hughes, Zora Neale Hurston, Richard Wright, and many others associated with this moment in African American literary production.[150] These lines from Hughes's poem "Lenox Avenue: Midnight" are exemplary of a literary manifestation of the urban-centered version of a blues/jazz aesthetic:

> The rhythm of life
> Is a jazz rhythm,
> Honey . . .
> The Broken heart of love
> The weary heart of pain,—
> > Overtones,
> > Undertones,
> > To the rumble of street cars,
> > To the swish of rain . . .[151]

The literary manifestation of a diaspora-inspired version of a blues aesthetic—a poetic expression of African American voices and experiences after their displacement from the South to the North—continues in the contemporary writing of African American authors. For example, it structures Walter Mosley's novel *RL's Dream*.[152] The "RL" in the novel is RL Johnson (a character in Sherman Alexie's novel, treated in chapter 4), a blues singer from the Mississippi delta, who died in 1938 at a young age. His impact on the blues is represented through a fictional disciple, Atwater Soupspoon Wise, who is dying of cancer in New York as the novel opens. Expelled from his flat, he is taken in and has medical assistance arranged (through creative fraud) by another displaced southerner, Kiki Waters, a white woman, who is also in pain because of a stabbing. Before the novel ends, Soupspoon seemingly captures the essence of RL's blues while performing in his last musical gig in a rundown gambling spot. The blues, which emerges first in the delta, manifests itself again as Soupspoon, having chased it all over the delta, following RL's tortured path of "sufferin' and singin'," finally catches up with it, far from home, near the end of his life.

Mosley's novel is not merely about the blues and some of the persons associated with it; his writing expresses it. The story of the two diasporic characters from the South, Soupspoon and Kiki, is scripted as "a prose ballad—a blues—of pain and redemption."[153] The blues-inflected "prose ballad" is articulated most frequently in the thoughts of Soupspoon—for example, in a moment when he awakened by Kiki's cries during a nightmare: "The blankets were kicked off her bed. Her naked behind was thrust up in the air because she was hunched over the pillow and some sheet." And Soupspoon reacts:

*A white woman; skinny butt stuck out at me like a ripe peach on a low branch.*
There was nobody left to tell. Nobody left to understand how strange it was,
how scary it was. Nobody to laugh and ask, "An' then what you did?" *An then
I died,* Soupspoon said to himself. There was nobody to hear him. And even if
there was—so what? That was the blues.[154]

## Rap/Hip-Hop: African American and Hawaiian Modalities

The contemporary impulse to preserve a distinctive and politically enabling
African American aesthetic articulates itself less through intricate coding
and evasion than through a direct form of musically expressed critique. The
diaspora to the North is now an old story. The "hood" and the street are
the new one. There are occasional fugitive elements of hip-hop that reveal
a genesis in the blues aesthetic, but, as Paul Gilroy points out, it is more
of a hybrid, world music; it combines African American vernacular culture
with Caribbean equivalents.[155] And, most significantly, much of its force derives from a different approach to the spaces of African American existence.
As Tricia Rose notes, rap music television articulates a decidedly African
American spatial predicate. Unlike heavy metal performances, for example,
which are simply shown on sound stages, the scenes of its performance as
well as its content reference the "hood, the street, posses." It displays an
explicit recognition of the terrain of African American habitation.[156]

As primarily a music of political critique, hip-hop was the result "a con-
certed effort by young urban blacks to use mass culture to facilitate communal discourse across a fractured and dislocated national community."[157]
And it has reached beyond an African American national community, as
hip-hop artists aspire to a dialogue that reaches a transnational, diasporic
black counter-public scattered throughout the globe.[158] However broad or
limited its global reach and political effectiveness among dispersed, black
counter-publics, hip-hop has migrated across the Pacific. And, as I have
noted, it has influenced the musical oppositionality of Australian Aboriginal
rap groups, as, for example, part of the "multicultural noise" of Maori activist
musicians in New Zealand;[159] and it has been incorporated into the contemporary musical expression of Hawaiian nationhood. Activist musicians,
who constitute one dimension of a growing, multidimensional Hawaiian
sovereignty movement, have recently produced a set of songs that convey an
indigenous political initiative aimed at reconvening a Hawaiian nation that
was destroyed at the time of the U.S. annexation at the end of the nineteenth
century.

In one of the pieces in the collection, *Big Island Conspiracy: Reflective
but Unrepentant,* Hawaiian activist/composer/performer Kelii W. "Skippy"
Ioane delivers the following lines (some of which constitute the epilogue

to chapter 1), which combine English and Hawaiian words in a hip-hop musical rhythm:

> Colonial thugs with their Bible and drugs—snitches,
> dopers, religious interlopers. The mission to seize
> secure *ka aina pa'a i ka* [the land that is held/secured in
> the] native pure. Cultures trampled, intellectual
> examples. Righteousness brought, the European
> thought. . . . Steal the soul of the man you steal the life of
> the land. American sugar, Pilgrim descendants. Broke
> the tribal laws of their own Ten Commandments. Thou
> shall not lie, thou shall not steal. From peaceful, friendly
> nations,—who's gods are real—touch that—*haina ia*
> *mai ana kapuana, o ka poe i ka aina* [tell the story of the
> people who love their land] —touch that.[160]

## Conclusion: The Musico–Literary Appropriations of Hawaiian Sovereignty

The musical poetics of Ioane's song resonate with the history of the Hawaiian lyrical tradition. It is a *mele,* a Hawaiian word that applies to equally music or poetry.[161] And the last quoted line (translated as: "tell the story of the people who love their land"), is from a Hawaiian protest song, *Kaulana ka puana,* composed in 1893 and "still sung today by *Kanaka Maoli* [Hawaiian people] as a call to sovereignty."[162] Moreover, the collection as a whole evokes a history of Hawaiian traditional musical forms: for example, a chant to the goddess Pele, entitled "Chant," and Hawaiian/popular music hybrids: for example, a ballad, "Samuela Texas," that combines chanted Hawaiian laments (*"Auwe, auwe, auwe"*), African American hymn-like moments ("Samuela Texas call Mr. Pharaoh, let the original people go"), and rap styles ("Annexation, constipation, Kanaka cities in a stolen nation"). The collection is of a piece with the modern trajectory of postcontact Hawaiian musical forms, for since the period of Western contact, through the moment of the annexation, and into the present, Hawaiian-Western musical hybrids have been part of a Hawaiian politico-aesthetic opposition to colonization. Music, as Elizabeth Buck has put it in her analysis of post-contact Hawaiian cultural politics, "has been a continuing site of resistance for Hawaiians."[163]

Without going into detail on the genealogy of Hawaiian hybrid musical forms, I want to call attention first to the composition of national anthems by a succession of Hawaiian royalty, for, as John Charlot has pointed out, "the Hawaiian national anthems are prime examples of bicultural religio-political thinking and expression."[164] And, more generally, like all post-contact musical forms, the music, although a Western form and written in a Western idiom, is appropriated to a project of preserving a Hawaiian nation at important historical moments. Among the exemplary instances of anthems as national political initiatives is the first "truly original Hawaiian anthem," *Hawaii Pono'i*,[165] written by King Kalakaua (1874–1891). Like the development of French grand opera earlier in the same century, the anthem effects a shift away from the cosmologically-oriented legitimation of a monarchy and nobility and toward a recognition of a social order and nation; it speaks to a nationhood that evokes a "people." However, because, in the Hawaiian case, the "people" are increasingly subjugated by a foreign power, the resistance dimensions of the music are esoteric (as has been the case with much African American music). For example, attempting to keep alive the historical consciousness necessary to maintain a Hawaiian national imaginary, Kalakaua's anthem contains a perspective of a "unified nation" while, at the same time, dissimulating its commitments "to exploit the gap between Hawaiian and non-Hawaiian understanding."[166] Although overlaid with a non-Christian, religious rhetoric, *Hawaii Pono'i* is primarily a political anthem. In addressing "Hawaii's own," and devoting attention to the specifics of the social order, the anthem is organized primarily around the problem of "the unity of the nation as well as its problems."[167]

The impulse to Hawaiian nationhood has remained alive in the increasingly Western–oriented musical forms since the annexation. The shift to Western instrumentation and primarily to English language vocals has not compromised the music's functioning within a Hawaiian collective imaginary. Post-contact Hawaiian musical forms are in effect akin to what Deleuze and Guattari have called a "minor literature" (treated in chapter 1). Focusing on Franz Kafka's texts, written in Prague by a minority writer in the dominant German language of the country, Deleuze and Guattari argue that those who write from a minoritarian perspective within major literatures provide a politicized mode of articulation; they "express another possible community and forge the means for another consciousness and another sensibility."[168] Writing from an alternative locus of enunciation, minority writers reinflect the words and expressions in the major language, giving themselves identity space they lack when the utterances come from the controlling majority. Put differently and more specifically, Hawaiian musical inscriptions are involved in what Russell Potter has called a "resistance vernacular . . . *deploying variance* in order to deform and reposition the rules of 'intelligibility' set up by the dominant [musical] language."[169]

Hawaii musical and poetic forms (as minor literatures in Deleuze and Guattari's sense and as "resistance vernaculars" in Potter's) have amplified their political nation-referencing impact by adopting diverse politico-aesthetic forms from other political movements. Skippy Ioane's incorporation of hip-hop into his Hawaiian sovereignty *mele* is the most recent in a history of politicized hybrid musico-literary appropriations that have accompanied a growing set of Hawaiian sovereignty movements.[170] From the late 1960s through the 1980s, for example, a blues aesthetic migrated into musical and poetic articulations of Hawaiian national consciousness. Like Ioane's recent incorporation of hip-hop styles in his "In Flagrante Delecto," an earlier Hawaiian anticolonial, nationhood movement was accompanied by an African American musical style, a blues aesthetic manifested in such songs as Liko Martin's and Thor Wold's "Nanakuli Blues," which includes the lines:

> The beaches they sell to build their hotels
> My fathers and I once knew
> Birds all alone, the sunlight at dawn
> Singing Nanakuli blues.[171]

The song served at the time (1968), as, among other things, an "anthem" to a Hawaiian nationhood movement spurred by the plight of Hawaiian farmers being displaced from their homesteads in Waihole and Waikane valleys on the north side of the Island of Oahu.[172] More generally, the major impetus of the blues-inflected *mele* from the Waihole-Waikane protests through the 1980s was a reaction against the desecration of Hawaiian places as a result of a tourist- and military-oriented political economy.

The application of a blues aesthetic is produced in Hawaiian poetry as well as song, as, for example, in these lines from Hawaiian activist/scholar Haunani Kay Trask's, "Agony of Place":

> There is always this sense:
> A wash of earth
> Rain, palm light falling
> Across ironwood ...
> and yet
> our love suffers ...
> in a land of tears
> where our people
> go blindly
> servants of another
> race, a culture of machines ...[173]

In the song form of the Hawaiian *mele*, the blues aesthetic was manifested in the 1980s by the continued popularity of "Nanakuli Blues," which, in the hands of various Hawaiian performers, became "Waimanalo Blues." On one occasion, when sung by Israel "Iz" Kamakawiwo'o'le and the Makaha sons of Ni'i'hau, Iz prefaced the song, which celebrates the beauty of the Hawaiian landscape and laments its destruction by the economic practices of colonizers, with the remark, "Dis song tell how them stu-u-pid *Haoles* [whites or foreigners] fight ovah land, when it not theirs to fight ovah."[174] Through its successive performances, the song aligns itself with a continuous tradition of political *mele,* a "thin fragile line of social protest in Hawaiian music that, since the annexation, had been kept alive mainly in the rural areas by a handful of respected artists."[175]

Finally, in the early 1990s, prior to Skippy Ioane's translation of the hip-hop impetus to the Hawaiian scene, a "Jawaiian" musical form emerged. It is a popular musical style that incorporates Reggae politico-aesthetics into a Hawaiian setting.[176] This development, like many of the indigenous translations/reinflections of world musics, bears comparison with Salman Rushdie's novelistic celebration of those forms of global rock music that defy or transcend the world forged by the spread of the European nation-state. However, unlike Rushdie's cosmopolitan political vision, which glimpses a post-national future, the indigenous usages of global, hybrid musical forms visit specific histories of wrong associated with the process of colonization. Potter's caution against neglecting the specific sites within which transcultural musical forms are developed is relevant here:

> It would be foolish ... to hail all transcultural or multicultural recordings or cross-influences, since the whole point of vernacular art forms is that they come from a particular place at a particular time, and are sites not only of invention and creativity, but of a history of resistance.[177]

The musical repertoires articulate attempts to restore forms of nation-hood that have been suppressed and have remained relatively uncoded in reigning official and academic political discourses. Just as the attach-ments supportive of nation-state formation were often aided and abetted by musico-literary cultural productions in the nineteenth century, of late the political initiatives that speak to alternative nationhood commitments are receiving musico-literary assists. New hybrid musics reflect an indige-nous locus of enunciation, and despite the considerable noise from the Tin Pan Alley-ization or commercialization of their music (against which African American resistant musical forms also had to struggle), manage to articulate compelling political voices of those who, throughout most of the post-contact history of Hawaii, have had no "right to be counted as speaking beings."[178]

The productive and exclusionary territorial and biopolitical practices, evident in the music-nationhood relationship, are also evident in visual genres and media. To explore this aspect of the production of nationhood, I turn, in chapter 4, to the creation of "landscapes," to the process of turning spaces and bodies into visual markers of nationhood.

# CHAPTER 4

# Landscape and Nationhood

## Introduction: Genre and Nationhood

Benedict Anderson's compelling case that nations, as "imagined communities," became objects of symbolic attachment and collective solidarity through mediating genres is worthy of emulation.[1] However, although my analysis in this chapter is edified by Anderson's contribution, I resist his presumption of a homogeneous national imaginary and his almost exclusive focus on print media. According recognition to the fragmenting sets of commitments that pull against a homogenous model of national imagining,[2] I treat both the consolidating, nation building, and resistant imaginaries that contend within state territories, while extending the nationhood-genre relationship Anderson addresses to visual media.[3] Visual media, like the literary genres and print media to which Anderson refers, articulate a spatiotemporality that facilitates collective identity, for a 'nation' emerges as a mode of "moulding and interpreting space," as well as a locus of attachment.[4] As Angela Miller puts it in her treatment of American landscape painting, "visual analogies were important precisely because they operated on the principle that what appeared to be discrete and fragmentary was in fact part of something larger." And, she adds, the formal aspect as well as the substance of the genre played a significant role; the compositional style of landscape painting aided the process of national identification (very much the way the newspaper's structure did, according to Anderson):

> Ambitious panoramic and composite techniques of composition, in which spatially discrete scenes and elements were synthesized into a unified whole, acted

out in artistic terms the political principle of *E pluribus unum,* or plurality of parts within a unifying framework.[5]

Inspecting the American case, as well as several others, my genre focus here is on pictorial works as modes of symbolic action that turn land or territory into "landscape." How can landscape be distinguished from land? Combining imagery from both writing and pictorial genres, Malcolm Andrews suggests that land becomes landscape when it acquires a frame and a narrative element or argument. "A frame," he asserts, "establishes the outer boundaries of the view; it gives the landscape definition,"[6] while the inclusions within the frame produce a thematic, as in the many treatments of Saint Jerome who, once embedded in the landscapes in Dutch Renaissance paintings, gives the view a spiritual significance,[7] as opposed to the more commercial thematics one finds in English eighteenth- and nineteenth-century landscape paintings, in which workers bring in harvests, giving the landscape a political economy significance. With respect to the latter, in several of John Constable's rural landscapes, men are shown laboring in such a way as to turn the countryside into "a kind of open air factory."[8]

Moreover, and most relevant for this analysis, beyond their affirmation of property ownership and commerce, many landscape paintings in the key nation-building centuries have symbolically converted land into *national* space. Miller demonstrates this connection in the American case, and Stephen Daniels elaborates the same connection in England, noting that "landscapes, whether focusing on single monuments or framing stretches of scenery, provide visible shape; they picture the nation."[9] Rather than mere depictions, landscape paintings often testify to "political intentions." Articulating with state designs, they summon nature to perform a "cultural purpose," to mark the frontiers of a state's territorial consolidation and the boundaries of its national culture.[10]

In short, beyond being merely an aesthetic activity, the production of landscape involves ideological gestures situated within historical nationhood struggles—for example, between those who want to maintain the land as a particular kind of social setting, one that privileges a nationhood image of property owners on landed estates, versus those whose national imagery privileges commercial expansion. Hence J.W.M. Turner's mid nineteenth-century canvases focus on circulation rather than property, as in his *Rain, Steam, and Speed—The Great Western Railway* (1844), which shows the train crossing the Thames River over Maidenhead Bridge. By "represent[ing] these two arteries and their conjunction, Turner is marking a system with regional, national, and international dimensions."[11] And by the early twentieth century, the "Vorticists," Wyndham Lewis and others, had wholly abandoned an Englishness based on rural landscapes. Their geographical England was a mechanized, "'industrial island machine . . . discharging itself into the sea.'"[12]

Turning to some other historical examples, the Swiss case is instructive because, among other things, it reflects a national imaginary that is more isolationist than the commercially expanding England constructed in Turner's later landscapes and in the subsequent modernist traditions. Rather than a single national language or a strong territorial association, what is central to Swiss national identity is alpine symbolism. As Oliver Zimmer puts it, "the Alps appear . . . as the physical dimension of the national past. As a way of conjoining landscape and nation."[13] Swiss landscape painters, notably the nineteenth-century artists Alexandre Calame and Francois Diday, expressed the significance of the Alps in Swiss identity formation with mountain scenes that reflected the developing discourse involved in the "nationalization of nature." This process was in evidence in a variety of states as the visual arts became involved in a general process, associated with the rise of national consciousness in some European countries, of changing the perspective "from nature as a more general idea to the more specific notion of landscape."[14]

In the American case, before the completion of the state's continental expansion, the major nation-building contributions of landscape artists was in the form of "middle landscapes," which featured "a rural Arcadia gently shaped by the hand of the farmer and aesthetically balanced between the extremes of wilderness and city."[15] These scenes of a harmonious nature seem to imply that nature itself endorses the expansion of Euro American settlement. The Native Americans in the scenes are usually accorded the role of awed spectators: "stupefied savage[s] confronting the signs of civilization on the march (as in the paintings of DeWitt Clinton Boutelle)"[16]

Subsequently, the most familiar and doubtless most significant nationhood-constituting landscape paintings (and photographs) have produced "the West as America."[17] "National destiny became tied to the natural world" as it was imagined in the far West, and the West that emerged in the most familiar nineteenth-century landscaping paintings was represented as "natural" and largely uninhabited. Those paintings that did include Native Americans tended, as in the case of George Catlin's landscapes, to depict an imperiled "race." With commercial and military initiatives, along with artistic and linguistic productions, the westward expansion of Euro American culture captured physically and symbolically the place-worlds of Native Americans. Inasmuch as the encounter of alternative modes of nationhood constitutes the most significant, but for many, the least evident contemporary political reality in the American West, I turn first to one of the primary implications of the Euro American westward expansion, the resulting fragmented "Indian country," which the familiar modes for constituting the contemporary western landscape rarely mark.

## "Indian Country"

In his story "Indian Country," Native American writer Sherman Alexie produces a provocative rendering of the contemporary Native American habitus in the U.S. For Alexie, contemporary Indian presence is both geographically and ethnologically ambiguous. The story's main character, Low Man Smith, a writer and doubtless a stand-in for Alexie, describes himself in one of the story's conversations as one who is "not supposed to be anywhere."[18] Moreover, his Indianness, along with that of the other Native American characters in the story, is highly diluted; a "Spokane," he speaks and understands no tribal languages, was born and raised in Seattle, and has visited his own reservation only six times. If viewed pictorially, the "Indian country" that emerges in Alexie's literary landscape would have to be a few faintly visible flecks of color on a map of the U.S.'s western states. Tellingly, the precarious and largely obscured visibility of that country is reinforced throughout the story's dialogues by continual challenges to traditional Indian practices of intelligibility. For example, when Low Man asks an older Indian, Raymond, if he is an elder, Raymond shifts to a non-Indian idiom: "elder than some, not as elder as others," he replies.[19]

The dimly etched and ambiguous Indian country that Alexie's story maps is the result of a history of effacement in which a variety of genres of Euro American practices of intelligibility, productions of landscape, among others, have been implicated. One of the earliest is Cotton Mather's "Exact Mapp of New England," an illustration in his narrative of New England church history, *Magnalia Christi Americana* (1702), where, "apart from two tribal choronyms in the heart of New England's dominions—Nipnak Country and Country of Naragansett—there are no further signs of actual Indian presence."[20] It is part of a text that participated in the process through which Euro Americans imposed a bio- as well as a territorial politics on the North American continent. Mather's complicity in the Euro American state's "ethnogenesis" (its totalizing continental presence) occurred both historically and geographically near the beginning of the process of the symbolic effacement of other forms of nationhood on the North American continent.[21]

Subsequently, Thomas Jefferson's geographical and ethnic mapping, in his *Notes on the State of Virginia,* conveyed the influential view that nature warrants a Euro American-dominated national future.[22] While his biopolitical conceits wholly excluded black bodies from the collective citizen body, Native Americans, despite in his view being developmentally inferior and in need of edification, were deemed part of his imagined national future.[23] However, by the mid nineteenth century, landscape painters, many of whom were influenced by Jefferson's romanticizing of America's pastoral habitus, tended to omit Native Americans; their imagery produced the new American state as a developing, wholly white national culture. For example, imagining a social rather than a religious New England, such landscape painters as Frederic Church were elaborating an "American era" that marked no Native American presence. The primary problem to which the landscapes were addressed was the relationship between local New England scenes and a white republican nationalism, between local scenery and a national sentiment.[24] Subsequently, while the westward expansion of the U.S. was displacing Native American inhabitants and recoding their lands, their landscape genres were being ignored, as Euro American textual practices performed the legitimation of the new Euro-style state's territorial and cultural expansion.

A century and a half after Mather's symbolic conversion of New England into a Christian imaginary, James Fenimore Cooper was complicit with a generation of landscape painters in contributing to a symbolic erasure of Indian presence, first in the eastern and Midwestern, and then in the western landscape. In an essay contributed to a coffee table book about "picturesque" landscapes, Cooper begins by noting that his essay is meant to enlighten those who cannot travel and must therefore be content to derive their information from "the pen, the pencil, and the graver."[25] He goes on to contrast an American landscape, which has "an air of freshness, youthfulness, and in many instances . . . rawness,"[26] with the landscapes of Europe "on which are impressed the teeming history of the past."[27]

Contrary to Cooper's conceits, the seemingly youthful and raw vistas of the West contained a rich history, which he was unable to discern because he wholly neglected a Native American perspective. Treating first the area of the Northwest through the Midwest, it is evident that the practices of the Iroquois nations provide evidence that is recalcitrant to Cooper's claims. In his historical reconstruction of the cultural history of the Iroquois, Matthew Dennis addresses the errors perpetuated by Euro American perceptions of Native American living areas:

> Many Europeans failed to recognize or acknowledge America as the product of centuries of cultural modification as a 'landscape' shaped by the desires of its denizens to provide themselves with a prosperous, secure, and fulfilling existence.[28]

Specifically, the shaping of the landscape was most evident near Iroquois villages—with clearings, plantings, and so on, while the landscapes more distant from the villages were left uncleared to facilitate the management of game. Further, the uplands were shaped for human habitation, a "protective zone of landscape that surrounded the core settlements of the Five Nations."[29]

Turning westward, it is evident that the practices of the Apaches also impeach Euro American presumptions. As the anthropologist Keith Basso learned when he was taught Apache cultural geography by native informants:

> For Indian men and women, the past lies embedded in features of the earth—in canyons and lakes, mountains and arroyos, rocks and vacant fields—which together endow their lands with multiple forms of significance that reach into their lives and shape the ways they think.[30]

To appreciate the epistemic and historical significance of western lands for Apaches, one would have to fill in a glaring omission in Cooper's list of genres of representation. Rather than "the pen, the pencil, and the graver," the western Apache's place worlds are collectively experienced through orality. The Apache naming of places is commemorative; it expresses significant episodes in tribal history. When the names are invoked in daily conversations, the landscape reemerges in commemorative symbolic enactments aimed at producing collective solidarity. Accordingly, Apaches practice a "history without authorities."[31] Their landscapes are place worlds that contain a "teeming history" of *their* past and are invisible to those who rely on built structures and on genres of writing. As Basso puts it, "[l]ong before the advent of literacy, to say nothing of 'history' as an academic discipline, places served humankind as durable symbols of distant events and as indispensable aids for remembering and imagining them—and this convenient arrangement, ancient but not outmoded, is with us still today."[32]

Cooper's scripted account of western landscape is therefore of a piece with the process through which the imposition of a European state model of social and political organization "overcoded"[33] the prior affiliations that were to become, cartographically speaking, a vanishing "Indian country." Shortly after Cooper's Eurocentric reading of a landscape (which he never visited), a team of surveyors and photographers accompanied Lieutenant George Wheeler on a survey of the American West. The team was part of the expansionist process through which the West was settled, "tamed," and effectively inscribed as the state recoded the territory, turning it into a white provenance and a resource that would aid in the process of industrialization.

The mapping process was, from the Native American point of view, an antagonistic cultural encounter "The act of mapping and naming was, in the eyes of the Indians, an act of trespass, not upon property but on religion, upon the sacred itself. The white man's maps threatened a whole way of life."[34]

This photograph (figure 1) by William Bell, one of the photographers accompanying Wheeler in his survey of the lands west of the 100th meridian, records an exemplary moment in the process of trespass. The view is named, and the act of inscription is represented within the view. A Euro American is

**Figure 1**   William Bell, *Grand Canyon of the Colorado River,* 1874.

seated in the foreground, writing on a tablet, exemplifying the possessive act: "The name lays claim to the view. By the same token, a photographic view attaches a possessable image to a place name"[34] Although the photographic practice of Wheeler's photographers, William Bell and Timothy O' Sullivan, was deemed to be a disinterested recording of scenes, the naming of the view, along with the representation of the writing process testifies eloquently to the dispossession of Native Americans from "Indian country." Of course, owing especially to the work and writings of Charles Mason and Jeremiah Dixon (creators of the famous Mason and Dixon line) in the eighteenth century, the use of the "survey" as a device that aided and abetted Euro America's imperial expansion had already become "assimilated into the discourse of landscape description."[35]

The surveys of Mason and Dixon transgressed the territorial and cultural boundaries of Native American nations in the East and Midwest, participating in an earlier episode of dispossession under the guise of the same disinterested science that animated the Wheeler western survey. Among the consequences of the historical trajectory of dispossession is the fractured and ambiguated "Indian country" Alexie describes. Certainly by the time the Lakota, Black Elk, wrote *his* commentary on what was left of the Indian country in 1930, he anticipated what Alexie was able to observe seventy years later. Black Elk's eloquent lament captures well the process through which the Indian country upon which Alexie reflected in his story had become so diminished: "They have made little islands for us ... and always, these islands are becoming smaller."[36] And, more recently, Native American writer Gerald Vizenor offers a equally eloquent lament, addressed to the consequences of the displacement of an oral by a written cultural practice:

> The sudden closures of the oral in favor of the scriptural are unheard, and the eternal sorrow of lost sounds haunts the remains of tribal stories in translation.[37]

### Landscape and Nationhood

The photographs taken during the Wheeler-led survey of the American West belong to an episode in the production of what W.C.T. Mitchell has called "imperial landscape," the pictorial and photographic representations through which European conquerors coded territories in a way that was congenial to their acts of possession/dispossession. In the U.S. those codes are increasingly contested, especially by the literary and artistic practices of Native Americans, which challenge the Euro American territorial imaginary and myth of a unitary national culture that became entrenched during its nation-building era. However, before treating the details of these artistic-political initiatives, I want to offer a cross-national comparative treatment of the role of landscape representations, which were as much involved in the consolidation of European nations as they were in their acts of external colonization.

In the English case, the relevant story begins in the sixteenth century. As Richard Helgerson points out, the genres implicated in the "Elizabethan writing of England," which were addressed to the issue of "who counts as a member of the nation,"[38] were as much outwardly focused on the peoples and places encountered during the voyages of exploration as they were on the domestic ethnoscape. Thus, for example, Richard Hakluyt's exemplary chronicle, *Prinicipll Navigations, Voiages, and Discoveries of the English Nation,* does not merely describe exotic otherness; it is implicated in inventing England as well as the world within which England is to be an agent:

> Hakluyt's task—the collective task of the various intersecting communities for which his name and his book stand as convenient markers—was thus not merely to record what the English had done and what the world was like . . . He also had to reinvent both England and the world to make them fit together."[39]

The invention of England subsequently proceeded in other genres, which manifested a similar effect: the invention of a collective nationhood while involved in elaborating an imperial imaginary. For example, the consolidation of what is now considered "English literature," instituted in British schools in the 1870s and "permeated by a rhetoric of national identity and moral purpose . . . ,"[40] occurred only after territorial expansion into unfamiliar cultural domains provoked reflection on England's cultural heritage and national past. In effect, in order to represent itself for purposes of imperial cultural governance, especially in India, a literary canon, which emphasized a "cultural heritage contained in the national past,"[41] was invented. As Gauri Visanathan puts it, "The Eurocentric literary curriculum of the nineteenth century was less a statement of the superiority of the Western tradition than a vital, active instrument of Western hegemony in concert with commercial expansion and military action."[42]

This "double movement," in which the invention of the non-English other was simultaneously an invention of the collective English self, was also enacted in the discourse on landscape in the eighteenth century. As Mitchell points out, while English landscape representations enlisted a view of nature to impose an English modernity abroad, it was also turning its own land into a "landscape" with a strong narrative element. In the view from England, landscape was perceived "as an inevitable, progressive development in history, an expansion of 'culture' and 'civilization' into a 'natural' space in a progress that is itself narrated as 'natural.' " But this imposition is "not confined to the external, foreign fields toward which the empire directs itself; it is typically accompanied by a renewed interest in the re-presentation of the home landscape." More specifically, the enclosure movement and its "accompanying dispossession of the English peasantry are an internal colonization of the home country," and it is simultaneously connected with a renewed interest in the landscape of the home or center.[43]

At a minimum, insight into the role of picturing the land in the European nation-building process requires a recognition of the interaction effects of the outward and inward gaze. In constituting themselves as nations, the European states were elaborating a world of landscapes and of included and excluded bodies, at home and abroad. Of late, some of the generations succeeding those excluded bodies, exemplified by contemporary Native American writers such as Sherman Alexie, Louise Erdrich, N. Scott Momaday, Leslie Silko, and James Welch, are reconfiguring landscapes to render themselves and their place-worlds visible. Before analyzing the implications of these efforts, however, I want to develop an elaborated perspective on the politics of the landscape-nationhood relationship by focusing on the complicit renderings of landscape that have aided and abetted a variety of nation-building projects.

### The European Scene

England is the state venue in which the role of landscape representations in elaborating national imaginaries has been most exhaustively investigated, for as Daniels has noted, the English landed estate [is] . . . the principal symbolic landscape . . . of national identity."[44] The symbolic, nation-building contribution of the English landscape painting tradition is prefigured in the evolution of European maps during the Renaissance, for "historically, the map precedes the landscape of property as national representation in Britain."[45] By the sixteenth century, official cartographers began to indicate a separation from the imprimaturs of emperors and monarchs. In England, specifically, cartographic representations had begun to diminish the space formerly assigned to "insignia of royal power," which had reflected identities based on "dynastic loyalty," and increasingly to emphasize markers of land configuration and national territory.[46] Landscape painters followed by emphasizing not merely land but proprietary holdings and, subsequently, the deployment of the bodies responsible for making those holdings valuable. And, while the "maps had attempted to comprehend and systematize many local knowledges within larger political and geographic orders, the landscapes that emerged in Britain drawing on Dutch and Italian example, limited what could be seen or imagined to the view of one person from one spot at one moment."[47] And landscape photography played a similar role, showing an England as "view, real estate, and locus of national identity."[48]

While landscape painters up through the early nineteenth century produced a political nation that privileged only well-to-do owners of landed estates, after 1832, some of them, particularly Turner, "offered middle-class consumers a way of possessing England (the land) and hence claiming membership in it (the nation)."[49] Struggle as well as possession is articulated on

Turner's canvases; his landscapes produce an England within which the terrain is contested—for example, his painted coastal scenes that depict the "activities of the lower classes" and thereby extend the political nation beyond the landed aristocracy.[50] Moreover, reception as well as production reflected contestation over the scope and character of the "political nation." For example, as Ann Bermingham points out, the tradition of painting enclosed estates with short vistas articulated with the idea of a politically privileged few. As a result, when landscape painters departed from this tradition by painting longer vistas, some critics associated the long vistas, which connected property with the rest of the landscape, as "equivalent to the levelling tendencies of democratic governments and revolutions."[51]

Nineteenth-century French landscape painting reflects a fundamental departure from the English case, primarily because of the way the genre addresses a fundamental difference in the French politics of nation building. As is evident in other genres—mapmaking and national theater and national opera initiatives especially—French landscape painting in the nineteenth century reflects a different mode of political legitimation from the English case. In contrast with nineteenth-century England's legacy of a limited political nation, reflected in the centrality of the landed estate, France had undergone a revolutionary change in the class basis of national legitimation. This change was in evidence in a shift in cartographic representations, which were aimed at displacing the spaces of aristocratic privilege with a uniform space in keeping with a republican ideal: "the uniform application of law and administration."[52] New national cartographic surveys repressed regional differences in order to depersonalize the formerly hierarchically-oriented social order.[53] In accord with the position of contemporary critical geographers that maps are ethico-political statements, the "redrawing of France's administrative boundaries in the late eighteenth century was a moral act inspired by and symbolizing the highest political ideals;" it reflected a state in the process of producing a modern politico-moral territoriality, one in which the "subordination of the bourgeoisie to the nobility and church" would be overturned.[54]

French cultural governance, aimed at fashioning a bourgeois republican national culture, proceeded on several fronts in the nineteenth century, for example, as I noted in chapter 3, the development of the government-controlled National Opera and National Theater. In particular, French grand opera, "a subtly used tool of state"[55] was, despite significant contention, oriented toward an emphasis on a new locus of sovereignty, "the voice of the 'people,'"[56] as it sought (in stark contrast with the case of the arts in England) to assimilate a proletarian constituency into the audience of national arts. Similarly, as I also noted (and also in contrast with the English case) by the mid nineteenth century, advocates of a national theater saw the *fêtes publiques* as a way to "invite the people into the nation."[57] French landscape, despite its wide variety of tendencies, was also subject to similar cultural governance initiatives. For example, a government arts policy in the 1860s "supported and privileged landscape painting" with purchases and distributions to museums. The initiative was "a clear expression of its wider aim—to cultivate an image of liberal pluralism and to appeal to the widest constituency of French citizens."[58]

Although in the English case there was not a comparable governmental initiative to link landscape painting to a nationalist project, in some respects the painters, whatever their ideological perspectives, produced scenes that articulated with governmental policy, or, more specifically, with the policies involved in the process of enclosure. Bermingham addresses the landscape painting-enclosure relationship, noting that after 1780, nature became reoriented, and articulated itself in a charged "relationship between the aesthetic of the painted landscape and the economics of the enclosed one."[59] Thus, for example, the rustic landscapes of Thomas Gainsborough, intended as celebrations of an imperiled country life, show a "shallow and fragmented landscape" that imposes a mode of perception that "profoundly accommodates the policy of enclosure."[60]

The rustic landscape tradition was displaced by subsequent trends, for example, a reactive one in which early nineteenth-century British landscape art displayed its distaste for the revolutionary events in France with "an appeal to nature's diversity and complex variety in order to legitimate and obscure its own political institutions and social hierarchies."[61] Nevertheless, the history of British landscape art, like other histories is "conjunctural" rather than linear.[62] The values and representational practices animating the rustic landscape tradition have persisted, and among the implications of this persistence is an invidious distinction between England and its Celtic fringe, particularly Ireland, which has been historically regarded as a wild, untamed landscape (and ethnoscape) in comparison with an orderly and civilized England. For much of the English aesthetic tradition, Ireland has shared the place of Britains colonial others, encouraging a reactive genre of landscape art, described by Daniels:

> The very regional reach of English imperialism, into alien lands, was accompanied by a countervailing sentiment for cosy home scenery, for thatched cottages and gardens in pastoral countryside. Inside Great Britain lurked Little England.[63]

Recall that (as noted in chapter 1) Michael Neill points out that Ireland has played a crucial role in the development of English nationhood, for Irish difference was "a prerequisite for the idea of an English National body politics in principle separable from the body of the monarch—the idea of the nation, that is, as a 'commonwealth; with an essential and permanent existence distinct from the King's estate and determined by something other than the dynastic accidents that fixed the boundaries of the feudal kingdoms . . ." And further "It was the Irish 'wilderness' that bounded the English garden, Irish 'barbarity' that defined English civility, Irish papistry and 'superstition' that warranted English religion; it was Irish 'lawlessness' that demonstrated the superiority of English law and Irish 'wandering' that defined the settled and centered nature of English society."[64]

Contemporary Irish artists are often energized by their awareness of Ireland's historical role as a disparaged other in the framing of the English national imaginary and the articulation of that role in aesthetic traditions. Here I want to call attention to one artistic reaction to what one commentator on a recent exhibition of Irish landscape art calls "a deeply implanted and widely projected sense of Ireland as a site of nature (God-given) rather than of culture (man-made)" because it supplies a transition to my primary political theme, the recovery of indigenous landscape perspectives that have been overcoded, with the aid of dominant landscape painting traditions, during the nineteenth- and early twentieth-century nation-building enterprises.[65] The work, executed by Caroline McCarthy, is entitled *Greetings!* Using two video monitors "with archetypal images of Irish landscape," into which the artists head occasionally intrudes (see figure 2), the images are intended, according to McCarthy, to show that "she has no purchase in this landscape of meaning" in which Ireland has been located as merely "a site of nature."[66]

The Irish exhibition is exceptional because in most European states, the encounter between nation-building initiatives and indigenous presence remains unrecorded in contemporary landscape art traditions. But before leaving the European scene for the former colonies, within which the encounter has been more evident, I want to touch on the case of Finland, where an indigenous presence has been shown to haunt the state's claim to control a territory that is coextensive with a unitary and coherent national culture. The Finnish case is especially pertinent because, "there is a remarkable consensus in Finland about which works of art best articulate Finnishness."[67] The images behind this consensus were produced by painters during "the golden age of Finnish Art," when the paintings of Albert Edelfelt, Akseli Gallen-Kallela, Eero Jarnefelt and Pekka Halonen turned Finnish land into landscape at the turn of the nineteenth century.

The significance of Finland as panoramic (and largely empty) landscape, viewed from a high vantage point, articulated in the major landscape painting collection at the Finnish National Gallery,[68] has been a more or less continuous thematic in the Finland's cultural governance ever since. In the mid nineteenth century, the influential Finnish writer/poet Zacharias Topelius edited a landscape album entitled *Finland Portrayed in Drawings,*

**Figure 2**   Caroline McCarthy, *Greetings,* 1996, Irish Museum of Modern Art, Dublin.

and wrote about the importance of northern paintings along with prescriptions for artists about how to represent Finland. Thereafter, through the nineteenth century, there were public education campaigns to encourage illustrations of "the programmatic construction of Finnishness." And in recent years, the Finnish state has continued to encourage the identification of the nation with the landscape. In 1993, the ministry of the environment disseminated national images in a published a survey entitled *kansallismaisema* (National Landscape)."[69]

Yet despite the seeming consensus, conveyed in the dominant landscape painting tradition of Finland as a "European cultural landscape and the unconquered, peripheral wilderness,"[70] the existence of the indigenous *Sami*

**Figure 3**    Jorma Puranen from the series *Imaginary Homecoming,* Untitled, 1994.

(Lapp) people disrupts this national imaginary. Jorma Puranen's photo-graphic montage (figure 3), in which *Sami* portraits are embedded in a landscape that has been mined, records this disruption. As Tutta Palin puts it, "by this simple method, an excerpt from nature is turned into an im-age of the colonising practices of Western culture." The image is especially powerful when one recognizes that "not one member of the Sami people can be found in the 'typically Finnish' folk depictions by the masters of the Golden Age of Finnish Art [because] in the bourgeois culture of the turn of the century, the Sami were invisible, except in illustrations to ethnographic studies and exotic travel journals written by foreigners."[71]

## Landscape and Distant Colonization

Turning now to the complicity of landscape painting with colonizing out-side of Europe, the Australian case provides a telling juxtaposition to that of Finland, because a significantly more influential, explicitly expressed in-digenous cultural politics has had a marked effect on the development of the Australian national imaginary. What is a mere haunting in the Finnish case is a seemingly continuous and often acknowledged ambivalence in the Australian. A treatment of the landscape-nationhood relationship in Australia requires us to revisit the problematic that Mitchell calls "imperial landscape." And Paul Carter's gloss on the European-Aboriginal encounter provides an apt context for the significance of landscape painter's symbolic role in aiding the production of Australia's Euro-oriented nationhood.

Carter's main focus is on language and, more specifically, on the discourses through which the "explorers" and subsequently the settlers transformed space into place, i.e., into spaces marked with their own cultural narratives. In general, as he notes, "the landscape emerges as an object of interest in so far as it exhibits a narrative interest.[72] The explorer's and settler's linguistic acts, especially the acts of naming, were part of a process of making an alien land into an intelligible landscape. Indeed, for some of the initial European explorers, for example, Joseph Banks's (the botanist accompanying Captain Cook on his voyages) acts of naming more or less exhausted the issue of knowing as it was initially framed.[73] But the subsequent, elaborated process through which Europeans sought to "know" Australia cannot be separated from the ultimate project of settling and then dominating what was to be meant by Australia. The initial acts of naming were meant to "inaugurate a form of possession that would render the dynamic of [the explorers] journeys invisible."[74] Thereafter, the agenda was one of possession, an intention, at the symbolic level, to make what was observed as formless and challenging to their modes of signifying space, intelligible. It was, in Carter's terms, an attempt "to enclose the mirage in a net of associations, to neutralize the otherness.... The euphonious but untranslatable names with which the Aborigines inhabited the landscape could have no epistemological place: they were not typical, obeyed no known rules, conveyed no useful facts."[75] But, although "exploration civilized the country by translating it into English," it was "language replete with misconceptions, repetitions: it was language in a primitive state of development;"[76] For white Australia, the territory remained partly enigmatic and difficult to incorporate comfortably into their nationhood conceits because of the ambiguous ways that indigenousness marked the landscape and ethnoscape of the emerging nation-state.

The linguistic ambiguities and ambivalences afflicting the European process of symbolic possession in Australia is markedly reflected in the history of their landscape painting. As Christopher Allen points out, Australian art developed in a specific context, the "construction of a new land" in the face of "the ambivalent background of the Aboriginal presence."[77] During the period of exploration, images were primarily "topological views of coastlines made as aids to navigation."[78] But after the fixation on the coastline and the inauguration of the period of settlement, landscape painters participated in the process of a nation-oriented domestication, a "nationalization of nature" with "colonial security" as the frame "from which the new land may be safely enjoyed."[79] The major genre was a version familiar in England, a picturesque landscape focusing primarily on domestic life, for example, John Glover's *A View of the Artist's House and Garden* (1835).

However, as the settler's gaze turned increasingly toward the territory's interior, the Aboriginal presence was largely discounted, in both commentaries and landscape paintings, as the Australian interior was described and depicted "as a barren wilderness or a desolate waste..." that contained qualities that were seemingly "resistant to familiarization."[80] Insofar as Aborigines appear in landscape paintings, they are depicted as part of a troubling mood, seeming to "mark some kind of malaise." The paintings show them at ease but deprive them of a proprietary purchase on the land. The paintings seem to say that "they live and survive in a difficult environment with apparent ease; and yet they do not actually 'occupy' the land in any way recognized as permanent by the European mind."[81]

Although as Australian landscape has ultimately displayed diverse attempts to have nature warrant Euro-Australian possession, one of the main landscape painting genres was produced by the group known as the Heidelberg School. Their main emphasis, on an "emotional range from the heroism of labour to the lyricism of landscape," is exemplary of the role of painting in the process of discounting Aboriginal cultural coherence and of territorially dispossessing Aboriginal peoples. Despite the wide range of emotional tone in their paintings, the narrative animating the Heidelberg School's symbolic construction of the new Australia was the founding of a "moral legitimacy" *vis á vis* Aborigines.[82] For example, one prominent focus is on the depiction of [white] "useful labor"—for example, Tom Robert's *Woodsplitters* (1886), and his *Shearing the Rams* (1890). As Allen notes, "the Aboriginal people virtually never appear in Heidelberg art" and it is not merely a matter of a racist nationalism he suggests. Rather, the "ideology of work" which the paintings convey perpetuates "the legitimacy of the settler's occupation" and "displace[s] ... concerns about Aboriginal familiarity with the land. Aborigines are at home in the sublime, but strangers to the world of work, as it is conceived by the settler."[83]

In response to their nonpresence, imposed in Euro Australian landscape traditions, there is a strong public art tradition in which Aborigines themselves turn land into landscape in ways that reassert their presence and challenge Euro Australian symbolic acts of dispossession. For example, the *Aboriginal Memorial,* a set of ritual poles that induces the observer to see a "'forest' of treelike forms" and induces "a pictorial sense of landscape,"[84] calls attention to a different Australia. Made by twenty Aboriginal men from the remote vicinity of Ramingining in Australia's Northern Territory,

**Figure 4**    Tom Roberts, *Shearing of the Rams,* 1890, National Gallery of Victoria, Melborne.

the memorial is intended as a survival statement of a culture that has been threatened by "the drive to white national unity" and as an assertion of the "presence of those peoples who will not fit into an imposed, colonial, fabricated nationality."[85]

Although there are numerous other relevant Aboriginal works, I want here to offer a brief example of a European artist's challenge to the trajectory of Euro Australia's painterly acts of possession, in which they make the nature testify to the legitimacy of their settlement. The English landscape painter, Michael Andrews (1928–1995), whose early work was produced in the U.K., traveled to Australia in 1983 and "fulfilled a longstanding ambition to visit Ayers Rock (know as Uluru to the Aborigines in central Australia).[86] Producing a series of paintings of the rock and its surrounding areas, Andrews saw his paintings as attempts at recovering the spiritual significance of the land in general and the rock in particular for Aborigines. One of his paintings, *Laughter Uluru (Ayers Rock)/The Cathedral* (1985), (figure 5) enacts a cultural translation as well as a recovery of the Aboriginal spiritual habitus and thereby issues a challenge to the Euro Australian landscape painting tradition. Recalling some lines from a Christian hymn, "Rock of Ages, cleft for me. Let me hide myself in thee," Andrews's version of the rock, with a large smiling mouth-like cleft, spiritualizes the landscape from

**Figure 5**   Michael Andrews, *Laughter Uluru (Ayers Rock), The Cathedral,* 1985, Tate Gallery, London/Art Resource, NY.

the points of view of both cultures. He also articulates the two cultural practices materially as well as symbolically:

> While at the Rock he gathered grasses and plants which he later used as stencils when applying spray paint. He also mixed soil taken from the site with paint . . .[87]

Unlike, for example, the influential Heidelberg landscape artists, who symbolically asserted the values of a monocultural nation within which indigenous people would have no qualified presence, Andrews creates a landscape that accords recognition to its Aboriginal connection; he depicts a land that speaks of Aboriginal sensibilities, while at the same time producing an uneasy synthesis, symbolically and materially, of Euro and Aboriginal spirituality.

Like the Australian case, the landscape traditions of European settlers in Canada speak to a national imaginary that is rendered ambiguous and ambivalent by the existence of indigenous peoples or, as they increasingly regard themselves in North America, "first nations." The Canadian case has significant resonances with the Australian because until well into the nineteenth century, Euro Canadians saw much of their territory as untamed wilderness: "The Canadian terrain was generally considered a vast, hostile, dimly seen, unpoetic mass" until "the celebration of untamed nature" began in literature and the arts from the middle nineteenth through the first half of the twentieth century.[88] Moreover, as was the case in Australia, landscape art was influenced more by conventions of European landscape painting than by a willingness to be influenced and edified by an unfamiliar territory. The European conventions that migrated into representations of Canadian territories "framed [the painter's] vision of the new environment he encountered rather than the environment which challenged that vision." Ignoring the art of indigenous peoples, which contained "a sophisticated statement of an integral relationship with their spiritual and material worlds," Euro Canadian painters juxtaposed "the disorderliness of the 'wilderness'" and "the cultivated and geometrical order of the domesticated world."[89]

By the early twentieth century, Canada's North had become a primary object of Canadian cultural nationalism, and the most familiar imagery associated with the nationalization of Canadian nature-as-the-North was produced by a group of Ontario artists known as the Group of Seven, whose "North" was largely "primordial" and "unpeopled."[90] Explicitly dedicated to Euro Canadian nation building, these artists declared (in the brochure of their 1921 exhibition) that theirs was an art that "sincerely interprets the spirit of a nation's growth."[91] Their contribution to this "spirit" has been pervasive. For example, the group's influence on the Canadian national imaginary was affirmed in 1958 during the successful election campaign of Prime Minister John Diefenbaker, who declared, "I see a new Canada . . . a Canada of the North."[92]

Diefenbaker's landscape imaginary, a pure unpeopled North, has been subjected to a number of significant challenges. Although details in the group's landscapes can be shown to have undermined a simplistic nationalist reading of North (for example, the ways in which some paintings call attention to the elements of their construction),[93] rather than offer a reading of group's paintings, I will focus on two of the challenges, both of which make use of photomontage techniques and explicitly evoke the influence of the group's version of the landscape.

One challenge comes from an indigenous artist. Because, in the early 1980s, the National Gallery of Canada faced criticism "for its failure to recognize native art in fulfilling its mandate to build collections of national and artistic importance,"[94] it acquired Carl Beam's *The North American Iceberg* (1985), (figure 6) which, given that it is a photomontage of an ethnoscape rather than a landscape, is an ironic commentary on the depopulating of

**Figure 6**   Carl Beam *North American Iceberg,* 1985, National Gallery of Canada, Ottawa.

the North in traditional Euro Canadian landscape painting. And because the photos include historical as well as contemporary figures (Geronimo, Anwar Sadat, and contemporary Inuit and Indian figures), the work challenges the temporality as well as the dominant spatial imaginary of Euro Canadian nationhood. As one commentary puts it:

> The cosmopolitan range of images in Beam's painting suggests a kind of human or cultural landscape, rather than a natural one, a landscape in which the conventional framework of space and time collapses as images from the past and present, near and far, are juxtaposed.[95]

Beam's juxtapositions challenge the contemporary, historically invested Canadian national imaginary by bringing together nineteenth-century Indians in a work with a rocket launch, which implies that the current, violence-aiding technologies of conquest are a legacy from the violence of the Euro Canadian founding. Taken as a whole, the work, with its emphasis on the institutionalized forgetfulness or blindness to the presence of other peoples, is a critique of the Canada whose image the Group of Seven helped to produce.

A similarly ironic work, which also challenges the Group of Seven's Canadian imaginary by inserting bodies into a landscape usually figured as barren, is Jin-me Yoon's *A Group of Sixty-Seven* (1986), which is titled in a way that explicitly evokes the legacy of the Group of Seven. While Beam's photomontage exposes "the obfuscation of the history of Canadian nation building and the resultant oppression of the native peoples,"[96] Yoon's challenges the contemporary conceit that Canada is a more or less monocultural nation. Like Beam, Yoon repopulates the land. Hers is also an ethnoscape, showing, in this case, Korean immigrants whose presence cannot be recovered as long as the dominant image of Canadian nationhood is the empty northern landscapes of the Group of Seven.

Speaking of her work, which "examines the production of 'minoritized' identities through the construction of signs of nationalist identity," Yoon is explicit about the critical challenge her photographic insertion of immigrant bodies (her's among others) into a northern landscape poses to the dominant image of Canadian nationhood: "I am interested in appropriating the genre of landscape photography to question the constructed 'nature' of Canadian identity. Imaged in the heroic setting of the Canadian Rockies, can I as a non-western woman enjoy a 'naturalized relationship to this landscape?"[97] As Erin Manning puts it, Yoon's *Group of Sixty-Seven* "interrupts the unitary and naturalized narrative of Canadian nationalism [focusing on] two icons [produced by Group of Seven artists] of Canadian art, *Maligne Lake, Jasper Park (* Lawren Harris, 1924), and *Old Time Coast Village* (Emily Carr, c. 1929–1930)." The critique is effected, she adds, through the "subversion of modes of representation foregrounded in these early works, where the landscape is associated with an unproblematized emptiness."[98]

### America as the West

While it was images of a vast and empty North that helped legitimate the Euro Canadian nation-building project, it was the emptiness of "the West" that played this role in the U.S. case. As in Canada, much of the dominant landscape painting tradition in the U.S. has obscured the nation-killing or peoples-destroying aspects of nation building.[99] Certainly, "the West of the imagination" had included a fabled ethnoscape well before President Thomas Jefferson purchased the area west of the Mississippi and sent his secretary, Meriwether Lewis, out to demystify the vast territory. French naturalists, with whom Jefferson was familiar, had already symbolically peopled the area with "inferior savages."[100] And the fable persisted despite the recalcitrant information that centuries of contact supplied. For example, Alexis de Tocqueville and Gustavo de Beaumont, while on their celebrated tour of America, selected an inland travel itinerary with the express purpose of glimpsing the "wilderness" and its wild denizens: "They were determined not to miss savages in a purely savage setting"[101]

As the nineteenth century progressed, and contact increasingly demystified, for many, the western landscape and ethnoscape, the landscape painting traditions accorded America's First Nations a minor role in the territories. But they were not present in an economically or politically qualified way. Tocqueville's remark about their presence echoes the dominant Euro American view:

> One could still properly call North America an empty continent, a deserted land waiting for inhabitants.[102]

Vastness and virtual emptiness (of a significant indigenous habitus) certainly dominates much of the landscape painting from the time that Tocqueville issued his observation until well into the twentieth century. The tendency in the paintings initially narrating the Euro American territorial and cultural expansion was to offer what Albert Boime calls a "magisterial gaze," which foregrounds a prospect from which Euro Americans can look from within their cultivated and organized spaces of domesticity toward a future in which they will organize and domesticate the vastness of the untamed West.[103] Exemplary of the earlier versions are the works comprising Thomas Cole's *The Course of Empire!*. Typical of Cole's composition is his *River in the Catskills* (1843), in which a young farmer is a stand-in for the spectator. He is looking across a wide vista below him, and:

> The foreground is strewn with thickets and a storm-blasted trees symbolizing the undomesticated landscape that the farmer prepares to clear. . . . The line of vision extends into the remote distance where smoke arises from scarcely seen manufactories on the horizon. Cole's picture tells us that the future lies over the horizon.[104]

Although the compositional structure violates the traditional east to west narrative associated with national expansion (the farmer should be looking in the opposite direction rather than back), as Boime suggests, "Cole's reversal is a metaphorical mirror of the pioneer's vision of the future prospects awaiting him."[105] What of the indigenous nations who are unprepared for this future? Native Americans in the paintings of the period are cast in the role of helplessly awed observers of a process running past them, for example, in DeWitt Clinton Boutelle's *The Indian Hunter* (1843), and *Indian Surveying the Landscape* (1855), in which "a cigar-store Indian" is the "imagined spectator . . . identified totally with the landscape that is all but conquered."[106]

Where are the African American's in nineteenth-century landscape art? The widely circulated *Harper's Monthly* magazine devoted some attention to plantation life and very little to slave immiseration (the engraving in the April 1899 issue, *Contrabands in the Swamps*, is an exception). While, as noted, Native Americans were often found in nineteenth-century landscape illustrations of the West, African Americans achieved much less visibility in the visual media constructing landscapes.[107] In the post-emancipation period, as former slaves traveled westward, "[v]isual space opened only gradually for black Americans."[108] When they did appear, it was in a "visual grammar" that had been the primary ideological legitimation for the Euro American movement westward. The paintings and illustrations integrated African Americans into "the national narrative of manifest destiny" (for example, in an illustration in the August 1866 edition of *Harper's Monthly* in which they are shown cutting a canal).[109] And rather than being incorporated into a story of mobility, as were Euro Americans, African Americans, particularly in the *Harper's Monthly* illustrations, were shown assembled in domestic tableux (for example, in *Harper's Monthly's* June 1876 illustration, *In Ole Virginny,* (figure 7) in which a large, extended family is shown clustered around their cabin).[110]

Once the westward expansion accelerated in the post Civil War period, the vistas to which landscape painters addressed themselves became both the official and commercial versions of America's West. For example, Emmanuel

**Figure 7**   *In Ole Virginny,* June 1876, *Harper's New Monthly Magazine.* Published in John Easten Cooke, "Virginia in the Revolution."

Leutze's thirty-foot mural, *Across the Continent, Westward the Course of Empire Takes Its Way,* was placed in the U.S. Capitol, and many similar landscape versions of the West were marketed by Currier and Ives to promote travel. In general, the paintings "turn[ed] their sights toward expansionist subjects . . . they quickly jumped the Mississippi" (or they returned to scenes of origin to suggest that the settling of the West was continuous with the historically authorized acts of original continental settlement).[111] Some, like Albert Bierstadt were producing a West cast as a "new Eden, announcing its scenic wonders and publicizing its staggering resources,"[112] while others were more focused on the dynamic of expansion and the replacement of a sparsely populated, 'natural' world with a bustling commercial one, for example, Fanny Frances Palmer's *Across the Continent: "Westward the Course of Empire Takes Its Way,"* (1868), published and widely distributed by Currier and Ives.

Like the painters Cole, Boutelle, and others of the Hudson School, whose works were images east of the Mississippi and looked toward a territorially and culturally enlarged Euro American future, the landscape painters imaging the far west continued with the project of "representing the expansionist process" in works that "offer a transparent view of what was then construed as a national purpose."[113] At a minimum, the West created by nineteenth-century landscape painters served as a dominant set of images of Euro American nationhood, ignoring a growing set of African American settlements and aiding and abetting the process of diminishing the significance of Native Americans, who, after the Marshall Court decisions in the1830s, had been officially transformed from recognized nations subject to "foreign policy" to domestically dependent peoples.[114]

Although the Native Americans in Palmer's landscape are dwarfed by the large panorama of a painting that is focused on Euro American nation building rather than on the indigenous provenances of the West, other Euro American landscape painters accorded the Indian nations more space and treated their war making, hunting practices, and living arrangements—for example, the romantically oriented canvases of Asher B. Durand, George Catlin, Karl Bodmer, and Thomas Moran in the nineteenth century and Frederick Remington in the twentieth. Nevertheless, although landscape painters addressed themselves in diverse ways to "the Indian problem," they all painted the Indian obituary in one way or another. On the one hand, for example, there is John Mix Stanley's *Last of Their Race* (1857), showing a small, forlorn-looking cluster of six Native Americans, appearing to be pushed to the shores of the Pacific, and, on the other, there are "a series of paintings representing acculturation themes," implying a peaceful assimilation into Euro American society.[115] Certainly, the dominant trajectory of Euro American landscape painting supports a story of cultural imperialism, a pictorial celebration of the appropriation of Indian lands.

Nevertheless, the obituaries, written and depicted in various ways by those who treated Indian subjects, are misleading. As Sherman Alexie's story implies, "Indian country," however ambiguous its locations, persists. Its persistence has in recent decades been attested to in the artistic contributions of Native Americans, in their ceremonies, poetry, fiction, paintings, and public installations.

### The Return of Indian Country

Although I have emphasized the ways in the Euro American landscape traditions producing the West, like much of the Euro American literary tradition, engaged in a symbolic overcoding of Native American relationships to their territories, I have also noted that Native American cultural geography remains active and, as was the case during the initial encounters, continues to participate in the conversation on American nationhood. As Frederick Remington's landscape, *The Interpreter Waved at the Youth* (1905) (figure 8) implies, the West-as-America emerged through a process of encounter and translation.[116]

There is certainly much to support Larzer Ziff's claim that Euro American literary genres were part of a "literary annihilation," of Indianness even though some of the writers, for example, Thomas Jefferson and Timothy Dwight, thought they were preserving it.[117] Some white textual versions of

**Figure 8**   Frederic Remington, *The Interpreter Waved at the Youth,* 1905, The Art Institute of Chicago.

Indian practices to which Ziff refers make his case, for example, Nicholas Biddle's version of the Mandan Buffalo Dance, parts of which are rendered in Latin and so distant from a "corporeal presence," that they effectively bury what they represent.[118] But others, for example, John Cremony's *Life Among the Apaches*, written later in the century, offers a West that his Apache informants helped him describe. Although Cremony, a U.S. army major assigned to a troop protecting a mining operation, wrote in English and in some respects never abandoned a Eurocentric version of Native American cultures as "savage" and ineligible to participate in a bicultural nation-building project, many of his observations are respectful of and edified by Apache forms of knowing. He ultimately learned Apache language and put it to use in his accounts of the land and of white-Indian encounters.[119]

Cremony's collaboration with Apaches represents a very small part of more general aspect of the making of the expanded American landscape. Native Americans have contributed significantly to diverse versions of what constitutes American nationhood. Despite episodes of "literary annihilation" or the dominance of a white monologue, which Ziff argues was resisted only in recent decades, "when Indian writers began representing their own culture,"[120] there was significant Native American literary participation in shaping the meaning of American nationhood in the nineteenth century. Analyzing the writings of William Apess, Black Hawk, George Copway, John Rollin Ridge, and Sarah Winnemucca, Cheryl Walker argues that not only was "America" an encounter of alternative nationhoods (for Native Americans had not understood nations as the Euros had come to define them"[121]), but also that America emerged as a political entity as a result of significant Native American participation in discussions of national identity.[122]

Certainly, since the initial encounters, in both white and Indian accounts, Native Americans have had an ambivalent place in the nation-state. During the period of intense contact, occasioned by the Euro American expansion, from the white perspective, "the unavoidable confrontation with the Indian problem frustrated attempts to create a unified, consistent idea of the nation."[123] In the case of Native American writing, the ambivalence registered itself in the way that Euro and Indian cultural presumptions are inter-articulated. As Walker's investigation shows, while mirroring "the prevailing image of America . . . some Native American writers, in the process of becoming literate, took to mimicking the discourse of the whites," while some wrote prose that was more fugitive or "mobile," emphasizing difference.[124]

Although there is much more to be contributed by attention to the centuries of Euro and Native American negotiations and translations involved in shaping and contesting versions of American nationhood, my focus in this last section is a return to the interventions constituted by contemporary

Native American literary and pictorial landscapes, which I initiated in my discussion of Sherman Alexie's version of "Indian country." To provide a political context for this return, I want to point to a particular aspect of the land that has been the ancestral home of part of the Navajo nation for centuries, an area that includes "Monument Valley," where John Ford filmed nine of his westerns and, in the process, created one of the most familiar images of "the West" (for example, it is still a primary location for the Philip Morris company's depiction of "Marlboro Country"). There, as well as in the lands of other Native American nations, since the 1940s, right after World War II, and for many years thereafter, the Manhattan Project and its successors mined uranium and tested nuclear weapons. In the case of the nuclearization near Los Alamos, in the area of the Laguna Pueblo reservation in New Mexico, the mining and testing had the effect of bringing, "even this remote patch of land into the pattern of nuclear holocaust."[125]

Although the "holocaust" expression may seem extravagant, evidence of the catastrophic effect of nuclearization on Native Americans abounds. For example, in January 2000, the Environmental Protection Agency (EPA) conducted tests on the radiation level from the closed uranium mines in Monument Valley (stretching from Utah to Arizona). The test results, which showed that the Navajos in the valley are exposed to more than 100 times the level considered safe, were released to the Navajo residents nine months later only after one of them, Elsie Begay, made a formal request for the results under the Freedom of Information Act.[126] Because the nuclearization of their lands has created the occasion for both literary and pictorial reactions that offer Native American accounts of their place in a landscape of danger, it provides a context for treating significant versions of the reassertion of an Indian country largely unrecorded in Euro American discourses. To engage this context, I turn first to Leslie Marmon Silko's novel *Ceremony*, the primary venue of which is a radiation-polluted landscape in the Laguna Pueblo territory and whose major character, Tayo, is, like the central character in Remington's *The Interpreter waved at the Youth*, is a "half-breed" and thus also a representative of an intercultural encounter.[127]

Silko's *Ceremony* provides, both thematically and formally, a counter text to Euro American versions of the western landscapes and ethnoscapes. The novel is about a purifying ceremony that turns its main character, Tayo, from a hallucinating and estranged "half breed," World War II veteran into a redemptive figure whose recovery has collective significance for his Native American people, as his "Indian" half takes over his personality and is finally acknowledged by the aunt who raised him.[128] At the same time, Silko's writing enacts a ceremony. In addition to being the author of the novel, she becomes a personage within it, a "thought-woman" (*Ts'itstsi'nato*), who is introduced as a storyteller in an epic poem with which the novel begins.

The storyteller is no mere narrator; she, like the shaman, Betonie, who heals Tayo in the novel, is one whose storytelling serves as a purifying ceremony, a role made evident in two more long poems within the novel.

Thematically, Tayo, who is half Laguna and half white (his father was white and his Laguna mother was a prostitute, who left Tayo with her sister when he was four), returns home from his service in the Pacific, where he fought against the Japanese in World War II. He returns to a territory undergoing a drought, which imperils the livelihoods of the cattle-raising Native Americans in his old community. Stressed, fatigued, and prey to hallucinations, Tayo often cannot distinguish his own people from the Japanese he fought against during the war. His hallucinations serve two functions; they initiate the primary narrative by necessitating his healing relationship with Betonie, the shaman, and they serve as a powerful political allegory, creating a victim homology between the Japanese and Native Americans, both of whom have suffered from the U.S. nuclear project.

Ultimately, the cure for Tayo's radical alienation is his reentry into the Native American cultural geography, a regaining of an intimacy with the landscape. Again, the form of the story parallels its theme. Silko's prose constitutes a Native American literary geography; it enacts its theme in several places. For example, her description of a lovemaking scene creates a parallel between male-female intimacy and person-land intimacy. When Tayo and the woman of Tse-pi'na make love, Tayo's experience of it is described as follows: "He eased himself deeper within her and felt the warmth close around him like river sand, soft giving way under foot, then closing firmly around the ankle in cloudy warm water."[129] And while the land is described as a living companion for Native Americans, for the white world it is merely a series of exploitable objects. As the shaman explains to Tayo, "They see no life when they look, they only see objects . . ."[130]

While Tayo's story asserts the significance that traditional ceremonies have for recovering the Native American landscape, as he regains an intimacy with the land, it is also a vehicle for noting how Native Americans were victimized by the reach of the atomic age into their territory. As is noted in the novel:

> Trinity site, where they exploded the first atomic bomb, was only three hundred miles to the southeast, at White Sands. And the top-secret laboratories where the bomb had been created were deep in the Jemez mountains, on land the Government took from Cochiti Pueblo.[131]

Tayo's cure involves a recognition of the consequences of the nuclearization of his tribal lands. Significantly, it is at an abandoned uranium mineshaft where he completes his personal ceremony and at the same time sees the destructive results of the mining and testing of nuclear weapons on Indian lands. Even as she has Tayo contemplating the destructiveness of uranium mining, Silko brings the poisoned landscape to life, giving it a Native American cultural significance by having Tayo perceive the way that life and death are intertwined in a piece of uranium ore, "a gray stone streaked with powdery yellow uranium, bright and alive as pollen."[132]

The simultaneous political and cultural connections between Native Americans and their exploited and endangered lands made in Silko's novel have also been made by Native American painters. Just as Silko's novel, written in English, can be construed as part of a "minor literature" that uses but reinflects the dominant language and thereby subverts the dominant practices of intelligibility articulated in "major literatures," contemporary Native American painters have appropriated and transformed European painting genres to subvert the traditional representations of their peoples and lands.[133] Noteworthy in this respect is Joe H. Herrera's "Pueblo Modernism," influenced by pop expressionism and adapted to Native American themes, for example, biomorphic figures associated with "nature and landscape, and thus, Pueblo ritual life."[134] Equally important and influential among Native American artists is Fritz Scholder's pop art style, for example, his *Indian with Beer Can* (1969), and *Indian Wrapped in Flag* (1976), which show Native Americans in passive positions (the nonspeaking but spoken-about Indian), which Scholder treats ironically. His paintings are a critique of the traditional making of Indian identity, the articulation of "romantic cliches" in the landscape paintings of the famous Taos School.[135]

Although there are abundant, additional relevant examples, I want to call particular attention to the work of the Kiowa/Caddo painter, T.C. Cannon, because some of his paintings treat the same nuclear polluted "Indian country" that is the venue for Silko's novel. Drawing, like Scholder, on the pop art/expressionist genre, Cannon's images are not only ironic commentaries on the tradition of representation but are also explicitly politically thematized. Like Silko's Tayo, Cannon, a Vietnam veteran (who died at age thirty-two in an auto accident), manifests bicultural attachments. He served alongside Euro Americans in a war but returned as a critic of the continuing oppression of Native Americans. His ambiguous location between cultures is powerfully depicted in a photo self-portrait in which he is flanked by pictures of Sitting Bull and Bob Dylan. And one of his paintings is a commentary on the split self; his *Soldiers* is a figure split down the middle, with a white cavalry officer left half and an Indian warrior right half.

But Cannon's main artistic focus is political rather than merely autobiographical. His most significant political art is a statement about the overcoding and destruction of Native American lands. Thus, his *Village with Bomb* (figure 9) simultaneously offers a critique of the stoic, nonspeaking Indian (objectified as the noble savage unsuited to modernity) and, like Silko's *Ceremony*, marks the impact of the nuclearism of the cold war on

**Figure 9** T.C. Cannon, *Summer Sun (Village With Bomb)*, 1972. Used with permission of Joyce Cannon Yi.

Native Americans and their lands. In addition to being a commentary on how nuclearism has constituted a recent chapter in the white oppression of Native Americans, Cannon's *Village with Bomb* is a powerful affront to the romantic expansion narrative produced by the dominant Euro American landscape traditions.

## Conclusion: Toward a Renewed Co-Invention

The historical trajectory of landscape painting I have offered is not a simple, historicist rendering of an aesthetic practice. Rather, I have emphasized historicity, situating different moments in landscape production historically in order to show how the visual culture of landscape production has been tied to the more general political projects with which they are associated. Hence, I have located European landscape genres within a nation-building project, within attempts at inventing and elaborating a homogenous national culture. At the same time, I have attempted to expose the dark side of those projects, the inattentiveness to the voices of indigenous nations, whose systems of intelligibility were not regarded as significant.

In a relevant and poignant autobiographical passage, Emmanuel Levinas treats this aspect of oppression, as he reports on his experience as one of a group of Jewish prisoners of war in Nazi Germany, a group regarded as "subhuman, a gang of apes":

> A small inner murmur, the strength and wretchedness of persecuted people, reminded us of our essence as thinking creatures, but we were no longer a part of the world. Our comings and goings, our sorrow and laughter, illnesses and distractions . . . all that passed in parenthesis. We were beings entrapped in our species; despite all their vocabulary, beings without language.[136]

Accordingly, I have selected landscape productions that constitute moments of resistance, episodes in which those who have been silenced by European nation builders have reacted and rearticulated their voluble presence. Indigenous nations have persisted in reminding the European conquerors that they are not creatures without language. And, of late, their literary and figurative landscapes have constituted a counter-narrative to the European nation-building and sustaining projects.

As Anne Farrar Hyde has pointed out, during the Euro Americans' initial encounters with the far western lands, their vocabularies proved inadequate. Before the symbolic acts of appropriation that resulted in their discourses on landscape and their formal framings and thematics in paintings and photographs, they were forthright in claiming that for them the territory was enigmatic. Historian Francis Parkman "saw nothing he could describe in European terms," and essayist and travel writer Bayard Taylor referred to the land's "indescribability."[137] As is well known, lacking an intimacy with Native American cultural geography, and therefore having no knowledge of the historical depth that western places have had for first nations, Euro American writers and artists resorted to either views that made the West alternatively barren or picturesque or narrative panoramas that made it part of a Euro American social, economic, and political future.

Yet, as I noted, Native Americans constituted a significant locus of enunciation in the conversations shaping the American nation in the nineteenth century. Although throughout most of the twentieth century, the importance of Native America's contributions to American nationhood has been neglected in mainstream, white-dominated literary and visual cultures, a contemporary renaissance of Native American scholarship and artistic production promises to restore a now complex and scattered "Indian country." Native Americans are making it increasingly evident that there is a continuing need to restore the frontier, understood as "a territory or zone of interpenetration" rather than simply the boundary of Euro America.[138] Only by paying heed to Native American perspectives, by allowing them a role in retranslating the meaning of the historical trajectory of the Native American life worlds, can they become effectively part of the political nation.

Accordingly, there is an episode with which I want to conclude because it involves a bicultural retranslation of some of the earliest known Native American landscape paintings in the American Southwest. In the early nineteenth century, French trappers and travelers collected Native American buffalo robes upon which Native American artists had painted landscapes, often in the form of narratives. The robes, which were originally both coats and works of art, are now displayed in various European museums, most notably a large collection in *Musée de l'Homme* in Paris. Sitting there for more than a century, the Paris collection had not until recently had the benefit of Native American interpretation. In 1990, a group of Native American scholars, connected with the Smithsonian's National Museum of the American Indian, traveled to Paris to begin a dialogue with French art historians, and ultimately to produce a volume, *Robes of Splendor*. The volume contains images of and commentaries on painted buffalo robes by Native American and French scholars, who collaborated to interpret these "examples of the nineteenth-century American Indian cultural patrimony."[139] The buffalo hides were not merely food casings and articles of clothing. For the Southwestern Native American nations, "the buffalo is the surveyor of the Native American's territory, just as the eagle or the nighthawk, geometrician of the sky, gauges the space from up above."[140] As a result, the cultural meanings of the frame add significantly to the imagery in the paintings.

Because the robes served as both articles of clothing and as narrative canvases upon which the artists described their world (see figure 10), the integration of the robes into Native American everyday life adds to their meanings. Moreover, unlike European landscape paintings, whose boundaries are constituted by a simple rectangular frame, the meaning of the painted images on buffalo robes benefit from the frame's varied contours: "On these painted hides, space is first defined by the very shape of the skin, its geometry. The neck and the tail mark the high and the low, the North and the South, verticality, while the opposing hooves suggest the directions of space."[141] And, most significantly, the painted robes constituted a mode of literacy, "a

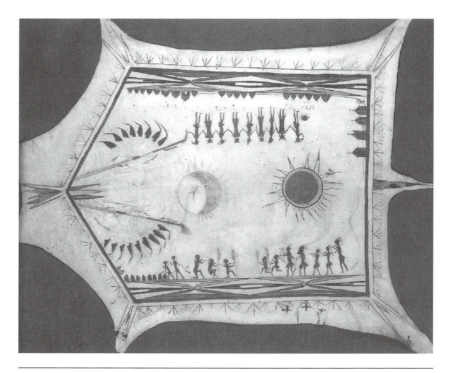

**Figure 10**  Daniel Ponsard, *Three Villages Robe,* from *Robes of Splendor* (New York: The New Press, 1993).

nonalphabetic form of writing that served as a social record and situated an individual within the group and society."[142] Moreover, through the robes' circulation from one wearer to another, they acquired additions to their narratives, revisions and additions that render them equivalent in to those texts from other cultures—for example, the Talmud—which grew through historical accretion.

While the collaborative event leading to the production of the volume on painted robes did not become newsworthy, it is nevertheless exemplary in terms of the possibilities it represents. At a minimum, it involved a process of translation that added producers to the art-historical construction of the American West. Its political significance articulates with the rationale for the creation of the National Museum of the American Indian, a place meant not merely for collecting artifacts but for "promoting and facilitating the active involvement of Native peoples in the representation and interpretation of their cultural materials."[143] This small episode, a retrospective enactment of the process of cultural translation and a recovery of a significant American literature/figuration, produced in the American West, is a step toward altering the distribution of voices heard on the characteristics of American nationhood. However, this small gesture of retranslation can hardly overcode the way the "American West" has achieved its dominant form of recognition—in feature films. I turn to that West as well as to the more general cinema-nationhood relationship in chapter 5.

CHAPTER **5**

# Film and Nation Building

## Cinematic Nationhood: A Brief Survey

One of the legacies of the "Western" political theory canon is the myth that the modern state emerged as a historically evolving contract, in which individual calculations, aimed at avoiding war, are responsible for translating individual security concerns into a collective sensibility that assembles and legitimates the body politic. Among the more articulate challenges to this enduring fable is Michel Foucault's. In a summary of his course on the theory of the state, he devotes his lectures to the task of putting aside the "false paternities" of the political theory canon in order to recover a violent past "beneath the form of institutions," and to show that contrary to the legendary histories such as Thomas Hobbes's, in which it is supposed that "non-war . . . founds the state," state-initiated law has followed in the wake of battles.[1] Although Foucault's field of reference is state formation on the European continent, a compelling case can be made for the validity of his view in the Americas as well.

For example, Richard Slotkin has linked the territorial extension of American national culture, through its expansion westward, to the rule of the gun. In his *Gunfighter Nation,* he makes a case for locating America's founding in its Indian wars and turns frequently to western films as the genre in which the westward-moving frontier of violence has been mythologized throughout the twentieth century.[2] Certainly, as one analyst of the history of the genre has put it, "guns constitute the visible moral center of the Western movie."[3] In this chapter, I focus on the continuing negotiation of U.S. nationhood within the genre of the western film and locate my analysis in a

**141**

comparative treatment of the cinema-nationhood relationship as it bears on state-impelled nationhood projects in diverse national settings.

To put it briefly at the outset, cinematic nationhood is the process through which film has been involved in the cultural articulation of the nation-building and sustaining projects of states. Yet, in a variety of global venues, especially in recent decades, the cinema has also been an arena of contestation, as films have challenged the territorial and biopolitical commitments historically involved in identifying national peoples. In addition to being subject to the shaping forces affecting all commercial media, film production and reception have been conditioned by attempts to deepen or to challenge various forms of national identity. There are two basic modes in which films have generated visual and narrative representations of national identity. They have done so in a grand way, through their reproduction of the symbols and foundational myths of nations (the dominant icons and stories through which nations recognize themselves), and in a banal way, through their treatment of aspects of everyday life.[4] The grander statements of national identity tend to be contained in epics, for example, D.W. Griffith's *Birth of a Nation* (1914), in the American case, and Sergei Eisenstein's *Alexander Nevsky* (1938), and *Ivan the Terrible* (1945), in the Soviet-Russian. The more banal statements are in evidence in a wide variety of film genres, for example, the ways in which Frenchness is articulated through simple gestures and everyday life scenes in comedies, as in the films featuring John-Paul Belmondo in the 1960s and Gerard Depardieu in the 1980s.[5]

During early periods of nation building, in many global locations, the nation-building epic had pride of place. It often served as a vehicle for transmitting the foundation myths through which states claim coherent cultural nationhood. The South African case is exemplary in this respect. One of its epic films, *De Voortrekkers* (The Trekkers, 1915), chronicles the story of a great trek, which began in 1836 with a migration northward from the British cape colony and ended with a victory over the Zulus. Like D.W. Griffith's *Birth of a Nation*, the film presents foundational assumptions about and legitimations for racial superiority and exclusion, an ideological frame that in the case of white South Africa, exhausted much of the narrative space of·its nationhood mythology.[6]

Since its appropriation for purposes of reinforcing foundation myths in the early part of the twentieth century, however, film has developed as an increasingly critical medium. As Robert Burgoyne has summarized the American case:

> In the contemporary period . . . many of the most hallowed myths of nation have been challenged and criticized in feature films that contest the basic premises of American ideology—the myth of manifest destiny . . . the progressive extension

of liberty to ever-increasing numbers of people . . . the power of national belonging to displace the lived identity of race, or the existence of a single homogenous nation extending from 'sea to shining sea.'[7]

This critical role of film, particularly as it is in evidence on the American scene in a recent genre, the "post-Western" film, which challenges the "hallowed myths" to which Burgoyne refers, is addressed at the end of this chapter. To provide an elaborate and comparative political frame at the outset, I begin with a brief sketch of the role of film in a variety of nation-building projects, noting the critical conjunctions between films and their historical contexts and the special contribution of cinema's narrative and imagistic capacities to its meaning production.

Although the Hollywood film emerged as the most globally pervasive and influential cinematic development, France is the nation where all the elements of cinematic nationhood were first critically enunciated—through film production, through film criticism, and through the development of a national film archive.[8] Because the cinema emerged in France in 1895, in a period in which French nationalism was especially prominent, the cinema's thematics were expressive of significant national "discursive events . . . moments in history when those producing a nation's cinema feels compelled to represent itself a 'real national cinema.'"[9] Yet, as Susan Hayward points out, "the cultural specificity of a nation changes over time," as a result "so do its artifacts, including cinema."[10] Thus, the class representatives in French films change "according to the social, economic, and political environments of the time" (hence, for example, the disparity between a Jean-Paul Belmondo in the 1960s and a Gerard Depardieu in the 1980s).[11] At a minimum, when addressing queries about how cinema "contribute[s] to the kinds of imaginings that sustain nation-states,"[12] it is necessary to specify the historical forces that shape a nation's most pervasive self-understandings at particular historical moments. To begin addressing this "how" question, along with the relevant historical specifications, I offer some brief examples of the historical forces shaping film in diverse national venues at particular moments, beginning with some observations about film in Latin America.

Early cinema in Latin American has to be understood in connection with a complex set of commercial and cultural relationships between Latin American countries and the United States. Because much of the impetus for nation building in Latin America involved the project of entering a modernity that the U.S. virtually defined, and because film was primarily a U.S. import, "the cinema fed the national self-confidence [in diverse Latin American national cultures] that its own modernity was 'in progress' by enabling viewers to share and participate in the experience of modernity developed elsewhere."[13] Nothing testifies to this voyeuristic aspect of national identity creation more than Argentine author (and filmmaker-turned-novelist), Manuel Puig's novel *Betrayed by Rita Hayworth,* in which a young Argentine boy imagines himself coming-of-age by becoming too sophisticated to be betrayed by women the way the American men are in Rita Hayworth films.[14] The novel is not only the story of a boy becoming a man but also an allegory of Argentina growing into modern nationhood.

However, in spite of the influence of U.S. cultural practices, conveyed in large measure through imported Hollywood films, early Latin American filmmakers developed a locally inflected cinema, featuring filmic symbols (scenes of national festivals), and filmic narratives (storylines celebrating specific Latin American revolutions and revolutionary leaders), that linked their films to "the distinctively Latin American project of modern nation building."[15] The context for the Latin American cinema-nationhood relationship was therefore ambivalent; it involved "complex negotiations between national events/traditions and foreign models and the demands of Westernization."[16] An exemplary modernity abroad was articulated with national projects, as Latin American films involved themselves in the enunciation of diverse forms of nationhood.

As in other global arenas, since the period of collaboration between filmmaking and nation building, Latin America cinema has become a critical medium, concerned in varying degrees and in diverse national venues with negotiating the nationhood-personhood relationship. For example, in the Cuban case, Tomaz Gutierrez Alea's *Hasta cierto punto* (Up to a Certain Point, 1988) and *Fresa i chocolate* (Strawberry and Chocolate, 1995), challenge the homophobia of contemporary Cuban macho nationalism. Also, as is the case with many contemporary Cuban films, they participate in a feature peculiar to the Castro period of Cuban cinema; the cinema has "asked its audience to read the discourse of nation *through* female characters."[17] For example, in *Hasta cierto punto* (Up to a Certain Point, 1983), the female character, Lina, provides the vehicle to articulate the cultural and political values associated with the Cuban revolution. Countering the machismo of the male characters, who are self-absorbed and forgetful of revolutionary values, Lina is identified metaphorically with a "bird in flight," which allows her not only to transcend her identity as a sexual object but also to become a figure of rededication to revolutionary ideals.[18]

The emergence of Turkish cinema provides a significant contrast to the dominant tendencies of early cinema in Latin American, because its earliest forms were shaped within the context of a very different nation-building project. As is evident in musical and visual arts in many Latin American countries, Latin American states have explicitly recognized their cultural nations as ethnically mixed: "Mestizaje, or mixture, both physical and cultural, is a master narrative of national identity for much of

Latin America."[19] In sharp contrast, national identity in a modernizing Turkey has disavowed diversity. Whereas in the Ottoman Empire there was "an astounding complexity of identity—multi-cultural, multi-confessional, multi-lingual," with its adoption of the French model of the nation-state—a state containing a homogeneous cultural nation—Turkey lost much of its "cultural cosmopolitanism."[20] In particular, by the twentieth century and the advent of Turkish cinema, the Kemalist state had extended its programs of cultural governance to control filmmaking, demanding that Turkish filmmakers "give thickness and substance" to the nation's founding ideals, which had been "thinly formulated."[21]

Nevertheless, some Turkish directors have resisted this demand. Yesim Ustaoglu's contemporary film *Gunese Yolculuk* (Journey to the Sun, 1999) deserves mention not only because it challenges the Turkish state's mythology of a mono-ethnic, national cultural coherence but also because of the way its spatial focus plays into that challenge. While Turkish films aiding and abetting the official version of Turkish national identity have emphasized national space, Ustaoglu's film enacts a spatial shift—to the city—that effectively undercuts the myth of a homogeneous ethnic nation. Her *Journey to the Sun* features the story of an migrant from Tire, Mehmet, who journeys to Istanbul and, after befriending a Kurd, becomes involved in misadventures associated with Turkey's persecution of its Kurdish minority. As Robbins and Aksoy have noted about such contemporary urban-focused Turkish films, *Journey to the Sun* effects "a transformation of imaginary space—from the nation to the city. In the imaginary space of the nation, it is possible to declare and assert the ideal . . . the illusion of cultural homogeneity and unity . . . [that] . . . is not at all possible in the imaginary space of the city."[22] Ustaolgu is sensitive to the racism and the denial of otherness within that is integral to the official Turkish model of nationhood. As she notes, she wanted to both "reveal the everyday racism" and show how racial discrimination against Kurds is "linked to the way in which the Turkish republic established a modern nation state and treated all other ethnicities as 'Other,' not as a mosaic . . . as it was in previous periods."[23]

The tendency of Turkish urban-focused films to run counter to the dominant Turkish national imaginary has resonances with the cinema-nationhood relationship in Britain. As in the Turkish case, in much of early British cinema, the dominant tendency in filmmaking was to produce film settings and narratives that were generally in step with the government's extension of cultural governance to the cinema. In 1927, a legislative measure in behalf of the film industry was contemplated in a bill before the House of Commons, stipulating governmental control of films because of the expressed sentiment that "the cinema is today the most universal means through which national ideas and national atmosphere can be spread, and even if those be intangible things, surely they are amongst the most important influences in civilisation."[24] In keeping with this sentiment, many of the British films in the 1920s were aimed at showing an England with traditional values and fixed social relationships, "a mythic rural England," displaying little identity stress, as the films' characters showed themselves to be comfortable within their various social stations.[25]

Certainly British cinema has since become a more critical medium, often at odds with the presumption of the "homogenising project of nationalism."[26] The more critical film projects address the U.K.'s national/cultural boundaries, treating the different nations that constitute Britain (for example, the modes of Scottish difference examined in *Train Spotting* (1996), the culturally centrifugal forces that are evident in the gulf between the prosperous south and depressed industrial North (examined in *Brassed Off*, 1997, and *The Full Monty*, 1997), and tensions both between and within white Englishness and a "colored" immigrant England, (explored especially in films set in London such as the Stephen Frears/Hanif Kureishi director/writer collaborations: *My Beautiful Laundrette* (1986), and *Sammy and Rosie Get Laid* (1987).

*Sammy and Rosie Get Laid* is especially relevant to this survey of cinematic nationhood because it explicitly effects the spatial shift from nation to city that has been the vehicle for contemporary Turkish cinema's challenge to the myth of homogeneous nationhood. As Sammy (a Pakistani immigrant married to Rosie, a white English social worker) puts it, "We are not British, we are Londoners." The cast of characters who disport themselves in the London scene—blacks and whites, immigrants and natives, heterosexuals and lesbians, capitalists and Marxist radicals—constitute a diversity that serves as a biopolitical challenge to the Thatcherite Britain in which the film is set. A plurality of ethnicities, diverse sexualities, different ways of treating the past, and varying degrees of contemporary identification with Britishness, contradict Thatcherite Britain's official attempts to impose a homogeneous national imaginary.

In addition to its focus on contemporary modes of ethnic difference, the film uses a critical temporal difference, articulated as a generational tension. The film's historical problematic becomes evident when, during a visit by Sammy's father, there is a discovery (by two fact-finding lesbians) that he was once complicit with imperialist violence back in Pakistan. The discovery disrupts a modern and unconventional family romance, shifting it to a fraught political story with historical depth, which it then resolves within a domestic frame. The film's resolution—after Sammy's father commits suicide, Sammy and Rosie's domesticity is reestablished—reflects the general tenor of contemporary British films. However challenging to British nationhood are the Celtic fringe, the northern locales, and the London scene, the imperial past, which haunts *Sammy and Rosie Get Laid,* remains domesticated within Britain's diverse (although politicized) ethnoscape. Even the critical films speak more to a conflicted present than to a need to come to terms with the role of a violent imperial past.

In contrast with postwar German cinema, for example, in large measure British cinema allows the nation to step back graciously from the more violent episodes in the trajectory of British nationhood. This resistance to historical reflection contrasts dramatically with German cinema's preoccupation with history. The contrast is worth pursuing, for it must deepen our appreciation of the historical contingencies of the cinema-nationhood relationship. To understand postwar German cinema, it is necessary to understand the uses to which cinema was put by the German propaganda minister, Joseph Goebbels, during the Nazi period. Impressed with both Hollywood film and the cinematic techniques in Sergei Eisenstein's rendering of key moments in Soviet history, Goebbels saw the cinema as the quintessential propaganda medium, especially when its montage effects are seamlessly effected. As Anton Kaes notes, Goebbels turned to film as an effective artistic propaganda medium because it is possible with film "to educate without revealing the purpose of education." Filmic technique, Goebbels asserted, can be employed in a way that "penetrates the whole of life without the public having any knowledge at all of the propagandistic initiative."[27]

As a result of the legacy of collective trauma from the Nazi period and Goebbels's notorious use of cinematic propaganda, much of postwar German film, in both East Germany and West Germany, became preoccupied with the articulation of history and cinematic narrative technique.[28] However, initially, before postwar German cinema began its critical reflection on the tensions between Germany's wartime experience and its present period of democratization, its geographically estranged segment, the city of Berlin, was in thrall to a U.S. dominated denazification process, which demanded that its film industry participate in democratization. What this meant in practice (a practice realized in a series of Berlin film festivals beginning in 1951) was that the industry show a preponderance of American films. The rethinking of German political culture, in this early stage, was to be realized through the importation of cinematic versions of the American thought-world.

Although state officials in the rest of West Germany were more concerned with developing a distinctly "national cinema."[29] the first versions of the new "national cinema" were very much like the old versions. The dominant early postwar film genre was the nostalgic *Heimatfilm,* "a peculiarly German genre with interwar antecedents."[30] It shows idealized spaces, especially forests and landscapes, with German people enacting their traditional folkways.[31] However, by the 1960s, a critical cinema was inaugurated both thematically and cinemagraphically by a generation that did not want to avoid the past—for example, in the films of Jean-Marie Straub and Daniele Huillet, who used "sudden unmarked flashbacks" to challenge conventional narrative form in a way that allowed for a conjoining of Germany's past and present.[32] Among the most familiar writer/directors of the critically oriented "new German cinema" was Rainier Werner Fassbinder. In his films, as in those of Straub and Huillet, the treatment of politics in postwar Germany is radically entangled with the politics of the mechanisms of storytelling, as flashbacks are used to articulate the past and present.[33]

The collective issues associated with nationhood are treated symbolically by Fassbinder within interpersonal relationships, as "public history keeps breaking into private stories."[34] Exemplary in this respect is one of his most famous films, *The Marriage of Maria Braun*, "a story about the labor of storytelling, of fabricating fictions."[35] Lacking an unambiguous narrating subject, the film achieves a historical rather than a merely personal focus and is thematically organized around the issue of forgetting. Maria's memory of her prewar marriage is idealized and distorted as she sustains an image of her marriage while, at the same time, having affairs with an American G.I. and a German industrialist and achieving a financially enabling and prestigious career. After leading a life based on a dissimulation of her personal history, Maria dies (shortly after being reunited with her husband) because she has lit a cigarette after having forgotten to turn off the gas on the stove. Ultimately, the private tragedy reflects a public issue; it is suggested that the price of forgetting is very high.[36]

As has been the case with German film, in Chinese cinema, as it has developed after the Chinese revolution, forgetfulness is a dominant issue. One aspect of forgetfulness has been state-imposed, as part of an attempt to impose a continuity of Chineseness in a state with a history of cultural as well as political division. State cultural governance through cinema has been especially evident at particular historical moments, for example, during the period following the Tiananmen Square massacre, when the governing elite wanted to obscure the differences that the violent confrontation reflected. Thus, *Dajueezhan* (Decisive Engagements, 1991) was produced in the post-Tiananmen period as an epic version of the Chinese revolution. A film about the civil war, it "strains to claim the legitimacy of the People's Republic as the (one and only) Chinese nation," and it represents the struggle with Chiang Kai-shek as "not between two quasi- or proto-national entities. Rather, on the one hand we have a national subject (the Chinese people), a nation (the People's Republic), and its agent (the People's Liberation Army), and on the other hand, we have a traitorous individual (Chiang Kai-shek), and his foreign master (the USA)."[37] In this film, the voice-overs and images actively work to forget the claims of other sociopolitical entities and "to eternalize the People's Republic."[38] For example, "Mao Zedong is shown walking alone in the hills of Hebei province, overlooking the frozen Yellow River. "As the river ice begins to melt and move to the accompaniment of sonorous cracks and crunches, the relentless progress of history is symbolized . . . [because] the Yellow River is the mythical birthplace of Chinese civilization." The imagery therefore "creates an association between Mao as representative of the nascent People's Republic and a much older, mythical, and transcendent culture."[39]

Nevertheless, as was the case in Germany after the war, the forgetfulness imposed in the films by filmmakers who are complicit with official cultural governance has been countered by a new cinema (the "new Chinese Cinema") in which there exists critical reflection on state nationhood projects. There has been a "tactful building-up of a profound complexity and ambivalence" in recent films that interrogate the grand myths perpetuated in earlier film history—"ethnic solidarity," and "the glorious revolution," among others.[40] Moreover, this same challenge to legitimation-oriented cinema has taken place in the "other China." In Taiwan, as on the Chinese mainland, official policy has sought to maintain an unbroken Chineseness from the mainland period to the Han Chinese presence in Taiwan. But Taiwanese filmmakers have been much more oppositional than their mainland counterparts. In such films as Hou Hsiao-Hsien's *Tongnian wangshi* (A Time to Live and a Time to Die, 1987), Taiwan is represented not as a linguistically and ethnically homogeneous national culture (the nationalist prerevolution films on the mainland privileged Han ethnicity and Mandarin language), but as a "space crisscrossed by a specific and intricate network of nuanced and subtle differences," linguistic, ethnic, and social.[41] And recently, there has even been cinematic attention to the aboriginal experience, perspective, and linguistic integrity in Taiwan (in *Man from Island West*, 1990, an independent film produced by Taiwanese).[42]

It is appropriate to end this review of cinematic nationhood with attention to another period of revolutionary nationalism, that which created the Soviet Union, not only because of the ways in which the period's major filmmaker, Sergei Eisenstein, lent his film art to the project of building a Soviet national imaginary, but also because Eisenstein's compositional approach to film, which he called "intellectual montage," inspires much of the analysis in this chapter. Eisenstein's compositional strategies were inspired by the film narrative innovations of D.W. Griffith and John Ford, both of whose work plays an important part in my analysis of the most pervasive cinema-nationhood relationship on the American scene, the symbolic creation of the American "West."

At a thematic level, Eisenstein's best known films are treatments of key moments in the Bolshevik revolution. Certainly his *Battleship Potemkin*

(1925), and *October* (1928), dramatic cinematic narratives of the events associated with the Bolshevik takeover, are unambiguous in their celebration of the new Soviet state. And even in his historical films, Eisenstein's primary thematic impetus is toward forging the link between state and nation. In his *Alexander Nevsky* (1938), and *Ivan the Terrible* (1945), he emphasizes the unity of the Russian people in the face of both foreign threats and domestic division. Effectively, the ways in which his films explore geopolitical space and ethnoscapes render his cinematic role comparable to the novelistic role of Sir Walter Scott in Britain; his filmic geography comprehends the state and its people and presents "compelling representations of key themes of national identity."[43]

But to appreciate *how* Eisenstein's film's accomplish their work of "cinematic nation-building," one must heed his approach to composition, his use of "intellectual montage."[44] The effective reality of events for Eisenstein are only grasped when one understands the structure of associations. For example, he notes how Griffith introduces a young gang leader by introducing a shot of the wall of his room, covered with naked women, in his film *Intolerance* (1916). Eisenstein refers to such film compositional moments in Griffith as instances of "parallel montage." By jumping from one image to another, Eisenstein, notes, Griffith's technique is truly "cinematic"; it is capable of "provoking the necessary association."[45] This kind of emphasis on the mapping of associations through cinematic composition was well elaborated in Eisenstein's *October,* in which he includes a montage sequence that cuts from shots of Kerensky to "close-ups of a crafted gold peacock, one of the precious objets d'art that filled the Winter Palace" in order to convey the idea that Kerensky's leadership is atavistic and self-absorbed rather than sensitive to his mass constituency.[46]

Eisenstein departed from a strict chronological reading of historical episodes not only, as was the case with Griffith, to produce a series of parallels, but also to exercise control over narrative sequence in order to effect the interpretation of the meaning of events by interrupting flows of action. Critical of Griffith's mere "drama of comparisons," Eisenstein sought to dramatize unifying ideas.[47] For montage to perform its realist function (explanatory, conceptual, and thematic), it must work not only through its juxtapositions but also by the way the composition as a whole produces a "generality, a synthesis of one's theme, that is an image embodying a theme."[48] Thematically/compositionally, Eisenstein saw his task as not simply one of narrating a patriotic story. Rather, he enlisted intellectual montage to produce an allegiance-producing political lesson for the viewer. The montage effects in his films were meant to make evident the cause and effect relationships and the overriding conceptions that allow one to perceive the historical continuity of Russian solidarity from the past to the present and to appreciate the contemporary collective significance of Soviet agriculture policy. With respect to the latter, he uses intellectual montage in *The Old and the New* (1929) "to make abstract economic planning intelligible, by cinematic means, to the millions" (for example, by cutting back and forth between industrial and agricultural scenes).[49]

## A John Ford Interlude

While he credited D.W. Griffith as the inventor of modern cinematic technique, Eisenstein was even more admiring of the cinematic skill of John Ford. Asked about films by Americans that fulfilled his criteria for good composition, Eisenstein responded that if a good fairy were to allow him magically to become the author of a film made by an American, he would, without hesitation, choose John Ford's *Young Mr. Lincoln* (1939).[50] Ford's film, he notes, is distinguished not simply by its "marvelous craftsmanship, where the rhythm of the montage corresponds to the timbre of the photography," but also by the way in which it enacts its "popular and national spirit."[51]

Given Eisenstein's penchant for nation-building cinema, it is not surprising that he drew inspiration from two of the American filmmakers most responsible for establishing cinematic approaches to American nationhood (primarily historical enactments of white America's politico-military and cultural territorial expansion), Griffith and Ford. As Eisenstein rightly perceived, the effectiveness of the cinematic nationhood that these American directors created is owed in large measure to their compositional skills. I turn here to one of John Ford's most stunning cinematic sequences, which occurs in his western, *My Darling Clementine* (1949), because it displays the compositional skill that Eisenstein admired and because it provides a threshold to my main focus, the cinematic creation of a mythic West, the cultural incorporation of which is seen as white America's ineluctable destiny.

The scene takes place in the town of Tombstone, which is framed by what remains as one of the dominant images of "the West": Monument Valley, where (as noted in chapter 4) Ford filmed nine of his westerns. Nothing testifies to the persistence of Monument Valley as the mythic West more than its continuing appearance in the Philip Morris company's long-running "Marlboro Man" cigarette advertisements. A recent one in, among other places, a two-page panorama in the very front of the July 2001 issue of *Harpers* shows a lone, mounted cowboy, galloping through a landscape that is both actual and mythic; it is in Utah, in John Ford's Monument Valley, the encompassing milieu for his western film narratives, most of which created a West that witnessed, with approval, the territorial and cultural expansion of white American nationhood.

**Figure 11**    Wyatt Earp meets the Clantons in Monument Valley, from *My Darling Clementine,* 1946, directed by John Ford.

Throughout *My Darling Clementine,* the viewer has seen many shots of the large buttes in the valley, whose panoramic expanse dominates the town of Tombstone. The sequence I want to describe begins just before the famous showdown at the O.K. Corral between Wyatt Earp, accompanied by his eldest brother and Doc Holliday, and the Clanton family, which has been responsible for killing two of Wyatt's brothers. The first killing, of the youngest brother, was responsible for luring Earp away from his life outside of the community into the town and into his role as Tombstone's marshal. The scene begins with the sun rising over the O.K. Corral. A dark shape that looks like one of the giant buttes in the valley comes slowly into view. However, as the light increases, it become evident that the shape the viewer sees is Pa Clanton's hat. Shortly afterward there is a cut to Wyatt, his brother, and Doc Holliday heading up the street to engage the Clantons in the final showdown. Over Wyatt's shoulder, one of the buttes whose shape matches Pa Clanton's hat is visible.

What Ford creates in this sequence is a homology between person and landscape, a cinematic gesture that is repeated in several scenes in *Clementine.* For example, when Earp rides out to install a headstone for his brother's grave, he is shown in profile with a low angle shot that creates an association between his head and the rocky outcroppings in the background of the frame.[52] But to fulfill Eisenstein's demand that intellectual montage convey a unifying theme, we have to inquire into the homology's implication. As was the case in all of Ford's westerns, he was exploring the interrelationships between characters and landscapes. Here, Wyatt Earp's delivery of lawfulness must take the detour of extralegal revenge in a setting that displays the two inseparable impediments to the expansion of a stable and peaceful domesticity to the West: the untamed landscape, which encompasses and dominates the lives of the West's people, and the hitherto untamed, violent characters, who have imposed the rule of the gun. This theme and its cinematic realization runs throughout Ford's westerns, although with varying ideological inflections.

However, before treating major themes in Ford's cinematic trajectory, I want to emphasize Ford's very brief cinematic commentary on "the Indian" in *My Darling Clementine,* because it provides a threshold for treating a primary consequence of white America's westward expanding nationhood: the destruction of Native American nationhood. When Wyatt Earp first comes into Tombstone from his encampment outside the town and stops at the barbershop, his shave is interrupted by bullets flying into the shop from the saloon across the street. The shots are being fired by a inebriated Native American customer named Indian Charlie, whom the local marshal is afraid to confront. After remarking about what kind of town would tolerate a drunken Indian, Earp sneaks into the saloon, subdues Charlie, and, after dragging him outside and heaving him into the street, he shouts, "Indian, get out of town and stay out." Earp's expulsion of the Indian is part of his character's assigned role. His movement from outside of town into the town and position of town marshal, which constitutes an extension of a pacified social order, spreading from east to west, requires the expulsion of all those who are unruly or culturally ineligible to participate in the new West.

Ford, his predecessors and successors, return to my narrative later. To appreciate the primary ethico-political significance of the early national-building westerns we must acknowledge the diminution of Indian country in the West (symbolized by Indian Charlie's expulsion from Tombstone), which is inseparable from white America's cinematic nationhood. It is a cinema-nationhood relationship—first elaborated within the films of D.W. Griffith—that produced "the myth of the West" and articulated the Euro American ethnogenesis elaborated in chapter 4. This myth constitutes film's primary contribution to white American nationhood. The nationhood vehicle in westerns, as film critic Peter Wollen has noted, is:

> an invented national history, with its monumental heroes, dramatic climaxes, narrative goals. The myth of the West—the ever expanding frontier, that manifest destiny that underlay America's westward dynamic . . .—stands alongside other

national myths that justified the unification of Germany, or the expansion of Tsarist Russia to the Pacific, or the scramble for Africa, or the imposition of the British raj in India.[53]

To specify the role of cinema in the mythic ethnogenesis, we must note that in both their silent realization and in their classic mode, westerns have articulated a white nationalist discourse by positing a hierarchy of appropriate character types, a "racial pyramid" in which the Euro American population is constituted as "the repositors of the national language and appearance."[54] Moreover, the bulk of westerns generate these racial hierarchies in the form of both the oppositional groups they confront and structures of attachment that form their life worlds. The tendency of western films has been to articulate Theodore Roosevelt's notion (treated in chapter 6) of the "winning of the West," which gives the English-speaking population a special worthiness for cultural and territorial dominance.[55] The filmic depiction of Native Americans as "savages," who are unworthy custodians of the land is well known. With some notable exceptions, westerns have tended to treat them not by elaborating the complexities of their life worlds but by treating them as hostile impediments to the "manifest destiny" animating the Euro American westward expansion. Although with Ford's *Fort Apache* (1948), and *Cheyenne Autumn* (1964), the Indian was rehabilitated as a coherent counterculture, worthy of respect, it is within the genre Andre Bazin has called the "super-western," from the early silent films through their most significant period of popularity (the 1970s), that westerns served primarily as vehicles of white, triumphal nationhood.

### The West of D.W. Griffith and John Ford

An inquiry into the beginning of cinema's role in supporting the western territorial and cultural expansion of white America must take us back to the era of the silent film and especially, to the western films of D.W. Griffith as well as John Ford's early films. In effect, the early western films, by their work of constructing a myth of national origin, supported federal Indian policy which, through such congressional initiatives as the Dawes Act (1887), had begun to efface the "Indian" as "a separate people, culture, and political economy"[56] (a policy that was partly reversed with the Wheeler Howard Act—aka the "Indian Reorganization Act"—of 1934, which "encouraged tribal organization" once again).[57] The early western films of Griffith, which focused on violent encounters while, at the same time, lamenting the victimization of a "proud race," depoliticized what was an international encounter by turning it "into a domestic tragedy (or farce) played out among individuals."[58]

In the silent films, there are two basic ways in which film narratives "encode[s] a mythology of national origin."[59] The first is evident in the battle clashes, as Indians attack trains, stagecoaches, covered wagons, and forts—in such films as Griffith's *The Last Drop of Water* (1911), and Ford's *The Iron Horse* (1924)—in which the cavalry arrives to rescue the Anglos and represent the nation's strength and expansionist perseverance (although Ford's view of the cavalry was to become less celebratory, as in his treatment of its brutal excesses in *The Searchers* (1956). The second is more biopolitical than geopolitical. As Virginia Wexman has put it, an important vehicle for "nationalist ideology" in Griffith and Ford westerns is the romantic, Anglo couple, "the family on the land," which stands as a bastion against the threat of interracial marriage and against a competing model of familial attachment, the Indians' clan or lineage-based system of intimacy and attachment.[60]

The Euro American founders, who were most prominent in producing the thought-world of white America, began with the presumption that a Christian marriage must underpin the society and that "legal monogamy benefitted social order."[61] Moreover, the ideal of Christian monogamy was juxtaposed to the practices of the Indian. For example, such Native American nations as the Iroquois did not make the nuclear family their primary psychological or economic unit, and "to Christian settlers, missionaries, and government officials, Indian practices amounted to promiscuity."[62] This presumption and juxtaposition, along with the more general commitment to a racial hierarchy, constructed racial intermarriage between whites and Indians as a threat to white American nationhood, a theme that is played out in Ford's *The Searchers* (treated at length in chapter 6), which articulates the theme while, at the same time, implicitly criticizing the racism manifested by the character with the most virulent anti-miscegenation attitude, John Wayne's Ethan Edwards.

Ultimately, what came to be the settled "West," as the domain of heroic Euro American conquest, as the location for the establishment of white familial domesticity, and as the pictorial icon of the territorial and cultural and economic consolidation of Euro America in general, is doubtless a set of images that owe as much to the films of John Ford as to any other genre. Combining a deep sensitivity to the interrelationships between persons and landscapes, an almost unmatched appreciation of the potential of film as a medium, and a nuanced understanding of the role of myth, Ford contributed, as much as any filmmaker, to "America's sense of itself."[63] A survey of Ford's entire corpus of western films is beyond the scope of this analysis. However, it is important to begin with attention to some aspects of his first Monument Valley film, *Stagecoach* (1939), in which he first displays his knack for synthesizing characters and landscapes.

Although *Stagecoach* lacks the later Ford treatment of clashing structures of intelligibility, which are especially prominent in his *The Man Who Shot*

*Liberty Valance,* it is the place where he begins making the landscape his most important player.[64] In the insightful terms supplied by Gilles Deleuze, Ford stages "intense collective moments" reflecting a historical social dynamic in a setting where "the milieu encompasses the people."[65] Instead of a founding moment, *Stagecoach* constructs a nation-sustaining moment; it addresses itself to social change. "For Ford . . . society changes, and does not stop changing, but the changes take place in an encompasser which covers them and blesses them with a healthy illusion as continuity of the nation."[66]

Ford's film is a cinematic version of a story he found in the magazine, *Colliers,* Ernest Haycock's "Stage to Lourdsburgh." It is clear that the way the West was constructed in *Colliers* had a profound influence on Ford (and others doing classic western films). Owen Wister's western stories in *Colliers,* which were illustrated by Frederic Remington (whose version of the West Ford explicitly acknowledged as one of his influences), offered a West that was an evolving social order.[67] Accordingly, the stagecoach journey, which occupies most of the film, is a microcosm of that evolving social order. Filled with a disparate and often feuding group of types—a prostitute, a soldier's pregnant wife, an outlaw, an alcoholic doctor, a liquor salesman, and a banker—the film has both historical and contemporary resonances. It is both a tribute to the historic expansion of a tolerant social democracy and "covert New Deal movie with constant appeals to collective wisdom," for in Ford's case, as in general, the contribution to cinematic nationhood must be understood as period-specific.[68]

Apart from the film's resolution, in which the law looks tolerantly on the character that made John Wayne famous, the Ringo Kid, who helps to hold off the Indian menace until the cavalry arrives, it also represents the successful incursion of white society into Indian country. At the end of the story, the ex-outlaw is left to his desired shift from loner to marriage partner—the new life he desires as a rancher and the husband of Dallas, the ex-prostitute. However, this story is not without ironic touches, for example the fright reaction of the travelers when they encounter an Indian woman, who is the wife of a Mexican managing one of the stagecoach stations. For the most part, however, the Indians are simply the most menacing part of the western landscape. Resisting their attack on the stagecoach helps to establish the communal character of its occupants and, through the rescue by the Seventh Cavalry, the reach of white governance into the "savage land."

The valley that Ford appropriated in his construction of a vanishing Indian country was to become a mythic celluloid location. The Indian had dropped out of dime novels by 1904 so that their principle venue (for purposes of white symbolic and commercial consumption) was in films, where they were codified as visual spectacles "within a nationalist ideology of race progress."[69] The pre-Ford Indians in Monument Valley, the Paiutes for whom the valley had been a home, had left, doubtless because the valley, known originally as "the Paiute strip . . . became a public domain, open homesteading" by 1922.[70] The remaining Indians in the valley were mostly Navajos, some of whom Ford hired to play various warlike Indian nations in *Stagecoach* and in subsequent films made in the valley ("Ford had about fifty Navajos that played all the Indians in his pictures, whether they were supposed to be Navajos, Comanches, or Mescaleros").[71]

As Ford's West became increasingly an annex of eastern culture, he became seemingly ambivalent about the demise of the Old West. Apart from the wildly shifting attitudes his films display with respect to the Indians, who remain largely at the margins of the western communities he constructs (appearing primarily framed as part of the vast landscape), it is clear that although Ford's main characters are primarily vehicles for extending a white nation westward, he is wistful about the demise of the West ruled by the gun, even as his film's narratives celebrate the establishment of a peaceful, democratic domesticity. The ambivalence is clearly displayed in *My Darling Clementine,* primarily through Ford's version of the historic Wyatt Earp. Having expelled Indian Charlie from the town of Tombstone, Wyatt's people problems occur after the racial exclusion has defined American citizenship; they are centered entirely within the white part of the West, whose characters the landscape alternatively dominates and mimics.

At a simple thematic level *Clementine* is a "community western;"[72] Although Wyatt Earp begins outside the community, and although the main action sequence, the showdown at the O.K. Corral, references an individual revenge motif, most the film narrative lies outside of the revenge story. Like Shakespeare's Hamlet, Wyatt delays his revenge, and the film belabors the settings rather than the antagonism. Indeed, Ford makes the link between Wyatt and Hamlet unmistakable. Shakespeare's play is brought to Tombstone by a touring theatrical company, and Wyatt becomes involved in re-collecting the actors after their performance is disrupted by a rowdy audience.[73] Filmed as a series of tableaux (the film is largely devoid of tracking shots or zooms) *Clementine*, as Bill Nichols rightly notes, "asserts spatial continuity, integrating characters into the same kind of space."[74] And as for the long middle section of the film, when very little happens: "hesitation marks Earp's function of bringing order-from-above; lingering allows Earp to integrate himself with the town's people."[75] Nothing speaks more to this communal bonding than the famous dance with Wyatt and Clementine. Diverse commentators have recognized its centrality. As John Kitses puts it, the dance is the "heart of Clementine"; it is "an epiphany, a hymn to harmony," and part of "an ideological operation which everywhere valorizes order and social regulation"[76] and in Michael Coyne, "the church-dance sequence stands as the apogee of American citizenship, and the final scene guarantees the civilizing process will continue," inasmuch as Clementine, who "functions as both nurse *and* schoolmarm is an . . . agent and essence of civilization," and decides to stay (as Earp heads out of town to bury his brothers).[77]

Wyatt and Clementine's dance is not the only "hymn to community harmony" dance scene in films about the West-as-America. As is noted in chapter 3, there is a communal dance scene in the film version of Rodgers and Hammerstein's *Oklahoma!,* which serves as a hymn to community harmony among cowmen and farmers. And Ford himself uses a communal dance scene as a social harmony trope in his *Wagon Master* (1950), another of his "community westerns" that celebrates the cultural and territorial expansion of white America. Yet despite all the positive valence that white America's nation building receives in some of Ford's most memorable filmic moments, in which Indians are socially and territorially abjected or disparate white characters are united, such moments do not exhaust Ford's cinematic contemplation of the values of unchallenged whiteness and the displacement of guns by legalisms.

With respect to the former, after Indian Charlie's unceremonious leave-taking from Tombstone in *Clementine,* Indians return within different contexts, for example, as a menace to American settlement and to white America's bloodlines, but also as objects of racism in *The Searchers,* a complex film in which John Wayne's Ethan Edwards is portrayed as both a hero and as a monomaniacal racist, and as unjustly treated victims in *Cheyenne Autumn.* In both of these films, Ford explores the ways in which white words, in the form of stories, legalisms, and policies, have been white America's "most potent weapon against Indians."[78] With respect to the legalisms, although James Stewart's Ransom Stoddard in *The Man Who Shot Liberty Valance* (1962), seems to represent the triumph of the law and the word over the gun, the gun remains part of the moral center of Ford's most complicated western and perhaps his most ambivalent treatment of the taming of the West by the spread of eastern culture and the territorial extension of the white American imaginary.[79] As Michael Coyne puts it, "*Liberty Valance* is a community Western in which the ideal of community darkens and sours irrevocably."[80]

Certainly there were signs in earlier films that Ford's view of the white American western habitus had begun to darken. In *The Searchers,* for example, the western setting is the same as it was in *Stagecoach,* but the white-Indian relationship is more ambiguous. Although as has been the case in the classic western film genre, "Indian country" remains a venue of menace and is radically separated from the spaces of white habitation and domesticity, John Wayne's Ethan Edwards, a rebel returned from the Civil War, and his adversary, the Comanche chief Scarface, both violent men, are not easy to distinguish morally. Scarface has abducted Ethan's niece, Debbie, but Ethan is so racist that he deliberately kills buffalo in order to destroy Indian culture, and although he finally demurs in his plan, he vows to kill Debbie once he finds her because she has been tainted by her relationship with Scarface. Indians have no presence in *Liberty Valance,* and the large landscapes that dominate Ford's earlier films are largely absent. What is retained is Ford's queries about the kids of people and the kinds of place America is to be. It is the film in which Ford's disillusionment with the sustaining myths of white American nationhood is most profoundly represented.

### On the Edge of Critique: Ford's *The Man Who Shot Liberty Valance*

Ford's *Valance,* like his earlier films, reflects aspects of national political issues. In *Stagecoach,* for example, one of the passengers, an embezzling banker, who "looks uncannily like a cross between Warren Harding and Herbert Hoover," presents for an America just emerging from the Great Depression, "the unacceptable face of the American Dream."[81] And it is likely, as Coyne suggests, that Ford's *Clementine* mirrors, to some extent, the postwar preoccupations of a country whose capacity for nuclear annihilation on the one hand and felt need for a masculinist security mentality, in conflict with a "'feminized' concept of negotiable coexistence" on the other, creates the quandaries reflected in Wyatt Earp's extended delay before the final showdown.[82] Doubtless, the racial and familial themes in *The Searchers* can be ascribed in part to national issues of race prejudice and familial instabilities.[83] And, finally, in one of Ford's post-*Valance* films, *Cheyenne Autumn,* it is likely that the post-Vietnam sensitivity to America's unethical use of its military capacity and its continuing unjust treatment of its racial minorities are allegorically at issue in Ford's rendering of the violent oppression of the Cheyenne nation during the episode of their attempt to return to their Dakota homeland.

If we locate the politics of Ford's *Valance* in a similar way, it is tempting to focus on the national issues that were current at the beginning of the 1960s. For example, Alan Nadel insists that while the film's main character, Ransom Stoddard, is framed by the turn-of-the-century American West, the film's presence in 1962 is framed by "the New Frontier administration" and that Ford represents "the Old West in such a way as to reconcile it to the rule of the Eastern establishment and suppress the acts of brute murder upon which the spread of a democratic nation was predicated."[84] Nadel is correct about the suppression of the violence toward first nations, which Ford was to address rather than suppress subsequently in his *Cheyenne Autumn.* But one can locate *Valance* within a more powerful and historically broader political register to provide a critical perspective on white American nation building as a whole. Ironically, myth in general, and the mythic West specifically, which Ford had been very much responsible for helping to produce, receive critical scrutiny in the film. And, crucially, the cultural winning of the West, through the growing dominance of the written word, and its manifestation in legal discourse, are represented as ambiguous rather than triumphal achievements. The film is not, for example, like *How the West Was Won* (released the same year), an unambivalent celebration of the spread of white national culture.

*Valance* begins with a train trip bringing Ransome Stoddard (James Stewart), and his wife Hallie (Vera Miles), back to the town of Shinbone where they had met. Stoddard, now a U.S. senator, and his wife have returned to attend the funeral of Tom Doniphon (John Wayne), who had played a crucial role in Stoddard's successful political career. A key to the story is an encounter with the local press, to whom Stoddard decides to tell the story of his relationship with Doniphon. But before we get the story told, there is a dissolve to the old, more wild West and a scene in which Stoddard's initial arrival in Shinbone is delayed by an ambush by outlaws led by the notorious Liberty Valance (Lee Marvin). When Valance takes a valued memento from one of the women passengers and Stoddard protests, uttering the venerable Ford query, "What kind of a man are you?" Valance issues the same query and responds by giving Stoddard a brutal beating.

Stoddard is subsequently found by Tom Doniphon and brought to Shinbone where he is nursed and then hired as a dishwasher in the restaurant run by Hallie and her Swiss immigrant parents. The rest of the story involves a deepening contrast between Stoddard and Doniphon, the only man capable of standing up to Valance and his cronies, who have been hired by the ranchers to intimidate the farmers and tradesmen so they cannot unite to achieve statehood and enjoy the commercial and political benefits of representation and transportation linkage with the rest of the country. Accordingly, in addition to the clash of character types (as the film considers the appropriate characters to forge the expanding democratic nation)— Stoddard is a man of the law who brings his law books to Shinbone and who teaches people, Hallie among others, to read and write, while Doniphon's prowess is with his gun—the spatial focus is significant. Unlike the emphasis on wide panoramas in Ford's earlier films, the shots emphasize the confining spaces of the town: the restaurant, the saloon, the newspaper office, and the main street. However, a larger spatial context has an off-screen presence. There are few outdoor scenes, and no long shots of the western landscape, but conveyances are emphasized (the stage and the train), and what the film gives up by way of its visualization of the expansive space of the West it redeems with an emphasis on another expanse: the network of communication and transportation linkages between the local town and both regional and national centers of authority and finance.

The story's central episode, indeed the key hinge of the story, is the shooting of Liberty Valance. After Valance challenges Stoddard to a gunfight because he has lost to Stoddard in a vote to send a candidate to the regional convention, and after Valance and his men have trashed the newspaper office that reported the result and have beaten the newsman, Dutton Peabody (Edmund O'Brien), Stoddard decides to take up the challenge. As Stoddard approaches the showdown, he is unaware that Tom Doniphon, who has tried to train him to shoot, but has also humiliated him in ways similar to Valance (for example, shooting a paint bucket above his head and getting his suit doused) is standing in an alley, ready to shoot Valance from the side. The fight takes place, Valance is killed, and Stoddard's subsequent fame as "the man who shot Liberty Valance" becomes the basis for his election as regional representative and subsequently his political career as senator. At the regional convention, Stoddard, who is about to reject the position because he is a man of the law and cannot accept an identity based on a violent act, changes his mind when Doniphon takes him aside and reveals the fact that he, not Stoddard, killed Valance.

Ultimately, what seemed like a simple, heroic nation-building narrative, a man from the East bringing law and order to a violent West and subsequently incorporating his region into the nation as a state, turns out to be a commentary on the role of myth in the nation-building process. The film's most famous line is uttered by the newsman who, near the end of the film, learns that Stoddard is not the man who shot Liberty Valance. When he's asked if he will print this revelation, he says, "This is the West, sir. When the legend becomes fact, print the legend."

Certainly, much of the rhetoric of the film, especially what is uttered by Peabody when he nominates Stoddard at the regional convention, emphasizes the film's nation-building narrative. Peabody begins with a gloss on the West's past, which dismisses its prior Native American inhabitants as lawless and violent savages. That West contained, he says:

> The vast herd of buffalo and savage redskins roaming our territory with no law to trammel them except the law of survival, the law of the tomahawk and the bow and arrow.

He then refers to the first wave of representatives of white America, who replaced one form of violence with another, more heroic, albeit now outmoded, variety:

> And then with the westward march of our nation came the pioneer and the buffalo hunter . . . and the boldest of these the cattlemen who seized the wide-open range as their personal domain . . . and their law was the law of the hired gun.

And, finally, he addresses himself to the present need for statehood in order to incorporate the territory into a populist, democratic nation:

> Now today have come the railroad and the people, the citizen, the homesteader, the shopkeeper, the builder of cities . . . and we need statehood to protect the rights of every man and woman however humble.

Peabody's genealogy of the characters whose presence have dominated the West at different historical junctures sets up the conclusion he seeks, the appropriateness of electing Ransom Stoddard, whom he identifies as one who "came to us not packing a gun but a bag of law books . . . a lawyer and a teacher . . ." and became subsequently: "a man who has become known in the last few weeks as a great champion of law and order."

But the misrepresentation that is central to Stoddard's identity impeaches the patriotic, nation-building tenor of Peabody's soliloquy. The "what kind of man" query that Stoddard aims at Liberty Valance early in the film effectively haunts Stoddard's misleading heroic existence and, by implication, America's nationhood as a whole. Nadel puts it well when he refers to Stoddard's "chronic inability to give authority to his assertions until be becomes the man who shot Liberty Valance . . . until he becomes the person he's not."[85] Ultimately, the reverence for words and books, for which Stoddard is an avatar, is undermined by the moral ambiguities afflicting his identity.

Ford's cinematic commentary on the ambiguous achievement of the coming of eastern words to the West is henceforth to be one of his central themes—for example, in *Cheyenne Autumn,* in which it is clear that the words are not to be trusted by the Cheyenne and that, more generally, the words that have won the West, assembled as they are in myth, cut two ways: "Myths sustain societies in Ford, but poison them as well. They define the limits of understandings, but are seldom perceived. They rule and regulate our lives."[86] Yet despite Ford's critical view of myth and his eventual appreciation of the ways in which the Indian story "is smothered by white stories," Ford's Indians, however tragic their existence is shown to be, are not allowed to tell their stories; their representation is primarily as a series of icons, "they are images constructed by the myths that we, the whites, have constructed."[87]

## Words and the West

Although Ford's Indians are relatively mute, his recognition of the white-red encounter as, among other things, a clash of intelligibilities moves in a promising direction for developing a political purchase on the consequences of American nation building/nation destroying. The critical route that Ford's cinematic corpus opens is one that Jim Jarmusch takes with his film

*Dead Man* (1995), one of the most important cinematic treatments of a politics of disjunctive intelligibilities as they bear on the encounter between nations in the American West. To set up a reading of the film's fictional enactment of such an encounter, I want to cut to a conversation that took place in the Southwest in the mid nineteenth century, because, along with Ford's *Valance* (to which *Dead Man* refers at various cinematic moments) it provides a proto-text to Jarmusch's film narrative.

The conversation, which reportedly took place in 1847, concerns disparate positions on the nature of a collective's political being, if one views "the political" in Carl Schmitt's terms as a society's relationship with its friends and enemies. The participants are John P. Cremony, a U.S. army major (mentioned in chapter 4), assigned to a troop protecting a mining operation, and a Comanche chief, Janamata (Red Buffalo), who had led a group of his warriors in an attack on a Mexican town across the *Rio Grande*. Cremony and his troop have ridden out to meet Janamata in order to dissuade him from further attacks in Mexico. In a dialogue that takes place in their only shared language, Spanish, he tells Janamata that he must recross the river and leave the Mexicans in peace. Janamata says in reply, "I hear your words and they are not pleasant. These Mexicans are our natural enemies," and, inasmuch as he is familiar with the history of the U.S.–Mexican War he adds, "they are also your enemies."

Cremony rejoins to the effect that the Mexicans are no longer U.S. enemies and explains that for white Americans, the friend-enemy relationship is a matter of reasons of state, not tradition or historical grievance. To this, Janamata responds that "your revenge is for yourself. It does not satisfy us for the blood of Comanches slain by Mexicans." There are thus two different imperatives *vis á vis* enemies at issue, one which stipulates an end to hostilities and one within which they must endure. Cremony, backed by credible force of arms, insists on privileging his reasons-of-state model for constituting enemies and suggests analogies that make no sense within the Comanche thought-world. Frustrated, Janamata decides that he can get nowhere talking with a man whose "tongue is double," and he speaks of his desire to avoid a war with "his American brothers." He therefore decides to retreat but asserts, nevertheless, that he will not promise not to return.

Despite his inability to recognize a fundamental political misunderstanding in his encounter with the Comanche chief (he assigns the disagreement to a failure of argumentation), Cremony at least understands the significance of tobacco in the Indian cultures of the West. At the beginning and end of his conversation with Janamata, he shares cigaritos with the chief, as a sign that it is a peaceful engagement.[88] By contrast, in Jim Jarmusch's *Dead Man,* William Blake (Johnny Depp), a young man from Cleveland who ends up traveling through a western landscape with a Native American named

Nobody (Gary Farmer), never understands the significance of tobacco in Indian country. When asked by Nobody on a few occasions if he has any tobacco, he says that he doesn't smoke; indeed these are his very last words in the film.

William Blake's obtuse responses to requests for tobacco highlight, at important moments, *Dead Man*'s most powerful rendering of the West, a place where the written word has never been reliable and especially where white words and white meaning-reception has never effectively come to terms with the discursive cultures of Native Americans. In contradistinction to the model of West-as frontier, "read through the narrow lens of nineteenth-century [white] American nationalism" by Theodore Roosevelt and Frederick Jackson Turner, a place in which white American nationhood develops and proves itself, is a model in which the western frontier is a place of encounter between disparate meaning cultures.[89] This frontier involved a coinvention, as whites and Indians alternatively fought and traded, struggled and cooperated to create "new landscapes, new property systems, new social relations."[90] But as the fluid situation of encounter gave way to an imposed regionalization, based on the extension of Euro American proprietary practices and political economy, the coinvention ended, and autocratic and unreliable white words took over the West.

The status of white words emerges early in *Dead Man,* which begins with a long train journey by Blake toward the far western town of Machine, where he has been led to believe, by correspondence, that he has a job as an accountant in the Dickinson steel mill. The journey westward by a man from the East bears superficial similarity to the plot in Ford's *Valance* in which the easterner Ransom Stoddard is bringing the words of the law to an untamed West: "Both features characters wearing suits, who arrive on trains from the east (Blake the accountant and Stoddard the attorney). And both are forced to adopt the violent codes of the West."[91] In *Dead Man,* the problem of the word is introduced in a conversation that Blake has with the train's stoker, who, upon learning of Blake's promised job, remarks, "I wouldn't trust no words written down on no piece of paper written by Dickinson out in Machine."

Jarmusch's approach to Blake's ride constitutes both a commentary on the classic western and an introduction to a critique of the vagaries of the white written word. Jarmusch, in fact, saw himself resisting the John Ford western, which he claims not to like "because he [Ford] idealizes his characters and uses westerns to enforce some kind of moral code."[92] Although here Jarmusch is failing to appreciate the moral ambiguities and ambivalence toward the written word's capture of the Old West in Ford's later films, there is one Fordian commitment that *Dead Man* effectively resists and parodies, the implicit valorization of the home and the heterosexual romantic couple.

**Figure 12**  Western garb on the train, from *Dead Man,* 1996, directed by Jim Jarmusch.

And although Ford's ambivalence to the written word cannot be dismissed, Jarmusch's West is far more anarchic with respect to all modes of articulation as well as with respect to social order.

The West toward which Blake travels—in a checkered suit and bowler hat—is among other things "a landscape that America has emptied of its natives and turned into a capitalist charnel house," as one reviewer deftly puts it.[93] Part of the process of that emptying is shown in the film's early narrative sequence. As Blake's train trip progresses, the landscape becomes a prairie, and the cast of characters looks increasingly western, for example, bearded men in buckskin outfits, carrying hunting rifles. In addition to the significance of the train itself, an "iron horse" that is arguably the major technology that transformed the West into a white provenance, at one point, the men with rifles rush to the windows and start shooting at a buffalo herd, a replay of the historical plan to destroy the plains Indians by killing off the basis of their sustenance.[94]

Nevertheless, as is the case in the later Ford films, much of *Dead Man*'s emphasis is on the politics of language. The unreliable letter from the Dickinson steel mill in the town of Machine is one of many signs that words, written or uttered, usually miss their targets. And the unreliability of white words is given special resonance. When Blake gets to the Dickinson steel mill he learns that the job is no longer available; doubtless the lack of a job for the new accountant reflects the lack of an openness in the West to an accounting of America's responsibility for its destruction of the Indian nations.

**Figure 13**   The three bounty hunters, from *Dead Man,* 1996, directed by Jim Jarmusch.

Contrary to one reading of the film, in which the writer insists that "*Dead Man*... disavows the guilt associated with the conquest," *Dead Man* is pervasively, although subtly/cinematically concerned with it.[95] Moreover, inasmuch as the words exchanged between Blake and the Indian, Nobody, reflect a fundamental lack of discursive rapport, it is made evident that this West is responsible for disavowing the relevance of Native American discursive practices.

The anarchic quality of the West, linguistic and otherwise, is apparent as soon as Blake alights from the train at his destination in Machine. Reversing the traditional discourse on savagery, the film displays a civilization of savage, gun-toting white men who fire their guns with little provocation. As Blake walks up the street, for example, a man getting a blow job in an alley points his gun at him; when he finally gets into Dickinson's office in the steel mill, Dickinson pulls out a rifle and shoots at him, and after he has a liaison with Thel, the fiancée of Dickinson's son, the son shoots at him, killing Thel and gravely wounding Blake, as Blake's bullet, fired from a gun that he found under Thel's pillow, kills the intruder. It is with this mortal wound that Blake meets up with Nobody, who travels through a wilderness with Blake, intending to bring him to the place where he will die (he is to be launched in a canoe in "the place where the sun meets the sky"). As his journey with Nobody begins, Blake is a dead man in two senses. First, he is taken by Nobody to be the long deceased poet, William Blake, and second, he will surely die from his gunshot wound if not sooner from other bullets because he is being pursued by three bounty hunters, hired by Dickinson to avenge the death of his son, as well as by two "lawmen" (named Lee and Marvin).

During their initial encounter, Nobody introduces the issue of Blake's words. Referring to Blake the poet, he says, "I discovered the words that you, William Blake, had written. They were powerful words, and they spoke to me." Doubtless, Blake's words affected Nobody so profoundly because of the dominant theme of his poetry—explorations of the relationship between innocence and experience. While a child, Nobody had been taken as a captive to England from his tribal homeland. Until he fastened onto the words of William Blake, he survived in his life as an exhibit among the English, he says, by "mimicking them, imitating their ways." He therefore needed the vehicle of poetry to mediate his innocence of Euro culture. Indeed, he quotes a line from Blake's *Auguries of Innocence:* "Some are born to sweet delights; some are born to endless nights."

However, Nobody's self-translation into the linguistic world of England ultimately estranges him from his Indian nation. He remains a loner when he returns to the West because his European sojourn and his resulting hybridized sense-making is not intelligible within his Native American culture, which has given him the name, "He Who Talks Loud, Says Nothing" (which he translates as "Nobody"). Nobody is therefore like Low Man Smith in Sherman Alexie's "Indian Country" (treated in chapter 4), one who "is not supposed to be anywhere." And also, like Smith, his conversations involve frequent miscommunications. Throughout the film, words are aimed in strange directions, and modes of reception are unreliable. For example, while hiring the bounty hunters to pursue Blake, Mr. Dickinson (Robert Mitchum) addresses many of his remarks to a stuffed bear in his office. And Nobody's speech is aphoristic, full of poetic and biblical references, and in various Native American languages as well as in English (to foreground the lack of linguistic unity that constitutes American, Jarmusch supplies no translations for the several Indian languages that Nobody uses in the film). At one point Blake says that he has not understood a single word Nobody has uttered. And, as I noted, even Nobody's most frequent, seemingly coherent utterance, which he directs to Blake: "Do you have any tobacco?" makes no sense to Blake, who had told him early on that he didn't smoke. Blake fails to understand the significance of exchanges of tobacco in an other America, long effaced in Cleveland but still very much a part of the far West.

Supplementing the anarchic linguistic world of the West in *Dead Man* is an anarchic mode of violence. The gun, which as noted "constitutes the visible moral center of the western movie," is not an effective instrument of justice or even of account settling in *Dead Man.* Bullets, like words, usually miss their targets. They are fired with little provocation, and the results cannot be recruited unambiguously into a coherent narrative, heroic or otherwise:

> Every time someone fires a gun at someone else in this film, the gesture is awkward, unheroic, pathetic; it's an act that leaves a mess and is deprived of any pretense at existential purity.[96]

Blake's wound results from a bullet aimed at someone else; One of the bounty hunters, Cole, shoots one of the others simply because the man had said, "fuck you;" Nobody shoots a trapper without aiming at him; and Blake acquires deadly aim only after his world is a blur because Nobody has taken his glasses and traded them. Moreover, there are no clear fiduciary responsibilities for the use of deadly force. Dickinson is an unprosecuted captain of the local industry despite being a homicidal maniac with several killings to his credit. And he sends off "lawmen" and bounty hunters ("the finest killers of men and Indians in this half of the world") alike in pursuit of Blake.

The anti-western impetus of *Dead Man* exists in many of its other moments and modes as well. Filmed in black, white, and grays (like *Liberty Valance,* its frequent referent), it displays an Indian country that, contrary to the Indian-as-menace of the classic westerns, is a result of the white menace. As Nobody leads Blake through a wilderness, the same landscape seems to appear repetitiously, not unlike the repetition of the same landscape in Ford's *Stagecoach.* But this wilderness is not about to be turned into a garden (as Hallie says of Ford's West in *Valance*). Rather, it contains scattered and destitute Indians, and whites who have never come to terms with the Indians or each other. Taken as a whole, it is a radically different commentary on the community theme of American nation building that is foregrounded in many classic westerns. Thel addresses herself to the theme before she is shot. When Blake asks her why she has a gun under her pillow, she says, "because this is America!"

In another significant way, its treatment of sexual intimacy, Jarmusch's film is not complicit with the mythic story of America's West as the venue in which a people has fulfilled its pre-scripted destiny. Instead, it offers a series of disjoint individual stories that intersect as a result of arbitrary encounters among their protagonists. It even counters the venerable nation-building theme that dates back even to the silent westerns. In these, as Wexman puts it, "Nationalist ideology as portrayed in westerns is wedded to the ideal of the romantic couple."[97] The most egregious affront to this corollary of American nationhood comes about when Blake almost becomes part of a "family." When he and Nobody encounter a party of three trappers with whom he tries to deposit Blake, under the apparent assumption that being "white men," they will make compatible living companions. The trappers turn out to be a non-traditional family. One of the men [Iggy Pop] is wearing a dress and bonnet and is doing the cooking.

The arrangement fails because a quarrel ensues over which one is to become Blake's sex partner. Nobody, with some assistance from the suddenly straight shooting Blake (to whom Nobody had said, prophetically, "I will make you a killer of white men"), kill them and continue their journey. For Jarmusch a West with this kind of family, which he likens to "a trace element of a family unit," makes sense "because these guys live out in the fuckin' nowhere."[98] And his cinematic answer addresses the issue of the family more extensively. Unlike those westerns that treat the romantic, hetero Anglo couple as the foundation of national culture, Jarmisch's film shows how a variety of forces and events, well outside "natural" inclinations and forces of attraction, create and dissolve familial structures in a setting with no cultural centrality, a place in which the "where" is ambiguous.

Accordingly, in the filmic narrative, the ties that bind are more the result of contingent circumstances than they are initiating forces. And Jarmusch's expression "fuckin' nowhere," is enacted in the film; none of the sex depicted is confined within the traditional nuclear family or the home. In addition to interrupting the blow job in the alley, when he alights from the train in the town of Machine, Blake interrupts another extra-familial episode of sexual intercourse—one on the ground in the forest between "Nobody" and a Native American woman. And in a further, more drastic commentary on the diremption between families and fucking, the bounty hunter Cole, we hear (when one of his companions speaks to another out of his earshot) had "fucked his parents" and, moreover, had proceeded to kill them, cut them up, and eat them.

Given the close association between images of the romantic couple and national mythologies, *Dead Man*'s commentary on amorous relationships is also a demythologizing treatment of the West as America. And inasmuch as the primary genre for the perpetuation of those myths has been the feature film, Jarmusch's *Dead Man* references specific moments from those films, especially John Ford's, as it challenges the traditional heroic nation-building narrative which many of these films perpetuate. While *Dead Man* contains many of the dimensions of the classic western—the easterner traveling west, the marginal and transitional cast of characters in the Western setting, the pervasiveness of gunplay, and the vagaries of the white-red encounter—it recontextualizes them to pursue a critique not only of white American nation building but also the role of film history in supporting the mythic versions of the national story.

In addition to the names of the marshals, Lee and Marvin, *Dead Man* contains some very specific references to classic westerns. For example, the pile of bones visible in the main street of Machine where Blake alights in the

West in Ford's *Valance* can be taken as a reference to the town of Shinbone, where Ransom Stoddard (another suited Easterner) shows up in the West. And the paper roses that Thel shows Blake when they first meet are doubtless a reference to the cactus roses with which Tom Doniphon courts Hallie (and with which Hallie reciprocates by putting some on his coffin) in *Valance*. However, many of the recontextualizations are accomplished cinematically. For example, while (like *Valance)* it is filmed in black and white, it also contains a "generous palette of greys" to draw attention, as Susan Maier suggests, to "the fragile instability of oppositional constructs." And, because "the film's aesthetics hovers . . . between a documentary-like realism and a strange artificiality," it portrays "the tenuous boundaries between history and myth.[99] *Dead Man* also accomplishes its critical commentary on nation-building myths and their realization in the classic western through the use of referential montage. Several scenes reflect earlier ones. In addition to the already-mentioned repetitions as Blake travels through the wilderness, with each pass revealing a different aspect of the depredations that anarchic violence has visited on the western landscape in general and the first nation's provenances more specifically, there is an important link between his first and last journeys on foot. The first one takes him down the main street of Machine and the second down the main thoroughfare of a destitute Kakiutl village. In addition to focusing on the fraught discursive practices in the West, the film supplies, side-by-side, alternative narratives—nation building on the one hand and nation destroying on the other.[100]

## Conclusion: A Continuing Encounter of Nationhoods

> The white man asked, *Where is your nation?* The red man said, *My nation is the grass and roots, the four-leggeds and six-leggeds and belly wrigglers and swimmers and the winds and all the things that grow and don't grow.* The white man asked, *How big is it?* The other said, *My nation is where I am and my people where they are and the grandfathers and their grandfathers and all the grandmothers and all the stories told, and it is all the songs, and it is our dancing.* The white man asked, *But how many people are there?* The red man said, *That I do not know.*[101]

The "white man's" query and the "red man's" response reveal alternative conceptions of nationhood. If we situate the query where it was doubt-less continually repeated—in the mid nineteenth century—it accords with Foucault's observation about the changing "governmentality" of the Euro-initiated state, which became preoccupied with the biopolitics of "the population" by the mid nineteenth century.[102] But we must recognize that more than one governmentality was involved. Reflecting on the story of this telling encounter of alternative models of nationhood, Cheryl Walker asserts that the story of America is not simply one of the western extension of Euro

American nationhood but a confrontation of nationhoods and, like Cronon and others, she notes that the nation-building process in the nineteenth century was an intercultural one, a "defining time" for both white and Indian nations as each absorbed some of the cultural and political practices of the other (although in varying degrees for the different Indian nations).[103]

If, in accord with Walker's suggestion, we view the development of the West as a series of internation encounters, we can move beyond the sympathy-for-a-vanishing-race perspective that the later classic westerns articulated and recognize instead the model that *Dead Man* and other post-westerns pose, a restoration of the ambiguities and incoherences in American nationhood. Apart from contesting the legitimacy of the Euro American appropriation of Indian lands, such films as Jarmusch's *Dead Man* and Robert Altman's *Buffalo Bill and the Indians* suggest that, as Walker puts it, "the American character has always been a contested matter. Perhaps we should say that there is no American character outside of the history of these contestations, which took place far earlier and across a broader spectrum of the American population than many of us once believed."[104]

*Dead Man* effectively restages the encounter between nationhoods and locates a fraught terrain, discursive and otherwise. Featuring arbitrarily aimed bullets, semen, and words, the film challenges the national, familial, and discursive codes, respectively, that classic western films have lent to the myths of American nation building. In its presentation of western types, the film reverses the traditional distinction that allocates civility to whites and savagery to Indians, but more significantly, it reveals the "insistence of the Indian," the way Indian presence continues to disrupt the American state's representation of itself as a unified cultural nation.[105] The insistence of the Indian is increasingly evident in the writings and films made by Native Americans, which destabilize the discourses of belonging and attachment. Their literary and cinematic initiatives are beginning to reverse the old supposition of the "vanishing race," which has been perpetuated in a history of a literary and cinematic annihilation of Indianness.

Before John Ford's cinematic representations, which merged characters and landscapes creating a parallel between the fate of the Indian and the fate of the landscapes of the Old West, Zane Grey provided the same imagery in the very last lines of his novel *Union Pacific* (a classic western train travel story that much of *Dead Man* parodies):

> Red and dusky, the sun was setting beyond the desert. The old chief swept aloft his arm, and then in his acceptance of the inevitable bitterness he stood in magnificent austerity, somber as death, seeing in this railroad train creeping, fading into the ruddy sunset, a symbol of the destiny of the Indian—vanishing—vanishing—vanishing.[106]

The train carrying William Blake westward in *Dead Man* brings him to a different West from that witnessing a vanishing. It brings him to a place of ambiguity, one that challenges the dominant American nation-building story. Now, insofar as Native American voices and artistic productions are increasingly available, there is a growing challenge to the ways in which the discourses of nationhood can finesse the role of the Native American presence. For example, Chris Eyre's film *Smoke Signals,* which, like Alexie's stories and novels, foregrounds the ambiguous contemporary Indian presence in the American West, features characters whose self-assertion must confront the white inventions of mythological Indians. Not what they once were, when subject primarily to the imaginative production by others, "Indians" are an ambiguous presence, testifying to an American nationhood (established violently—a theme pursued in chapter 6) that cannot be consolidated within the mythic trajectory: the ethnogenesis on the continent to which classic western films disproportionately contributed.

# CHAPTER 6

# "The Nation-State and Violence"
## *Wim Wenders Contra Imperial Sovereignty*

### The World Trade Center Towers Come Down; Bin Laden Is Wanted "Dead or Alive"

September 11, 2001: After al Qaida operatives hijacked U.S. passenger planes and crashed them into the towers of the World Trade Center in lower Manhattan, the horrific results of the attack on civilian targets were witnessed by millions around the world. Included in the continually repeated televised sequence was a body falling through the air from more than ninety stories up; a doomed worker, hopelessly waving a white flag from a window near the top of one of the towers, and, most stunningly, the two towers imploding with thousands still trapped inside. Because viewers saw these events continually repeated in video footage on television screens, it played like a disaster movie (in video release) without a touch of redemption. But however horrendous it may have seemed, it was (to borrow a phrase from Don DeLillo) "an aberration in the heartland of the real."[1] A nation with the world's most powerful defensive and destructive capabilities had thousands of its citizens victimized by a small group of men with low tech weapons.

U.S. President George W. Bush's initial reaction was to evoke a Wild West scenario. He wanted the alleged mastermind of the attack, Osama bin Laden, "brought to justice" in the manner the world has come to know through western movies. bin Laden, said Bush, was "wanted, dead or alive." And the scenario of the Hollywood western persisted: "On the eve of the Iraqi invasion [March 19, 2003] the president's advisors were working hard to embed George W. Bush inside the script of the American Western."[2] President Bush's resort to the codes of the West (as Hollywood has made them) is not a singular gesture. As I noted in chapter 5, Richard Slotkin points out that the U.S. is a "gunfighter nation" in one of its dominant collective imaginaries. Pointing to western films as the genre within which the territorial extension of Euro American national culture (the westward-moving frontier of violence) has been mythologized and celebrated throughout the twentieth century, Slotkin dismisses the more pacific, contractual models of the evolution of American nationhood and locates the elaborate of the U.S. as a nation-state in its acts of violent possession.[3] Certainly, the Hollywood version of the "gunfighter nation" looms large in popular as well as official culture. In an episode of the HBO production, *The Sopranos.* Tony Soprano's Uncle Junior says to his head hit man, who is thirsting for violent revenge against some of Tony's overly exuberant minions, "Take it easy, we're not making a Western here."

Doubtless, aspects of America's western experience can provide compelling historical analogies for the events after 9/11, but with varying political inflections, some of which escape the historical frame that the Bush administration sought to impose. One can, for example, revisit the revenge-happy antics that emerged throughout the U.S. in America's centennial year, right after General George A. Custer and his cavalry regiment were wiped out by Crazy Horse and his Sioux warriors. Evan Connell's remarks, in his account of the events following the battle of Little Big Horn, resonate with some of the official and popular reactions to 9/11:

> Reaction throughout the country was no different in 1876 than it is today upon receipt of similar news: shock, followed by disbelief, fury, and a slavering appetite for revenge.[4]

In the 1876 episode, "volunteers popped up like daisies in April" (in "of all places," Sioux City and in Salt Lake City, Springfield, Illinois, and throughout several states, including Arkansas, Nevada, Tennessee, and Texas), egged on by a revenge-lusting media. Among the more incendiary statements in the press was an editorial in the *Chicago Tribune:* "In every case where an inoffensive citizen is slain, let 100 of these red brutes feel the power of a rope properly adjusted under their chins." And in an statement reminiscent of President Bush's, "a group of schoolboys [in Custer's birthplace of New Rumsley, Ohio] took an oath—'each with his right hand upraised over a McGuffey First Reader'—to kill Sitting Bull on sight."[5]

Connell's gloss on one of America's earlier violent episodes points to a danger that President Bush doubtless neglected in his precipitous evocation of the cinematic "Wild West." Eager to respond to the event with an analogy that legitimates a revenge scenario, he turned to a genre that threatens the legitimation he sought. Robert Burgoyne's observations about westerns and America's self actualizing narratives disclose that threat. Drawing on a remark by the Cherokee artist and writer Jimmie Durham, who writes, "America's narrative about itself centers upon, has its operational center in a hidden text concerning its relationship with American Indians . . . the part involving conquest and genocide, [which] remains sacred and consequently obscured." Burgoyne adds that "one of the most durable and effective masks for the disguised operational center of the nation-state has been the western, a genre that has furnished the basic repertoire of national mythology."[6] At a minimum, as noted in chapter 5, the classic western films treat, in politically ambiguous ways, an extended episode of Euro America's expanding (imperial) sovereignty. But to evoke their messages is not necessarily to legitimize a contemporary version, as an inspection of both a classic and a post-western will show. However, before turning to the western to examine how two of them, John Ford's *The Searchers* (briefly treated in chapter 5), and Wim Wenders's *Paris, Texas*, negotiate and renegotiate the Euro American imperial expansion, I offer an interpretive frame for the historical trajectory of "imperial sovereignty."[7]

## Establishing Imperial Sovereignty

In 1876, the biopolitics providing the context for the post-Little Big Horn revenge scenario was already in place, having emerged from the Euro American nation-building project. As I noted in chapter 4, a white American ethnogenesis had already largely disqualified the political eligibility of Native American nations. Whether lamented as a "vanishing race" or abjured as impediments to a commercial model of land use, the "savage" bodies were either dangers to be eliminated or problems for the Euro American "Indian policy." In contrast, the main contemporary biopolitical conceits are post nation-building ones. The bodies to be protected and those to be under surveillance and attacked or excluded reflect a genealogy of security practices. To achieve a critical political purchase on the post-9/11 attack on Afghanistan, primarily by U.S. and British forces, aimed at punishing the regime that harbored Osama bin Laden, on the subsequent security initiatives that involve domestic as well as global forms of criminalization and intelligence gathering (while planning for the preemptive use of force), and on the American and British led attack on Iraq, one must appreciate the historical changes in state sovereignty practices.

As the twentieth century drew to a close, many surmised that war in the post cold war era would be increasingly framed and influenced by a post sovereignty, globalized set of political and economic forces. While it is certainly the case that capital expansion is not wholly controlled by national decision makers and that many of the "deadly quarrels"[8] recognized as wars in the post cold war era have resulted in the summoning of multinational forces—for example, UN peace keepers and NATO forces—sovereignty commitments have remained central to peacekeeping/war making. To the extent that contemporary warfare has achieved the prefix post-it is postindustrial rather than post sovereign. Instead of preparing for a clash of heavily armed tanks and massed armies, those nation-states most involved in managing global conflict are reconceiving the character and tasks of alliance structures and are developing global surveillance technologies to perceive threats (hence Paul Virilio's characterization of modern war as "the logistics of perception")[9] and weapons technologies that allow for (allegedly) accurate strikes from a great distance and, when "manned," involve a limited contingent of forces on the ground.

With the industrialization of warfare, spanning the period from World War I to World War II, the tank became the signature weapon, serving not only as a warfare instrument but also, in its various versions, as nationhood icons. As Patrick Wright puts it: "Nations have long been defined by their creeds, languages and literatures, but in modern times they've come to be known by their tanks, too [as evidenced by their names—after historical heroes in some cases and mythic founders of national culture in others]."[10] Of course, the primacy of the tank was premised on the clashing of massed land armies on battlefields. Its effectiveness was a realization of an industrial power that supplied an effective kill ratio. Without going into the nuances of a subsequent history of weapons systems, one can assume at a minimum that their design and judicious use reflect the users' assumptions about what kinds and locations of bodies are to be violently confronted. Hence, for example, since the major powers have been intervening in civil wars that are often deployed within dense urban venues rather than on large open battlefields, the large tank on metal treads has been increasingly displaced by smaller wheeled versions of armored vehicles (such as the Humvee), which can maneuver in narrow streets. And recently, the clandestine terrorist cell, not amenable to battlefield weapons, is a primary focus. They become targets of long-range guided missiles in some cases and in others of special forces, who employ assassination technologies rather than the killing force of battlefield weapons.

Doubtless, we can learn as much about the biopolitics of contemporary sovereignty moves by heeding the minutiae of ballistics and delivery systems as we can from the pronouncements of "defense intellectuals" about what lives are at stake, where danger lies, and who are the enemies. Weapons design is, among other things, an implementation of sovereignty's approach to sustaining and eliminating forms of life. For example, when James Puckel invented a many-chambered machine gun in the early eighteenth century (a time before the development of the biopolitics of populations), he dedicated his invention to "Defending KING GEORGE your COUNTRY and LAWES."[11] But the "in-be-half-of" is only one side of the biopolitics of weaponry. The delivery of their killing power has also involved biopolitical commitments. For example, Winston Churchill wrote about the nineteenth-century battle of Omdurman in 1898 (between a "great Dervish army" in the Sudan and English lancers), he referred to "the most signal triumph ever gained by the arms of science over barbarians."[12] And roughly at the same time, when the dumdum bullet (named for the Indian factory in Dum Dum, near Calcutta, where it was manufactured)—with a lead core to create larger wounds and thus more stopping power—it was designated for use in the colonies, especially Africa. Its use was prohibited between (what European powers called) "civilized" states.[13]

In the interpretive elaboration of danger, reflected in battle plans as much as in implements, there is also a cartographic component involved. In the contemporary construction of global conflict, in which eligible and ineligible, worthy and unworthy forms of life are being distinguished, to know dangerous bodies is also to know how the landscape of terrorism is being mapped. Inasmuch as terror can strike anywhere, the terrain of battle must extend to the terrains of everyday life (e.g., to urban environments).[14] To put the issue in general terms, there is a correlation between changing conceptions of the landscape of danger and engagement and alterations in approaches to the recognition and location of bodies: those that are dangerous, those that are vulnerable, those that are regarded as politically eligible (those whose voices are heeded as civically relevant and whose bodies require protection), and those who are either primordially or contingently politically unqualified.

At a minimum, sovereign violence began intensifying after 9/11. Lacking unambiguous venues and easily discernible antagonists, the representation of threat entered a frantic and expansive mode. Paradox abounded as violent choices were made in order to defend (politically qualified) humanity from violence, and the juridical concepts of law and justice was invoked in the process. Jean Baudrillard's remark is apropos:

> What kind of State is that which is able to nip terrorism in the bud and eliminate it ... ? Does it not have to equip itself with its own terrorism and in doing so simply generalize terror at all levels? What is the real price for such security and are we all seriously dreaming about this?[15]

Certainly, however, the process of criminalizing geopolitical antagonists and intensifying intelligence networks predates 9/11. Especially in the U.S. case, ever since the cold war, there has been an increasing ambiguity between conducting warfare and fighting crime. While fighting both the Taliban fighters and al Qaida operatives in Afghanistan in 2001, the Bush administration refused to grant their adversaries unqualified military status. The assault hovered ambiguously between a search for specific culprits and a military campaign aimed at ending a regime's (the Taliban's) control over the country. At the outset of the war, Secretary of Defense Donald Rumsfeld admitted perplexity about where and what to strike, noting that Afghanistan lacks "high value targets." And after killing hundreds of fighters and at least as many civilians, scores of captives were imprisoned at Guantanamo Bay, Cuba, kept in a legal limbo, a zone of juridical indistinction between prisoner of war and criminal status.

The ambiguous status of the captives reflects what two analysts have noted as a post cold war trend:

> [a] growing gap between traditional security concepts and paradigms and the contemporary practice of security policy... the coercive apparatus of the state has been reconfigured and redeployed.... [producing a] growing fusion between law enforcement and national security missions, institutions, strategies, and technologies.[16]

Whereas the cold war "security paradigm" distinguished sharply between the external military security of states and its "internal policing functions," the practical and conceptual internal/external separation, which arose historically after states had in varying degrees monopolized force capabilities and largely disarmed their populations, is now being reconceived.[17]

One of the better known versions of the history of states' monopolization of violence is supplied in Anthony Giddens's sociological gloss on the modern state. His widely accepted treatment of the modern state's history of violence is one of a successful process of the "pacification" of state populations and a subsequent "withdrawal of the military from direct participation in the internal affairs of the state."[18] However appropriate to the history of European states Giddens's linear narrative may be—certainly, episodes of militarization in a wide variety of global venues suggests that "military withdrawal from domestic affairs" has not been continuous—trends in post cold war sovereignty and security practices present a new challenge to the narrative. In addition to a growing use of military technologies for crime fighting, domestically and abroad (for example, in U.S. anti-narcotic assaults in Columbia), post-9/11 developments in "homeland security" and the elaboration of a domestic intelligence network, which reconfigures CIA and FBI investigatory functions, permit unprecedented levels of domestic surveillance (under the Patriot Act of October 2001), and insinuate military tribunals into the domestic juridical network in the U.S., dissolve many of the former distinctions between domestic crime fighting and global warfare.[19]

Along with the territorial ambiguities that the new warfare-as-crime-fighting entails, a new biopolitics is emerging. The criminalization of military adversaries has been accompanied by a biometric approach to intelligence and surveillance. The significance of this change becomes evident if one contrasts Giddens's treatment of the surveillance technologies that paralleled the modern state's monopolization of violence with the current ones. Throughout his discussion Giddens refers primarily to the use of paper trails. He begins with a treatment of the state's use of writing, proceeds to their "coding of information," (47) and concludes with some observations about cultural governance, the sponsoring of printed materials, not only for surveillance but also to enlarge the scope of the public sphere (179). Certainly, the paper trail and/or its electronic realization in the form of computer files remains significant, but the new modes of warfare-as-crime fighting involve the development of a biological rather than merely a paper trail, as new genetic tracing discoveries are being recruited into intelligence gathering.

Is the biometric, designer weapon far behind? Anticipating the role of biometric coding in futuristic forms of warfare, science fiction writer William Gibson began his novel *Count Zero,* with this passage:

> They set a SLAMHOUND on Turner's trail in New Delhi, slotted it to his pheromones and the color of his hair. It caught up with him on a street called Chandni Chauk and came scrambling for his rented BMW through a forest of bare brown legs and pedicab tires. Its core was a kilogram or recrystallized hexogene and flaked TNT.[20]

Thanks to advanced cloning technology in Gibson's futuristic war world, "Turner" is reassembled from some of his own parts and some others (eyes and genitals bought on the open market). He lives on as the novel's main character, a commando, operating in a war over R&D products. Whether or not the military logistics of biometric warfare is now underway, the surveillance dimension is being rapidly developed. And the use of pheromones in the Gibson account is technologically anachronistic. The technology of DNA tracing, now well developed, is complementing the photograph and paper trial to surveill and intercept dangerous bodies. Shortly after the destruction of the Taliban regime in Afghanistan, U.S. Attorney General. John Ashcroft, sought changes in federal law "to allow the Federal Bureau of Investigation to maintain a DNA databank of profiles taken from al Qaida and Taliban fighters detained in Afghanistan and Cuba."[21] Subsequently, "forensic experts" were dispatched to Afghanistan to test the human tissue found in one of the battlefields to see if any of the dead included bin Laden or his top associates.[22]

Of course, policy makers face legitimization issues when introducing new modes of surveillance and criminalization. When those operating the "reasons of state" are involved in implementing a historically unorthodox "governmentality"—in this case an extraordinary mode of surveillance and management of the global order and the domestic population—they have to produce warrants for the new policy initiatives. Accordingly, after the 9/11 episode, the Bush administration began operating on two fronts to solicit acquiescence to their simultaneous intensification of domestic surveillance and preparation for global military incursions (a strategy of "preemptive defense").[23] On the one hand, there was a feverish search for legal precedents, hence the designation of an America citizen as an "enemy combatant" to apply a law of war that was earlier applied only to foreign nationals, and on the other, the administration approached film and television producers seeking to encourage them to create patriotic feature films and TV dramas, designed to elicit public support for the new policies.

This latter part of the administration strategy, its cultural governance initiatives aimed at managing popular culture, particularly films and television, occupies much of this chapter's analysis. But to appreciate what the media was being summoned to provide a warrant for, it is necessary first to heed additional dimensions of the historical context, especially the historical changes in the practices of state sovereignty that have ultimately led to the policies for which the administration was seeking compliance. First and foremost what must be understood is the paradoxical nature of the George Bush/Tony Blair attack on Afghanistan's Taliban regime and Saddam Hussein's Iraqi regime, along with the structures of surveillance that has been put in place both in the U.S. and globally.

In their treatment of "imperial sovereignty," their designation for the post cold war proliferation of "micro conflicts,"[24] Michael Hardt and Antonio Negri emphasize the new biopolitics: "The realization of modern sovereignty," they assert, "is the birth of biopower."[25] The concept of biopower belongs initially to Foucault, who associates it with modernity's reigning governmentality, the increasing concern with managing populations. But it involves a militant, expansionist dimension as well, inasmuch as the modern security state, seeking to protect its population, has increasingly seen the need to preempt threats abroad. For imperial sovereignty, the entire world is both "within its domain and at the frontiers."[26] As the Hardt-Negri quotations imply, sovereignty is both a spatial and a biopolitical phenomenon. While the spatial or territorial aspect is a familiar feature of political theorizing, belonging as it does to a history of nation-state formation, the biopolitical aspect has been under-theorized.

Simply put, understanding the biopolitical aspect of state security practices, ranging from the administrative to the violent, requires an approach to sovereignty that treats its non-juridical dimensions, its constructions of worthy versus unworthy human life. In a brief but suggestive section of his investigation of the history of sexuality, Michel Foucault addresses the biopolitics of war in the modern era, asserting that whereas wars were once "waged in the name of the sovereign who must be defended," now, "they are waged in behalf of the existence of everyone . . . the decision that initiates them and the one that terminates them are in fact increasingly informed by the naked question of survival"; killing takes place "in the name of life necessity."[27]

However, Foucault's treatment of the biopolitics of the sovereignty-war connection is underdeveloped and merely suggestive. Giorgio Agamben provides an elaboration of Foucault's introduction of the biopolitical dimension of governing by elaborating Foucault's insight about the change in the legitimation of war from protecting the inviolability of the sovereign to implicating a broader model of life. This broadening of the issue permits analysis of a wide range of state actions aimed at "administering life,"[28] In particular, Agamben argues that modern sovereignty has been reinflected by the "politicization of life."[29] Sovereignty, at the level of executive decision making, he notes, operates in a process of making exceptions in order to use extralegal force (in violation of territorial sovereignty) in behalf of some aspect of human existence. Rather than functioning wholly within a legal framework, it exists in a zone of "indistinction" between violence and the law.[30] This topology of sovereignty, a paradoxical conjunction of force and judiciousness, achieved clear expression in a Bush-quoting banner headline in *USA Today* on October 10, 2001: "Bombs 'Tighten the net of Justice.'"

To appreciate what appears to be paradoxical—the sovereignty-affirming significance of a violation of territorial sovereignties—one must recognize with Agamben that sovereignty-as-enactment exists in "the intersection between the juridico-legal and biopolitical models of power."[31] Moreover, Agamben's approach effaces the inside boundary, for in his model, expendable lives are included exclusions. Sovereignty's biopolitical imperatives, realized in the making of exceptions (contemporary historical examples include U.S. missile strikes in the Sudan, and NATO's "humanitarian intervention" in Kosovo, as well as a joint "allied" strike on Afghanistan), are derived from the power to administer life. To invoke Agamben's terms, sovereign power is deployed to distinguish "bare life" (that part of humanity that is excluded from political protection) from politically qualified life and thus, as Agamben puts it, to kill without committing homicide.[32]

Yet Agamben's approach to sovereignty, like Foucault's, is underspecified with respect to current changes in political orders, especially as they affect legitimations for war. As William Connolly has put it, Agamben's attention to "the modern intensification of biopolitics . . . pays little heed to the changed global context."[33] In a global context, the most significant post cold war change in the model of life upon which sovereignty's approach to peacekeeping/war making is predicated is from a biopolitics of "population" (the collective identity to which Foucault was referring when he spoke of war in behalf of "the existence of everyone"), to a biopolitics of "humanity." In this latter conception of life, those who must be defended (as well as those who are criminalized) constitute a new class of bodies to be protected and a new set of threatening ones to confront. Thus, for example, British Prime Minister Tony Blair, a leading proponent of contemporary "peacekeeping," introduces the concept of "positive engagement" (as opposed to the cold war concepts of defense and deterrence) to refer to intervention in behalf of an endangered *humanity* rather than simply the *population* of the U.K., or even of the populations of the states within the NATO alliance.[34] And some months after 9/11, President Bush claimed that the defense of the U.S. will require military responses to "evil" regimes that harbor or support "terrorism."

Bush's and Blair's approach to war and peace exemplifies the new way of construing sovereignty within the Western alliance. Rather than abandoning a system of state sovereignty, it is an expansive, cooperative venture in which cooperation is no longer constituted as merely an alliance against a common threat. It involves, instead, preparation for engagement with what are regarded as disruptive modes of violence (threats to "peace") within sovereign territories. The new venture requires, in the words of one analyst, whose observation fits the attacks on Afghanistan and Iraq, "a coalition of war and humanitarianism," where politics is deployed in the form of humanitarian war (the U.S. war slogans in the Iraqi case refer to liberating the Iraqi people).[35] This expansive, imperial sovereignty has echoes from the pasts of both countries. It harks back to the territorial and biopolitical aspects of the imperial expansion involved in the establishment of the British Empire and the United States, respectively. The echoes resound, in the former case from Elizabethan England and, in the latter, from the nineteenth century, moving "American frontier." And both historical epochs bear significant comparison with the present. They involve an expansionary militarization, a surveillant biopolitcs, and "cultural governance"—the support of diverse genres of expression that can be staged to warrant the emerging sovereignty practices and the inhibition of those that do not.

### The Case of Elizabethan England

In the sixteenth century, Elizabethan England experienced a reign of state terror provoked in part by its "decisive break from Roman Catholicism" and implemented by a "Cecilian regime," Sir William Cecil's (aka Lord Burghley) and his progeny's "construction of a Protestant State Church as a precondition for both domestic repression and external aggression."[36] In the process of creating a tightly controlled, surveillant, and militarized Protestant state, the Cecilian regime established an early modern version of the national security state by expanding both its military adventures and by developing an internal security network of clients and informants. England's external militance under the Cecilian regime was directed primarily against Spain and Portugal, a project that involved episodes of plunder at sea, primarily by government-approved merchant privateers, rather than full-scale clashes of fleets or land armies.

These episodes mark the beginning of the Elizabethan maritime expansion, which ultimately provided the major technology enabling British imperialism. Although the Cecilian regime's reliance on privateering merchant adventurers would seem to distance their militarization from the contemporary case, a version of privateering is being entertained as a contemporary option. For example, two writers (one a "think tank" security analyst and the other a journalist), pondering the ways to prosecute the "war on terrorism," have advocated a return to privateering.[37] They recognize that (as was the case with powerful merchants in earlier historical periods ) large corporations have the requisite power to and interest in lending considerable resources to the pursuit of the state's enemies. For example, although they are not directly involved in hot war privateering, Halliburton, a large oil service company (where Vice President Richard Cheney was the former CEO), "bedeviled lately by an array of accounting and business issues," is profiting significantly from the "war on terrorism." It's participation has included building cells for detainees at Guantanamo Bay in Cuba, feeding troops in Uzbekistan, and serving as a logistics supplier for the navy.[38] And subsequently, they were awarded a contract to extinguish Iraqi oil fires and repair damaged wells to help restore Iraq's postwar oil industry.[39]

The relevance of the Elizabethan case to the present is also evident at the level of domestic oppression. Given the religious cleavage involved in its battle for European hegemony, the Cecilian regime regarded Protestantism as synonymous with patriotism.[40] Although there was no significant standing army, the militias, formed through levies and used primarily for service abroad, were also employed for domestic pacification.[41] At the same time a growing intelligence system had developed, using "human resources." A vast network of informants was employed to identify those involved in subversive acts. And laws were in place to provide the required judicial leverage. As I noted in chapter 2, "[t]he scope of treason was extended by acts of 1534 and 1536, principally to encompass treason by word as well as overt deed." [42] Because of what was increasingly seen as a Catholic threat, anyone associated with that threat was surveilled by the network of spies that had been recruited to curtail domestic subversion. Many English Catholics and many associated with Spain were turned into traitors.

The covert domestic battle's external counterpart was a series of military initiatives, both to "facilitate subjugation of Scotland and Ireland" and to attack Spanish and French interests. Ultimately, "the very structure of government was built upon human surveillance and its intended inducement of paranoia among servants of the crown."[43] As is the case with the contemporary intensification of military adventurism and domestic surveillance, the Cecilian regime was involved in a struggle to legitimate its imperial sovereignty. The primary genres used to evince ideological support for the extensive militarization taking place were the book and the pamphlet, carrying "military treatises" and "pro-military propaganda" respectively.[44] But, on the side of a generalized encouragement for England's imperial expansion, arguably no genre or set of texts was more influential than Richard Hakluyt's treatises: *Discourse on Western Planting* (1584), and *Principall Navigations, Voisges, and Discoveries of the English Nation* (1589). In *Discourse on Western Planting*, Hakluyt juxtaposes England's global role with that of Spain, inveighing against Spanish tyranny in "the New World" and suggesting a more effective commercial English version of global hegemony.[45] Hakluyt also saw global economic and military expansion as a way to manage the domestic population. The colonies, he said, would be a place where England's "waste people" and "idle people" could be employed to avoid the damage they would otherwise do at home.[46]

As noted in chapter 4, Hakluyt's travel narratives helped to encourage a more expansive England. He was among those who were involved in "the articulation of England itself," celebrating English navigation on the one hand and promoting its expansion on the other.[47] And because Hakluyt's views of the nation's domestic issues and its imperial aspirations were congenial to those of the ruling elite, he was sponsored by them. Rewarding his complicity with the cultural governance of the Cecilian regime, Walsingham, the head of the state spy network, (to whom Hakluyt dedicated the initial edition of *Principll Navigations*) "bore at least part of the expense of the publication." And Sir Robert Cecil was one of Hakluyt's patrons (to whom subsequent editions of *Principll Navigations* were dedicated.[48]

However, Hakluyt's nation- and empire-building texts (and the other complicit books and pamphlets), which were absorbed into the Cecilian regime's cultural governance strategies, were not the only genres addressing the newly militarized and surveillant state. Elizabethan drama was significantly implicated in both affirming and criticizing the Cecilian regime's domestic terrorizing of the population as well as its foreign adventures. The dramatist most famously involved in the regime's terror and militarization was Christopher Marlowe. On the basis of equivocal evidence, it has often been assumed that Marlowe, who was patronized by Francis Walsingham's cousin, Thomas, participated in the regime's covert spying activities.[49] Moreover, the traditional reading of his play, *Massacre at Paris* (1592), sees it as an unequivocal and passionate expression of horror about the slaughter of Huguenots by French Catholics. But others see a subversive element in the play, for example, Curtis Breight's point that it "deploys Catholic propaganda written not by the French Catholic league but by English Catholic exiles [in a] direct and powerful attack on the Cecilian regime." He regards Marlowe's violent death as a political assassination by agents of a Protestant-dominated regime that read such nuances in the play as subversive to a Protestant hegemony.[50]

The evidence in the historical plays with respect to the Shakespearean position on the regime's surveillance and militarization is ambiguous. Although some see Shakespeare as a pro-monarchy patriot, on another view, Shakespeare's historical dramas, particularly his Henriad and his Richards, are allegorical; on this view the plays are read as treatments of contemporary Elizabethan politics and as implicitly critical commentaries on the effects of state terror and military adventurism on commoners. In the case of the Henriad, the dire effects of military recruitment are shown; for example, "Falstaff's recruiting practices and the ultimate destruction of his men" are represented, reflecting the fact that many commoners died not in battles but as a result of the hardships of service.[51] And *Coriolanus* "boldly exposes what the Henriad could only imply by accretion—that war functioned to dispose of commoners."[52] In addition, Shakespeare's historical plays reflect on the abuses of the security apparatus. "Under the guise of historical remoteness," they map aspects of the Elizabethan culture of surveillance and manifest a concern with the "lower-class victims of upper-class conflict."[53] In a close reading of the histories, Breight argues that rather than siding with the monarchy and its aristocratic henchmen, Shakespeare effectively "delineate[s] how the medieval modern state helps to manufacture itself by destroying alternative conceptions and practices of power," in this case regional communities with inconvenient religious affiliations led by traditional elites. But on another reading, Richard Helgerson's, Shakespeare is a loyal monarchist. His plays manifest a doubleness. They show "kingship in a narrative and dramatic medium that not only displayed power but revealed the sometimes brutal and duplicitous strategies by which power maintained itself." They both celebrate authority and "bear a subversive potential,"[54] while playing to audiences representing a range from commoners to kings. But for the "discursive community" of the theater, which Helgerson states, was "far removed from the councils of power," the plays (especially in Shakespeare's case) were not subversive but rather "contributed at once to the consolidation of central power, [and] . . . to the cultural division of class from class.[55]

## The American Scene

The transition from the Cecilian hegemony, which was central to the emergence of English imperialism, to the American scene has taken many forms, aided and abetted from both sides of the Atlantic. On the one hand, the colonization of North America was part of the British imperial project. Even though the war of independence created a historical rift in the "imperial transfer,"[56] the mythography emanating initially from both English and American historiography, and subsequently from novels and films, has created an articulation of an Anglo-American ideological project, which is especially evident in cinematic versions of Elizabeth's reign. As Breight summarizes it, "Elizabethan England was deployed in cinema as both a model and a warning: a model of heroic resistance to some potent external threat." And the films "provide a myth of innocent origins well suited to the rise of imperial America."[57]

But imposing a smooth historical continuity on the English-American forms of nation building and expansion has had to face a disruptive historical event. As Breight points out, the American Revolution constituted a daunting problem for the imperial transfer. The fact of the revolt of the American colonies creates a rift in the transfer narrative. Breight argues that "the mythmakers" [who sought narratively to heal the rift] "turned to Elizabethan England as the true origin of both Britain and the United States"[58] and he sees that mythography deeply embedded in a series of feature films about Queen Elizabeth's England, in which English and American actors together challenge the Spanish tyranny and, seemingly, hint that it constitutes an earlier version of the tyranny Adolph Hitler sought to impose on twentieth-century Europe.

Although twentieth-century cinema has played a significant role, the Anglo-American ideological project of smoothing the transfer was effected in the nineteenth century, in a quintessential American literary project, James Fenimore Cooper's novels, which were among the most popular pieces of fiction in both England and America (often outselling the novels of Sir Walter Scott).[59] However formidable may be the mythography that Breight attributes to the trajectory of historiographic and cinematic treatments of Elizabethan England, arguably Cooper's mythicizing of America, his construction of "the nation's 'ideal' history," looms even larger.[60] While, as he wrote, Euro America was involved in pacifying the new continent, Cooper, "a believer in [the] ritual of national consensus," pacified the violence at an ideational level.[61]

In his *Leatherstocking Tales*, and most notably in his *The Pioneers*, Cooper finesses both the rift caused by the American Revolution and the national legitimation issue arising from the dispossession of Native American nations. Writing at a time when Indians were a recognized challenge to the moral and legal legitimacy of the American nation, Cooper addressed *The Pioneers* to the question: "Who has the right to own and govern the land originally possessed by the Indians?"[62] As I noted in chapter 2 but want to elaborate here, to answer that question, Cooper articulates a discourse on inheritance with a discourse on the law to justify the dispossession. With respect to the discourse on the law, Cooper's complicity with the Euro American expansion and appropriation of Indian provenances simulates much of the legal process responsible for that appropriation. In particular the Supreme Court's decision in Johnson v. McIntosh, the year of *The Pioneers* publication (1823), covered the same issue of rights to land that Cooper addresses in his novel. In the case, the "landmark" opinion by Chief Justice John Marshall ranges beyond the validity of Euro-Indian relations to treat the U.S.-England relationship from which he extracts "rights of conquest" that allow Euro Americans to inherit the results of the English invasion.[63] Similarly, in *The Pioneers*, after struggling with a disjuncture between natural and positive law, where the former, enjoying Natty Bumppo's advocacy, would establish Indian land claims, Cooper relegates the "natural" world (including Natty Bumppo himself) to a generational past and seals the dispossession by turning to inheritance. He creates a family lineage through adoption, which connects England with Native America and thereby finesses the revolutionary rupture.[64] Susan Scheckel summarizes the legitimating effect of Cooper's inheritance ploy:

> In making inheritance the basis of a legitimate claim to the American land, Cooper shifts emphasis away from the Revolution as the crucial defining moment in American national history.[65]

After Cooper's contribution to the affirmation of an Anglo-American imperialism, and before a rapidly expanding participation by film in the Euro American ethnogenesis, key texts in the British American "imperial transfer" are Theodore Roosevelt's, Owen Wister's, and Frederick Remington's, in the form of an epic, a novel, and stories and illustrations, respectively. Roosevelt's pseudo (what he calls a "perfectly continuous") history of "English-speaking peoples" in his four-volume epic, *The Winning of the West* (briefly treated in chapter 3), alternatively depopulates and repopulates the West. He justifies the expansion of white America in some places by claiming that they are occupying "waste" spaces visited only "a week or two every year,"[66] and in others by having "savage and formidable foes"[67] fighting heroic settlers with "fierce and dogged resistance,"[68] virtually every step of the way. Adding a biopolitical corollary to his romantic *soldatesque* and reproducing the anti-Spanish sentiment that was integral to English imperialism, Roosevelt praises "the English race" for maintaining its ethnic integrity by exterminating or driving off the Native Americans rather than, like the Spanish in their colonial venues, "sitting down in their midst" and becoming a "mixed race."[69] Subsequently, Roosevelt implemented his contempt for Spanish colonial practices by taking a leading role in a war (the Spanish-American) that both dispossessed Spain of its colonies and constituted a signature event in the Anglo-American imperial transfer.

Roosevelt's friend, the writer Owen Wister (whom I summoned briefly in chapters 3 and 5), shared and popularized Roosevelt's view of Anglo Saxon superiority in his fiction. In his brief story "The Course of Empire," (rewritten as "The Evolution of the Cow-Puncher," noted in chapter 3), Wister places an English nobleman in Texas and has him adapt rapidly, using his already developed skills as a horseman and marksman.[70] The "object lesson" to be drawn, according to Wister, is that once "the English nobleman smelt Texas, the slumbering untamed Saxon awoke in him," so that he was able to display himself as "a born horseman," and a "perfect athlete." The adaptation is explicable for Wister as a racial characteristic: "The man's outcome typifies the way of his race from the beginning."[71] And, seconding Roosevelt's dread of racial mixing, Wister decries the hybrid character of "our own continent":

> No rood of modern ground is more debased and mongrel with its hoards of encroaching alien vermin, that turn our cities to Babels and our citizenship to a hybrid farce, who degrade our commonwealth from a nation into something half pawn-shop, half broker's office.[72]

Like his cow puncher, Wister's commercial blockbuster (and avowedly neocolonial), *The Virginian,* also features a character whose superiority is a function of his racial purity and class background.[73] Unlike the "formula western" (in literature and film) spawned by Wister's novel, and in accord with the legitimation for Indian dispossession in Cooper's novels, *The Virginian* deploys an image of a "nation governed by those few whose natural superiority is a function of breeding and inheritance."[74] Throughout the novel the Virginian is juxtaposed to lessor men, for example, Shorty, who manifest a "featureless mediocrity," a "countenance like thousands." Whereas Roosevelt had evacuated most of the Native Americans from the western ethnoscape, Wister's novel effectively evacuates the non-Anglo cowboys. Along with Frederick Remington, whose illustrations adorn Wister's novels and stories (and a Roosevelt commentary), Wister invents a whitened West as a venue for imperialist adventurers.

From the point of view of an imperialist imaginary, Remington presents a more ambiguous case than Roosevelt and Wister. A friend of both men, his illustrations in Wister's *The Virginian* and in Roosevelt's serialized publication *Ranch Life and the Hunting Trail* (1888), for *Century Magazine* portray the cowboy-as-natural-aristocrat that Wister and Roosevelt invented. Nothing testifies more strikingly to Remington's view of the cowboy as a legacy of English aristocracy than his *Last Cavalier* (1895) painting (figure 14), in which a cowboy is on horseback in the foreground while the background

**Figure 14**   Frederic Remington, *The Last Cavalier,* 1895. Private Collector, Cincinnati, Ohio. Used with permission.

consists in a faded panorama of historical horsemen, of which the most prominent are generations of English knights.

This painting along with numerous others in Roosevelt's book as well as, for example, the illustrations for several of Wister's cowboy stories in *Harper's* and *Colliers,* helped invent the popular culture image of the West. And like Cooper, Wister, and Roosevelt, Remington portrayed a vast cultural gulf between Euro and Native Americans. Unlike those three, however, Remington, in both his illustrations and writings, displayed an ethnographic as well as an imperialist mentality; he sought to study and represent an "Indian character," which, however, given his unalterable Euro-oriented gaze, romanticized primitivism.[75]

Ultimately, Remington's contributions, at least as much as Roosevelt's and Wister's, contributed to the "imperial transfer" by constructing a primarily Europeanized West, featuring heroic and aristocratic white cowboys, horsemanship, and guns at the moral center of the new West. In addition to his vast corpus of paintings and drawings (numbering 2,750),[76] as well as sculptures and writings, he served as a journalist in two episodes of U.S. imperial expansion. On the continental front, he served as an "artist war correspondent" with General Nelson A. Miles in his campaign against the Apaches in 1886.[77] And, subsequently, he helped to sell the U.S. takeover of Spanish colonial possessions, helping to build anti-Spanish sentiment before and during what he called "the Cowboy's War" by providing illustrations for William Randolph Hearst's *New York Journal,* for example, his drawing of a strip search of an American woman by "the evil Spaniards," and his famous painting of the war, *Charge of the Rough Riders at San Juan Hill,* arguably another version of his "'last Cavalier' myth."[78]

## Cinema: The New History-Making Genre

While Remington participated in legitimating Euro America's imperial consolidation, primarily with drawing and painting technologies at the turn of the century, the film genre was to take over that role throughout the twentieth century. Perhaps the most significant linkage is between Remington's role and that of John Ford's, a connection that is most manifest in the way the two rendered the social history of the West. Remington rendered the process of Euro American settlement and the Native American resistance by exploring types. In his celebration of imperial expansion, he represented not only the cowboy and the Indian warrior but also the old mountain man, the French Canadian trapper, and the Mexican vaquero, among others.[79] This version of the biopolitics of the expansion westward was to be taken up by John Ford in his first epic western film, *Stagecoach,* which I treat briefly in chapter 5.

As I noted, in *Stagecoach,* Ford, like Cooper and Wister, constructs the American West as an evolving social order, which is represented both within the stagecoach itself (a microcosm of that evolving order) and by the types that Ford treats as those to be superceded (caricatures of Mexicans and Indians).[80] *Stagecoach* is therefore primarily a celebration of Euro American expansion. Despite the few satiric moments in which the film anticipates the complications Ford was to insinuate into the West's racial-spatial order in his later films, for the most part, *Stagecoach* evinces no ambivalence about the displacement of Native American nationhood. However, subsequently, in arguably one of the most significant twentieth-century films, *The Searchers* (also treated briefly in chapters 4 and 5), Ford's West becomes more complicated. Most notably, John Wayne, who is unambiguously heroic in *Stagecoach* as the Ringo Kid (saving the stage's passengers from an attack by menacing Indians), becomes, as Ethan Edwards, both hero and anti-hero in *The Searchers.* He is at once an Indian-hating racist and an exemplar of heroic masculinity, wise in the ways of his adversaries and protective of those with whom he is associated.

The details of the family drama in the film—it is implied that Ethan has had a romantic attachment to his brother's wife—are less important than the historical context and social setting. Ford's film maps the expanding world of post-Civil War America and reenacts the encounters among white settlers, Spanish aristocrats, and Indian nations, shortly after Texas had become independent. The film's historical moment is right after Texas had violently extracted itself from Mexican control and was in a period of ongoing war with Comanches (who were not defeated until the Red River Indian War of 1874–1875). In the film, a Comanche war party, led by Scarface, kills Ethan's brother and wife, rapes, mutilates, and kills their eldest daughter, Lucy, and carries off Debbie, the younger daughter. The episode precipitates a captivity narrative (one of the oldest modes of American literature). The main searchers are Ethan and young Martin Pawley, a part Cherokee, whose Indianness is constantly disparaged by Ethan during their quest to find Debbie and exact revenge for the massacre. The search proceeds for five years, allowing Ford to present the articulation of generational and historical times. Ethan's paternal relationship with Martin (which he resists until making his will near the end of the film) sets a background for his anti-miscegenation fixation and sets in motion the same biopolitical forces at work in Cooper's novels. Although Ethan ultimately resists the impulse, he has sworn to kill Debbie when he finds her because she has become an intimate of a Comanche and, in his words, is "no longer white." Although Ford's film is somewhat more ambivalent about the ethnogenesis of the Euro American state than Cooper's novels, he offers a similar resolution, put into the mouth of Mrs. Joergenson, the mother of Martin Pawley's "intended," Lucy. She remarks at one point that the West will have a white future, but perhaps not until "all their bones are in the ground."

Nevertheless, Ford's film is not simply a narrative of white civilization displacing savage Indianness in the West. As is the case with Ford's films in general, a strictly narrative account misses the play of opposing forces and worldviews that clash in the film. Indeed, Ford's film anticipates the "dysnarrative" aspect of later, so-called "experimental cinema;"[81] *The Searchers* contains a resolution-inhibiting encounter between two different orders of coherence, the narrative and the structural. While in the narrative register, a resolution occurs because Ethan decides to bring Debbie home rather than killing her, Structurally, much of the imagery—stark juxtapositions between dark domestic interiors and a wide, seemingly untamable landscape— suggests that the space is too large to afford easy incorporation into the cultural habitus of any group. Moreover, there is no clear dividing line between Euro and Native Americans. Certainly Euro American practices of exchange are juxtaposed to Native American trading practices, most notably the difference between the double eagle coins that Ethan throws around and the trade that Martin effects for a blanket (while he is unaware that he is also acquiring a wife). But Ethan and his adversary, Scarface, operate with similar revenge motifs. And Ethan, despite his articulated contempt for Indians, displays many instances of Indianness, for example, speaking Comanche, desecrating a corpse to compromise its spiritual future, and scalping the dead Scarface. And the different groups are also similar in their violence. The scene of Ethan's family's burned farmhouse and dead bodies is parallel to a scene of a burned Indian village with dead bodies, courtesy of the Seventh Cavalry.

Most significantly, the antagonisms and boundary protection exhibited by Ethan Edwards is juxtaposed to that of a searcher who is seemingly peripheral to the main search—old Mose Harper, the man who, without even trying, actually finds the missing Debbie (and whose various appearances constitute a dysnarrative). Although the humorous antics of Mose tend to be treated by viewers as mere comic relief (for example, while he and the other Texas Rangers are under fire during a ferocious Indian attack, he exclaims, "thank thee Lord for what we are about to receive), Mose can be seen instead as one who operates outside of the racial-spatial order and its attendant antagonisms. While controlling territory, seeking revenge, and, in general, having one's ethnos dominate the landscape is what drives Ethan and Scarface, Mose is unimpressed with boundaries and enemies. In one scene, when chasing Indians is on the agenda, he begins an Indian dance rather than grabbing a weapon. And when he appears at each key juncture in the story, first at the farmhouse when the rangers form a posse in search of stolen cattle, then as he returns to see the farmhouse burned, and toward the end when he is asked to report on Debbie's whereabouts, a rocking chair is central to the scene. In the first, he sits in a rocker inside the house and, on taking his leave, thanks his hostess for the chair (while the others mention only the coffee). In the second, he finds the rocker outside the burned out farmhouse, and while the others are dealing with their anger and grief, he sits down to rock. Finally, in the third, he offers the information to Ethan about how to find Debbie in exchange for a promise of his very own rocking chair. Rather than merely exhibiting a demented and lazy loafer, through the character Mose, Ford's film offers a different kind of life world, one in which the drive is to abide without ethnic enmity and territorial displacement. For this reason among others, the film cannot be easily enlisted along with those texts that warrant or celebrate the nineteenth-century version of Euro American imperial expansion.

Subsequently, the more critical "post-westerns," which emerged in the last two decades of the twentieth century, have also addressed themselves to the consequences of the Euro American imperial expansion in the west, often with cinematic references to Ford's westerns (as in Jarmusch's references to Ford's *Liberty Valance* in his *Dead Man,* treated in chapter 5). Among these, German director Wim Wenders's *Paris, Texas,* is especially noteworthy here because it begins with a cinematic reflection on *The Searchers.* Certainly, in

**Figure 15**    Mose Harper in rocking chair, from *The Searchers*, 1956, directed by John Ford.

*The Searchers,* as in Ford's other westerns, the Indians are primarily props. Within the narrative register of the films (at times undercut with visual moments), white stories are foregrounded and Indians have primarily "iconic" roles.[82] In one of his later films, *Cheyenne Autumn* (1964), the Cheyenne, oppressed while attempting to return to their homelands in the north, become somewhat more central to the story than the Indians in other Ford westerns. And in an observation that helps to frame Wenders's cinematic disruption of the mythic west in *Paris, Texas,* Ford makes the point in *Cheyenne Autumn* that white language constitutes a cognitive imperialism; it is undoubtedly the most effective weapon used to conquer Indianness in the west. Although the signs of an Indian presence in Wenders's West are minimal, the hints of their former presence incorporate Ford's observation about the role of language and align his film with Burgoyne's earlier noted treatment of the western as "one of the most durable and effective masks for the disguised operational center of the nation-state" ... [its] ... "hidden text concerning its relationship with American Indians."

### *Paris, Texas*

Reminiscent of the opening scene in *The Searchers* (after a song about what makes a man wander accompanies the opening credits, the first scene in *The Searchers* shows John Wayne riding in from a vast panorama in Monument Valley), Wenders's film begins with a man, Travis, wandering over a large western landscape, close to the Mexican border, before he collapses in a small isolated gas station store where he has sought something to drink. Seemingly affirming Ford's insight into the role of language, when Travis's brother, Walt, comes from California to fetch him, Travis is speechless for much of their journey; he has wandered "beyond the frontiers of language."[83] Although some of the film's narrative can be quarantined within a Freudian family story, (particularly one oriented around patriarchal violence), the implied historical narrative (and dysnarrative) it contains provides a more effective political gloss.[84] Travis and his brother begin their journey to California without dialogue and with significantly different relationships to language. Travis is without speech, and Walt, who summons him back into language, is a not simply a prototypical middle-class man mouthing unremarkable platitudes, but also someone whose company makes roadside billboards.

Walt's vocation reflects Ford's *Cheyenne Autumn* point about white words taking over the West but with a decidedly Wenders inflection. Wenders's West is "*the* place [in America] where things fall apart."[85] For Wenders, the West has been abandoned—"civilization simply passed through"—so that now, for example, instead of a lot of people, "in the middle of a desert you come across a road sign reading: 375 Street."[86] As Wenders puts it, the West holds "names and writing . . . a lot of signboards, cinema facades, billboards half worn away by the elements, already falling apart."[87] Given this version of the West, *Paris, Texas*'s Walt represents Euro America's contemporary habitus. Instead of the settlers' homes, around which the action in Ford's films take place, there are signs and billboards. As Wenders notes, "a man will paint a big sign first of all, and then the sign counts for more than the building."[88] And Los Angeles, Walt's place of residence, represents the ultimate in an ersatz relationship with place (where representations trump built structures): "I was walking around in downtown Los Angeles, and all of a sudden down this dead end I saw a painted wall with its make-believe windows and a dainty awning."[89]

Wenders exhibits America's contemporary name-dominated habitus in his filming of *Paris, Texas*. The dominating imagistic aspect of the film's focus on signs is reflected in the "location scouting" stills, taken before the filming began; they include motel signs, road signs, abandoned café buildings with names in large lettering and, most tellingly, a small, almost effaced sign in the midst of an empty desert tract that reads, "Western World Development Tract 6271."[90] Rather than seeing America's "world of names" as merely a commentary on a contemporary rift between person and place, *Paris, Texas,* offers hints of a history of violent displacement that the naming-dominated white American habitus overcodes. Here Wenders is likely influenced by the Austrian novelist, Peter Handke, for the expressions "world of names" and "places of names" appear often in Handke's novelette, *The Long Way*

*Around,* which features a contrast between the Native American mode of dwelling in Alaska and the Euro American mode of dwelling in cities such as Berkeley (where apartment buildings have "colonized woods"), Denver ("Mile High City"), and New York ("The Big Apple"). In this latter mode, for example, the Northern Lights, which for Native Americans has cosmological significance, is reduced to the name of a street, "Northern Lights Boulevard" in a California city.[91]

To discern this aspect of the film, one must recognize the relays it creates between individual and collective stories. At the individual level, Travis, once he is summoned back into language, recovers the memory of his violence toward his wife, Jane. At the end of his personal search, which is consummated when he restores the relationship between Jane and their son, Hunter, he is able to verbalize his past violent acts and take responsibility for them. At another level, the film ponders Euro America's collective violence, primarily through images rather than with its major narrative thread. When Travis returns to his son after a long encounter with his wife, the film cuts to an alley where the worlds "RACE, BLOOD, LAND" are written on a wall. At roughly the same time, the camera shows a large head of a Native American woman, as part of a mural on the wall and an African American version of the Statue of Liberty. And yet another aspect of the history of imperialism is thematized. When Travis finally converses with his brother, Walt, we learn that they are Hispanic on their mother's side. Subsequently, Travis sings a melancholy Spanish song while in Walt's home, and later he renews his familiarity with his Hispanic side in a conversation with his brother and sister-in-law's Mexican maid, Carmelita, who asks him identity questions to help him select a mode of dress and a body language.

One ready-to-hand interpretation of the mixture of cultural and national codes—including the disjunctive Paris-Texas, a German doctor who treats Travis after he collapses, Walt's wife, who is French, and the Spanish maid, Carmelita—is to evoke the idea of cultural conflict.[92] While cultural conflict is one of Wenders's cinematic signatures (it is also central to his *An American Friend,* and is very much a part of this film) the concept of *critical translation* should be applied as well. After Walter Benjamin's insight (noted in chapter 1) that the translator is coming to terms with her/his own national-cultural-linguistic self-understanding while making sense of a foreign text, one can read Wenders's approach to Euro America's violent past as not only a recovery of American history but also as a reflection on Germany's Nazi past. Wenders's disjunctive assemblage of signs from both a German and an American past makes present, albeit ambiguous, the process through which memory becomes "history."

Again, Handke's *The Long Way Around* provides a proto-text. His main character, Austrian geologist Valentin Sorger, discovers the violence of names

**Figure 16**   Native American Image, from *Paris, Texas*, 1984, directed by Wim Wenders.

**Figure 17**   African American "Statue of Liberty," from *Paris, Texas*, 1984, directed by Wim Wenders.

**Figure 18**   Travis's macho lesson, from *Paris, Texas*, 1984, directed by Wim Wenders.

on the American continent while, at the same time seeking to come to terms with the violence of the Nazi period in Germany and Austria. Attempting, through his simultaneous reading of America and Europe, to evince a "science of peace" in the present, Handke's Sorger discovers that he must first free himself from being an unreflective part of his national patrimony, from being "the faithful replica of death-cult masters."[93] Like Handke (and also like novelist Thomas Pynchon, who offers a similar translation, linking the Nazi death machine and American violence within a satyric assault on 1960s America's domestic repression and violent imperialism—in his *Gravity's Rainbow*),[94] Wenders effects a simultaneous treatment of Nazi German and Euro America's racial violence. He does it most dramatically through the earlier noted slogans and figures on the wall, but he also evokes the violence of Germany's past through the doctor, who treats Travis, who, after his collapse, "falls literally into the world of language."[95] The doctor turns out to be "corrupt and greedy"; his demand of a large payment from Walt as a ransom for Travis is another aspect of Wenders's critical look backward at the biopolitics of Germany during the Nazi period.

Nevertheless, along with its moments of disruptive imagery, Wenders's *Paris, Texas*, contains a strong narrative similarity to Ford's *The Searchers* inasmuch as both searchers, Ethan and Travis, remain loners at the ends of the stories. But in *The Searchers,* Ford, as in his other westerns, displays an ambivalent position on myth, seeing it as both destructive and necessary ("print the legend" as he says through a newspaper editor in *The Man Who Shot Liberty Valance*). His films have continued to produce a West that by 1893, as Slotkin notes, had been historically "closed," as "a geographical place and a set of facts requiring historical explanation." Instead, it is ready-to-hand for people (for example, President Bush) to use as an unproblematic mythic West, "a set of symbols that *constituted* an explanation of history."[96] By contrast, Wenders is unambivalently hostile to national myth, both Germany's and America's. And, unlike Ford, he is unambivalently hostile to violence, which for Wenders has no heroes. As a result, in *Paris, Texas,* he restores the West as a place whose history must be reopened, as a set of symbols requiring critical explanation.

## Hollywood at War

Wenders returns to the issue of American violence in his *The End of Violence.* However, before examining that film, which is prescient with respect to America's contemporary "war on terrorism," I return to Ford, to the historic cinema-war relationship more generally, and then to Hollywood's role in what CNN has called "America's New War." Ford's *The Searchers* and some of his subsequent westerns both technically and narratively produce a West that cannot be unambiguously articulated with a heroic or democratic account of the U.S.'s developing continental nationhood in the nineteenth century. In particular, the films make it evident that America's Indian wars, along with the less violent aspects of the Euro-Native American encounter, constitute a troubled past that haunts attempts at either celebrating or exonerating subsequent war policies. The recent World War II film, *Windtalkers* (2002), which honors the role of Navajo code talkers, enlisted to stymie Japanese intelligence, is doubtless aimed at creating a more hospitable Euro American-Native American relationship by emphasizing a collaboration in a (relatively) morally unambiguous war, at a time when the U.S.'s increasingly aggressive war policy faces severe domestic and global criticism.

For much of the twentieth century, regimes involved in warring violence looked to film as a genre well-positioned to encourage national allegiance. Ford himself was enlisted in the making of documentaries supportive of the Allied cause in World War II (as were others major film directors such as Howard Hawks and Frank Capra). As noted in chapter 5, Joseph Goebbels, the Nazi propaganda minister, enthralled by the reality effects and their subtle persuasiveness in Hollywood films, created a substantial cinema propaganda campaign, which has been subjected to critical commentary ever since. For example, well aware of the film-war policy relationship in general and the case of Nazi Germany in particular, critical theorist and film director Alexander Kluge locates those film and television dramas that seem to provide a "universalistic representation of reality," as especially insidious. They belong, he argues, to a "pseudo public sphere," which aids and abets the "imperialism of consciousness" that is mandated in state projects of cultural governance.[97]

As is well known, such mandates are intensified in wartime. For example, in the British case, there was an unchallenged celebration of the war effort in feature films during World War II. In particular, such films as *For Freedom, Convoy, Ships with Wings, In Which We Serve, We Dive at Dawn,* and *San Demetrio, London,* combined patriotic drama and realism "to find a formula for the war narrative that would prove acceptable to audiences and critics."[98] Hollywood's U.S. role during World War II is similar. For example, the "B movie crime fighter," Ronald Reagan, who, as Michael Rogin famously shows, subsequently took his "Hollywood identity to Washington," made patriotic films during the war (before turning to his role as an unambiguous hero in westerns).[99]

The Washington-Hollywood romance had cooled considerably by the 1960s, especially as a result of the critical Vietnam War feature films, which made it difficult to incorporate that war into a patriotic scenario.[100] However, by the 1990s, after the Gulf War helped cure what pro-military people called "the Vietnam syndrome" (a popular resistance toward military adventurism), the U.S. "defense" establishment sought to enlist Hollywood in its training as well as it public relations projects. In August of 1999, in what the designer of the relationship called "a marriage made in heaven," "an unprecedented collaboration between the Pentagon and Hollywood" was effected. The U.S. army announced the formation of an "Institute for Creative Technologies" at the University of Southern California (chosen because of its close ties to Hollywood"). As a *Los Angeles Times* business reporter put it "the entertainment industry is expected to use [cutting edge technologies] to improve its motion special effects, make video games more realistic ... [and] to help the creators of military simulations develop better story lines that are believable and engaging."[101]

The new and friendly military-Hollywood relationship was in the news again after the September 11 attack and subsequent U.S.—British assault on the Taliban regime in Afghanistan. The Bush administration approached Hollywood film directors to enlist their talents in the "war on terrorism." In early November, 2002, the media carried a story about a meeting between White House advisor Karl Rowe and several dozen top television and film executives. Aware of the film industry's role in World War II, the Bush administration wanted "patriotic war movies that characterized the early years of that war.[102] After that meeting, "nearly a dozen" patriotic war movies were under production (for example, the above-mentioned *Windtalkers*), and television dramas followed suit. Among the most notable of the TV genre was an episode of *JAG* (a CBS drama about military lawyers). The April 30, 2002, episode, produced with the Pentagon's help, featured a trial of a defiant al Qaida terrorist (doubtless modeled after Zacarias Moussaoui, the alleged twentieth hijacker) by a military tribunal at which he receives a "fair trial" (a promise by Defense Secretary Rumsfeld to the media after the tribunal plan was floated). As one commentary notes:

> [T]he strategy behind the "Tribunal" episode is more transparent than ever: the show creates the wish-fulfillment fantasy of capturing a terrorist responsible for the attacks, depicts an idealized military, yet ends with an ominous threat of more terror in the works, affirming the government's real-life message that American must remain vigilant.[103]

Extending the media campaign to trials is not surprising given the extraordinary legal quandary the government is in. Alleged plotters are to be tried by military tribunals that operate without the accused's presumption of innocence and on the basis of some evidence that their attorneys cannot see. In some cases, U.S. citizens are being held without trial, as the Bush administration places intelligence gathering above the rights of the accused, arguing that a state of war justifies the abrogation of rights. As intelligence gathering by FBI agents is creating a pervasive climate of intimidation, even extended to surveillance of people's library borrowing profiles and Internet searches, and as the White House encourages the population at large to take on a surveillant attitude, passing information on what they see as suspicious activities to government agencies (a "human resource spy network reminiscent of the earlier mentioned Cecilian hegemony in Elizabethan England), the entertainment industry is being suborned. For example, Hollywood stars are shown answering phones for September 11 charities in three-minute trailers released in theaters throughout the country. And, in general, the relationship between the Bush administration and studio executives is positive. Hollywood, notes one White House official, is "way out in front of us in getting patriotic messages out just like the Hollywood community was in World War II."[104] In light of these developments, I summon Wim Wenders again, this time to reflect on the current episode of imperial violence and as an antidote to the U.S. entertainment industry's complicity in it.

### Wim Wenders's *The End of Violence*

After having treated, allegorically, much of Euro America's initial enactment of imperial sovereignty in *Paris, Texas,* Wenders undertook a powerful meditation on an attempt to eliminate all violent crime in *The End of Violence* (1997). His approach in the film articulates cinematically with what Baudrillard has suggested about ending terror, when (as noted above) he remarks that to "nip terror in the bud," a state would have "to equip itself with its own terrorism and in doing so simply generalize terror at all levels." *The End of Violence* is set in a Los Angeles that has been equipped to surveill and totally eliminate all violent crime. But at the same time, through one of the characters, a Salvadorean woman hired to spy on a surveillance technician, the film treats the issue of U.S. imperial sovereignty, especially as it aids and abets both domestic and foreign aspects of state violence.

The film addresses it self to a parallel system of power and violence, that articulated by the Hollywood film industry and that of a panoptic surveillant, and ultimately terrorist government. Two management-of-violence persona and their venues are featured at the outset. First, there is Hollywood producer Mike Max, whose specialty is violent crime thrillers. He manages his film production empire from a distance, connecting with his staff with his laptop computer, while seated on his Malibu patio, overlooking the Pacific Ocean. At the same time Ray Bering manages an anti-crime project in which satellites

**Figure 19**  Ray Bering in the observatory, from *The End of Violence*, 1996, directed by Wim Wenders.

monitor Los Angeles streets with hidden cameras whose visual data are processed in his planetarium-like building on a Los Angeles hilltop (the Griffith Observatory).

The two become connected when Max gets an email from Bering, which details the satellite monitoring of the city. Because Max's vocation is suspect and Ray himself is under surveillance, Max is subsequently abducted by henchmen sent to kill him. They fail to carry it out when, after Max delays them with promises of wealth, they are mysteriously shot, after which Max goes underground, becoming part of the work crew of Mexican gardeners who manage the grounds of his estate. Once Ray is ultimately murdered (because his scrutiny of the stills from the killing of the henchmen is reported by the suborned Salvadorean woman, posing as a cleaning woman, hired to spy on him), it becomes clear that the process of seeking to end violence is a cure more violent than its objects of attention.

At the same time that the narrative carries the film forward, making clear that the brave new world of a crime-free Los Angeles is far more horrific than the prior version, Wenders's film provides two levels of intimacy in a world increasingly reliant on distance. Cinematically, the painterly dimension of the film (for example, a diner scene that evokes Edward Hopper's *Nighthawks* [1942]) evokes an aesthetics of the city that is unavailable on the digitalized versions that make their way onto Max's and Bering's screens. And at another level, Max and Bering are shown in their respective moments of intimate attachment. For Bering, his devoted and caring relationship with his father (who is shown in a room full of books and working with an older technology, a typewriter) contrasts with his distant relationship with the rest of the city. And, when his extension of his intimacy to the Salvadorian cleaning woman, with whom he has an affair, ends in his death (when she reports his suspicious activity), it is implied that ending violence also radically compromises the possibility of intimate attachments.

In Max's undercover sojourn, living with his Mexican gardeners, the film supplies a another episode of intimacy. In contrast with his earlier laptop-mediated distance form Los Angeles' infrastructure, Max enjoys an episode of comradely and familial belonging, which contrasts dramatically with the cold distance in his broken marriage. The making of violent representations had kept the life world of Mike Max at a distance. In particular, he had not been in touch with a laboring infrastructure, which results from transnational relationships and, among other things, made possible his leisurely poolside working style. Although no global structural supplements are offered to tell us how the gardeners are recruited into their profession, the transnational relationships that attend "the end of violence" in Los Angeles are supplied through the implied biography of Bering's maid/lover, Mathilda.

Mathilda, whose family was wiped out by death squads (supported, as history has shown, by U.S. policy) has scars which, until they become intimate, Ray Bering admits that he had never noticed. At the end of the film, the anti-crime FBI unit that has been responsible for killing Bering also threatens to kill Matilda. Following the logic of a totalizing approach to ending all violence, the antiviolence organization turns out to be threatened by its own employees, at least one of whom, ironically, is recruited because of the complicity of an antiviolence organization in global violence. Through "the domestic" Mathilda, then, the boundary between domestic and global violence is effaced. The antiviolence project has eventuated in a vast, secret, and largely unseen organization of state terror.

## Conclusion: Cultural Governance and Political Critique

> Listen ... listen: this is war's evensong, the War's canonical hour, and the night is real.
>
> Thomas Pynchon, *Gravity's Rainbow*

After 9/11, life began imitating Wenders's feature film *The End of Violence,* as the Bush administration's "war on terror" turned to the creation of a domestic surveillance network, a suspension of due process for both citizen and noncitizen suspects, and a set of plans, (implemented with the March 2003 attack on Iraq) for military assaults on countries that support "terrorists" in direct or indirect ways. Among other things, the CIA-FBI nexus, which is part of the administration's new "Homeland Security" office, is at least as intimidating as the end-of-violence organization that Wenders depicts in his film. Wenders's film is not moralistic. Instead of harping on a specific message, it begins with a query to director Mike Max from an off-screen voice: "Define violence. You're making a movie about it. Shouldn't you know what it is?" Max resists a definitive answer. And, similarly, rather than defining violence, Wenders's film ponders it, treating especially the relays between shooting (in a filmic sense) and shooting to kill.

Another dimension of cinematic shooting, however, is shooting to influence. Much of *The End of Violence* focuses on artistic media. For example, the film's meditation on the violence-artistic media relationship includes an episode of artistic readings at a Los Angeles performance venue, where Ade, an African American poet, mimes a white teenager being molested by her father. And at another point, a character ponders the question of whether observing nuclear particles can affect their behavior. Such moments speak to the question of the power of the arts to affect how people act. While that issue will always escape definitive conclusion, certainly one can place more confidence in the effect of the arts on how people think. It is doubtless that assumption that drives the Bush administration's attempt to enlist the entertainment industry to produce patriotic, policy-friendly features and dramas.

Yet, as I noted with respect to Bush's turn to the classic western, artistic productions are open to continuing interpretation. Thus, for example, although the Jerry Bruckheimer/Ridley Scott treatment of the U.S. intervention in Somalia, *Black Hawk Down,* drew optimistic administration support (the Washington premier was attended by Secretary of Defense Rumsfeld and Vice President Cheney),[105] the film does not unambiguously provide the romantic *soldatesque* that the administration expected. Although the film portrays an (unsuccessful attempt) to eliminate a political leader involved in violence unfavorable to American interests (now part of the administration's war agenda), it does not clearly valorize the policy or the attempt. Certainly, its version of good guys (American soldiers engaged in resolute duty and often heroic mutual support) and the bad guys (murderous Somali mercenaries) plays into the administration's hands, but at the same time, no clear point of view on the policy or its failed implementation strikes the viewer. Ultimately, at a historical moment when a government is seeking support from the arts to extend its sphere of imperial violence while, at the same time, closing what has been one of history's most open societies, the arts can be mobilized to resist. Its archives remain open to a process in which memory can never be constructed as definitive history. Those who would use films in particular or the arts in general to achieve quiescence can never rest assured.

# Notes

## Preface

1. Among the most notable of these are Jean Baudrillard, Pierre Bourdieu, Gilles Deleuze, Jacques Derrida, Michel Foucault, Jean-Francois Lyotard, and Jean-Luc Nancy.
2. Walter Mignolo, "The Geopolitics of Knowledge and the Colonial Difference," *South Atlantic Quarterly* 101: 1 (2002), p. 67.
3. Nestor Garcia Canclini, *Hybrid Cultures: Strategies for Entering and Leaving Modernity*, trans. Christopher L. Chiappari and Silvia L. Lopez (Minneapolis: University of Minnesota Press, 1995), p. 43.
4. Gilles Deleuze, "Having an Idea in Cinema," trans. Eleanor Kaufman, in Eleanor Kaufman and Kevin Jon Heller, eds., *Deleuze and Guattari: New Mappings in Politics, Philosophy, and Culture* (Minneapolis: University of Minnesota Press, 1998), p. 17.
5. Franz Fanon, *Black Skin, White Masks*. Trans. Charles Lam Markmann (London; Pluto, 1986), pp. 17–18.
6. Epeli Hau'ofa, "Our Sea of Islands," in *A New Oceania: Rediscovering Our Sea of Islands* (Suva, Fiji: University of the South Pacific, 1993), pp. 6–7.
7. Antonio Benetz-Rojo, "The Repeating Island," in Gustavo Perez Firmat, ed., *Do the Americas Have a Common Literature?* (Durham, NC: Duke University Press, 1990), p. 93.
8. *Ibid.*, p. 86.
9. Quotation from Walter Mignolo, *The Darker Side of the Renaissance: Literacy, Territoriality, and Colonization* (Ann Arbor: University of Michigan Press, 1995), p. 5.
10. See *Ibid.*, p. 9.
11. Dipesh Chakrabarty, "Marxism After Marx: History, Subalternity and Difference," in Saree Makdisi et al., eds., *Marxism Beyond Marxism* (New York: Routledge, 1996), p. 67.
12. Georges Didi-Huberman, "The art of not describing; Vermeer—the detail and the patch," *History of the Human Sciences* 2: 2 (June 1989), p. 141.
13. *Ibid.*
14. See Michel Foucault's early and comprehensive treatment of discourse production: *The Archaeology of Knowledge*, trans. A.M. Sheridan Smith (New York: Pantheon, 1972).
15. Michel Foucault, "What is Critique?" trans. Lysa Hochroth, in Michel Foucault, *The Politics of Truth*, eds., Sylvere Lotringer and Lysa Hochroth (New York: Semiotext(e), 1997), p. 59.
16. Michel Foucault, *The Archaeology of Knowledge*, trans. A.M. Sheridan Smith (New York: Pantheon, 1972), p. 120.
17. Akhil Gupta and James Ferguson, "Beyond 'Culture': Space, Identity, and the Politics of Difference," pp. 65–80 in Jonathan Xavier Inda and Renato Rosaldo, eds., *The Anthropology of Globalization* (Malden, MA: Blackwell, 2002), p. 65.

## Chapter 1

1. Sally Engle Merry, *Colonizing Hawai'i: The Cultural Power of Law* (Princeton, NJ: Princeton University Press, 2000), p. 22.
2. Edouard Glissant, *Poetics of Relation*, trans. Betsy Wing (Ann Arbor: University of Michigan Press, 1997), p. 16.
3. See John W. Burgess, *The Foundations of Political Science* (New Brunswick, NJ: Transaction, 1994), p. 6.
4. See "Documents: Letters of Sanford B. Dole and John W. Burgess," *The Pacific Historical Review* (March 1936), pp. 71–75.
5. Burgess, *The Foundations of Political Science*, p. 40.

6. In 1898, after the overthrow of the Hawaiian monarchy and President William McKinley's signing of a resolution annexing Hawai'i, roughly two million acres of government and crown lands were ceded to the federal government.
7. William H. Burgess, "Federal recognition will result in legal apartheid," *The Honolulu Advertiser,* October 1, 2000, p. B–1.
8. *Ibid.,* p. B–4.
9. Haunani-Kay Trask, "Sovereignty stolen by U.S. must be restored," *Honolulu Advertiser,* October 1, 2000, p. B–1.
10. *Ibid.,* p. B–4.
11. Patrick D. Reagan, *Designing a New America* (Amherst, University of Massachusetts Press, 1999), p. 57.
12. *Ibid.,* p. 4.
13. Charles Merriam, "Progress Report of the Committee on Political Research," *American Political Science Review* 17: 2 (May 1923), p. 279.
14. *Ibid.,* p. 280.
15. Ellen Herman, *The Romance of American Psychology* (Berkeley: University of California Press, 1995), p. 138. See also Michael E. Latham, *Modernization as Ideology: American Social Science and 'Nation-Building' in the Kennedy Era* (Chapel Hill: University of North Carolina Press, 2000).
16. Timothy Mitchell, "Society, Economy, and the State Effect," in George Steinmetz, ed., *State/Culture* (Ithaca, NY: Cornell University Press, 1999), p. 77.
17. Gabriel A. Almond, Taylor Cole, and Roy C. Macridis, "A Suggested Research Strategy in Western European Government and Politics," *American Political Science Review* 49: 4 (December 1955), p. 1043.
18. *Ibid.*
19. Vincente Rafael, "The Cultures of Area Studies," *Social Text* 41 (1994), p. 3.
20. *Ibid.,* p. 6.
21. Kay Warren, *Indigenous Political Movements and Their Critics* (Princeton, NJ: Princeton University Press, 1998), p. 19.
22. Walter Mignolo, *Local Histories/Global Designs* (Princeton, NJ: Princeton University Press, 2000), p. 251.
23. *Ibid.,* p. 261.
24. *Ibid.,* pp. 262–63.
25. See Pierre L. Van Den Berghe, "The Modern State: Nation-Builder or Nation Killer," *International Journal of Group Tensions* 22: 3 (fall 1992), 191–208.
26. *Ibid.,* p. 197.
27. Historian Donald Grubbs, quoted in Clyde Woods, *Development Arrested: Race, Power, and the Blues in the Mississippi Delta* (New York: Verso, 1998), p. 3.
28. *Ibid.,* pp. 4–5.
29. *Ibid.,* p. 30.
30. *Ibid.,* p. 20.
31. *Ibid.,* p. 50.
32. *Ibid.,* p. 19.
33. *Ibid.,* p. 50.
34. *Ibid.,* p. 205.
35. *Ibid.,* p. 241.
36. See Jacques Ranciere, *Disagreement,* trans. Julie Rose (Minneapolis: University of Minnesota Press, 1998).
37. *Ibid.,* p.27.
38. Woods, *Development Arrested,* p. 260.
39. Daniel Lerner, "Preface," in Daniel Lerner, ed., *The Human Meaning of the Social Sciences* (New York: Meridian, 1959), p. 22.
40. See Daniel Lerner's panegyric on the Truman administration's "Four Point Program," in "Communication and Development," in Daniel Lerner and Lyle M. Nelson, eds., *Communication Research—A Half-Century Appraisal* (Honolulu: University of Hawaii Press, 1977), p. 148.
41. The quotations are from Saskia Sassen, "Globalization after September 11," *The Chronicle of Higher Education* 1/18/2002, p. B-11.

42. Herbert I. Schiller, *Culture, Inc.: The Corporate Takeover of Public Expression* (New York: Oxford University Press, 1989), pp. 137–138.

43. Quotations are from Jan Nederveen Pieterse, who supplies a critical history of the "political development" orientation and its successors: *Development Theory: Constructions/Reconstructions* (Thousand Oaks, CA: Sage, 2001), p. 28.

44. See *Ibid.*, pp. 45–50.

45. *Ibid.*, p. 7.

46. The best examples of historical treatments of changes in the "will to knowledge" are by Michel Foucault. The quotations in this section are from Gilles Deleuze's remarks on Foucault's work, from his essay "Life as a Work of Art," in Gilles Deleuze, *Negotiations,* trans. Martin Joughin (New York: Columbia University Press), p. 96.

47. Didi-Huberman, "The art of not describing," pp. 144–145.

48. *Ibid.*, p. 146.

49. *Ibid.*, p. 155.

50. *Ibid.*, p. 156.

51. Michael Fried, *Realism, Writing, Disfiguration: On Thomas Eakins and Stephen Crane* (Chicago: University of Chicago Press, 1987), p. 11.

52. *Ibid.*, p. 42.

53. The quotations are from Deleuze, *Negotiations,* p. 63.

54. Gilles Deleuze, *Cinema 2,* trans. Hugh Tomlinson and Robert Galeta (London: Athlone, 1989), p. 7.

55. *Ibid.*, p. 38.

56. For example, treating the U.S., ethnoscape, Albert Murray refers to it as "incontestably mulatto." See his *The Omni-Americans* (New York: E.P. Dutton, 1970), p. 22. The quotation on creolization is from Sydney Mintz, "Enduring Substances, Trying Theories: The Caribbean Region as Oikoumene," *Journal of the Royal Anthropological Institute* 2: 2 (June 1996), p. 302.

57. Lerner, "Preface," p. 23.

58. Carl E. Pletsch, "The Three Worlds, or the Division of Social Scientific Labor, circa 1950–1975," *Comparative Studies in Society and History* 23: 4 (October 1981), p. 568.

59. *Ibid.*, p. 33.

60. Daniel Lerner, *The Passing of Traditional Society: Modernizing the Middle East* (New York: Free Press, 1958), p. 45.

61. *Ibid.*, p. 113.

62. Walter G. Andrews, "Singing the Alienated 'I': Guattari, Deleuze and Lyrical Decodings of the Subject in Ottoman Poetry," *The Yale Journal of Criticism* 6: 2 (fall 1993), p. 197.

63. *Ibid.*

64. *Ibid.*, pp. 203–215.

65. See Kevin Robbins and Asu Aksoy, "Deep Nation: the national question and Turkish cinema culture," in Hjort and MacKenzie, eds., *Cinema & Nation,* p. 204, and Nicholas Monceau, "Confronting Turkey's Social Realities: An Interview with Yesim Ustaoglu," *Cineaste* 26: 3 (summer 2001), p. 30.

66. Douglas Frantz, "Turkish Court Hobbles a Popular Pro-Islamic Politician," *New York Times,* January 10, 2002, p. A-5.

67. Lerner, *The Passing of a Traditional Society,* p. 113.

68. Reinhard Schulze, "The Birth of Tradition and Modernity in 18th and 19th Century Islamic Culture—The Case of Printing," *Culture & History* 16 (1997), p. 29.

69. *Ibid.*, p. 41.

70. *Ibid.*, p. 52.

71. *Ibid.*, p. 43.

72. *Ibid.*, p. 31.

73. Lerner, *The Passing of a Traditional Society,* p. 48.

74. This point is made by, among others, Walter Mignolo, "I Am Where I Think: Epistemology and the Colonial Difference," *Journal of Latin American Cultural Studies* 8: 2 (November 1999), p. 238.

75. Dipesh Chakrabarty, "Marxism after Marx," p. 68.

76. Canclini, *Hybrid Cultures,* p. 9.

77. *Ibid.*, p. 41.

78. Achille Mbembe, *On The Postcolony* (Berkeley: University of California Press, 2001), pp. 7–9.

79. *Ibid.*, p. 15.
80. *Ibid.*, p. 17.
81. *Ibid.*, p. 9.
82. *Ibid.*, p. 4.
83. *Ibid.*, p. 10.
84. John Borneman, "American Anthropology as Foreign Policy," *American Anthropologist* 97: 4 (December 1995), p. 665.
85. *Ibid.*, p. 666.
86. James Clifford, "Identity in Mashpee" in *The Predicament of Culture* (Cambridge, MA: Harvard University Press, 1988), p. 277.
87. *Ibid.*, p. 318.
88. *Ibid.*, p. 306.
89. *Ibid.*
90. Walter Benjamin, "Critique of Violence," in *Reflections,* trans. Edmund Jepthcott (New York: Schocken, 1978), p. 287.
91. *Ibid.*, pp. 299–300.
92. Beatrice Hanssen, *Critique of Violence: Between Poststructuralism and Critical Theory* (New York: Routledge, 2000), p. 4.
93. Michel Foucault, "Nietzsche, Genealogy, History," in Paul Rabinow, ed., *The Foucault Reader* (New York: Pantheon, 1984), p. 88.
94. Jacques Derrida, "Force of Law," in Drucilla Cornell, Michael Rosenfeld, and David Gray Carlson, *Deconstruction and the Possibility of Justice* (New York: Routledge, 1992), p. 24.
95. *Ibid.*, p. 21.
96. The expression appears initially in Michael Omi and Howard Winant, *Racial Formation in the United States: From the 1960s to the 1990s* (New York: Routledge, 1995) (first edition in 1986). A recent elaborated using the expression is in David Theo Goldberg, *The Racial State* (Malden, MA; Blackwell, 2002).
97. See Paul Gilroy, *Against Race: Imaging Political Culture beyond the Color Line* (Cambridge, MA: Harvard University Press, 2000), pp. 58–59.
98. Goldberg, *The Racial State*, p. 4.
99. Anthony Marx, *Making Race and Nation* (New York: Cambridge University Press, 1998), p. 3.
100. See J. Kehaulani Kauanui, *Rehabilitating the Native: Hawaiian Blood Quantum and the Politics of Race, Citizenship, and Entitlement,*" Doctoral dissertation in the program in the history of consciousness (Santa Cruz: University of California-Santa Cruz, 2000).
101. *Ibid.*, p. vi.
102. *Ibid.*, p. 26.
103. See Cheryl Harris, "Whiteness as Property," *Harvard Law Review* 106 (1993), pp. 1709–1791.
104. Kauanui, *Rehabilitating the Native*, p. 34.
105. The quotations are from David Theo Goldberg, "States of Whiteness," in David Theo Goldberg, Michael Musheno, and Lisa Bower, eds., *Between Law and Culture: Recasting Legal Studies* (Minneapolis, University of Minnesota Press, 2001), p. 177.
106. Ronald Dworkin, *Sovereign Virtue: The Theory and Practice of Equality* (Cambridge, MA: Harvard University Press, 2000), p. 3.
107. *Ibid.*, p. 5.
108. Michel Foucault, "What is Critique?" trans. Lysa Hochroth, in Sylvere Lotringer and Lysa Hochroth, eds., *The Politics of Truth* (New York: Semiotext(e), 1997), p. 42.
109. Dworkin, *Sovereign Virtue*, p. 17.
110. *Ibid.*, p. 71.
111. *Ibid.*, p. 77.
112. Ranciere, *Disagreement*, p. 11.
113. *Ibid.*, p. 30.
114. Jacques Ranciere, "Politics, Identification, and Subjectivization," *October* 61 (summer 1992), pp. 59–60.
115. *Ibid.*, p. 63.
116. *Ibid.*
117. *Ibid.*, p. 15.
118. *Ibid.*, p. 39.

119. *Ibid.*, p. 101.
120. *Ibid.*, p. 77.
121. *Ibid.*, p. 79.
122. For an application of Ranciere's insights under this rubric, see Benjamin Arditi and Jeremy Valentine, *Polemicization* (Edinburgh: Edinburgh University Press, 1999).
123. "Integration" is the term Jurgen Habermas employs to treat a narrative of nation building. See his "The European Nation-State: On the Past and Future of Sovereignty and Citizenship," trans. Ciaran Cronin, *Public Culture*, 10: 2 (winter 1998), pp. 397–416. And see Timothy Mitchell's challenge to Habermas's narrative: "Nationalism, Imperialism, Economism: A Comment on Habermas, *Public Culture*, 10: 2 (winter 1998), pp. 417–423, in which he notes that contrary to Habermas's implication, imperialism was the context that shaped the nationalist movements involved in the creation of the modern nation-state.
124. See Matt Malkia, "Conceptual Analysis for the Social Sciences," on the web at http://www.uta.fi/laitokset/hallinto/cocta/Future_Plans.htm, p. 4.
125. Judith Butler, "Restaging the Universal," in Judith Butler, Ernesto Laclau, and Slavoj Zizek, *Contingency, Hegemony, Universality* (New York: Verso, 2000), p. 37.
126. James Clifford, *Routes: Travel and Translation in the Late Twentieth Century* (Cambridge, MA: Harvard University Press, 1997), p. 11.
127. Walter Benjamin, "The Task of the Translator," trans. Harry Zohn in *Illuminations* (New York: Schocken, 1968), p. 81.
128. Carol Jacobs, *In the Language of Walter Benjamin* (Baltimore: Johns Hopkins University Press, 1999), p. 76.
129. The implication I am deriving is close to that suggested by Jacques Derrida in *The Ear of the Other: Otobiography, Transference, Translation*, trans. Avital Ronell and Peggy Kamuf (New York: Schocken, 1985).
130. *Ibid.*, p. 32.
131. Harold Bloom and David Rosenberg, *The Book of J* (New York: Grove Weidenfeld, 1990).
132. Mignolo, *Local Histories/Global Designs*, p. 263.
133. *Ibid.*, p. 17.
134. *Ibid.*, p. 264.
135. Andrea Opitz, "James Welch's *Fools Crow* and the Imagination of Precolonial Space," *American Indian Quarterly* 24: 1 (winter 2000), p. 129.
136. *Ibid.*, p. 126.
137. *Ibid.*, p. 131.
138. *Ibid.*, p. 133.
139. *Ibid.*
140. Michelle Cliff, *Free Enterprise* (New York: Dutton, 1993).
141. On minor literature, see the original development of the concept in Gilles Deleuze and Felix Guattari, *Kafka: Toward a Minor Literature*, trans. Reda Bensmaia and Dana Polan (Minneapolis: University of Minnesota Press, 1986).
142. Anne Donadey "The Multilingual Strategies of Postcolonial Literature: Assia Djebar's Algerian Palimpsest," *World Literature Today* 74: 1 (winter 2000), p. 31.
143. *Ibid.*, p. 29. Donadey is quoting from Djebar's *Fantasia*.
144. Quotations from Samia Mehrez, "Translation and the Postcolonial Experience: The Francophone North African Text," in Lawrence Venuti, ed., *Rethinking Translation: Discourse, Subjectivity, Ideology* (New York: Routledge, 1992), p. 121.
145. *Ibid.*, p. 122.
146. *Ibid.*, p. 127.
147. This point is inspired by Jacques Derrida's reading of Benjamin's essay, which, after Benjamin, argues that translation must start from history: "*Des Tours de Babel*," trans. Joseph F. Graham, in Joseph F. Graham, ed., *Difference in Translation* (Ithaca, NY: Cornell University Press, 1985), pp. 165–207.
148. Emily Apter, "Crossover Texts/Creole Tongues: A Conversation with Maryse Condé," *Public Culture* 13: 1 (winter 2001), p. 95.
149. There are many usages of the concept of counter-memory. It is applied to Michel Foucault's work; see, for example, Donald E. Bouchard, ed., *Language, Counter-Memory, Practice*, trans. Donald F. Bouchard and Sherry Simon (Ithaca, NY: Cornell University Press, 1977). For a recent well articulated usage, see Louise Bernard, "Countermemory and Return: Reclamation

of the (Postmodern) Self in Jamaica Kincaid's *The Autobiography of My Mother* and *My Brother*," *Modern Fiction Studies* 48: 1 (spring 2002), pp. 113–138.

# *Chapter 2*

1. Mario Vargas Llosa, *The Notebooks of Don Rigoberto*, trans. Edith Grossman (New York: Penguin, 1999), p. 170.
2. The quotation is a line from Walter Kendrick's review of the novel (in the *New York Times Book Review*) excerpted on the back of the book.
3. Jacqueline Rose supplies a similar insight about the role of fantasy in the state's perpetuation of its reality. To fulfill "the requirement to make *sure* of itself," the state, she suggests, must invade its peoples' fantasies. It must rely not simply on raw coercion but also on "the inner meaning it holds for its subjects or the subjective belief they attach to it." See her *States of Fantasy* (Oxford: The Clarendon Press, 1996), p. 8. And Etienne Balibar, like Vargas Llosa, sees the nationalizing of a nation's social formation as a work of fiction. A nation-state, he notes, continuously fabricates a "fictive ethnicity": "The Nation Form: History and Ideology," in Etienne Balibar and Immanuel Wallerstein, *Race, Nation, Class: Ambiguous Identities* (London: Verso, 1991), p. 96. The most comprehensive treatment of nationhood as a product of narrative forms is in Homi Bhabha's edited collection, *Nation and Narration* (New York: Routledge, 1990).
4. The quoted expressions belong to Gayatri Chakravorty Spivak, "Woman in Difference: Mahashweta Devi's 'Douloti the Bountiful,'" in Parker, Mary Russo, Doris Sommer, and Patricia Yaeger, eds., *Nationalism and Sexualities* (New York: Routledge, 1992), p. 101.
5. Michael Hardt and Antonio Negri, *Empire* (Cambridge, MA: Harvard University Press, 2000), pp. 95–96.
6. Rogers Brubaker adopts a similar position when he suggests that one treat the "nation" as a category of practice, not of analysis: in *Nationalism Reframed* (New York: Cambridge University Press, 1996), p. 7.
7. The introduction of the concept of the imaginary to refer to the abstract attachments as-sociated with nationalism belongs to Benedict Anderson. See his *Imagined Communities*, extended and revised edition (New York: Verso, 1991). Anderson's most significant contri-bution is his treatment of the role of writing technologies and their realization in such genres as the novel and the newspaper in engendering national consciousness.
8. Peter Guardino and Charles Walker, "The State, Society, and Politics in Peru and Mexico in the Colonial and Early Republican Periods," *Latin American Perspectives* 73: 19 (spring 1992), p. 12.
9. David Nugent, "Building the State, Making the Nation: The Bases and Limits of State Cen-tralization in 'Modern' Peru," *American Anthropologist* 96: 2 (June 1994), pp. 338.
10. *Ibid.*, p. 337.
11. For example, as Nugent points out, in one region, the Chachapoyas in the northern Sierra, there were two different periods with respect to reactions to state centralizing initiatives. In the 1930s, the state was regarded as a "protector and potential liberator of a self-defined 'moral community'" so that the local, marginalize groups used the state to resist the local power brokers and assisted the state in the process of integrating the region and nationalizing the regional population but in the second phase, of centralization in the 1970s, the same 'moral community' regarded the state's expansionist policies as immoral and mobilized to thwart its attempt to impose greater control: *Ibid.*, p. 333.
12. Tracy Lynne Devine, "Indigenous Identity and Identification in Peru: *Indigenismo*, Education and Contradictions in State Discourses," *Journal of Latin American Cultural Studies* 8:1 (June 1999), p. 64.
13. *Ibid.*, p. 68.
14. In referring to state biopolitical initiatives, I am influenced by Giorgio Agamben's analysis of the topology of sovereignty. According to Agamben, sovereignty exists in "the intersection between the juridico-legal and biopolitical models of power." In addition to its legal supports and legitimations, it is situated in a complex topology of lives, both inside and outside its jurisdiction. Giorgio Agamben, *Homo Sacer: Sovereign Power and Bare Life*, trans. Daniel Heller-Roazen (Stanford, CA: Stanford University Press, 1998), p. 6.

15. *Ibid.*, p. 69.

16. Joseph Roth, "Rare and ever rarer in this world of empirical facts . . ." in *The Collected Stories of Joseph Roth,* trans. Michael Hofmann (New York: W.W. Norton, 2002), pp. 66–70.

17. The quotations are from Sarah A. Radcliffe, "Frontiers and popular nationhood: geographies of identity in the 1995 Ecuador-Peru border dispute," *Political Geography* 17: 3 (March 1998), p. 275.

18. The quotations are, successively, from Mark Thurner, "'*Republicanos*' and '*la Comunidad de Peruanos*': Unimagined Political Communities in Postcolonial Andean Peru," *Journal of Latin American Studies* 27: 2 (May 1995), pp. 291, 292, and 293.

19. *Ibid.*, p. 302.

20. *Ibid.*, p. 318.

21. *Ibid.*, p. 291.

22. *Ibid.*, p. 295.

23. Mario Vargas Llosa, "Questions of Conquest," *Harper's* 281: 1687 (December 1990), p. 51.

24. Mario Vargas Llosa, *A Fish in the Water,* 1st ed., trans. Helen Lane (New York: Farrar, Straus and Giroux, 1994), pp. 44–45.

25. Neil Larsen "Mario Vargas Llosa: The Realist as Neo-Liberal," *Journal of Latin American Cultural Studies* 9: 2 (August 2000), p. 162.

26. Quoted in Alberto Moreira, "The Order of Order: On the Reluctant Culturalism of Anti-Subalternist Critiques," *Journal of Latin American Cultural Studies* 8: 1 (June 1999), p. 141.

27. José Maria Arguedas, "Introduction" (from a lecture Arguedas delivered in 1965 at a public gathering in Arequiopa, June 14, 1965), in José Maria Arguedas, *Deep Rivers,* trans. Frances Horning Barraclough (Austin: University of Texas Press, 1978), p. x.

28. John V. Murra, "Introduction," in José Maria Arguedas, *Deep Rivers,* trans. Frances Horning Barraclough (Austin: University of Texas Press, 1978), p. xi.

29. *Ibid.*, p. xii.

30. *Ibid.*, p. xii.

31. Arguedas, *Deep Rivers,* p. 25.

32. Quotation from Mario Vargas Llosa, "Afterword," in *Ibid.*, p. 239.

33. Walker Connor, "When Is a Nation," *Ethnic and Racial Studies* 13:1 (January 1990), p. 99. It should be noted in addition that the recognition of an incomplete nationalizing process is often part of a state's nation-building strategy. As David Lloyd and Paul Thomas have pointed out, the state's justification for the need to continue the forging of a harmonious national order encourages it to locate itself in a narrative of an "asymptotically deferred harmony," *Culture and the State* (New York: Routledge, 1998), p. 33.

34. See Timothy Mitchell's use of the expression in "Society, Economy, and the State Effect," in George Steinmetz, ed., *State/Culture* (Ithaca, NY: Cornell University Press, 1999), pp. 76–97.

35. Brubaker, *Nationalism Reframed,* p. 16.

36. Ana Maria Alonso, "The Politics of Space, Time and Substance: State Formation, Nationalism, and Ethnicity," *Annual Review of Anthropology* 23 (1994), p. 381.

37. Anderson, *Imagined Communities.*

38. See Gilles Deleuze and Felix Guattari, *Anti-Oedipus: Capitalism and Schizophrenia,* trans. Robert Hurley, Mark Seem, and Helen R. Lane (New York: Viking, 1977), pp. 139–153.

39. *Ibid.*, p. 140.

40. This way of formulating Deleuze and Guattari's approach to the state's coding of bodies belongs to Paul Patton, *Deleuze and the Political* (London: Routledge, 2000), pp. 140–141.

41. For this aspect of the state-as-"apparatus of capture," see Gilles Deleuze and Felix Guattari, *A Thousand Plateaus: Capitalism and Schizophrenia,* trans. Brian Massumi (Minneapolis: University of Minnesota Press, 1987), pp. 424–473.

42. I treat the temporality of the state more extensively in Michael J. Shapiro, "National Times and Other Times," chapter 5 in *For Moral Ambiguity: National Culture and the Politics of the Family* (Minneapolis: University of Minnesota Press, 2001), pp. 112–138.

43. Henk van Woerden, "The Assassin," *Granta* 69 (spring 2000), p. 15.

44. *Ibid.*, p. 19.

45. *Ibid.*, p. 17.

46. The concept of a structure of feeling is Raymond Williams's. It is used variously in his writings, but is closest to the sense in which I am employing it in his *The Long Revolution*

(Harmondsworth: Penguin, 1961), and *Politics and Letters* (London: Verso, 1979). My discussion here borrows from the critique of Williams by David Simpson, who has followed assiduously the different meanings of "structure of feeling" throughout Williams's writings. See his "Raymond Williams: Feeling for Structures, Voicing 'History,'" *Social Text* 30 (1992), pp. 9–26.

47. The quotation is from Simpson, *Ibid.*, p. 20.
48. Van Woerden, "The Assassin," p. 20.
49. The quotation is from Cornell West's treatment of the contributions of Raymond Williams: "The Legacy of Raymond Williams," *Social Text* 30 (1992), p. 7.
50. Van Woerden, "The Assassin," p. 48.
51. *Ibid.*, p. 50.
52. *Ibid.*, p. 55.
53. For a discussion of "biopolitics," see Giorgio Agamben, *Homo Sacer: Sovereign Power and Bare Life,* trans. Daniel Heller-Roazen (Stanford, CA: Stanford University Press, 1998).
54. Van Woerden, "The Assassin," p. 55.
55. *Ibid.*, p. 58.
56. *Ibid.*, p. 73.
57. Gilles Deleuze and Felix Guattari, *Anti-Oedipus*, pp. 139–153.
58. James C. Scott, *Seeing Like a State* (New Haven, CT: Yale University Press, 1998), p. 52.
59. This way of formulating Deleuze and Guattari's approach to the state's coding of bodies belongs to Paul Patton, *Deleuze and the Political* (London: Routledge, 2000), pp. 140–141.
60. For this aspect of the state-as-"apparatus of capture," see Deleuze and Guattari, *A Thousand Plateaus,* pp. 424–473.
61. I am drawing on an account of the event in Samira Kawash, "Men: Moving Bodies, or the Cinematic Politics of Deportation," in Eleanor Kaufman and Kevin Jon Heller, eds., *Deleuze and Guattari: New Mappings in Politics, Philosophy, and Culture* (Minneapolis: University of Minnesota Press, 1998), pp. 127–141.
62. The political significance of the condition of being perceptible but not representable is elaborated in Gilles Deleuze, *Cinema 2: The Time Image,* trans. Hugh Tomlinson and Robert Galeta (Minneapolis: University of Minnesota Press, 1989).
63. *Ibid.*, p. 137.
64. *Ibid.*, p. 136.
65. David Campbell, *National Deconstruction* (Minneapolis: University of Minnesota Press, 1998), p. 23.
66. *Ibid.*, p. 53.
67. Robert K Schaeffer, *Severed States: Dilemmas of Democracy in a Divided World* (Lanham, MD: Rowman and Littlefield, 1999), p. 1.
68. *Ibid.*, p. 15.
69. Robert Getso, *Peace Review* 11: 4 (December 1999), p. 592.
70. Friedrich Nietzsche, *Thus Spoke Zarathustra,* trans. Walter Kaufman (New York: Viking, 1966), p. 48.
71. Urvashi Butalia, *The Other Side of Silence* (New Delhi: Penguin, 1998), p. 3.
72. *Ibid.*, p. 45.
73. Schaeffer, *Severed States,* p. 1
74. Amri Beso, "*Bosnian Blues,*" in Misha Berson, "Bosnia Blues," *American Theater* 13: 1 (January 1996), p. 18.
75. Robert M. Hayden, "Imagined communities and real victims: self-determination and ethnic cleansing in Yugoslavia," *American Ethnologist* 23: 4 (November 1996), p. 783.
76. *Ibid.*, p. 784.
77. Semezdin Mehmedinovic, *Sarajevo Blues,* trans. Ammiel Alcalay (San Francisco: City Lights, 1998).
78. *Ibid.*, p. 78.
79. *Ibid.*, p. 107.
80. *Ibid.*, p. 110.
81. *Ibid.*, p. 90.
82. Mieke Bal, *Death and Dissymmetry: The Politics of Coherence in the Book of Judges* (Chicago: University of Chicago Press, 1988), p. 170.
83. *Ibid.*

84. Butalia, *The Other Side of Silence,* p. 21.
85. The expression belongs to Julia Kristeva. See her "Women's Time," trans. Alice Jardine and Harry Blake *Signs* 7, no. 1 (spring 1981), 18–27.
86. See the series collected in the *New York Times* under the rubric of "How Race Is Lived in America:" on the web at http://www.nytimes.com/library/national/race/textindex.html.
87. Mirta Ojito, "Best of Friends, Worlds Apart," in *Ibid.*
88. *Ibid.*
89. Eric J. Hobsbawm, *Nations and Nationalism Since 1780* (New York: Cambridge University Press, 1990).
90. Reinhardt Koselleck, *Futures Past: On the Semantics of Historical Time,* trans. Keith Tribe (Cambridge, MA: MIT Press, 1985), pp. 10–12.
91. Philip Corrigan and Derek Sayer, *The Great Arch* (Oxford: Basil Blackwell, 1985), p. 49. The Corrigan and Sayer investigation of emerging British nationhood points out that the English portion of the United Kingdom has been a relatively unified state for a longer period than any other European state, and that the consolidation involved "cultural forms" as well as the fiscal administration of land divisions involved in that consolidation.
92. Among the analyses that emphasize the shift from the premodern to the modern state as one involving a frontier versus border practice respectively is Anthony Giddens's *The Nation State and Violence* (Cambridge, England: Basil Blackwell, 1983).
93. The treatment from which the quotations are drawn is in Richard Helgerson, "The Land Speaks: Cartography, Chorography, and Subversion in Renaissance England," *Representations* 16: 4 (fall 1986), p. 56.
94. *Ibid.,* p. 62.
95. Josef W. Konvitz, "The Nation-state, Paris and cartography in eighteenth- and nineteenth-century France," *Journal of Historical Geography* 16: 1 (January 1990), p. 5.
96. *Ibid.,* p. 4.
97. *Ibid.,* p. 5. Interestingly, the displacement of nobility-oriented territoriality with bourgeois-friendly cartography was reflected in other modes of enunciation. For example, in the early nineteenth century, the painter Ingres, who had specialized in portraits of the nobility (for example, the Duc d'Orlean) began painting bourgeois political notables, for example, Louis-Francois Bertin, the publisher of a political journal. See *Les Portaits d' Ingres* (Paris: Ministere de la Culture, 1985), pp. 71–75.
98. Loren Kruger, *The National Stage: Theater and Cultural Legitimation in England, France, and America* (Chicago: University of Chicago Press, 1992), p. 3.
99. *Ibid.,* p. 6.
100. *Ibid.,* p. 33.
101. *Ibid.,* p. 83.
102. *Ibid.,* p. 185.
103. Michael Neill, "Broken English and Broken Irish: Nation, Language, and the Optics of Power in Shakespeare's Histories," *Shakespeare Quarterly* 45: 1 (spring 1994), p. 3.
104. *Ibid.*
105. *Ibid.,* p. 14.
106. *Ibid.,* p. 15.
107. Carla Mazzio, "Staging the Vernacular: Language and the Nation in Tomas Kyd's *The Spanish Tragedy*," *Studies in English Literature 1500–1900* 38: 2 (spring 1998), p. 207.
108. *Ibid.,* p. 208.
109. Quotations are from Jochen Achilles, "'Homesick for Abroad': The Transition from National to Cultural Identity in Contemporary Irish Drama," in *Modern Drama* 38 (winter 1995), p. 436.
110. Quotations are from Josephine Lee, "Linguistic Imperialism, the Early Abbey Theater, and the *Translations* of Brian Friel," pp. 164–181, in J. Ellen Gainor, ed., *Imperialism and Theater* (New York: Routledge, 1995), p. 272.
111. Brian Friel's *Translations . . .* , p. 417.
112. *Ibid.,* p. 418.
113. Lee, "Linguistic Imperialism," p. 174.
114. Friel's play is one among many in which a Brechtian theatrical orientation, i.e., one that encourages critical thought in the audience rather than emotional identification with the characters, is enlisted to subvert the structures of intelligibility that have served imperialism

and nationalism. See, for example, the discussion in Aparna Dharwadker, "John Gay, Bertold Brecht, and Postcolonial Antinationalisms," *Modern Drama* 38: 4 (spring 1995), pp. 4–21.

115. Quotation from Diana Taylor's excellent treatment of Buenaventura's dramas: *Theater of Crisis: Drama and Politics in Latin America* (Louisville: University Press of Kentucky, 1991), p. 185.

116. *Ibid.*, p. 134.

117. *Ibid.*, p. 138.

118. *Ibid.*, p. 136.

119. Susan Scheckel, *The Insistence of the Indian: Race and Nationalism in Nineteenth-Century American Culture* (Princeton, NJ: Princeton University Press, 1998), p. 15.

120. *Ibid.*

121. See Scheckel's gloss on Cooper's *The Pioneer's* in *Ibid.*, pp. 15–35.

122. *Ibid.*, p. 45.

123. *Ibid.*, p. 54.

124. Quotations are from Rebecca Blevins Faery, *Cartographies of Desire: Captivity, Race, and Sex in the Shaping of An American Nation* (Norman: University of Oklahoma Press, 1999), p. 152.

125. Daniel K. Richter, *Facing East from Indian Country* (Cambridge, MA: Harvard University Press, 2001), p. 77.

126. Monique Mojica, *Pocahontas and the Blue Spots* (Toronto: Women's Press, 1991).

127. "A modern Chilean-born woman who carries her history of resistance from the survival of the Andean women, to the 'Amanda' guerillas, to her own story as a refugee. As a woman of the Americas, she accompanies Contemporary Woman #1 on her journey." *Ibid.*, p. 59.

128. Franco Moretti, *Atlas of the European Novel: 1800–1900* (New York: Verso, 1998), p. 14.

129. *Ibid.*, p. 35.

130. *Ibid.*, p. 40.

131. *Ibid.*, p. 22.

132. Georg Lukacs, perhaps the best known critical commentator on Scott's novels, also recognized the role of the novels, particularly the historical novel, in Britain's nation-building project. He saw in Scott novels an inscription of "the complex and intricate path that led to England's national greatness and to the formation of the national character": *The Historical Novel,* trans. Hannah and Stanley Mitchell (New York: Humanities Press, 1965), p. 54.

133. See Katie Trumpener, *Bardic Nationalism: The Romantic Novel and the British Empire* (Princeton, NJ: Princeton University Press, 1997).

134. Nina Gerassi-Navarro, *Pirate Novels: Fictions of Nation Building in Spanish America* (Durham, NC: Duke University Press, 1999), p. 109.

135. *Ibid.*, p. 7.

136. *Ibid.*, p. 8.

137. *Ibid.*, p. 119. The identity practices of the former colonial states have in effect reciprocated the uses of the other reflected in these novels. As Michael Kearney points out, these states intensified their biopolitical practices to supplement its territorial management. They became "social, cultural, and political form[s]" with "absolute geopolitical and social boundaries inscribed on territories and persons, demarcating space and those who are members from those who are not": Michael Kearney, "Borders and Boundaries of State and Self at the End of Empire," *Journal of Historical Sociology* 4: 1 (March 1991), p. 54.

138. Quotation from Mary N. Layoun, *Travels of a Genre: The Modern Novel and Ideology* (Princeton, NJ: Princeton University Press, 1990), p. xii.

139. See *Ibid.* for treatments of Kafani and other Middle Eastern writers, located within an analytic frame that speaks to the homology between narration deformation and antiimperialism.

140. The quotation (and the perspective I am offering on the special situation of the Lebanese and Palestinian novel) belongs to Edward Said. See his "Foreword," to Elias Khoury, *Little Mountain,* trans. Maria Tabet (Minneapolis: University of Minnesota Press, 1989), p. xv.

141. Khoury, *Little Mountain,* p. 62.

142. Rhonda Cobham, "Misgendering the Nation: African Nationalist Fictions and Nuhruddin Farah's *Maps,*" in Parker, Russo, Sommer, and Yaeger, eds., *Nationalisms and Sexualities,* p. 43.

143. See Catherine Bestemen, "Violent politics and the politics of violence: the dissolution of the Somali nation-state," *American Ethnologist* 23: 3 (August 1996) pp. 579–596.

144. My analysis here is influenced by the discussion in Derek Wright, "Nations as Fictions: Postmodernism in the Novels of Nuhruddin Farah," *Critique* 38: 3 (spring 1997), pp. 193–204.

145. Nuhruddin Farah *Maps* (New York: Pantheon, 1986), p. 18.

146. *Ibid.*, pp. 40–41.

147. *Ibid.*, p. 216.

148. Jurgen Habermas, "The European Nation-State: On the Past and Future of Sovereignty and Citizenship," *Public Culture* 10: 2 (winter 1998), pp. 397–416.

149. Timothy Mitchell. "Nationalism, Imperialism, Economism: A Comment on Habermas," *Public Culture* 10: 2 (winter 1998), p. 413.

150. Among the "official" texts that consigned U.S. racial inequality to a narrow policy problematic was the infamous Moynihan report. Daniel Patrick Moynihan issued his report on "the Negro family" in 1965. For a review of its implications and the controversy it attracted, see Lee Rainwater and William L. Yancey, *The Moynihan Report and the Politics of Controversy* (Cambridge, MA: MIT Press, 1967). For a treatment of the role of American social science in psychologizing rather than politicizing racism within a historical and structural frame, see Ellen Herman, *The Romance of American Psychology* (Cambridge, MA: Harvard University Press, 1995).

151. Jean Muteba Rahier, "Body Politics in Black and White: *Senoras, Mujeres, Blanqueamiento* and Miss Emeraldas 1997–1998, Ecuador," *Women & Performance* 11: 1 (March 1999), p. 106.

152. For a general treatment of this relationship, see Andrew Parker, Mary Russo, Doris Sommer, and Patricia Yaeger, eds., *Nationalisms and Sexualities* (New York: Routledge, 1992).

153. Anne McClintock, "No Longer a Future Heaven: Women and Nationalism in South Africa," *Transition* 51 (1991), p. 104.

154. Donna J. Guy, "'White Slavery,' Citizenship and Nationality in Argentina," in Parker, Russo, Sommer, and Yaeger, eds., *Nationalisms and Sexualities*, p. 202.

155. Mahasweta Devi, "The Author in Conversation" (with Gayatri Chakravorty Spivak) in *Imaginary Maps*, trans. Gayatri Chakravorty Spivak (New York: Routledge, 1995) p. xi.

156. *Ibid.*, p. xix.

157. *Ibid.*, p. xxii. Ironically, wealthy land holders and money lenders have also been anti-development historically. In the late Victorian period both found usury to be far more profitable than agricultural production, a situation related to the coercive levies that the English had imposed on Indian agriculture. See Mike Davis, "The Origin of the Third World," *Antipode* 32: 1 (January 2000), pp. 67–68.

158. The expression is Spivak's in "Woman in Difference," p. 98.

159. *Ibid.*, pp. 101–102.

160. Mahashweta Devi, "Douloti The Bountiful" in *Imaginary Maps*, p. 93.

161. Spivak, "Woman in Difference," p. 112.

162. Quotation from Michael Kammen, *In the Past Lane: Historical Perspective on American Culture* (New York: Oxford University Press, 1997), p. 175.

163. The quotation is from David Noble, *The Eternal Adam and the New World Garden* (New York: George Braziller, 1968), p. ix. The exceptionalist ideology has been subject to numerous critiques, most notably in David Veysey's influential essay, where he dismissed the notion of an American distinctiveness and asserts that contrary to the presumption of a generalized, unique, and singular American character (and mission), "we are but one fractional (and internally fractionated) unit in a polyglot world, and that social history is composed of a vast number of separate and distinct pieces, like a mosaic that seldom stops at international boundaries lines . . . " (Quoted in Kammen, *In the Past Lane*, p. 179).

164. Lauren Berlant, *The Anatomy of National Fantasy* (Chicago: University of Chicago Press, 1991), p. 34.

165. Sacvan Bercovitch, *The American Jeremiad* (Madison: University of Wisconsin Press, 1978), p. 205.

166. Toni Morrison, *Paradise* (New York: Plume, 1999). Hawthorn also inspires Philip Roth's *The Human Stain*, a novel he explicitly haunts, for Roth's Nathan Zukerman resides in Hawthorne territory in the Berkshires of Massachusetts and is evoked as a predecessor by the writer who says he would like to "find sustenance in *people* like Hawthorn." And the novel contrasts the troubled life of a part-black, assumed-to-be-white academic, who is so committed to passing

as white that he hides his "mixed" origins with his young lover, Faunia Farley, who "is not deformed by the fairy tale of purity."

167. Morrison discovered the basis for her story when, as she says, "I was looking at the book of photographs, *Ghost Towns of Oklahoma*," and noticed that, "it scarcely mentions any of the black ones." Quoted in "Morrison's West," *Vanity Fair* 450 (February 1998), p. 144.
168. Morrison, *Paradise*, p. 194.
169. *Ibid.*, p. 217.
170. *Ibid.*, p. 5.
171. *Ibid.*, p. 217.
172. See M.M. Bakhtin, "Discourse in the Novel," in *The Dialogic Imagination* (Austin: University of Texas Press, 1981), pp. 259–422.
173. Tobin, *Time and the Novel*, p. 6.
174. Morrison, *Paradise*, p. 217.
175. *Ibid.*, pp. 6–7.
176. Marc-Alain Ouaknin, *The Burnt Book: Reading the Talmud*, trans. Llewellyn Brown (Princeton, NJ: Princeton University Press, 1995), pp. xi–xii.
177. *Ibid.*, pp. 170–171.
178. Morrison, *Paradise*, p. 85.
179. *Ibid.*, p. 86.
180. Ouaknin, *The Burnt Book*, p. 158.
181. See Michel Foucault, "Of Other Spaces," trans. Jay Miscowiec, *Diacritics* 16 (spring 1986), p. 22.
182. Morrison, *Paradise*, p. 318.

## *Chapter 3*

1. The hyphenated term, "musico-literary" is borrowed from David Michael Hertz, who applies it to the convergence of the poetry and music of the French symbolist movement in the nineteenth century. See *The Tuning of the Word: The Musico-Literary Poetics of the Symbolist Movement* (Carbondale: Southern Illinois University Press, 1987).
2. The expression is Simon Frith's in his "Introduction" to *World Music, Politics and Social Change* (New York: Manchester University Press, 1989), p. 2.
3. I am indebted to my colleague, Sankaran Krishna, for pointing out the connection between the actual Rai and the fictional Rai.
4. Salman Rushdie, *The Ground Beneath Her Feet* (New York: Henry Holt, 1999), p. 203.
5. *Ibid.*, p. 24.
6. Salman Rushdie, *Imaginary Homelands* (New York: Penguin, 1992), p. 14.
7. *Ibid.*, p. 15.
8. My use of the term "hybridity" is based on its application to novelistic utterances by M.M. Bakhtin, who defines the hybrid character of novelistic discourse as "a mixture of two social languages within the arena of an utterance." See Bakhtin, "Discourse in the Novel," p. 358. Among the more critical uses of the concept of "hybridity"—in a broad cultural sense— are Homi K. Bhabha's in *The Location of Culture* (New York: Routledge, 1994), and Garcia Canclini's in *Hybrid Cultures*.
9. Rushdie, *The Ground Beneath Her Feet*, p. 20.
10. *Ibid.*, p. 93.
11. *Ibid.*, pp. 95–96.
12. See Tony Mitchell, "Indigenous Music and Music television in Australia," *Perfect Beat* 1:1 July 1992), pp. 1–16.
13. The quotation, based on an interview with Djur Djura, is from Timothy D. Taylor, *Global Pop* (New York: Routledge, 1997), p. 90.
14. Rushdie, *The Ground Beneath Her Feet*, p. 157.
15. Habermas, (1998) "The European Nation-State." p. 406.
16. Rushdie, *The Ground Beneath Her Feet*, p. 458.
17. Robin Balinger "Sounds of Resistance," in Ron Sakolsky and Fred Wei-Han Ho, eds., *Sounding Off! Music as Subversion/Resistance/Revolution* (Brooklyn, NY: Autonomedia), p. 15. James Clifford's analysis of diasporas is relevant here. He points out that "specific

cosmopolitanisms articulated by diasporic discourses are in constitutive tension with nation-state/assimilationist ideologies. They are also in tension with indigenous, and especially with autochthonous claims." See James Clifford, "Diasporas," *Cultural Anthropology* 9: 3 (August 1994), p. 308.

18. George Lipsitz, *Dangerous Crossroads: Popular Music, Postmodernism and the Poetics of Place* (New York: Verso, 1994), p. 138.

19. *Ibid*, p. 145. See also Andrew Goodwin and Joe Gore, "World Beat and the Cultural Imperialism Debate," in Sakolsky and Ho, eds., *Sounding Off!*, p. 125.

20. See Ian Maxwell, "Sydney Style: Hip Hop Down Under Comin' Up," in Tony Mitchell, ed., *Global Noise: Rap and Hip-Hop Outside the USA* (Middletown, CT: Wesleyan University Press, 2001), p. 270. See also Lipsitz, *Dangerous Crossroads*, p. 143.

21. The contrast between the assimilation Jewish American, Irving Berlin, and the African American, anti-assimilation, LeRoi Jones, is reflected in their name changes. Irving Berlin was originally named Israel Baline. LeRoi Jones Africanized his name to become Amiri Baraka.

22. Jacques Attali, *Noise: The Political Economy of Music,* trans. Brian Massumi (Minneapolis: University of Minnesota Press, 1985), p. 6.

23. Peter Wade, "Music, blackness and national identity: three moments in Columbian history," *Popular Music* 17: 1 (January 1998), p. 4

24. *Ibid.*, p. 7.

25. Ralph Vaughan Williams, ""Should Music be National?" in his *National Music and Other Essays* 2nd edition (New York: Oxford University Press, 1987), p. 1.

26. Attali, *Noise*, p. 55.

27. Attali states, for example, that "with music is born power and its opposite: subversion," *Ibid.*, p. 6.

28. Linda Hutcheon and Michael Hutcheon., "Otherhood Issues: Post-National Operatic Narratives," *Narrative* 3: 1 (January 1995), p. 1.

29. Jane F. Fulcher, *The Nation's Image: French Grand Opera as Politics and Politicized Art* (New York: Cambridge University Press, 1987) p. 1.

30. *Ibid.*, p.8.

31. *Ibid.*, p. 202.

32. *Ibid.*, p. 116.

33. See Nancy Vogeley, "Italian Opera in Early National Mexico," *Modern Language Quarterly* 57: 2 (June 1996), pp. 279–288. In another North American state venue, Canada, which also offers a postcolonial pluricultural context, the migration of the operatic genre was inserting, in one historical instance, into a different political problematic.

34. Quotations and description in Linda Hutcheon and Michael Hutcheon, "Imagined Communities: Postnational Canadian Opera," in Richard Dellamora and Daniel Fischlin, eds., *The Work of Opera: Genre, Nationhood, and Sexual Difference* (New York: Columbia University Press, 1997), p. 239.

35. Hertz, *The Tuning of the Word,* p. 13.

36. *Ibid.*, pp. 17–18.

37. Debussy was explicit about seeking to achieve with his music what symbolist poets were doing with words. As John R. Clevenger notes, Debussy "sought to forge purely musical correlates for Symbolist poetic techniques." See John R. Clevenger, "Debussy's Rome Cantatas," in Jane Fulcher, ed., *Debussy and His World* (Princeton, NJ: Princeton University Press, 2001), p. 93.

38. Hertz, *The Tuning of the Word,* p. 23.

39. Hertz, *The Tuning of the Word,* p. 16.

40. *Ibid.*, p. 57.

41. *Ibid.*, p. 78.

42. *Ibid.*, p. 117.

43. I am indebted to the ethno-musicologist Ricardo Trimelos for these insights into Debussy's liberties with tonality.

44. Clevenger, "Debussy's Rome Cantatas," p. 16.

45. See Hertz, *The Tuning of the Word,* p. 78, for this formulation with respect to Mallarme.

46. Clevenger, "Debussy's Rome Cantatas," p. 53.

47. The quotation and material on Bruneau's reaction to Debussy's music are from Jane F. Fulcher, *French Cultural Politics and Music* (New York: Oxford University Press, 1999), p. 44.

48. Philip Roth, *I Married a Communist* (New York: Vintage, 1999), p. 39.

49. Sam B. Girgus, *The New Covenant* (Chapel Hill: University of North Carolina Press, 1984).
50. M.M. Bakhtin, "The *Bildungsroman*," in Caryl Emerson and Michael Holquist, eds., *Speech Genres and Other Late Essays,* trans. Vern W. McGee (Austin: University of Texas Press, 1986), pp. 22–23.
51. Girgus, *The New Covenant,* p. 12.
52. *Ibid.,* p. 66.
53. *Ibid.,* p. 183.
54. Irving Berlin: quoted in John Lahr, "Revolutionary Rag," *The New Yorker,* March 3, 1999, p. 78.
55. Christian Appy, "'We'll Follow the Old Man': The Strains of Sentimental Militarism in Popular Films of the Fifties," in Peter J. Kuznick and James Gilbert, eds., *Rethinking Cold War Culture* (Washington, DC: Smithsonian, 2001), p. 8.
56. "Jake! Jake! The Yiddisher Ball-Player," words by Blanche Merrill, music by Irving Berlin in Charles Hamm, ed., *Irving Berlin: Early Songs,* Vol. 3, 1913–1914 (Madison, WI: A-R Editions, 1994), pp. 74–77.
57. Eric Rolf Greenberg, *The Celebrant* (New York: Everest House, 1982).
58. *Ibid.,* p. 14.
59. *Ibid.,* p. 135.
60. Girgus, *The New Covenant,* p. 18.
61. Quotation from David Monod, "Disguise, Containment and the *Porgy and Bess* Revival of 1952–1956," *Journal of American Studies* 35: 2 (August 2001), p. 285.
62. This point is made by Mark Steyne in *Broadway Babies Say Good Night* (Boston: Faber and Faber, 1997), p. 75.
63. See *The Songs of Irving Berlin: Patriotic Songs* (Milwaukee, WI: Hal Leonard, 1991).
64. Charles Hamm, "Genre, performance, and ideology in the early songs of Irving Berlin," *Popular Music* 13: 2 (May 1994), p. 145.
65. Quotation from Michael Denning, *The Cultural Front: The Laboring of American Culture in the Twentieth Century* (New York: Verso, 1996), p. 284.
66. Blitzstein dedicated *The Cradle Will Rock* to Bertold Brecht, whose conversations with Blitzstein influenced the play. The Brechtian *Songspiel* served as a model for Blitzstein, who noted that his play "was to be a colloquial piece; but it was also to be an opera" (quoted in *Ibid.,* p. 289).
67. The details of the play's initial staging are described in *Ibid.,* p. 285.
68. The Euro American composers in the nineteenth and early twentieth centuries who sought to contribute to a unitary and ethnically blind national culture were those involved in producing symphonic forms. However, Tin Pan Alley composers, those producing the Broadway form of musical theater, took over by the 1940s. For details on the earlier nationalistic initiatives of symphony composers, see Alan Howard Levy, *Musical Nationalism: American Composers' Search for Identity* (Westport, CT: Greenwood Press, 1983).
69. Paul Filmer, Val Rimmer, and David Walsh, *Oklahoma!:* ideology and politics in the vernacular tradition of the American musical," *Popular Music* 18: 3 (October 1999), p. 383.
70. Robert Day, "'Sooners' or 'Goners,' they were hellbent on grabbing free land," *Smithsonian* 20: 8 (November 1989), p. 193.
71. The so-called "civilized tribes" from the East brought black slaves and black relatives with them ("thousands of Negroes were neighbors or slaves of the Five Civilized Tribes"), and many became cowboys. See Philip Durham and Everett L. Jones, *The Negro Cowboys* (New York: Dodd, Mead & Co., 1965), pp. 18–19.
72. Filmer, Rimmer, and Walsh, "*Oklahoma!,*" p. 386.
73. *Ibid.,* p. 387.
74. The quotation is from the celebratory introduction to a selection of Wister's stories by Robert L. Hough in his *The West of Owen Wister* (Lincoln: University of Nebraska Press, 1972), p. vii.
75. Owen Wister, "The Evolution of the Cow-Puncher," *Harper's Monthly* 91 (September 1895), 602–617.
76. From Daniel F. Littlefield, Jr., *Alex Posey: Creek Poet, Journalist and Humourist* (Lincoln: University of Nebraska Press, 1992 (originally appearing in *Indian Journal,* December 14, 1894).

77. See the analysis of Posy's style in Alexia Kosminder, *Tricky Tribal Discourse: The Poetry, Short Stories, and Fus Fixico Letters of Creek Writer Alex Posey* (Moscow: University of Idaho Press, 1998).

78. The quotations are from Michael Jarrett, "The Tenor's Vehicle: Reading *Way Out West*," *LIT* 5: 3–4 ( 1994), p. 233.

79. The story of Oklahoma popular music and the movement of jazz musicians from Oklahoma to Kansas City is told in William W. Savage, Jr., *Singing Cowboys and All That Jazz* (Norman: University of Oklahoma Press, 1983).

80. Paul Carter provides an apt juxtaposition of the musical, *Oklahoma!* and Altman's *Kansas City*. He contrasts "imperial history," which is based on a "theatrical assumption that historical individuals are actors, fulfilling a higher destiny," with "spatial history," which, instead of treating historical spaces as "natural, passive and objectively there," focuses on the journeys through which spaces are shaped (p. xxi). And, he notes, in addition, that "spatial history ... does not organize its subject matter into a nationalist enterprise (p. 294). See his *The Road to Botany Bay* (Chicago: University of Chicago Press, 1987).

81. See Nathan W. Pearson Jr., "Political and Musical Forces that Influenced the Development of Kansas City Jazz," *Black Music Research* 9: 2 (fall 1989), p. 182.

82. Filmer, Rimmer, and Walsh, "*Oklahoma!*," p. 385

83. *Ibid.*

84. Quoted in Woods, *Development Arrested*, p. 3.

85. Paul Gilroy, *The Black Atlantic: Modernity and Double Consciousness* (Cambridge, MA: Harvard University Press, 1993), p. 3.

86. Noel Burch, "Spatial and Temporal Articulations," in *Theory of Film Practice*, trans. Helen Lane (New York: Praeger, 1973), p. 17.

87. LeRoi Jones (Amiri Baraka), *Blues People* (New York: Morrow, 1999), p. 57.

88. Robert Sterritt, "Director Builds Metaphor for Jazz in *Kansas City*," in David Sterritt, ed. *Robert Altman: Interviews* (Jackson: University of Mississippi Press, 2000), p. 211.

89. Connie Byrne and William O. Lopez, "*Nashville*," in *Ibid.*, p. 20.

90. The quotation is from Krin Gabbard's review of the film: *Kansas City, The American Historical Review* 102: 4 (October 1997), pp. 1274–1275.

91. See the Altman interview in Byrne and Lopez, *Nashville*, p. 21.

92. Quoted in Sterritt, "Director Builds Metaphor for Jazz in *Kansas City*," p. 213.

93. Sterritt's observation in *Ibid.*, p. 212.

94. Ibid.

95. On the blues fidelity in Southwestern jazz bands, see Jones, *Blues People*, p. 167.

96. See Ben Sidran, *Black Talk* (New York: Da Capo, 1971).

97. Lipsitz, *Dangerous Crossroads*, p. 63.

98. *Ibid.*, p. 61.

99. Houston A. Baker, Jr., *Modernism and the Harlem Renaissance* (Chicago: University of Chicago Press, 1987), p. 71.

100. The quotations are from David Horn, "From Catfish Row to Granby Street: contesting meaning in *Porgy and Bess*," *Popular Music* 13: 2 (March 1994), p. 170.

101. See Monod, "Disguise, Containment and the *Porgy and Bess* Revival of 1952–1956," pp. 305–306.

102. Quoted in Denning, *The Cultural Front*, p. 313.

103. John Gennari, "Jazz Criticism: Its Development and Ideologies," *Black American Literary Forum* 25: 3 (fall 1991), p. 449.

104. "Musicking" is Christopher Small's term, which he uses to distinguish an improvising approach to performance. See his *Music of the Common Tongue: Survival and Celebration in African American Music* (New York: River Run Press, 1987).

105. On this contrast between European and African American music see Bruce Johnson, "Hear me talkin' to ya: problems of jazz discourse," *Popular Music* 12: 1 (January 1993), pp. 1–12.

106. See Burrill Crohn, director, *The Coltrane Legacy* (New York: Video Artists International, 1985).

107. Small, *Music of the Common Tongue*, p. 382.

108. My use of the term "semiosis," is inspired by Walter Mignolo's discussion of colonial semiosis in his *The Darker Side of the Renaissance* (Ann Arbor: University of Michigan Press, 1995), where he treats the semiotic interactions between European conquerors and indigenous

meso-Americans, an interaction between incommensurate practices of signification in "radically different cultural traditions.

109. Coltrane's remarks on *Alabama* are reported in Sacha Feinstein, "From *Alabama,* to *A Love Supreme:* The Evolution of the John Coltrane Poem," *The Southern Review* 32: 2 (April 1996), pp. 315–327.

110. Attali, *Noise,* p. 58.

111. The quotation is from Mike Zwerin "Remembering John Coltrane," on the web at http://www.culturekiosque.com/jazz/miles/rhemile.htm.

112. Attali, *Noise,* p. 59.

113. Quoted in Zwerin, "Remembering John Coltrane."

114. Gilles Deleuze, *Difference and Repetition,* trans. Paul Patton (London: Athlone, 1994), p. 10.

115. *Ibid.,* p. 8.

116. Michel Foucault, *Death and the Labyrinth: The World of Raymond Roussel,* trans. Charles Ruas (New York: Doubleday, 1986), p. 16.

117. *Ibid.* p. 177.

118. Raymond Roussel, *How I Wrote Certain of My Books,* trans. Trevor Winkfield (New York: Sun, 1977), p. 3.

119. When he was thirteen, Roussel went to the Paris Conservatory, where he studied piano. Stating, however, that for him "words came easier than music," he turned to the novel as the genre within which he was to explore sounds and meanings. See John Ashbery's preface to Foucault's *Death and the Labyrinth,* p. xv.

120. Roussel, *How I Wrote Certain of My Books,* p. 11.

121. *Ibid.,* p. 9.

122. Quotation from Leon Botstein, "Beyond the Illusions of Realism: Painting and Debussy's Break with Tradition," in Fulcher, ed., *Debussy and His World,* p. 150.

123. Roman Jakobson and Morris Halle, *Fundamentals of Language* (The Hague: Mouton, 1971), p. 69.

124. *Ibid.,* p. 74.

125. *Ibid.*

126. Nathaniel Mackey, "Other: From Noun to Verb," in Krin Gabbard, ed., *Jazz Among the Discourses* (Durham, NC: Duke University Press, 1995), p. 85.

127. The quotation is from Bill Cole, *John Coltrane* (New York: Da Capo, 1993), p. 57.

128. For a discussion of the horizontal versus vertical approach to improvisation in hard bop or free jazz, see Paul F. Berliner, *Thinking in Jazz: The Infinite Art of Improvisation* (Chicago: University of Chicago Press, 1994), p. 128. It should be noted, however, that Coltrane's explorations were not entirely vertical. Influenced by both Miles Davis and Thelonious Monk, he also explored melodic and rhythmic changes, seeking "more plasticity, more viability, more room for improvisation in the statement of the melody itself" (Nat Hentoff, quoted in Mackey, "Other: From Noun to Verb," p. 78.

129. See in particular Slavoj Zizek's description of Schumann's piano piece *Carnaval* in "Robert Schumann: The Romantic Anti-Humanist," in his *The Plague of Fantasies* (New York: Verso, 1997), p. 200.

130. See Henry Louis Gates, Jr., *The Signifying Monkey: A Theory of Afro-American Literary Criticism* (New York: Oxford University Press, 1988), p. 52.

131. *Ibid.*

132. Mackey, "Other: From Noun to Verb," p. 83.

133. See Carl Woideck, *The John Coltrane Companion* (New York: Schirmer, 1998), p. 35.

134. *Ibid.,* p. 43.

135. *Ibid.,* p. 44.

136. Quoted in Cole, *John Coltrane,* p. 58.

137. Jakobson and Halle, *Fundamentals of Language,* p. 92.

138. Touré "Hip-hop Nation: In the End, Black Men Must Lead," *New York Times* on the web, 8/22/99.

139. Ranciere, *Disagreement,* p. 27.

140. Jones, *Blues People,* p. 66.

141. *Ibid.,* p. 35.

142. See "The Freedom Train" in *The Songs of Irving Berlin: Patriotic Songs,* pp. 20–23.

143. See Bryan Garman's treatment of the influence of Guthrie's music on Springsteen: "The Ghost of History: Bruce Springsteen, Woody Guthrie, and the Hurt Song," *Popular Music and Society* 20: 2 (summer 1996), pp. 69–117.

144. Jones, *Blues People*, p. ix.

145. *Ibid.*, p. 95.

146. *Ibid.*, p. 141.

147. Jones's expression in *Ibid.*, p. 57.

148. On the African heritage of African American signifyin' in both literary and musical forms, see Henry Louis Gates, Jr., *The Signifying Monkey* (New York: Oxford University Press, 1988).

149. See Mackey, "Other: From Noun to Verb," p. 83.

150. For a treatment of the manifestation of a blues aesthetic in African American writing, see Houston A. Baker, Jr., *Blues Ideology and Afro-American Literature* (Chicago: University of Chicago Press, 1984.

151. Langston Hughes, "Lenox Avenue: Midnight," in *The Weary Blues* (New York: Alfred A. Knopf, 1926), p. 39.

152. Walter Mosley, *RL's Dream* (New York W.W. Norton, 1995).

153. The quotation, which captures the essence of the style, is from the book jacket copy: *Ibid.*

154. *Ibid.*, p. 74.

155. Gilroy, *The Black Atlantic*, p. 32.

156. See Tricia Rose, *Black Noise: Rap Music and Black Culture in Contemporary America* (Hanover, NH: University Press of America, 1994), p. 10.

157. Mark Anthony Neal, *What the Music Said*, (New York: Routledge, 1999), p. 136.

158. See *Ibid.*, p. 165.

159. Tony Mitchell, "*Kia Kaha* (Be Strong): Maori and Pacific Islanders Hip-Hop in Aotearoa— New Zealand," in Mitchell, ed., *Global Noise*, p. 283.

160. Kelii W. "Skippy" Ioane, "In Flagrante Delecto," in *Big Island Conspiracy: Reflective but Unrepentent* (Honolulu: Deep Ka'a Ka'a Records, 1999). The translation of the Hawaiian expressions are by Noenoe Silva.

161. That the *mele* is either a musical or poetic form was noted in early Western analyses of Hawaiian lyrical practices. See, for example, Nathaniel Emerson, *Unwritten Literature of Hawaii: The Sacred Songs of the Hula* (Honolulu: Mutual, 1998). For a contemporary treatment from a Hawaiian perspective on the *mele,* see Noenoe Silva, *Ke Ku' E Kupa'aloa Nei Makou: Kanaka Maoli Resistance to Colonization* (Honolulu: University of Hawaii department of political Science, unpublished doctoral dissertation, 1999), especially chapter 4, "The Merrie Monarch: Genealogy, Cosmology, and Performance Art as Resistance," pp. 109–153.

162. Silva, *Ke Ku' E Kupa'aloa Nei Makou: Kanaka Maoli Resistance to Colonization,* p. 167.

163. Elizabeth Buck, *Paradise Remade: The Politics of Culture and History in Hawai'i* (Philadelphia: Temple University Press, 1993), p. 118.

164. John Charlot, *The Hawaiian Poetry of Religion and Politics* (Honolulu: Institute for Polynesian studies, 1985), p. 15.

165. *Ibid.*, p. 23.

166. *Ibid.*

167. *Ibid.*, p. 20.

168. Deleuze and Guattari, *Kafka: Toward a Minor Literature*, p.17.

169. Russell A. Potter, *Spectacular Vernaculars: Hip-Hop and the Politics of Postmodernism* (Albany: State University of New York Press, 1995), p. 68.

170. Despite significant division in the local Hawaiian community, there are at present there are at least "40 native Hawaiian groups actively promoting the restoration of the Native Hawaiian Nation." R.D.K. Herman, "Hawai'i at the Crossroads," in D.W. Woodcock, ed., *Hawai'i: New Geographies* (Department of Geography, University of Hawaii-Manoa, 1999), p. 80.

171. "Nanakuli Blues," written by Liko Martin and Thor Wold became the better known "Waimanalo Blues." recorded by various artists, including Gabby Pahinui, Country Comfort, and arlo Couthrie.

172. The anthem reference and suggestion about the efficacy of the song is taken from Jon Osorio, "Songs of Our Natural Selves: The Enduring Voice of Nature in Hawaii Music," unpublished paper, (Honolulu: department of Hawaiian studies, University of Hawaii).

173. Haunani Kay Trask, "Agony of Place," in Joseph P. Balaz, ed., *Ho'omanoa* (Honolulu: Ku Pa'a Inc., 1989), pp. 8–9.

174. George H. Lewis, "Don' Go Down Waikiki: Social Protest and Popular Music in Hawaii," in Reebee Garfalo, ed., *Rockin' the Boat: Mass Music and Mass Movements* (Boston: South End Press, 1992), p. 171.
175. *Ibid.*, p. 180.
176. See Andrew N. Weintraub, "Jawaiian Music and Local Cultural Identity Hawaii," in Philip Hayward, ed., *Sound Alliances* (New York: Cassell, 1998), pp. 78–88.
177. Potter, *Spectacular Vernaculars*, p. 145.
178. Ranciere, *Disagreement*, p. 27.

# *Chapter 4*

1. Benedict Anderson, *Imagined Communities: Reflections on the Origin and Spread of Nationalism*, rev. ed. (New York: Verso, 1991). Subsequently, Anderson treated the way in which print media, especially newspapers, made for a relatively coherent supranational, global imaginary. See his *The Spectre of Comparisons* (New York: Verso, 1998).
2. As implied by Partha Chatterjee's query, "whose imagined community?" in *The Nation and Its Fragments* (Princeton, NJ: Princeton University Press, 1993).
3. *Ibid.*
4. Quotation from Colin Williams and Anthony D. Smith. "The National construction of social space," *Progress in Human Geography* 7: 4 (December 1983), p. 504.
5. Angela Miller, *The Empire of the Eye: Landscape Representation and American Cultural Politics 1825–1875* (Ithaca, NY: Cornell University Press, 1993), p. 15.
6. Malcolm Andrews, *Landscape and Western Art* (Oxford: Oxford University Press, 1999), p. 5.
7. *Ibid.*, p. 26.
8. Ann Bermingham, *Landscape and Ideology: The English Rustic Tradition, 1740–1860* (Berkeley: University of California, 1986), p. 142.
9. Stephen Daniels, *Fields of Vision: Landscape Imagery and National identity in England and the United States* (New York: Polity, 1993), p. 5.
10. See Martin Warnke, *Political Landscape: The Art History of Nature* (Cambridge, MA: Harvard University Press, 1995), pp. 10–13.
11. Daniels, *Fields of Vision*, p. 126.
12. The quotation is from a Vorticist manifesto treated in Paul Edwards, "Wyndham Lewis and the *Rappel a l'ordre*: Classicism and Significant Form, 1919–21," in David Peters Corbett, Ysanne Holt, and Fiona Russell, eds., *The Geography of Englishness* (New Haven, CT: Yale University Press, 2002), p. 142.
13. Oliver Zimmer, "In Search of Natural Identity: Alpine Landscape and the Reconstruction of the Swiss Nation," *Comparative Studies in Society and History* 40: 4 (October 1998), p. 644.
14. *Ibid.*, pp. 639–644.
15. Miller, *The Empire of the Eye*, p. 13.
16. Albert Boime, *The Magisterial Gaze: Manifest Destiny and American Landscape Painting* c. *1830–1865* (Washington, DC: Smithsonian Institution Press, 1991), p. 79.
17. I take this expression from a collection based on a Smithsonian exhibit on western landscape. See William H. Truettner, ed., *The West as America: Reinterpreting Images of the Frontier, 1820–1920* (Washington, DC: Smithsonian Institution Press, 1991).
18. Sherman Alexie, "Indian Country," *The New Yorker* (March 13, 2000), p. 82.
19. *Ibid.*, p. 77.
20. Quotation from William Boelhower, "Stories of Foundation, Scenes of Origin," *American Literary History* 5: 3 (fall 1993), p. 391.
21. The terms belong to Boelhower in *Ibid.*, p. 392.
22. See Thomas Jefferson, *Notes on the State of Virginia*, ed. Frank Shuffelton (New York: Penguin, 1999).
23. My discussion of Jefferson here is influenced by Catherine Holland's reading of Jefferson's *Notes*. See her "Notes on the State of America: Jeffersonian Democracy and the Production of a National Past," *Political Theory* 29: 2 (April 2001), pp. 190–216.
24. Exemplary of Church's landscapes is his *New England Scenery*. My discussion of Church is indebted to Miller's discussion in *The Empire of the Eye*, pp. 171–173.

25. James Fenimore Cooper, "American and European Scenery Compared," in Motley F. Deakin's facsimile reproduction of *The Home Book of the Picturesque: Or American Scenery, Art, and Literature. Comprising a Series of Essays by Washington Irving, W.G. Bryant, Fenimore Cooper, and Others* (1952), this edition (Gainesville, FL: Scholars' Facsimiles & Reprints, 1967), p. 51.
26. *Ibid.*, p. 68.
27. *Ibid.*, p. 52.
28. Matthew Dennis, *Cultivating a Landscape of Peace,* p. 17.
29. *Ibid.*, p. 4.
30. Keith H. Basso, *Wisdom Sits in Places: Landscape and Language Among the Western Apache* (Albuquerque: University of New Mexico Press, 1996), p. 34.
31. *Ibid.*, p. 32.
32. *Ibid.*, p. 7.
33. The concept of overcoding belongs to Gilles Deleuze and Felix Guattari. See their *A Thousand Plateaus.*
34. The quotation is from Alan Trachtenberg, "Naming the View," in *Reading American Photographs* (New York: Hill and Wang, 1989), p. 12.
34. *Ibid.*
35. The quotation is from David Seed, "Mapping the Course of Empire in the New World," in Brooke Horvath and Irving Malin, eds., *Pynchon and Mason & Dixon* (Newark: University of Delaware Press, 2000.), p. 87.
36. *Black Elk Speaks.*
37. Gerald Vizenor, "The Ruins of Representation: Shadow Survivance and the Literature of Domination," Alfred Arteaga, ed., An Other Tongue (Durham, NC: Duke University Press, 1994), p. 142.
38. Richard Helgerson, *Forms of Nationhood,* p. 10.
39. *Ibid.*, p. 153.
40. Gauri Viswanathan, *Masks of Conquest: Literary Study and British Rule in India* (NewYork: Columbia University Press, 1989), p. 142.
41. *Ibid.*, p. 118.
42. *Ibid.*, pp. 166–167.
43. W.J.T. Mitchell, "Imperial Landscape," in W.J.T. Mitchell, ed., *Landscape and Power* (Chicago: University of Chicago Press, 1994), p. 17.
44. Stephen Daniels, *Fields of Vision: Landscape Imagery and National Identity in England and the United States* (New York: Polity, 1993), p. 3.
45. Elizabeth Helsinger, "Land and National Representation in Britain," in Michael Rosenthal, Christiana Payne, and Scott Wilcox, eds., *Prospects for the Nation: Recent Essays in British Landscape* (New Heaven, CT: Yale University Press, 1997), p. 14.
46. The perspective and quotations here are from Richard Helgerson, "The Land Speaks: Cartography, Chorography, and Subversion in Renaissance England," *Representations* 16: 4 (fall 1986), p. 56. It was also the case, more generally in England that, by the end of the sixteenth century, the process of consolidating the state form was accompanied by "an unprecedented explosion in the making of maps." See Corrigan and Sayer, *The Great Arch,* p. 70.
47. Helsinger, "Land and National Representation in Britain," p. 15.
48. Jennifer Green-Lewis, "Picturing England: On Photography, Landscape, and the End(s) of Imperial Culture," *Genre* 29 (spring/summer 1996), p. 34.
49. Elizabeth Helsinger, "Turner and the Representation of England," in Mitchell, ed., *Landscape and Power,* p. 106.
50. *Ibid.*, p. 116.
51. Ann Bermingham, "System, Order, and Abstraction: The Politics of English Landscape Drawing around 1795," in Mitchell, ed., *Landscape and Power,* p. 83.
52. Josef W. Konvitz, "The Nation-state, Paris and cartography in eighteenth- and nineteenth-century France," *Journal of Historical Geography* 16: 1 (January 1990), p. 5.
53. *Ibid.*, p. 4.
54. *Ibid.*, p. 5. Interestingly, the displacement of nobility-oriented territoriality with bourgeois-friendly cartography was reflected in other modes of enunciation. For example, in the early nineteenth century, the painter Ingres, who had specialized in portraits of the nobility (for example, the Duc d'Orlean) began painting bourgeois political notables, for example,

Louis-Francois Bertin, the publisher of a political journal. See *Les Portaits d' Ingres* (Paris: Ministere de la Culture, 1985), pp. 71–75.
55. Fulcher, *The Nation's Image*, p. 1.
56. *Ibid.*, p. 8.
57. *Ibid.*, p. 33.
58. John House "Authority versus independence: the position of French landscape in the 1870s." in Richard Tomson, ed. *Framing France: The Representation of Landscape in France, 1870–1914* (Manchester England: Manchester University press, 1998), pp. 16–18.
59. Bermingham *Landscape and Ideology*, p. 1.
60. *Ibid.*, p. 2.
61. Ann Bermingham, "System, Order, and Abstraction: The Politics of English Landscape Drawing around 1795," in Mitchell, ed., *Landscape and Power*, p. 98.
62. The term conjunctural, is applied to the history of commerce by Fernand Braudel. See his *Afterthoughts on Material Civilization and Capitalism* (Baltimore: Johns Hopkins University Press, 1979) for an explication of his point of view.
63. Daniels, *Fields of Vision*, p. 6.
64. Michael Neill, "Broken English and Broken Irish: Nation, Language, and the Optics of Power in Shakespeare's Histories," *Shakespeare Quarterly* 45: 1 (spring 1994), pp. 1–32.
65. The quoted expression is from Declan McGonagle, "Renegotiating the Given," in Declan McGonagle, Fintan O' Toole, and Kim Levin, *Irish Art Now: From the Poetic to the Political* (London: Merrell Halberton, 1999), pp. 10–11.
66. *Ibid.*
67. Tutta Palin, "Picturing a Nation" in Tuomas M.S. Lehtonen, *Europe's Northern Frontier*, trans. Philip Landon (Jyvaskyla, Finland: PS-Kustannus, 1999), p. 208.
68. As noted in *Ibid.*, p. 219: "The paradigmatic Finnish landscape is a sublime panorama of lakes and forests, as seen from a high hill, or a ridge or mound, or from a purpose-built observation tower—any vantage point from where the eye can take in a large tract at a single glance."
69. *Ibid.*, p. 232.
70. *Ibid.*, p. 219.
71. *Ibid.*, p. 224.
72. Paul Carter, *The Road to Botany Bay*, p. 69.
73. *Ibid.*, p. 29.
74. *Ibid.*, p. 56.
75. *Ibid.*, p. 61.
76. *Ibid.*, p. 63.
77. Christopher Allen, *Art in Australia: From Colonization to Postmodernism* (London: Thames and Hudson, 1997), p. 12.
78. *Ibid.*, p. 19.
79. *Ibid.*, p. 24.
80. *Ibid.*, pp. 30–31.
81. *Ibid.*, p. 68.
82. *Ibid.*, p. 64.
83. *Ibid.*, p. 68.
84. Terry Smith, "Public Art between Cultures: The *Aboriginal Memorial*, Aboriginality, and Nationality in Australia," *Critical Inquiry* 27: 4 (summer 2001), pp. 648–649.
85. *Ibid.*, pp. 635–636.
86. Quotation from the brochure of the exhibition at the Tate Gallery in London: Paul Moorhouse and Ben Tufnell, *Michael Andrews* (London: Tate Gallery, 2001).
87. *Ibid.*
88. Quotations from Eric Kaufmann, "'Naturalizing the Nation': The Rise of Naturalistic Nationalism in the United States and Canada," *Comparative Studies in Society and History* 40: 4 (October 1998), pp. 682 and 679, respectively.
89. Quotations from Brian S. Osborne, "The iconography of nationhood in Canadian art," in Cosgrove and Stephen Daniels, eds., *The Iconography of Landscape* (New York: Cambridge University Press, 1988), pp. 163–165.
90. *Ibid.*, p. 169.
91. Quoted in *Ibid.*, p. 169.

92. Quoted in Eric Kaufmann, "'Naturalizing the Nation': The Rise of Naturalistic Nationalism in the United States and Canada," *Comparative Studies in Society and History* 40: 4 (October 1998), p. 689.
93. As Erin Manning points out, the landscapes of the Group of Seven "retain a nuance" in terms of both "the ways in which they negotiate the conflation between the territorial and the national" as well as "their inevitable critical interaction with contemporary artistic landscapes." See her *Ephemeral Territories* (Minneapolis: University of Minnesota Press), forthcoming (quotation from the doctoral dissertation version by the same title, University of Hawaii, 2000), p. 53.
94. Diana Nemiroff, Robert Houle, and Charlotte Townsend-Gault, *Land Spirit Power: First Nations at the National Gallery of Canada* (Ottawa: National Gallery of Canada, 1992), p. 16.
95. *Ibid.*, p. 17.
96. Quotation from Manning, *Ephemeral Territories*, p. 45.
97. Quotations from Diana Nemiroff, Nikos Papastergiadis, Hou Hanru, and Germaine Koh, *Crossings* (Toronto: National Gallery of Canada, 1998) [Exhibition, 7 August–1 November 1998], p. 182.
98. Manning, *Ephemeral Territories*, p. 46.
99. See Pierre L. Van Den Berghe, "The Modern Nation State: Nation-Builder or Nation-Killer," *International Journal of Group Tensions* 22: 3 (fall 1992), pp. 191–208, and Walker Connor, "Nation-Building or Nation-Destroying? *World Politics* 24: 1 (January 1972), pp. 319–355.
100. See William H. Goeztmann and William N. Goeztmann, *The West of the Imagination* (New York: W.W. Norton, 1986). As they note, Jefferson had engaged in a debate with the French naturalist, Comte de Buffon, about the "nature of the new world" and resisted Buffon's fantasy that the "savages" were "distinctly lacking in 'amative powers'" (p. xiii).
101. Harry Liebersohn, "Discovering Indigenous Nobility: Tocqueville, Chamisso, and Romantic Travel Writing," *American Historical Review* 99: 3 (June 1994), p. 754.
102. Tocqueville, *Democracy in America*, vol. 1, p. 25.
103. See Albert Boime, *The Magisterial Gaze: Manifest Destiny and American Landscape Painting* c. 1830–1865 (Washington, DC: Smithsonian Institution, 1991).
104. *Ibid.*, p. 8–10.
105. *Ibid.*, p. 10.
106. *Ibid.*, p. 79.
107. For a good review of the appearance of African Americans in *Harper's Monthly*, see Kathleen Diffley, *Home on the Range: Turner, Slavery, and the Landscape Illustrations in* Harper's New Monthly Magazine, *1861–1876* in Jack Salzman, ed., *Prospects: An Annual Review of American Cultural Studies*, vol. 14 (New York: Cambridge University Press, 1989), pp. 175–202.
108. *Ibid.*, p. 194.
109. *Ibid.*, p. 192–193.
110. *Ibid.*, p. 185.
111. William H. Truettner, Introduction: "Ideology and Image: Justifying Westward Expansion," in Truettner, ed., *The West as America: Reinterpreting Images of the Frontier, 1820–1920*, p. 30.
112. *Ibid.*, p. 35.
113. *Ibid.*, p. 34.
114. For description of this change, see Borneman, "American Anthropology as Foreign Policy."
115. Truettner, Introduction: "Ideology and Image: Justifying Westward Expansion," p. 44.
116. Remington's illustration accompanies a drama whose theme is the dangers of trading with violent and unscrupulous "savages." The picture can nevertheless be read allegorically. As David Murray notes, the use of a half-breed, a "crucial mediating figure," points to the "process of translation," and the self-effacement of the interpreter—his gesture draws attention away from himself—reflects a more general process of the ideological effacement of Indianness. See David Murray, *Forked Tongues: Speech, Writing and Representation in North American Indian Texts* (London: Pinter, 1991), p. I.
117. Larzer Ziff, *Writing in the New Nation* (New Haven, CT: Yale University Press, 1991), p. 172.
118. *Ibid.*, p. 165.
119. See John C. Cremony, *Life Among the Apaches* (New York: Indian Head Books, 1991).
120. Ziff, *Writing in the New Nation*, p. 173.
121. Cheryl Walker, *Indian Nation* (Durham, NC: Duke University Press, 1997), p. 4.
122. *Ibid.*, p. 7.

123. Scheckel, *The Persistence of the Indian,* p. 10.
124. Walker, *Indian Nation,* p. 16.
125. Quotation from Robert M. Nelson, *Place and Vision: The Function of Landscape in Native American Fiction* (New York: Peter Lang, 1993), p. 35.
126. For details see http://www.navajoboy.com/radiat.html.
127. Leslie Marmon Silko, *Ceremony* (New York: Penguin, 1977).
128. As Cheryl Walker points out, characters in Native American writings tend to differ from those in Euro American texts. In "Native American national allegory" (for example, the contemporary novels of Arnold Krupak), the self is represented as a "synecdochic self," as an "individual whose worth is determined not by autonomous acts but by his or her capacity to represent the group" (in contrast with the white American, liberal self, whose actions reflect on individual worth): Walker, *Indian Nation,* p. 12.
129. Silko, *Ceremony,* p. 181.
130. *Ibid.,* p. 135.
131. *Ibid.,* p. 245.
132. *Ibid.,* p. 246.
133. The introduction of the concept of minor literature and a treatment of its political implications is in Deleuze and Guattari, *Kafka: Toward a Minor Literature.*
134. See Margaret Archuleta and Dr. Rennard Strickland, *Shared Visions: Native American Painters and Sculptors in the Twentieth Century* (New York: New Press, 1991), pp. 12–13.
135. *Ibid.,* p. 16.
136. Emmanuel Levinas, "The Name of a Dog, or Natural Rights," in *Difficult Freedom: Essays on Judaism,* trans. Sean Hand (Baltimore: Johns Hopkins University Press, 1990), p. 53.
137. Anne Farrar Hyde, *An American Vision: Far Western Landscape and National Culture, 1820–1920* (New York: New York University Press, 1990), pp. 41–42.
138. The quoted expression is from Annette Kolodny, "Letting Go Our Grand Obsessions: Notes Toward a New Literary History of American Frontiers," *American Literature* 64: 1 (March 1992), p. 4.
139. George P. Horse Capture, Anne Vitart, Michael Waldberger, and W. Richard West, Jr., *Robes of Splendor* (New York: The New Press, 1993), p. 15.
140. *Ibid.,* p. 20.
141. *Ibid.,* p. 22.
142. *Ibid.,* p. 44.
143. *Ibid.,* p. 12.

## Chapter 5

1. See Michel Foucault, "War in the Filigree of Peace," trans. Ian Mcleod, *Oxford Literary Review,* 4: 1 (autumn 1979), pp. 15–19.
2. Richard Slotkin, *Gunfighter Nation: The Myth of the Frontier in Twentieth-Century America* (New York: Atheneum, 1992).
3. Robert Warshow, "Movie Chronicle: The Westerner," in Jim Kitses and Gregg Rickmen, eds., *The Western Reader* (New York: Limelight, 1998), p. 37.
4. A discussion of the banal aspects of national identity in film is in Mette Hjort, "Themes of a Nation," in Mette Hjort and Scott MacKenzie, eds., *Cinema & Nation* (New York: Routledge, 2000), pp. 103–117. The concept of banal nationalism, upon which she draws, is developed in Michael Billig, *Banal Nationalism* (London: Sage, 1995).
5. This point is made in Susan Hayward, "Questions of National Cinema," in Keith Cameron, ed., *National Identity* (Exeter, England: Intellect, 1999), p. 101.
6. See Jane M. Gaines, "Birthing Nations," in *Ibid.,* pp. 298–316.
7. Robert Burgoyne, *Film Nation* (Minneapolis: University of Minnesota Press, 1997), p. 7.
8. Hayward, "Questions of National Cinema," p. 96.
9. *Ibid.,* p. 98.
10. *Ibid.,* p. 106.
11. *Ibid.,* p. 103.
12. Mette Hjort and Scott MacKenzie, "Introduction," in *Cinema & Nation,* p. 3.
13. Ana M. Lopez, "Early Cinema and Modernity in Latin America," *Cinema Journal* 40: 1 (2000), p. 48.

14. Manuel Puig, *Betrayed by Rita Hayworth*, trans. Suzanne Jill Levine (New York: E.P. Dutton, 1971).
15. Lopez, "Early Cinema and Modernity in Latin America," p. 65.
16. *Ibid.*, p. 72.
17. Marvin D'Lugo, "'Transparent Women': Gender and Nation in Cuban Cinema." in John King, Ana M. Lopez, and Manuel Alvarado, *Mediating Two Worlds: Cinematic Encounters in the Americas* (London: BFI, 1993), p. 279.
18. *Ibid.*, pp. 283–284.
19. Wade, *Music, Race, and Nation*, p. 15.
20. The quotes are from the Lebanese historian Georges Corm, in Kevin Robbins and Asu Aksoy, "Deep Nation: the national question and Turkish cinema culture," in Hjort and MacKenzie, eds., *Cinema & Nation*, p. 204.
21. *Ibid.*, p. 211.
22. Robbins and Aksoy, "Deep Nation," p. 216.
23. Nicholas Monceau, "Confronting Turkey's Social Realities: An Interview with Yesim Ustaoglu," *Cineaste* 26: 3 (summer 2001), p. 30.
24. Quoted in Kenton Bamford, *Distorted Images: British National Identity and Film in the 1920s* (London: I.B. Taurus, 1999), p. 15.
25. *Ibid.*
26. Quotes are from Paul Willemen, *Looks and Frictions: Essays in Cultural Studies and Film Theory* (Bloomington: Indiana University Press, 1994), p. 212.
27. Anton Kaes, *From Hitler to Heimat: The Return of History as Film* (Cambridge, MA: Harvard University Press, 1989), p. 5.
28. As Kaes points out, film production in the two zones took different paths. While the Western zone was heavily shaped by attempts at making the West Germany a market for U.S. films, the films in the Eastern zone were more directly aimed at attacking the characteristic of national socialism—*Ibid.*, p. 11.
29. See Heide Fehrenbach, *Cinema in Democratizing Germany* (Chapel Hill: University of North Carolina Press, 1995), pp. 254–259.
30. *Ibid.*, p. 256.
31. See Kaes, *From Hitler to Heimat*.
32. *Ibid.*, p. 20.
33. *Ibid.*, p. 19.
34. *Ibid.*, p. 83.
35. *Ibid.*, p. 89.
36. *Ibid.*, p. 90.
37. Chris Berry "A Nation T(w/o)o: Chinese Cinema(s) and Nationhood(s)" in Wimal Dissanayake, ed., *Colonialism and Nationalism in Asian Cinema* (Bloomington: Indiana University Press, 1994), p. 47.
38. *Ibid.*
39. *Ibid.*
40. Yingjin Zhang, "From 'Minority Film' to 'Minority Discourse': Questions of Nationhood and Ethnicity in Chinese Cinema," in Sheldon Hsiao-peng Lu, ed., *Transnational Chinese Cinema* (Honolulu: University of Hawaii Press, 1997), p. 93.
41. Berry, "A Nation T(w/o)o," p. 57.
42. *Ibid.*, p. 60.
43. The quotation is from Anthony Smith, "Images of the Nation: Cinema, art and national identity," in Hjort and MacKenzie, eds., *Cinema & Nation*, p. 57. Smith suggests some useful comparisons between Eisenstein's cinematic tableaux and the way in which historical paintings celebrate national historical events.
44. The expression "cinematic nation-building" is used by Noel Carroll and Sally Banes, "Cinematic Nation-Building: Eisenstein's *The Old and the New*," in Hjort and MacKenzie, eds., *Cinema & Nation*, pp. 121–138. Eisenstein discusses intellectual montage in many of his writings. See, for example, his "Methods of Montage," in *Film Form*, trans. Jay Leyda (New York: Meridian, 1957), pp. 72–83.
45. *S.M. Eisenstein: Selected Works, Vol. 1, 1922–34,* ed. and trans. Richard Taylor (London: BFI, 1988), p. 42.
46. The quotation and example are taken from James Goodwin, *Eisenstein, Cinema, and History* (Urbana: University of Illinois Press), p. 86.

47. Sergei Eisenstein, "Dickens, Griffith, and the Film Today," in *Film Form,* trans. Jay Leyda (New York: Meridian, 1970), pp. 195–255.
48. Sergei Eisenstein, "Montage," in Leon Moussiac, *Sergei Eisenstein,* trans. D. Sandy Petrey (New York: Crown, 1970), pp. 94–95.
49. This example from *The Old and the New* is taken from Carroll and Banes, "Cinematic Nation-Building: Eisenstein's *The Old and the New,*" pp. 126–127.
50. Sergei Eisenstein, "Mr, Lincoln by Mr. Ford," in Jay Leyda, ed., *Film Essays and a Lecture by Sergei Eisenstein,* (Princeton, NJ: Princeton University Press, 1982), p. 139.
51. *Ibid.,* p. 140.
52. My reading of this scene is influenced by Stanley Corkin's in "Cowboys and Free Markets: Post-World War II Westerns and U.S. Hegemony," *Cinema Journal* 39: 3 (spring 2000), p. 73.
53. Peter Wollen, *Signs and Meaning in Cinema* (Bloomington: Indiana University Press, 1969), p. 14.
54. Virginia Wright Wexman, "The Family on the Land: Race and Nationhood in Silent Westerns," in Daniel Bernardi, ed., *The Birth of Whiteness* (New Brunswick, NJ: Rutgers University Press, 1996), p. 130.
55. See Theodore Roosevelt, *The Winning of the West* (New York: G.P. Putnam's Sons, 1889).
56. Gregory S. Jay, "'White Man's Book No Good': D.W. Griffith and the American Indian," *Cinema Journal* 39: 4 (summer 2000), p. 8.
57. See Jacqueline Kilpatrick, *Celluloid Indians: Native Americans and Film* (Lincoln: University of Nebraska Press, 1999), pp. 40–41.
58. *Ibid.,* p. 7.
59. Wexman, "The Family on the Land," p. 132.
60. *Ibid.,* p. 131.
61. Nancy F. Cott, *Public Vows: A History of Marriage and the Nation* Cambridge, MA: (Harvard University Press, 2000), p. 10.
62. *Ibid.,* p. 25.
63. The quotation is from Scott Eyman, *Print the Legend: The Life and Times of John Ford* (Baltimore: Johns Hopkins University Press, 1999), p. 21.
64. In his biography of Ford, Scott Eyman states that from his earliest films, Ford was already "making the landscape a character," See his *Print the Legend,* p. 73.
65. Gilles Deleuze, *Cinema 1,* p. 146.
66. *Ibid.,* p. 148.
67. For an analysis of the Cooper-Wister contrast and its influence on westerns, see John Cawelti, *The Six-Gun Mystique Sequel* (Bowling Green, OH: Bowling Green University Popular Press, 1999), p. 66.
68. The quotation is from Eyman, *Print the Legend,* p. 205.
69. Richard Abel, "'Our Country'/ Whose Country? The 'Americanisation' Project of Early Westerns," in Edward Buscombe and Roberta E. Pearson, eds., *Back in the Saddle Again: New Essays on the Western* (London: BFI, 1998), pp. 86–87.
70. Reported in *Ibid.,* p. 195.
71. *Ibid.,* p. 207.
72. See Michael Coyne's *The Crowded Prairie: American National Identity in the Hollywood Western* (New York: I.B. Tauris, 1997), where he identifies "community Westerns" as those "predisposed to reflect national and societal concerns" (p. 7).
73. For an analysis of the Shakespearean connection in *Clementine,* see Scott Simmon, "Concerning the Weary Legs of Wyatt Earp: The Classic Western According to Shakespeare," in Kitses and Rickman, eds., *The Western Reader,* pp. 149–166.
74. Bill Nichols, "Style, Grammar, and the Movies," p. 616.
75. *Ibid.,* p. 617.
76. Jim Kitses, "Introduction," in Kitses and Rickman, eds., *The Western Reader,* p. 22.
77. Coyne, *The Crowded Prairie,* p. 51.
78. The expression belongs to Tag Gallagher, "Angels Gambol Where They Will: John Ford's Indians," in Kitses and Rickman, eds., *The Western Reader,* p. 274.
79. As I noted above, the idea that the gun is "the moral center of the Western," is expressed in Warshow, "Movie Chronicle: *The Westerner,*" p. 37.
80. Coyne, *The Crowded Prairie,* p. 108.
81. Quotations are from *Ibid.,* p. 20.

82. *Ibid.*, p. 37.

83. Again, see *Ibid.*, pp. 81–82.

84. Alan Nadel, *Containment Culture: American Narratives, Postmodernism, and the Atomic Age* (Durham, NC: Duke University Press, 1995), p. 197.

85. *Ibid.*, p. 195.

86. The quotation is from Tag Gallagher, "Angels Gambol Where They Will: John Ford's Indians," in Kitses and Rickman, eds., *The Western Reader*, p. 273.

87. *Ibid.*

88. The details of the conversation are reported in John C. Cremony, *Life Among the Apaches* (New York: Indian Head Books, 1991), pp. 13–14.

89. The quoted segment is from John Faragher, "Americans, Mexicans, Metis: A Community Approach to the Comparative Study of North American Frontiers," in William Cronon, George Miles, and Jay Gitlin, eds., *Under an Open Sky: Rethinking America's Western Past* (New York: W.W. Norton, 1992), p. 90.

90. William Cronon, George Miles, and Jay Gitlin, "Becoming West," in *Ibid.*, p. 7.

91. Vincent Tocce, "Is It Shot Or Is It Dead?: The Western According To Virgil and Shakespeare," *CINE* 344 (December 15, 1998), p. 3.

92. Quoted in *Ibid.*, p. 1.

93. Kent Jones, Review of *Dead Man* in *Cineaste* 2: 2 ( spring 1996), p. 45.

94. As Jarmusch notes in an interview, "I think in 1875 well over a million were shot and the government was very supportive of this being done, because 'No buffalo, no Indians.' They were trying to get the railroad through and were having a lot of trouble with the Lakota and different tribes." From: Jonathan Rosenbaum, "A Gun Up Your Ass: An Interview with Jim Jarmusch," *Cineaste* 22: 2 (spring 1996), p. 21.

95. The quotation is from Mary Katherine Hall, "Now You Are a Killer of White Men: Jim Jarmusch's *Dead Man* and Traditions of Revisionism in the Western," *Journal of Film and Video* 52: 4 (winter 2001), p. 13.

96. This remark is made by Jonathan Rosenbaum in "A Gun Up Your Ass."

97. Wexman, "The Family on the Land: Race and Nationhood in Silent Westerns," p. 130.

98. See Jonathan Rosenbaum, "A Gun Up Your Ass: An Interview with Jim Jarmusch," *Cineaste* 22:2 (1996), p. 23.

99. See Susan Maier, "'Stranger in a Strange Land': Jim Jarmusch's *Dead Man* and the Technology of the American Western," *Node* 9: 1 (March 1997), p. 3.

100. For an argument that the state developed as a nation killer, see Pierre L. Van Den Berghe, "The Modern State: Nation-Builder or Nation-Killer," *International Journal of Group Tensions* 22: 3 (fall 1992), pp. 191–208.

101. William Least Heat Moon, *PrairyErth (A Deep Map)* (Boston: Houghton Mifflin. 1991), p. 16.

102. Michel Foucault, *The History of Sexuality,* trans. Robert Hurley (New York: Pantheon, 1978), p. 25.

103. Cheryl Walker, *Indian Nation* (Durham, NC: Duke University Press, 1997), p. 6.

104. *Ibid.*, p. 205.

105. The quoted expression is taken from Susan Scheckel, *The Insistence of the Indian: Race and Nationalism in Nineteenth-Century American Culture* (Princeton, NJ: Princeton University Press, 1998).

106. Zane Grey, *Union Pacific,* p. 471.

# *Chapter 6*

1. DeLillo was commenting on an earlier history making/shaking event, the assassination of President John F. Kennedy. See Don DeLillo, *Libra* (New York: Viking, 1988), p. 15.

2. The quotation is from Susan Faludi, "A Myth Rides into the Sunset," *Honolulu Advertiser,* April 1, 2003, p. A–8.

3. See Richard Slotkin, *Gunfighter Nation* (New York: Atheneum, 1992).

4. Evan Connell, *Son of the Morning Star: Custer and the Little Bighorn* (New York: Harper Collins, 1984), p. 330.

5. *Ibid.*, pp. 331–332.

6. Robert Burgoyne, *Film Nation: Hollywood Looks at U.S. History* (Minneapolis: University of Minnesota Press, 1997), p. 48.
7. Michael Hardt and Antonio Negri use the concept of "imperial sovereignty" to identify the post cold war conflicts that, they argue, are not organized around one central conflict but rather through a flexible network of microconflicts." *Empire*, p. 201. I am expanding the concept to identify all episodes of state violence undertaken in the name of shaping and sustaining its territorial and biopolitical coherence.
8. The quoted expression comes from Lewis Frye Richardson, *Statistics of Deadly Quarrels* (Pittsburgh: Boxwood Press, 1960).
9. Paul Virilio *War and Cinema: The Logistics of Perception,* trans. Patrick Camiller (New York: Verso, 1989).
10. Patrick Wright, *Tank* (New York: Viking, 2002), p. 17.
11. John Ellis, *The Social History of the Machine Gun* (Baltimore: Johns Hopkins University Press, 1975), p. 13.
12. See Sven Lindqvist, *"Exterminate All the Brutes,"* trans. Joan Tate (New York: The New Press, 1996), p. 67.
13. *Ibid.,* p. 52.
14. Among those articulating this war imaginary is Ralph Peters, "Our Soldiers, Their Cities," *Parameters* 26: 1 (spring 1996), pp. 43–50.
15. Jean Baudrillard, "The Seismic Order," (1991). On the web at http://www.uta.edu/english/apt/collab/texts/sedismic.html.
16. Peter Andreas and Richard Price, "From War Fighting to Crime Fighting: Transforming the American National Security State," *International Studies Review* 3: 3 (fall, 2001), p. 31.
17. Quotations in *Ibid.*, p. 33.
18. Anthony Giddens, *The Nation-State and Violence* (Berkeley: University of California Press, 1985), p. 192.
19. For example, on June 11, 2002, the *New York Times* reported the arrest of an American citizen, whom the attorney general alleges to be an al Qaida operative. Commenting on his legal status, Ashcroft said he is an "enemy combatant. . . . We have acted with legal authority both under the laws of war and clear Supreme Court precedent, which establishes that the military may detain a United States citizen who has joined the enemy and has entered our country to carry out hostile acts." And Deputy Defense Secretary Paul F. Wolfowitz said that the suspect, Mr. Al-Mujahir, was being held "under the laws of war." David Stout, "U.S. Arrests Man Accused of 'Dirty Bomb' Attack," *New York Times* on the web at http://www.nytimes.com/2002/06/10/national/10CND-TERROR.html.
20. William Gibson, *Count Zero* (New York: Ace Books, 1987), p. 1.
21. David Johnson, *"Law Change* Sought to Set Up DNA Databank for Captured Qaida Fighters," *New York Times,* March 2, 2002, on the web at http:www.nytimes.com/2002/ 03/06/national/06DNA.html.
22. Dexter Filkins, "U.S. Is Studying DNA of Dead Al Qaida and Taliban Combatants," *New York Times,* March 15, 2002, on the web at http://www.nytimes.com/2002/03/15/international/asia/15AFGH.html.
23. *New York Times,* 6/17/2002, p. 1.
24. Hardt and Negri, *Empire*, p. 201.
25. *Ibid.*, p. 89.
26. *Ibid.*, p. 171.
27. Michel Foucault, *History of Sexuality,* trans. Robert Hurley (New York: Vintage, 1998), p. 137.
28. *Ibid.*
29. Agamben, *Homo Sacer,* pp. 119–125.
30. *Ibid.*, p. 19.
31. *Ibid.*, p. 6.
32. *Ibid.*, p. 83.
33. William E. Connolly, "The Complexity of Sovereignty," (unpublished paper), p. 23.
34. Exemplary is Tony Blair's speech, "Enlightened Patriotism," (at the lord mayor's banquet, London, Monday 13 November 2000), on the web at http://www.fco.gov.uk/news/speechtext.asp?4374.

35. Robert Redeker, "In Place of Politics: Humanitarianism and War," in Tariq Ali, ed., *Masters of the Universe? NATO's Balkan Crusade* (New York: Verso, 2000), p. 172 .
36. The quotations are from Curtis C. Breight, *Surveillance, Militarism and Drama in the Elizabethan Era* (New York: St. Martins, 1996). Much of my treatment of the Elizabethan case is drawn from Breight's study.
37. Nikolas K.Gvosdev and Anthony A. Cipriano, "Patriotism and Profit Are Powerful Weapons," *Honolulu Advertiser,* 7/21/2002, p. B-4.
38. Jeff Gerth and Don Van Natta Jr., "In Tough Times a Company Finds Profits in Terror War," *New York Times,* on the web at http://www.nytimes.com/2002/07/13/bisiness/13Hall.html.
39. Reported in the *New York Times,* on the web at http://www.nytimes.com/2003/03/25/international/worldspecial/25HALI.html.
40. See *Ibid.,* p. 31.
41. *Ibid.,* p. 57.
42. Corrigan and Sayer, *The Great Arch,* p. 49.
43. Breight, *Surveillance, Militarism and Drama in the Elizabethan Era,* p. 51.
44. *Ibid.,* p. 59.
45. See Helgerson on Hakluyt in his *Forms of Nationhood,* p. 183.
46. Breight, *Surveillance, Militarism and Drama in the Elizabethan Era,* p. 33.
47. Helgerson, *Forms of Nationhood,* p. 152.
48. Historical details and quotations are from "Hakluyt, Richard," in *Catalogue of the Scientific Community,* on the web at http://es.rice.edu/ES/humsoc/Galileo/Catalogue/Files/hakluyt.html.
49. Breight, *Surveillance, Militarism and Drama in the Elizabethan Era,* p. 127. Much of the evidence supplied is circumstantial, for example, the fact that "contemporaneous with Marlowe's absences [from his college] was the plotting of the most dangerous conspiracy . . . the Babington plot" [an allegedly Catholic conspiracy against Queen Elizabeth that Marlowe was supposedly sent to monitor] Quotations from *The Marlow Society,* on the web at http://www.marlowe-society.org/16agent.htm.
50. Breight, *Surveillance, Militarism and Drama in the Elizabethan Era,* p. 116.
51. *Ibid.,* p. 210.
52. *Ibid.,* p. 237.
53. *Ibid.,* pp. 172–173.
54. Helgerson, *Forms of Nationhood,* p. 244.
55. *Ibid.,* p. 245.
56. The expression "imperial transfer" belongs to Christopher Hitchens; see his *Blood, Class, and Nostalgia: Anglo-American Ironies* (New York: Farrar, Straus & Giroux,1990). The expression is used by Breight, *Surveillance, Militarism and Drama in the Elizabethan Era,* pp. 15–17, to treat the genre history—especially feature films—of Elizabethan militarization.
57. Breight, *Surveillance, Militarism and Drama in the Elizabethan Era,* p. 17. The films include *Elizabeth the Queen,* or *The Private Lives of Elizabeth and Essex* (1939), *Young Bess* (1953), and *The Virgin Queen* (1955).
58. *Ibid.,* p. 14.
59. See John Cawelti, "Cooper and the Frontier Myth and Anti-Myth," in Paul Verhoeven, ed., *James Fenimore Cooper: New Historical and Literary Contexts* (Amsterdam: Rodopi, 1993), p. 151.
60. Quotation from Paul Verhoeven, "Neutralizing the Land: The Myth of Authority, and the Authority of Myth in Fenimore Cooper's *The Spy,*" in *Ibid.,* p. 73.
61. Quotation from *Ibid.,* p. 75.
62. Quotation from Susan Scheckel, "'In the Land of His Fathers': Cooper, Land Rights, and the Legitimation of American National Identity," in Verhoeven, *James Fenimore Cooper,* p. 126.
63. Here I am following Scheckel's discussion in "Cooper and National Identity," another version of *Ibid.* in her *The Insistence of the Indian: Race and Nationalism in Nineteenth-Century American Culture* (Princeton, NJ: Princeton University Press, 1998), p. 17.
64. See *Ibid.,* pp. 33–34.
65. Scheckel, "In the Land of His Fathers," p. 147.
66. Roosevelt, *The Winning of the West,* p. 119.
67. *Ibid.,* p. 30.

68. *Ibid.*, p. 40.
69. *Ibid.*, p. 30.
70. Owen Wister, "The Evolution of the Cow-Puncher," in Robert Murray Davis, ed., *Owen Wister's West* (Albuquerque: University of New Mexico Press, 1987), pp. 33–53.
71. *Ibid.*, p. 37.
72. *Ibid.*
73. Owen Wister, *The Virginian: A Horseman of the Plains* (New York: Macmillan, 1902). Apropos of its neo-imperial character, Wister refers to his novel as "a colonial romance" in the preface (p. ix). By 1990, more than two million copies of the novel had been sold (noted in Jane Kuenz "The Cowboy Businessman and 'The Course of Empire,'" *Cultural Critique* 48 (spring 2001), p. 120.
74. The quotations are from Jane Kuenz's reading of Wister's *The Virginian* and his other literary supports of imperialism in *Ibid.*, p. 101.
75. In addition to his western paintings, see Remington's *The Way of the Indian* (1906).
76. Noted in William H. Goetzmann and William N. Goetzmann, *The West of the Imagination* (New York: W.W. Norton, 1986), p. 238.
77. *Ibid.*, p. 241.
78. *Ibid.*, p. 251.
79. *Ibid.*, p. 242.
80. In his analysis of the Cooper-Wister contrast and its influence on westerns, John Cawelti employs the expression "evolving social order" and argues that Cooper's West neglected it, simply juxtaposing a civilized East with natural West: *The Six-Gun Mystique Sequel* (Bowling Green OH: Bowling Green University Popular Press, 1999), p. 66.
81. On the anti-diegetic aspects of experimental cinema, see Andre Gardies, *Le Cinema de Robbe-Grillet: Essai semiocritique* (Paris: Albatross, 1983).
82. This point is made by Tag Gallagher, "Angels Gambol Where They Will: John Ford's Indians, in Jim Kitses and Greg Rickman, eds., *The Western Reader* (New York: Limelight, 1998), p. 273.
83. The phrase belongs to Peter Handke in *The Afternoon of a Writer,* p. 4
84. Certainly Sam Shepard, who wrote the screenplay, is known for his psychological Freudian-oriented plots. For a treatment that offers a psychoanalytic reading of the film, see Donald L. Carveth, "The Borderland Dilemma in *Paris, Texas:* Psychoanalytic Approaches to Sam Shepard," *Psyart: A Hyperlink Journal for Psychological Study of Arts,* on the web at http:www.clas.ufl.edu/ipsa/journal/articiles/psyart1997/carvet01.htm.
85. Conversation with Alain Bergala in Wim Wenders, *Written in the West* (Munich: Shirmer, 1987), p. 11.
86. *Ibid.*
87. *Ibid.*, p. 9.
88. *Ibid.*, p. 13.
89. *Ibid.*, p. 16.
90. The "location scouting" stills can be seen in Chris Sievernich, ed., *Wim Wenders-Sam Shepard: Paris, Texas* (Nordlinger, Germany: Greno, 1984), pp. 98–99.
91. Peter Handke, *The Long Way Around,* one of three novelettes in *Slow Homecoming* (New York: Farrar/Straus/Giroux, 1985), p. 76. Both authors of the screenplay of *Paris, Texas,* Wenders and Sam Shepard, are familiar with Handke's novels. Wenders worked with Handke on a screenplay for one of Handke's earlier novels (*The Anxiety of the Goaltender during the Penalty Kick*), and Shepard reviewed *Slow Homecoming* in the *New York Times Book Review.*
92. This is the interpretive resort of Phillip Kolker and Peter Beicken, in their excellent reading of the film in their "*Paris, Texas:* Between the Winds," in Kolker and Beicken, *The Films of Wim Wenders: Cinema as Vision and Desire* (New York: Cambridge University Press, 1993), p. 125.
93. Handke, *Slow Homecoming,* p. 114.
94. Thomas Pynchon, *Gravity's Rainbow* (New York: Viking, 1973).
95. This apt expression is in Kolker and Beicken, "*Paris, Texas:* Between the Winds," p. 120.
96. Quotations from Slotkin, *Gunfighter Nation,* p. 212.
97. Alexander Kluge "On Film and the Public Sphere," trans. Thomas Y. Levin and Miriam B. Hansen *New German Critique,* pp. 24–25 (fall/winter, 1981–1982), p. 21.
98. James Chapman, *The British at War: Cinema State and Propaganda, 1939–1945,* p. 181.

99. Michael Rogin, *Ronald Reagan, the Movie and Other Episodes in Political Demonology* (Berkeley: University of California Press, 1987), p. 37.

100. See for example, Karen Rasmussen and Sharon D. Downey, "Dialectical Disorientation in Vietnam War Films: Subversion of the Mythology of War," *Quarterly Journal of Speech* 77: 2 (May 1991), pp. 176–195, and for a more general treatment, which locates the Vietnam War film in a historical trajectory of war-film relationships, see Tom Englehardt, *The End of Victory Culture* (New York: Basic Books, 1995).

101. Karen Kaplan, "Anita Jones' Proposal Links up Army and USC, *Los Angeles Times*, August 18, 1999.

102. Rick Lyman, "White House Sets Meeting with film Executives to Discuss War on Terrorism," *New York Times*, November 8, 2001, p. B-8.

103. Caryn James, "TV's Take on Government in a Terror-Filled World," *New York Times*, April 30, 2002, on the web at http://www.nytimes.com/2002/04/30/arts/30JAME.html.

104. "Act II: Hollywood waves the flag—and is redeemed": cover story in *Christian Science Monitor*, 12/21/2001, p. 1.

105. See Geoffrey Gray, "'Black Hawk' Damned," *The Village Voice* 47: 6 (February 12, 2002), p. 26.

# Bibliography

Abel, Richard. "'Our Country'/ Whose Country? The 'Americanisation' Project of Early Westerns." in Edward Buscombe and Roberta E. Pearson eds. *Back in the Saddle Again: New Essays on the Western.* London: *BFI,* 1998.

Achilles, Jochen."'Homesick for Abroad': The Transition from National to Cultural Identity in Contemporary Irish Drama." *Modern Drama.* No. 38:432–443, 1995.

Agamben, Giorgio. *Homo Sacer: Sovereign Power and Bare Life.* Trans. Daniel Heller-Roazen. Stanford, CA: Stanford University Press, 1998.

Alexie, Sherman. "Indian Country." *The New Yorker.* March 13,: 76–84, 2000.

Allen, Christopher. *Art in Australia: From Colonization to Postmodernism* (London: Thames and Hudson), 1997.

Almond, Gabriel A., Taylor Cole, and Roy C. Macridis, "A suggested research Strategy in Western European Government and Politics." *American Political Science Review* 49, no. 4, 1955.

Alonso, Ana Maria. "The Politics of Space, Time and Substance: State Formation, Nationalism, and Ethnicity." *Annual Review of Anthropology.* No. 23: 378–389, 1994.

Anderson, Benedict. *Imagined Communities.* Extended and Revised Edition. New York: Verso, 1991.

Andreas, Peter and Richard Price, "From War Fighting to Crime Fighting: Transforming the American national Security State." *International Studies Review.* 3, No. 3: 29–41, 2001.

Andrews, Malcolm. *Landscape and Western Art.* Oxford: Oxford University Press, 1999.

Andrews, Walter G., "Singing the Alienated 'I': Guattari, Deleuze and Lyrical Decodings of *the Subject* in Ottoman *Divan* Poetry." *The Yale Journal of Criticism* 6, no. 2: 195–207, 1993.

Appy, Christian. "'We'll Follow the Old Man': The Strains of Sentimental Militarism in Popular Films of the Fifties." in Peter J. Kuznick and James Gilbert eds. *Rethinking Cold War Culture.* Washington DC: Smithsonian, 2001.

Apter, Emily. "Crossover texts/ Creole Tongues: A Conversation with Maryse Condé.'" *Public Culture.* 13, No. 1: 94–97, 2001.

Archuleta, Margaret and Dr. Rennard Strickland. *Shared Visions: Native American Painters* and Sculptors*in the Twentieth Century.* New York: New Press, 1991.

Arditi, Benjamin and Jeremy Valentine. *Polemicization.* Edinburgh: Edinburgh University Press, 1999.

Arguedas, Jose Maria. *Deep Rivers.* Trans Frances Horning Barraclough. Austin: University of Texas Press, 1978.

Attali, Jacques. *Noise: The Political Economy of Music.* Trans. Brian Massumi. Minneapolis: University of Minnesota Press, 1985.

Baker, Houston A. Jr. *Blues Ideology and Afro-American Literature.* Chicago: University of Chicago Press, 1984.

———. *Modernism and the Harlem Renaissance.* Chicago: University of Chicago Press, 1987.

Bakhtin, M. M. "Discourse in the Novel," in *The Dialogic Imagination.* Trans. Caryl Emerson and Michael Holquist. Austin: University of Texas Press. 1981.

———. "The *Bildungsroman*." in Caryl Emerson and Michael Holquist eds. *Speech Genres & Other Late Essays.* Trans. Vern W. McGee. Austin: University of Texas Press, 1986.

Bal, Mieke. *Death & Dissymmetry: The Politics of Coherence in the Book of Judges.* Chicago: University of Chicago Press, 1988.

Balibar, Etienne. "The Nation Form: History and Ideology," in Etienne Balibar and Immanuel Wallerstein. *Race, Nation, Class: Ambiguous Identities.* London: Verso, 1991.

Balinger, Robin. "Sounds of Resistance," in Ron Sakolsky and Fred Wei-Han Ho eds. *Sounding Off: Music as subversion/Resistance/Revolution.* Brooklyn, NY: Autonomedia, 1996.

Bamford, Kenton. *Distorted Images: British National Identity and Film in the 1920's.* London: I. B. Taurus, 1999.

Basso, Keith H. *Wisdom Sits In Places: Landscape and Language Among the Western Apache.* Albuquerque: University of New Mexico Press, 1996.

Baudrillard, Jean. "The Seismic Order," (1991). Found on the web at http://www.uta.edu/english/apt/collab/texts/sedismic.html.

Benetz-Rojo, Antonio, "The Repeating Island," in Gustavo Perez Firmat ed., *Do the Americas Have a Common Literature?* Durham: Duke University Press, 1990.

Benjamin, Walter. "The Task of the Translator." Trans. Harry Zohn in *Illuminations.* (New York: Schocken), 1968.

———. "Critique of Violence." in *Reflections.* Trans. Edmund Jepthcott. New York: Schocken, 1978.

Bercovitch, Sacvan. *The American Jeremiad.* Madison: University of Wisconsin Press, 1978.

Berlant, Lauren. *The Anatomy of National Fantasy.* Chicago: University of Chicago Press, 1991.

Berliner, Paul F. *Thinking in Jazz: The Infinite Art of Improvisation.* Chicago: University of Chicago Press, 1994.

Bermingham, Ann. *Landscape and Ideology: The English Rustic Tradition, 1740–1860.* Berkeley: University of California Press, 1986.

———. "System, Order, and Abstraction: The Politics of English Landscape Drawing around 1795," in W. J. T. Mitchell ed. *Landscape and Power.* Chicago: University of Chicago Press, 1994.

Bernard, Louise. "Countermemory and Return: Reclamation of the (Postmodern) Self in Jamaica Kincaid's *The Autobiography of My Mother* And *My Brother. Modern Fiction Studies.* 48: No. 1: 113–138, 2002.

Berry, Chris. "A Nation T(w/o)o: Chinese Cinema(s) and Nationhood(s) in Wimal Dissanayake ed. *Colonialism and nationalism in Asian Cinema.* Bloomington: Indiana University Press, 1994.

Beso, Amri. "*Bosnian Blues,*" in Misha Berson, "Bosnia Blues." *American Theater.* 13, No. 1: 18, 1996.

Bestemen, Catherine. "Violent politics and the politics of violence: the dissolution of the Somali nation-state." *American Ethnologist.* 23, No. 3: 579–596, 1996.

Bhabha, Homi K. ed. *Nation and Narration.* New York: Routledge, 1990.

———. *The Location of Culture.* New York: Routledge, 1994.

Billig, Michael. *Banal Nationalism* (London: Sage), 1995.

Bloom, Harold and David Rosenberg. *The Book of J.* New York: Grove Weidenfeld, 1990.

Boelhower, William. "Stories of Foundation, scenes of Origin." *American Literary History.* 5, No. 3: 389–401, 1993.

Boime, Albert. *The Magisterial Gaze: Manifest Destiny and American Landscape Painting* c. *1830–1865.* Washington DC: Smithsonian Institution Press, 1991.

Borneman, John. "American Anthropology as Foreign Policy." *American Anthropologist.* 97. No. 4: 662–667, 1995.

Botstein, Leon. "Beyond the Illusions of Realism: Painting and Debussy's Break with Tradition." in Jane Fulcher ed. *Debussy and His World.* Princeton, NJ: Princeton University Press, 2001.

Braudel, Fernand. *Afterthoughts on Material Civilization and Capitalism.* Baltimore: Johns Hopkins University Press, 1979.

Breight, Curtis C. *Surveillance, Militarism and Drama in the Elizabethan Era.* New York: St, Martins, 1996.

Brubaker, Rogers. *Nationalism Reframed.* New York: Cambridge University Press, 1996.

Buck, Elizabeth. *Paradise Remade: The Politics of Culture and History in Hawai'i.* Philadelphia: Temple University Press, 1993.

Burch, Noel. *Theory of Film Practice.* Trans. Helen Lane. New York: Praeger, 1973.

Burgess, John W., *The Foundations of Political Science.* New Brunswick, N.J.: Transaction, 1994.

Burgess, William H., "Federal recognition will result in legal apartheid." *The Honolulu Advertiser,* October 1, 2000, p. B-1.

Burgoyne, Robert. *Film Nation.* Minneapolis: University of Minnesota Press, 1997.

Butalia, Urvashi. *The Other Side of Silence.* New Delhi: Penguin, 1998.

Butler, Judith. "Restaging the Universal." in Judith Butler, Ernesto Laclau and Slavoj Zizek. *Contingency, Hegemony, Universality.* New York: Verso, 2000.

Campbell, David. *National Deconstruction.* Minneapolis: University of Minnesota press, 1998.

Carroll, Noel. and Sally Banes. "Cinematic Nation-Building: Eisenstein's *The Old and the New.*" in Hjort, Mette and Scott MacKenzie eds. *Cinema & Nation.* New York: Routledge, 2000.

Carter, Paul. *The Road to Botany Bay.* Chicago: University of Chicago Press, 1987.

Carveth, Donald L. "The Borderland Dilemma in *Paris Texas:* Psychoanalytic Approaches to Sam Shepard." *Psyart: A Hyperlink Journal for Psychological Study of Arts* at: http:www.clas.ufl.edu/ipsa/journal/articles/psyart1997/carvet01.htm.

Cawelti, John. "Cooper and the Frontier Myth and Anti-Myth." in Paul Verhoeven ed. *James Fenimore Cooper: New Historical and Literary Contexts.* Amsterdam: Rodopi, 1993.

———. *The Six-Gun Mystique Sequel.* Bowling Green, OH: Bowling Green University Popular Press, 1999.

Chakrabarty, Dipesh. "Marxism After Marx: History, Subalternity and Difference," in Saree Makdisi et al eds. *Marxism Beyond Marxism.* New York: Routledge, 1996.

Charlot, John. *The Hawaiian Poetry of Religion and Politics.* Honolulu: Institute for Polynesian studies, 1985.

Chapman, James. *The British at War: Cinema State and Propaganda, 1939–1945.* (London: I.B. Tauris), 1999.

Chatterjee, Partha. *The Nation and its Fragments.* Princeton, NJ: Princeton University Press, 1993.

Clevenger, John R. "Debussy's Rome Cantatas." in Jane Fulcher ed. *Debussy and His World.* Princeton, NJ: Princeton University Press, 2001.

Cliff, Michelle. *Free Enterprise.* New York: Dutton, 1993.

Clifford, James. "Identity in Mashpee." in *The Predicament of Culture.* Cambridge, MA: Harvard University Press, 1996.

———. "Diasporas," *Cultural Anthropology.* 9, No. 3: 305–315, 1994.

———. *Routes: Travel and Translation in the Late Twentieth Century.* Cambridge, MA: Harvard University Press, 1997.

Cobham, Rhonda. "Misgendering the Nation: African Nationalist Fictions and Nuhruddin Farah's *Maps.*" Andrew Parker, Mary Russo, Doris Sommer and Patricia Yaeger eds. *Nationalism and Sexualities.* New York: Routledge, 1992.

Cole, Bill. *John Coltrane.* New York: Da Capo, 1993.

Connell, Evan. *Son of the Morning Star: Custer and the Little Bighorn.* New York: Harper Collins, 1984.

Connor, Walker. "Nation-Building or Nation-Destroying? *World Politics* 24, No. 1: 319–355, 1972.

———. "When is a Nation." *Ethnic and Racial Studies.* 13, No. 1: 96–105, 1990.

Cooper, James Fenimore. "American And European Scenery Compared," in Motley F. Deakin's facsimile reproduction of *The Home Book of the Picturesque: Or American scenery, Art, and Literature. Comprising a Series of Essays by Washington Irving, W. G. Bryant, Fenimore Cooper, and Others.* (1952) this edition. Gainesville Florida: Scholars' Facsimiles & Reprints, 1967.

Corbett, David Peters, Ysanne Holt, and Fiona Russell eds. *The Geography of Englishness.* New Haven, CT: Yale University Press, 2002.

Corkin, Stanley. in "Cowboys and Free Markets: Post-World War II Westerns and U. S. Hegemony." *Cinema Journal.* 39, No. 3: 68–80, 2000.

Corrigan, Philip and Derek Sayer. *The Great Arch.* Oxford: Basil Blackwell, 1985.

Cott, Nancy F. *Public Vows:* A History of Marriage and the Nation. Harvard University Press, 2000.

Coyne, Michael. *The Crowded Prairie: American national Identity in the Hollywood Western.* New York: I. B. Tauris, 1997.

Cremony, John C. *Life Among the Apaches.* New York: Indian Head Books, 1991.

Crohn, Burrill. *The Coltrane Legacy.* New York: Video Artists International, 1985.

Cronon, William, George Miles, and Jay Gitlin. "Becoming West." in William Cronon, George Miles, and Jay Gitlin eds. *Under an Open Sky: Rethinking America's Western Past.* New York: W. W. Norton, 1992.

Daniels, Stephen. *Fields of Vision: Landscape Imagery and National identity in England and the United States.* New York: Polity, 1993.

Day, Robert. "'Sooners' or 'Goners,' they were hellbent on grabbing fee land." *Smithsonian.* 20, No. 8: 190–194. 1989.

Deleuze, Gilles. *Cinema 1.* Trans. Hugh Tomlinson. London: Althlone, 1986.

———. *Cinema 2.* Trans Hugh Tomlinson and Robert Galeta. London: Athlone, 1989.

———. *Difference and Repetition.* Trans. Paul Patton. London: Athlone, 1994.

———. "Life as a Work of Art," in *Negotiations.* Trans. Martin Joughin. New York: Columbia University Press, 1997. 96.

————. " Having an Idea in Cinema." Trans. Eleanor Kaufman in Eleanor Kaufman and Kevin Jon Heller eds. *Deleuze and Guattari: New Mappings in Politics, Philosophy, and Culture.* Minneapolis: University of Minnesota Press, 1998.

Deleuze, Gilles and Felix Guattari. *Anti-Oedipus: Capitalism and Schizophrenia.* Trans. Robert Hurley, Mark Seem, and Helen R. Lane. New York: Viking, 1977.

————. *Kafka, or Towards a Minor Literature.* Trans. Reda Bensmaia and Dana Polan. Minneapolis: University of Minnesota Press, 1986.

————. *A Thousand Plateaus: Capitalism and Schizophrenia.* Trans. Brian Massumi. Minneapolis: University of Minnesota Press, 1987.

DeLillo, Don. *Libra.* New York: Viking, 1988.

Dennis, Matthew. *Cultivating a Landscape of Peace.* Ithaca, NY: Cornell University Press, 1993.

Denning, Michael. *The Cultural Front: The Laboring of American Culture in the Twentieth Century.* New York: Verso, 1996.

Derrida, Jacques. *The Ear of the Other: Otobiography, Transference, Translation.* Trans. Avital Ronell and Peggy Kamuf. New York: Schocken, 1985.

————. *"Des Tours de Babel."* Trans. Joseph F. Graham in Joseph F. Graham ed. *Difference in Translation.* Ithaca, NY: Cornell University Press, 1985.

————. "Force of Law," in Drucilla Cornell, Michael Rosenfeld and David Gray Carlson, *Deconstruction and the Possibility of Justice.* New York: Routledge, 1992.

Devi, Mahasweta. "The Author in Conversation" (with Gayatri Chakravorty Spivak) in *Imaginary Maps.* Trans. Gayatri Chakravorty Spivak. New York: Routledge, 1995.

Devine, Tracy Lynne. "Indigenous Identity and Identification in Peru: *Indigenismo,* Education and Contradictions in State Discourses." *Journal of Latin American Cultural Studies.* 8, No. 1: 61–73, 1999.

Dharwadker, Aparna. "John Gay, Bertold Brecht, and Postcolonial Antinationalisms." *Modern Drama.* 38, No. 4: 4–21, 1995.

Didi-Huberman, Georges. "The art of not describing; Vermeer—the detail and the patch," *History of the Human Sciences* 2, No. 2, 1989. 141.

Diffley, Kathleen. "*Home on the Range: Turner, Slavery, and the Landscape illustrations in* Harper's New Monthly Magazine, *1861–1876*" in Jack Salzman ed. *Prospects: An Annual Review of American Cultural Studies.* Vol. 14: 175–202. New York: Cambridge University Press, 1989.

D'Lugo, Marvin. "'Transparent Women': Gender and Nation in Cuban Cinema." in John King, Ana M. Lopez, and Manuel Alvarado. *Mediating Two Worlds: Cinematic Encounters in the Americas.* London: BFI, 1993.

Donadey, Anne. "The Multilingual Strategies of Postcolonial Literature: Assia Djebar's Algerian Palimpsest." *World Literature Today.* 74, No. 1: 27–36, 2000.

Durham, Philip and Everett L. Jones. *The Negro Cowboys.* New York: Dodd, Mead & Co., 1965.

Eisenstein, Sergei. *Film Form.* Trans. Jay Leyda. New York: Meridian, 1957.

————. "Dickens, Griffith, and the Film Today." in *Film Form.* Trans. Jay Leyda. New York: Meridian, 1970.

————. "Montage," in Leon Moussiac, *Sergei Eisenstein.* Trans. D. Sandy Petrey. New York: Crown, 1970.

————. "Mr, Lincoln by Mr. Ford." in Jay Leyda ed. *Film Essays and a Lecture by Sergei Eisenstein.* Princeton, N.J.: Princeton University Press, 1982.

————. *Selected Works Vol 1 1922–34* ed. and trans. Richard Taylor (London: BFI), 1988.

Ellis, John. *The Social History of the Machine Gun.* Baltimore: Johns Hopkins University Press, 1975.

Englehardt, Tom. *The End of Victory Culture.* New York: Basic Books, 1995.

Eyman, Scott. *Print the Legend: The Life and Times of John Ford.* Baltimore: Johns Hopkins University Press, 1999.

Faery, Rebecca Blevins. *Cartographies of Desire: Captivity, Race, and Sex in the Shaping of An American Nation.* Norman: University of Oklahoma Press, 1999.

Faragher, John. "Americans, Mexicans, Metis: A Community Approach to the Comparative Study of North American Frontiers." in William Cronon, George Miles, and Jay Gitlin eds. *Under an Open Sky: Rethinking America's Western Past.* New York: W. W. Norton, 1992.

Fanon, Franz. *Black Skin, White Masks.* Trans. Charles Lam Markmann. London: Pluto, 1986.

Fehrenbach, Heide. *Cinema in Democratizing Germany.* Chapel Hill: University of North Carolina Press, 1995.

Feinstein, Sacha. "From *Alabama,* to *A Love Supreme:* The Evolution of the John Coltrane Poem." *The Southern Review.* 32, No. 2: 315–327, 1996.

Dexter Filkins, "U.S. Is Studying DNA of Dead Al Qaida and Taliban Combatants." *The New York Times on the Web.* March 15, 2002: http://www.nytimes.com/2002/03/15/international/asia/15AFGH.html.

Filmer, Paul, Val Rimmer and David Walsh. *Oklahoma!:* ideology and politics in the vernacular tradition of the American musical." *Popular Music.* 18, No. 3: 389–390, 1999.

Foucault, Michel. *The Archaeology of Knowledge.* Trans. A. M. Sheridan Smith. New York: Pantheon, 1972.

———. *Language, Counter-Memory, Practice* Trans. Donald F. Bouchard and Sherry Simon. Ithaca, NY: Cornell university Press, 1977.

———. *The History of Sexuality.* Trans. Robert Hurley New York: Pantheon, 1978.

———. "War in the Filagree of Peace." Trans. Ian Mcleod. *Oxford Literary Review.* 4, No. 1: 15–19, 1979.

———. "Nietzsche, Genealogy, History." in Paul Rabinow ed. *The Foucault Reader* New York: Pantheon, 1984.

———. *Death and the Labyrinth: The World of Raymond Roussel.* Trans. Charles Ruas. New York: Doubleday, 1986.

———. "Of Other Spaces." Trans. Jay Miscowiec. *Diacritics* No. 16: 19–27, 1986.

———. "What is Critique?" Trans. Lysa Hochroth in Michel Foucault, *The Politics of Truth* ed. Sylvere Lotringer and Lysa Hochroth. New York: Semiotext(e), 1997.

Frantz, Douglas."Turkish Court Hobbles a Popular Pro-Islamic Politician." *New York Times,* January 10: A-5, 2002.

Fried, Michael. *Realism, Writing, Disfiguration: On Thomas Eakins and Stephen Crane.* Chicago: University of Chicago Press, 1987.

Frith, Simon. *World Musics, Politics and Social Change.* New York: Manchester University Press, 1989.

Fulcher, Jane F. *The Nation's Image: French Grand Opera as Politics and Politicized Art.* New York: Cambridge University Press, 1987.

———. *French Cultural Politics & Music.* New York: Oxford University Press, 1999.

Gabbard, Krin. "Kansas City," *The American Historical Review.* 102, No. 4: 1274–1275, 1997.

Gallagher, Tag. "Angels Gambol Where They Will: *John Ford's Indians.*" in Jim Kitses and Gregg Rickman eds. *The Western Reader.* New York: Limelight, 1998.

Garcia Canclini, Nestor, *Hybrid Cultures: Strategies for Entering and Leaving Modernity.* Trans. Christopher L. Chiappari and Silvia L. Lopez. Minneapolis: University of Minnesota Press, 1995.

Gardies, Andre. *Le Cinema de Robbe-Grillet: Essai semiocritique.* Paris: Albatross, 1983.

Garman, Bryan "The Ghost of History: Bruce Springsteen, Woody Guthrie, and the Hurt Song." *Popular Music and Society.* 20, No. 2: 69–117, 1996.

Gates, Henry Louis Jr. *The Signifying Monkey: A Theory of Afro-American Literary Criticism.* New York: Oxford University Press, 1988.

Gennari, John. "Jazz Criticism: Its Development and Ideologies," *Black American Literary Forum.* 25, No. 3: 447–458, 1991.

Gerassi-Navarro, Nina. *Pirate Novels: Fictions of Nation Building in Spanish America.* Durham, NC: Duke University Press, 1999.

Gerth, Jeff and Don Van Natta Jr. "In Tough Times a Company Finds Profits in Terror War." *New York Times* on the web at: http://www.nytimes.com/2002/07/13/bisiness/13Hall.html.

Gibson, William. *Count Zero.* New York: Ace Books, 1987.

Giddens, Anthony. *The Nation State and Violence.* Cambridge: Basil Blackwell, 1983.

Gilroy, Paul. *The Black Atlantic: Modernity and Double Consciousness.* Cambridge: Harvard University Press, 1993.

———. *Against Race: Imaging Political Culture Beyond the Color Line.* Cambridge, MA: Harvard University Press, 2000.

Glissant, Edouard. *Poetics of Relation.* Trans. Betsy Wing. Ann Arbor: University of Michigan Press, 1997.

Goetzmann, William H. and William N. Goetzmann. *The West of the Imagination.* New York: W. W. Norton, 1986.

Goldberg, David Theo. "States of Whiteness," in David Theo Goldberg, Michael Musheno, and Lisa Bower eds. *Between Law and Culture: Recasting Legal Studies.* University of Minnesota Press, 2001.

Goldberg, David Theo. *The Racial State.* Malden, MA: Blackwell, 2002.

Goodwin, Andrew and Joe Gore. "World Beat and the Cultural Imperialism Debate." in Ron Sakolsky and Fred Wei-Han Ho eds. *Sounding Off: Music as subversion/Resistance/Revolution.* Brooklyn, NY: Autonomedia, 1996.

Goodwin, James. *Eisenstein, Cinema, and History.* Urbana: University of Illinois Press, 1993.

Gray, Geoffrey. "'Black Hawk' Damned" *The Village Voice* 47, No. 6: 26, 2002.

Greenberg, Eric Rolf. *The Celebrant.* New York: Everest House, 1982.

Green-Lewis, Jennifer. "Picturing England: On Photography, Landscape, and the End(s) of Imperial Culture." *Genre* No. 29: 30–41, 1996.

Guardino, Peter and Charles Walker. "The State, Society, and Politics in Peru and Mexico in The Colonial and Early Republican Periods." *Latin American Perspectives.* 73, No. 19: 8–19. 1992.

Gupta Akhil and James Ferguson. "Beyond 'Culture': Space, Identity, and the Politics of Difference," in Jonathan Xavier Inda and Renato Rosaldo eds. *The Anthropology of Globalization.* Malden, MA: Blackwell, 2002.

Girgus, Sam B. *The New Covenant.* Chapel Hill: University of North Carolina Press, 1984.

Guy, Donna J. "'White Slavery,' Citizenship and Nationality in Argentina." in Andrew Parker, Mary Russo, Doris Sommer and Patricia Yaeger eds. *Nationalism and Sexualities.* New York: Routledge, 1992.

Gvosdev, Nikolas K. and Anthony A. Cipriano "Patriotism and Profit are Powerful Weapons." *Honolulu Advertiser.* July 7: B-4, 2002.

Habermas, Jurgen. "The European Nation-State: On the Past and Future of Sovereignty and Citizenship," Trans Ciaran Cronin. *Public Culture.* 10, No. 2: 397–416, 1998.

Hamm, Charles. ed. *Irving Berlin: Early Songs* Vol. III 1913–14. Madison, WI: A-R Editions, 1994.

———. "Genre, performance and ideology in the early songs of Irving Berlin." *Popular Music.* 13, No. 2: 141–155: 1994.

Peter Handke. *Slow Homecoming.* Trans. Ralph Manheim. New York: Farrar/Straus/Giroux, 1985.

Handke, Peter. *The Afternoon of a Writer.* New York: Farrar Straus & Giroux, 1989.

Hanssen, Beatrice. *Critique of Violence: Between Poststructuralism and Critical Theory.* New York: Routledge, 2000.

Hardt, Michael and Antonio Negri. *Empire.* Cambridge, MA: Harvard University Press, 2000.

Harris, Cheryl. "Whiteness as Property." *Harvard Law Review* No. 106:1709–1791, 1993.

Hau'ofa, Epeli. "Our Sea of Islands," in *A New Oceania: Rediscovering Our Sea of Islands.* Suva, Fiji: University of the South Pacific: 5–11, 1993.

Hayden, Robert M. "imagined communities and real victims: self-determination and ethnic cleansing in Yugoslavia." *American Ethnologist.* 23, No. 4: 779–786, 1996.

Hayward, Susan. "Questions of National Cinema." in Keith Cameron ed. *National Identity.* Exeter, England, intellect, 1999.

Helgerson, Richard. "The Land Speaks: Cartography, Chorography, and Subversion in Renaissance England." *Representations.* 16, No. 4: 47–60, 1986.

———. *Forms of Nationhood.* Chicago: University of Chicago Press, 1992.

Helsinger, Elizabeth. "Turner and the Representation of England." in W. J. T. Mitchell ed. *Landscape and Power.* Chicago: University of Chicago Press, 1994.

———. "Land and National Representation in Britain," in Michael Rosenthal, Christiana Payne, and Scott Wilcox eds. *Prospects for the Nation: Recent Essays in British landscape.* Yale University Press, 1997.

Herman, Ellen. *The Romance of American Psychology.* Berkeley: University of California Press, 1995.

Hertz, David Michael. *The Tuning of the Word: The Musico-Literary Poetics of the Symbolist Movement.* Carbondale: Southern Illinois University Press, 1987.

Hitchens, Christopher. *Blood, Class, and Nostalgia: Anglo-American Ironies.* New York: Farrar, Straus & Giroux, 1990.

Hjort, Mette and Scott MacKenzie eds. *Cinema & Nation.* New York: Routledge, 2000.

Hobsbawm, Eric J. *Nations and Nationalism Since 1780.* New York: Cambridge University Press, 1990.

Holland, Catherine. "Notes on the State of America: Jeffersonian Democracy and the Production of a National Past." *Political Theory*. 29, No. 2: 190–216, 2001.

Horn, David. "From Catfish Row to Granby Street: contesting meaning in *Porgy and Bess*." *Popular Music*. 13, No. 2: 167–178, 1994.

Horse Capture, George P., Anne Vitart, Michel Waldberg, and W. Richard West, Jr., *Robes of Splendor*. New York: The New Press, 1993.

Hough, Robert L. *The West of Owen Wister*. Lincoln: University of Nebraska Press, 1972.

House, John. "Authority versus independence: the position of French landscape in the 1870's." in Richard Tomson ed. *Framing France: The Representation of Landscape in France, 1870–1914*. Manchester: Manchester University press, 1998.

Hughes, Langston. *The Weary Blues*. New York: Alfred A. Knopf, 1926.

Hutcheon, Linda and Michael Hutcheon. "Otherhood Issues: Post-National Operatic Narratives," *Narrative*. 3, No. 1: 1–14, 1995.

———. "Imagined Communities: Postnational Canadian Opera." in Richard Delamore and Daniel Fischlin eds. *The Work of Opera: Genre, Nationhood, and Sexual Difference*. New York: Columbia University Press, 1997.

Hyde, Anne Farrar. *An American Vision: Far Western Landscape and National Culture, 1820–1920*. New York: NYU Press, 1990.

Ioane, Kelii W. (Skippy). "In Fla Grante Delecto." in *Big Island Conspiracy: Reflective but Unrepentent*. Honolulu: Deep Ka'a Ka'a Records, 1999.

Jacobs, Carol. *In the Language of Walter Benjamin*. Baltimore: Johns Hopkins University Press, 1999.

Jakobson, Roman and Morris Halle. *Fundamentals of Language*. The Hague: Mouton, 1971.

James, Caryn. "TV's Take on Government in a Terror-Filled World," *New York Times* on the web at http://www.nytimes.com/2002/04/30/arts/30JAME.html.

Jarrett, Michael. "The Tenor's Vehicle: Reading *Way Out West*." *LIT* 5, Nos. 3–4: 229–238, 1994.

Jay, Gregory S. "'White Man's Book No Good': D. W. Griffith and the American Indian." *Cinema Journal*. 39, No. 4: 1–14, 2000.

Jefferson, Thomas. *Notes on the State of Virginia*. ed. Frank Shuffelton. New York: Penguin, 1999.

Johnson, Bruce. "Hear me talkin' to ya: problems of jazz discourse." *Popular Music*. 12, No. 1, 1–12, 1993.

Johnson, David. "Law Change Sought to Set UP DNA Databank for Captured Qaida Fighters." *The New York Times on the Web*. March 2, 2002: http://www.nytimes.com/2002/03/06/national/06DNA.html.

Jones, Kent. Review of *Dead Man*. *Cineaste*. 2, No. 2: 44–45, 1996.

Jones, LeRoi (Amiri Baraka). *Blues People*. New York: Morrow, 1999.

Kaes, Anton. *From Hitler to Heimat: The return of History as Film*. Cambridge, MA: Harvard University Press, 1989.

Kammen, Michael. *In the Past Lane: Historical Perspective on American Culture*. New York: Oxford University Press, 1997.

Kaplan, Karen. "Anita Jones' Proposal Links up Army and USC. *Los Angeles Times,* August 18: A: 12, 1999.

Kauanui, J. Kehaulani. *Rehabilitating the Native: Hawaiian Blood Quantum and the Politics of Race, Citizenship,* and Entitlement," Doctoral Dissertation in the Program in The History of Consciousness. Santa Cruz: University of California, Santa Cruz, 2000.

Kaufmann, Eric. "'Naturalizing the Nation': The Rise of Naturalistic Nationalism in the United States and Canada." *Comparative Studies in Society and History*. 40, No. 4: 676–688, 1998.

Kawash, Samira. "Men: Moving Bodies, or The Cinematic Politics of Deportation." in Eleanor Kaufman and Kevin Jon Heller eds. *Deleuze and Guattari: New Mappings in Politics, Philosophy, and Culture*. Minneapolis: University of Minnesota Press, 1998.

Kearney, Michael. "Borders and Boundaries of State and Self at the End of Empire." *Journal of Historical Sociology*. 4, No. 1: 49–58, 1991.

Khoury, Elias. *Little Mountain*. Trans. Maia Tabet. Minneapolis: University of Minnesota Press, 1989.

Kilpatrick, Jacqueline. *Celluloid Indians: Native Americans and Film*. Lincoln: University of Nebraska Press, 1999.

Kluge, Alexander. "On Film and the Public Sphere." Trans. Thomas Y. Levin and Miriam B Hansen. *New German Critique*. Nos. 24–25: 19–25, 1981–82.

Kolodny, Annette. "Letting Go Our Grand Obsessions: Notes Toward a New Literary History of American Frontiers." *American Literature*. 64, No. 1: 1–14, 1992.

Konvitz, Josef W. "The Nation-state, Paris and cartography in eighteenth- and nineteenth century France." *Journal of Historical Geography*. 16, No. 1: 1–17, 1990.

Koselleck, Reinhardt. *Futures Past: On the Semantics of Historical Time*. Trans. Keith Tribe Cambridge, MA: MIT Press, 1985.

Kosminder, Alexia. *Tricky Tribal Discourse: The Poetry, Short Stories, and Fus Fixico Letters of Creek Writer Alex Posey*. Moscow: University of Idaho Press, 1998.

Kristeva, Julia. "Women's Time." Trans. Alice Jardine and Harry Blake. *Signs*. 7, No 1: 18–27, 1981.

Kruger, Loren. *The National Stage: Theater and Cultural Legitimation in England, France, and America*. Chicago: University of Chicago Press, 1992.

Kuenz, Jane. "The Cowboy Businessman and 'The Course of Empire'." *Cultural Critique*. No. 48: 118–129, 2001.

Larsen, Neil. "Mario Vargas Llosa: The realist as Neo-Liberal." *Journal of Latin American Cultural Studies*. 9, No. 2: 162–170, 2000.

Lahr, John. "Revolutionary Rag." *The New Yorker*. March 3rd: 78–79, 1999.

Latham, Michael E. *Modernization as Ideology: American Social Science and 'Nation-Building' in the Kennedy Era*. Chapel Hill: University of North Carolina Press, 2000.

Layoun, Mary N. *Travels of a Genre: The Modern Novel and Ideology*. Princeton, NJ: Princeton University Press, 1990.

Lee, Josephine. "Linguistic Imperialism, The Early Abbey Theater, and the *Translations* of Brian Friel," in J. Ellen Gainor ed. *Imperialism and Theater*. New York: Routledge, 1995.

Lerner, Daniel. *The Passing of Traditional Society: Modernizing the Middle East*. New York: Free Press, 1958.

———. "Preface," in Daniel Lerner ed. *The Human Meaning of the Social Sciences*. New York: Meridian, 1959.

———. "Four Point Program," in "Communication and Development," in Daniel Lerner and Lyle M. Nelson eds. *Communication Research—A Half Century Appraisal*. Honolulu: University of Hawaii Press: 148, 1977.

Levinas, Emmanuel. *Difficult Freedom: Essays on Judaism*. Trans. Sean Hand. Baltimore: Johns Hopkins University Press, 1990.

Levy, Alan Howard. *Musical Nationalism: American Composers' Search for Identity*. Westport, Ct.: Greenwood Press, 1983.

Lewis, George H. "Don' Go Down Waikiki: Social Protest and Popular Music in Hawaii, in Reebee Garfalo ed. *Rockin' the Boat: Mass Music and Mass Movements*. Boston: South End Press, 1992.

Liebersohn, Harry. "Discovering Indigenous Nobility: Tocqueville, Chamisso, and Romantic Travel Writing." *American Historical Review*. 99, No. 3: 752–769, 1994.

Lindqvist, Sven. "*Exterminate All the Brutes.*" Trans. Joan Tate. New York: The New Press, 1996.

Lipsitz, George. *Dangerous Crossroads: Popular Music, Postmodernism and the Poetics of Place*. New York: Verso, 1994.

Littlefield, Daniel F. Jr. *Alex Posey: Creek Poet, Journalist & Humourist*. Lincoln: University of Nebraska Press, 1992.

Lloyd, David and Paul Thomas. *Culture and the State*. New York: Routledge, 1998.

Lopez, Ana M. "Early Cinema and Modernity in Latin America." *Cinema Journal*. 40, No. 1: 45–56, 2000.

Lukacs, Georg. *The Historical Novel*. Trans. Hannah and Stanley Mitchell. New York: Humanities Press, 1965.

Lyman, Rick. "White House Sets Meeting With Film Executives to Discuss War on Terrorism." *New York Times*, November 8: B-8, 2001.

Mackey, Nathaniel. "Other: From Noun to Verb," in Krin Gabbard ed. *Jazz Among the Discourses*. Durham, North Carlina: Duke University Press, 1995.

Maier, Susan. "'Stranger in a Strange Land': Jim Jarmusch's *Dead Man* and the Technology of the American West/ern." *Node*. 9, No. 1: 1–12, 1997.

Malkia, Matt "Conceptual Analysis for the Social Sciences," at http://www.uta.fi/laitokset/hallinto/cocta/Future_Plans.htm.

Manning, Erin. *Ephemeral Territories*. Minneapolis: University of Minnesota Press, 2003.

Marx, Anthony. *Making Race and Nation*. New York: Cambridge University Press, 1998.

Mazzio, Carla. "Staging the Vernacular: Language and the Nation in Tomas Kyd's *The Spanish Tragedy*." *Studies in English Literature 1500–1900*. 38, No. 2: 205–116, 1998.

Maxwell, Ian. "Sydney Style: Hip Hop Down Under Comin' Up," in Tony Mitchell ed. *Global Noise: Rap and Hip Hop Outsid3e the USA*. Middletown, CT: Wesleyan University Press, 2001.

Mbembe, Achille. *On The Postcolony*. Berkeley: University of California Press, 2001.

McClintock, Anne. "No Longer a Future Heaven: Women and Nationalism in South Africa." *Transition* No. 51: 100–112, 1991.

McGonagle, Declan, Fintan O' Toole, and Kim Levin. *Irish Art Now: From the Poetic to the Political*. London: Merrell Halberton, 1999.

Mehmedinovic, Semezdin. *sarajevo blues*. Trans. Ammiel Alcalay. San Francisco: City Lights, 1998.

Mehrez, Samia. "Translation and the Postcolonial Experience: The Francophone North African Text." in Lawrence Venuti ed. *Rethinking Translation: Discourse, Subjectivity, Ideology*. New York: Routledge, 1992.

Merriam, Charles. "Progress Report of the Committee on Political Research." *American Political Science Review:* 17, No. 2: 278–289, 1923.

Merry, Sally Engle. *Colonizing Hawai'i: The Cultural Power of Law*. Princeton, N.J.: Princeton University Press, 2000.

Mignolo, Walter. *The Darker Side of the Renaissance: Literacy, Territoriality, & Colonization*. Ann Arbor: University of Michigan Press, 1995.

———. "I am Where I Think: Epistemology and the Colonial Difference." *Journal of Latin American Cultural Studies*. 8, No. 2: 236–239, 1999.

———. *Local Histories / Global Designs*. Princeton, NJ: Princeton University Press, 2000.

———. "The Geopolitics of Knowledge and the Colonial Difference." *South Atlantic Quarterly*. 101, No. 1: 65–77, 2002.

Miller, Angela. *The Empire of the Eye: Landscape Representation and American Cultural Politics 1825–1875*. Ithaca, NY: Cornell University Press, 1993.

Sydney Mintz. "Enduring Substances, Trying Theories: The Caribbean Region as Oikoumene," *Journal pf the Royal Anthropological Institute*. 2, No. 2: 297–315.

Mitchell, Timothy. "Society, Economy, and the State Effect," in George Steinmetz ed. *State/Culture*. Ithaca, New York: Cornell University Press: 74–85, 1999.

———. "Nationalism, Imperialism, Economism: A Comment on Habermas. *Public Culture*. 10, No. 2: 417–423, 1998.

Mitchell, Tony. "Indigenous Music and Music television in Australia." *Perfect Beat*. 1, No. 1: 1–16, 1992.

Mitchell, W. J. T. "Imperial Landscape," in W. J. T. Mitchell ed. *Landscape and Power*. Chicago: University of Chicago Press, 1994.

Mojica, Monique. *Pocahontas and the Blue Spots*. Toronto: Women's Press, 1991.

Monceau, Nicholas. "Confronting Turkey's Social Realities: An Interview with Yesim Ustaoglu." *Cineaste* 26, No. 3: 30, 2001.

Monod, David. "Disguise, Containment and the *Porgy and Bess* Revival of 1952–1956." *Journal of American Studies*. 35, No. 2: 282–214, 2001.

Moon, William Least Heat. *PrairyErth (a deep map)*. Boston: Houghton Mifflin. 1991.

Moreira, Alberto. "The Order of Order: On the Reluctant Culturalism of Anti-Subalternist Critiques," *Journal of Latin American Cultural Studies*. 8, No. 1: 138–149, 1999.

Moretti, Franco. *Atlas of the European Novel: 1800–1900*. New York: Verso, 1998.

Morrison, Toni. *Paradise*. New York: Plume, 1999.

Mosley, Walter. *RL's Dream*. New York W. W. Norton, 1995.

Murray, Albert. *The Omni-Americans*. New York: E. P. Dutton, 1970.

Murray, David. *Forked Tongues: Speech, Writing and Representation in North American Indian Texts*. London: Pinter, 1991.

Nadel, Alan. *Containment Culture: American Narratives, Postmodernism, and the Atomic Age*. Durham, NC: Duke University Press, 1995.

Neal, Mark Anthony. *What the Music Said*. New York: Routledge, 1999.

Nederveen Pieterse, Jan. *Development Theory: Constructions/ Reconstructions*. Thousand Oaks, CA: Sage, 2001.

Neill, Michael. "Broken English and Broken Irish: Nation, Language, and the Optics of Power in Shakespeare's Histories." *Shakespeare Quarterly*. 45, No. 1: 1–14, 1994.

Nelson, Robert M. *Place and Vision: The Function of Landscape in Native American Fiction*. New York: Peter Lang, 1993.

Nemiroff, Diana, Robert Houle, and Charlotte Townsend-Gault. *Land Spirit Power: First Nations at the National Gallery of Canada*. Ottawa: National Gallery of Canada, 1992.

Nietzsche, Friedrich. *Thus Spoke Zarathustra,*. Trans. Walter Kaufman. New York: Viking, 1966.

Noble, David. *The Eternal Adam and the New World Garden*. New York: George Braziller, 1968.

Nugent, David. "Building the State, Making the Nation: The Bases of Limits of State Centralization in 'Modern' Peru." *American Anthropologist*. 96, No. 2: 336–347, 1994.

Ouaknin, Marc-Alain. *The Burnt Book: Reading the Talmud*. Trans. Llewellyn Brown. Princeton, NJ: Princeton University Press, 1995.

Omi, Michael and Howard Winant. *Racial Formation in the United States: From the 1960s to the 1990s*. New York: Routledge, 1995.

Opitz, Andrea. "James Welch's *Fools Crow* and the Imagination of Precolonial Space." *American Indian Quarterly*. 24, No. 1: 123–132, 2000.

Osborne, Brian S. "The iconography of nationhood in Canadian art," in Denis Cosgrove and Stephen Daniels eds. *The Iconography of Landscape*. Cambridge University Press, 1988.

Palin, Tutta. "Picturing a Nation" in Tuomas M. S. Lehtonen,. *Europe's Northern Frontier*. Trans. Philip Landon. Jyvaskyla, Finland: PS-Kustannus, 1999.

Patton, Paul. *Deleuze and the Political*. London: Routledge, 2000.

Pearson, Nathan W. Jr. "Political and Musical Forces that Influenced the Development of Kansas City Jazz." *Black Music Research*. 9, No. 2: 178–188, 1989.

Peters, Ralph. "Our Soldiers, Their Cities." *Parameters*. 26, No. 1: 43–50, 1996.

Pletsch, Carl E. "The Three Worlds, or the Division of Social Scientific Labor, circa 1950–1975." *Comparative Studies in Society and History*. 23:, No. 4: 564–577, 1981.

Potter, Russell A. *Spectacular Vernaculars: Hip-Hop and the Politics of Postmodernism*. Albany: State University of New York Press, 1995.

Puig, Manuel. *Betrayed By Rita Hayworth*. Trans. Suzanne Jill Levine. New York: E. P. Dutton, 1971.

Pynchon, Thomas. *Gravity's Rainbow*. New York: Viking, 1973.

Rafael, Vincente. "The Cultures of Area Studies." *Social Text* No. 41: 1–12, 1994.

Rahier, Jean Muteba. "Body Politics in Black and White: *Senoras, Mujeres, Blanqueamiento* and Miss Emeraldas 1997–1998, Ecuador." *Women & Performance*. 11, No. 1:101–110, 1999. 106.

Rainwater, Lee and William L. Yancey. *The Moynihan Report and the Politics of Controversy* Cambridge, MA: M.I.T. Press, 1967.

Ranciere, Jacques. "Politics, Identification, and Subjectivization." *October* No. 61: 53–64, 1992.

———. *Disagreement*. Trans. Julie Rose. Minneapolis: University of Minnesota Press, 1998.

Rasmussen, Karen and Sharon D. Downey. "Dialectical Disorientation in Vietnam War Films: Subversion of the Mythology of War." *Quarterly Journal of Speech*. 77, No. 2:176–95, 1991.

Reagan, Patrick D. *Designing a New America*. Amherst, University of Massachusetts Press, 1999.

Redeker, Robert. "In Place of Politics: Humanitarianism and War." in Tariq Ali ed. *Masters of the Universe? NATO's Balkan Crusade*. New York: Verso, 2000.

Richardson, Lewis Frye. *Statistics of Deadly Quarrels*. Pittsburgh: Boxwood Press, 1960.

Richter, Daniel K. *Facing East from Indian Country*. Cambridge, MA: Harvard University Press, 2001.

Robbins, Kevin and Asu Aksoy. "Deep Nation: the national question and Turkish cinema culture," in Mette Hjort and Scott MacKenzie eds. *Cinema & Nation*. New York: Routledge, 202–213, 2000.

Rogin, Michael. *Ronald Reagan, the Movie and Other Episodes in Political Demonology*. Berkeley: University of California Press, 1987.

Roosevelt, Theodore. *The Winning of the West*. New York: G. P. Putnam's sons, 1889.

Rose, Jacqueline. *States of Fantasy*. Oxford: The Clarendon Press, 1996.

Rose, Tricia. *Black Noise: Rap Music and Black Culture in Contemporary America*. Hanover, Hew Hampshire: University Press of America, 1994.

Rosenbaum, Jonathan. "A Gun Up Your Ass: An Interview with Jim Jarmusch." *Cineaste*. 22, No. 2: 21–22, 1996.

Roth, Joseph. "Rare and ever rarer in this world of empirical facts . . ." in *The Collected Stories of Joseph Roth*. Trans. Michael Hofmann. New York: W.W. Norton, 2002.

Roth, Philip. *I Married a Communist*. New York: Vintage, 1999.

Roussel, Raymond. *How I Wrote Certain of My Books*. Trans. Trevor Winkfield. New York: Sun, 1977.

Rushdie, Salman. *Imaginary Homelands.* New York: Penguin, 1992.
———. *The Ground Beneath Her Feet.* New York: Henry Holt, 1999.
Sassen, Saskia. "Globalization After September 11." *The Chronicle of Higher Education* 1/18: B-11, 2002.
Savage, William W. Jr. *Singing Cowboys and All That Jazz.* Norman: University of Oklahoma Press, 1983.
Schaeffer, Robert K. *Severed States: Dilemmas of Democracy in a Divided World.* Lanham, MD: Rowman and Littlefield, 1999.
Scheckel, Susan. "'In the Land of His Fathers': Cooper, Land Rights, and the Legitimation of American National Identity. in Paul Verhoeven ed. *James Fenimore Cooper: New Historical and Literary Contexts.* Amsterdam: Rodopi, 1993.
———. *The Insistence of the Indian: Race and Nationalism in Nineteenth Century American Culture.* Princeton University Press, 1998.
Schiller, Herbert I. *Culture, Inc.: The Corporate Takeover of Public Expression.* New York: Oxford University Press, 1989.
Schulze, Reinhard. "The Birth of Tradition and Modernity in 18th and 19th Century Islamic Culture—The Case of printing." *Culture & History. No.* 16: 25–38, 1997.
Scott, James. *Seeing Like a State.* New Haven: Yale University Press, 1998.
Shapiro, Michael J. *For Moral Ambiguity: National Culture and the Politics of the Family.* Minneapolis: University of Minnesota Press, 2001.
Seed, David. "Mapping the Course of Empire in the New World," in Brooke Horvath and Irving Malin eds. *Pynchon and Mason & Dixon.* Newark: University of Delaware Press, 2000.
Sidran, Ben. *Black Talk.* New York: Da Capo, 1971.
Sievernich, Chris. ed. *Wim Wenders-Sam Shepard: Paris Texas.* Nordlinger, Germany: Greno, 1984.
Silko, Leslie Marmon. *Ceremony.* New York: Penguin, 1977.
Silva, Noenoe. *Ke Ku' E Kupa'aloa Nei Makou: Kanaka Maoli Resistance to Colonization.* Durham, NC: Duke University Press, 2004.
Simmon, Scott. "Concerning The Weary Legs of Wyatt Earp: *The Classic Western According to Shakespeare*." in Jim Kitses and Gregg Rickmen eds. *The Western Reader.* New York: Limelight, 1998.
Simpson, David. "Raymond Williams: Feeling for Structures, Voicing 'History'." *Social Text* No. 30: 9–26, 1992.
Slotkin, Richard. *Gunfighter Nation: The Myth of the Frontier in Twentieth Century America.* New York: Atheneum, 1992.
Small, Christopher. *Music of the Common Tongue: Survival and Celebration in African American Music.* New York: River Run Press, 1987.
Smith, Anthony. "Images of the Nation: Cinema, art and national identity." in Hjort, Mette and Scott MacKenzie eds. *Cinema & Nation.* New York: Routledge, 2000.
Smith, Terry. "Public Art between Cultures: The *Aboriginal Memorial,* Aboriginality, and Nationality in Australia." *Critical Inquiry.* 27, No. 4: 635–650, 2001.
Spivak, Gayatri Chakravorty. "Woman in Difference: Mahashweta Devi's '*Douloti the Bountiful.*'" in Andrew Parker, Mary Russo, Doris Sommer and Patricia Yaeger eds. *Nationalism and Sexualities.* New York: Routledge, 1992.
Sterritt, Robert. "Director Builds Metaphor for Jazz in *Kansas City*." in David Sterritt ed. *Robert Altman: Interviews.* Jackson: University of Mississippi Press, 2000.
Steyne, Mark. *Broadway Babies Say Good Night.* Boston: Faber and Faber, 1997.
Stout, David. "U.S. Arrests Man Accused of 'Dirty Bomb' Attack." *New York Times* on the web: http://www.nytimes.com/2002/06/10/national/10CND-TERROR.html.
Taylor, Diana. *Theater of Crisis: Drama and Politics in Latin America.* Louisville: University Press of Kentucky, 1991.
Thurner, Mark. "'*Republicanos*' and '*la Comunidad de Peruanos*': Unimagined Political Communities in Postcolonial Andean Peru." *Journal of Latin American Studies.* 27, No. 2: 290–305, 1995.
Tocce, Vincent. "Is It Shot Or Is It Dead?: The Western According to Virgil and Shakespeare." *CINE* No. 344: 3–15, 1998.
Trachtenberg, Alan. *Reading American Photographs.* New York: Hill and Wang, 1989.
Trask, Haunani Kay. "Agony of Place," in Joseph P Balaz ed. Ho'omanoa. Honolulu: Ku Pa'a Inc 1989.

Truettner, William H. ed. *The West as America: Reinterpreting Images of the Frontier, 1820–1920*. Washington DC: Smithsonian Institution Press, 1991.

Trumpener, Katie. *Bardic Nationalism: The Romantic Novel and the British Empire*. Princeton, NJ: Princeton University Press, 1997.

Trask, Haunani-Kay. "Sovereignty stolen by U.S. must be restored." *Honolulu Advertiser*, October 1: B-1, 2000.

Van Den Berghe, Pierre L. "The Modern State: Nation-Builder or Nation Killer." *International Journal of Group Tensions*. 22, No. 3:191–208, 1992.

van Woerden, Henk. "The Assassin." *Granta* No. 69: 7–80, 2000.

Vargas Llosa, Mario. "Questions of Conquest," *Harper's* No. 281: 51, 1990.

———. *The Notebooks of Don Rigoberto*. Trans. Edith Grossman. New York: Penguin, 1999.

———. *A Fish in the Water*, 1st ed. Trans. Helen Lane. New York: Farrar, Straus and Giroux, 1994.

Vaughan Williams, Ralph. *National Music and Other Essays* 2nd edition. New York: Oxford University Press, 1987.

Verhoeven, Paul. "Neutralizing the Land: The Myth of Authority, and the Authority of Myth in Fenimore Cooper's *The Spy*." in Paul Verhoeven ed. *James Fenimore Cooper: New Historical and Literary Contexts*. Amsterdam: Rodopi, 1993.

Virilio, Paul. *War and Cinema: The Logistics of Perception*. Trans Patrick Camiller. New York: Verso, 1989.

Viswanathan, Gauri. *Masks of Conquest: Literary Study and British Rule in India*. New York: Columbia University Press, 1989.

Vizenor, Gerald. "The Ruins of Representation: Shadow Survivance and the literature of Domination." in Alfred Arteaga ed. *An Other Tongue*. Durham, NC: Duke University Press, 1994.

Vogeley, Nancy "Italian Opera in Early National Mexico." *Modern Language Quarterly*. 57, No. 2: 279–288, 1996.

Wade, Peter. "Music, blackness and national identity: three moments in Columbian history." *Popular Music*. 17, No. 1: 1–13, 1998.

———. *Music, Race, & Nation*. Chicago: University of Chicago Press, 2000.

Walker, Cheryl. *Indian Nation*. Durham, NC: Duke University Press, 1997.

Warnke, Martin. *Political Landscape: The Art History of Nature*. Cambridge, MA: Harvard University Press, 1995.

Warren, Kay. *Indigenous Political Movements and Their Critics*. Princeton, NJ: Princeton University Press, 1998.

Warshow, Robert. "Movie Chronicle: *The Westerner*." in Jim Kitses and Gregg Rickmen eds. *The Western Reader*. New York: Limelight, 1998.

Weintraub, Andrew N. "Jawaiian Music and Local Cultural Identity Hawaii." in Philip Hayward ed. *Sound Alliances*. New York: Cassell, 1998.

Wenders, Wim. *Written in the West*. Munich: Shirmer, 1987.

West, Cornell. "The Legacy of Raymond Williams." *Social Text* No. 30: 5–12, 1992.

Wexman, Virginia Wright. "The Family on the Land: Race and nationhood in Silent Westerns." in Daniel Bernardi ed. *The Birth of Whiteness*. New Brunswick, NJ: Rutgers University Press, 1996.

Williams, Colin and Anthony D. Smith. "The National construction of social space." *Progress in Human Geography*. 7, No. 4: 503–512, 1983.

Williams, Raymond. *The Long Revolution*. Harmondsworth: Penguin, 1961.

———. *Politics and Letters*. London: Verso, 1979.

Willemen, Paul. *Looks and Frictions: Essays in Cultural Studies and Film Theory*. Bloomington: Indiana University Press, 1994.

Wister, Owen. "The Evolution of the Cow-Puncher," *Harper's Monthly*. No. 91: 602–617, 1895.

Wister, Owen. *The Virginian: A Horseman of the Plains*. New York: Macmillan, 1902.

Woideck, Carl. *The John Coltrane Companion*. New York: Schirmer, 1998.

Wollen, Peter. *Signs and Meaning in Cinema*. Bloomington: Indiana University Press, 1969.

Woods, Clyde. *Development Arrested: Race, Power, and the Blues in the Mississippi Delta*. New York: Verso, 1998.

Wright, Derek. Nations as Fictions: Postmodernism in the novels of Nuhruddin Farah." *Critique* 38, No. 3: 193–204., 1997.

Wright, Patrick. *Tank*. New York: Viking, 2002.

Zhang, Yingjin. "From 'Minority Film' to 'Minority Discourse': Questions of Nationhood and Ethnicity in Chinese Cinema." in Sheldon Hsiao-peng Lu ed. *Transnational Chinese Cinema.* Honolulu: University of Hawaii Press, 1997.

Ziff, Larzer. *Writing in the New Nation.* New Haven, CT: Yale University Press, 1991.

Zimmer, Oliver. "In Search of Natural Identity: Alpine Landscape and the Reconstruction of the Swiss Nation." *Comparative Studies in Society and History.* 40, No. 4: 639–648, 1998.

Zwerin, Mike. "Remembering John Coltrane," on the web at: http://www.culturekiosque.com/jazz/miles/rhemile.htm.

# Index